The Politics of Catherinian Russia

The Politics of Catherinian Russia :

The Panin Party

David L. Ransel

ix, 327p.

New Haven and London, Yale University Press, 1975

Published with assistance from the
Mary Cady Tew Memorial Fund.

Library of Congress catalog card number: 74–29736
International standard book number: 0–300–01795–2

Designed by John O. C. McCrillis
and set in Baskerville type.
Printed in the United States of America by
Vail-Ballou Press, Inc., Binghamton, N. Y.

Published in Great Britain, Europe, and Africa by
Yale University Press, Ltd., London.
Distributed in Latin America by Kaiman & Polon,
Inc., New York City; in India by UBS Publishers' Distributors Pvt.,
Ltd., Delhi; in Japan by John Weatherhill, Inc., Tokyo.

To My Father and the Memory of My Mother

Contents

Acknowledgments

While it is impossible to recognize all those who have contributed to this effort, I want to single out a few of the most important. For encouragement and helpful criticism along the way I am deeply indebted to my graduate supervisor Firuz Kazemzadeh, and to Marc Raeff, Isabel de Madariaga, Herbert Kaplan, V. A. Petrova, M. T. Beliavskii, and not least to the late S. B. Okun', my research adviser at Leningrad State University, who several times pressed me to go forward with a book on the Panins when the task seemed all but hopeless. Special thanks are due John T. Alexander, Frederic C. Jaher, and Thomas Krueger for reading the entire manuscript and making many improvements in style and content, and to Ralph T. Fisher, Jr., Michael Metcalf, George Yaney, Benjamin Uroff, and James T. Flynn for their helpful suggestions on various chapters. Many librarians and archivists have given invaluable assistance. I am particularly grateful for the services of Laurence Miller and his staff and the University of Illinois Library's Special Languages Division and the staffs of the national archives of Sweden and Denmark, the Leningrad Section of the Institute of History of the Soviet Academy of Sciences, the Manuscript Division of the Lenin Library and the Central State Archive of Ancient Acts in Moscow.

I hasten to add that the research was made possible through the generous support of the Inter-University Committee on Travel Grants (now the International Research and Exchanges Board), which enabled me to spend nine months in Leningrad and Moscow. The Danforth Foundation, the University of Illinois Research Board, and the Russian and East European Center at Illinois all provided financial assistance at various stages of research and writing. My research assistant of one year, Olga Yokoyama, added much to the overall effort, and typists Irene Blenker and Janice Draper provided their skills and unflagging good nature through the preparation of several drafts. Finally, I want to thank my wife, Terry, whose critical insights immeasurably strengthened the work while her patience and understanding carried me over many a rough spot.

Abbreviations

AGS	Arkhiv gosudarstvennogo soveta
AKV	Arkhiv kniazia Vorontsova
Arkhiv Kurakina	Arkhiv kniazia F. A. Kurakina
Chteniia	Chteniia v imperatorskom obshchestve istorii i drevnostei rossiiskikh
Despatches Buckingham	The Despatches and Correspondence of John, Second Earl of Buckinghamshire, Ambassador to the Court of Catherine II of Russia 1762–1765
DRa	Danske Rigsarkivet (Danish National Archive)
FSS	D. I. Fonvizin, Sobranie sochinenii
GBL	Gosudarstvennaia Biblioteka im. Lenina, Ruko-pisnyi Otdel
GPB	Gosudarstvennaia Publichnaia Biblioteka, Len-ingrad, rykopisnyi otdel
IPS	Istoriia Pravitel'stvuiushchego Senata za dvesti let, 1711–1911
LOII	Leningradskoe Otdelenie Instituta Istorii Akademii Nauk SSSR
PSZ	Polnoe sobranie zakonov rossiiskoi imperii
RBS	Russkii biograficheskii slovar'
SIRIO	Sbornik imperatorskogo russkogo istoricheskogo obsh-chestva
SRa	Svenska Riksarkivet (Swedish National Archive)
TsGADA	Tsentral'nyi Gosudarstvennyi Arkhiv Drevnikh Aktov
Williams Correspondence	Correspondence of Catherine the Great with Sir Charles Hanbury-Williams

Note on Dates and Transliteration

Unless otherwise specified, all dates follow the Julian calendar, which in the eighteenth century ran eleven days behind the Gregorian. On many diplomatic dispatches both dates are included. The transliteration of Russian terms follows the modified Library of Congress system. First names with common English equivalents have been rendered in English (thus: Catherine, rather than Ekaterina, and Paul, rather than Pavel).

1

Introduction

The theoretically unlimited power of the Russian autocracy was in fact very narrowly circumscribed. In the absence of legal administrative system and corporately organized social estates, the articulation of tsarist will depended upon the familial and personal patronage networks that dominated the court and upper administration. These "parties" constituted the main sphere of policy development, supervised the recruitment and training of personnel for high office, and supplied the organizational cohesion that made for effective policy implementation. Personal, rather than institutional, loyalty held the government together—or, alternately, frustrated and paralyzed it. This is scarcely surprising, since without a constitution or operative legal system, the familial patronage alliances afforded the chief protection of personal security, goods, career and status, freedom of expression, or any other material interests. They likewise provided the main avenue for realizing ambitions of increased power, wealth, and status.

These groups were not mere cliques but powerful personal networks that extended into many areas of government and society. Among the most prominent in the middle eighteenth century was the Vorontsov clan in Empress Elizabeth's reign, which, in cooperation with the favorite, Shuvalov, and his family, dominated the leading institutions for foreign and domestic affairs as well as Moscow University and the principal cultural organs. In Catherine II's reign two hierarchies, one based on the Panin family with its collateral ties to the Kurakin and Nepliuev clans, and another formed around the five Orlov brothers and their intimates, divided authority until the middle 1770s, when both were supplanted by a new hierarchy organized under the favorite G. A. Potemkin. In addition to a dominant position at court, Potemkin could boast a substantial territorial base in southern Russia, where he and his clients ruled with little interference from the central government. Hence, the reach of

1

these groups was often impressive. There was also considerable internal cohesion in the patronage hierarchies. They were cemented by strong personal and kinship loyalties that rendered them resistant to penetration. Even in the absence of material sanctions from a group in decline, personal allegiances were frequently strong enough to cause members to scuttle their own careers in preference to switching loyalties and bringing down on their heads the hostility of the group. Of course, rulers could manipulate the groups and under certain circumstances even replace one competing clientele network with another more responsive to the imperial will. But rulers could not govern without them and rely solely upon bureaucracy. Those who tried, like Peter III and Paul I, enjoyed but brief and stormy careers cut short by assassination.[1]

Little has been done on these groups and their most prominent leaders;[2] the purpose of this book is to detail and analyze the activities of one of the most important and neglected of them, the Panin party of Catherine II's time. The approach used here will be biographical, viewing the role of the party through its leader, Nikita Ivanovich Panin. Like most of the prominent figures of Catherine's reign, he has yet to receive serious attention from scholars. Apart from a brief review of Panin's career in the *Russian Biographical Dictionary*, not a single scholarly work has appeared on his life and political activity.[3] Yet he occupied responsible posts from the early years of Elizabeth's reign (1741–61), served for over twelve years as Russian envoy to Copenhagen and Stockholm (1747–60), was governor and tutor of the Grand Duke Paul (later Paul I), played a central role in the coup d'etat that brought Catherine II to power in 1762, and then served as senator, imperial councilor, and foreign minister during twenty of the most productive years of Catherine's reign.

[1]See the illuminating comments on this point by Marc Raeff, "The Domestic Policies of Peter III and His Overthrow," *American Historical Review*, 75 (June 1970), 1289–1310.

[2]This is scarcely to be wondered at when one considers that even Catherine II has not received an adequate biography. Alexander Brückner's *Istoriia Ekateriny Vtoroi*, 3 vols. (St. Petersburg, 1885), fell short of scholars' needs even at the time it was written. A projected ten-volume study by V. A. Bil'basov, *Istoriia Ekateriny II*, 2 eds. (London, 1895 and Berlin, 1900), showed great promise, but it failed to progress beyond the second volume, covering only the first two years of Catherine's reign.

[3]A. I. Braudo, "Nikita Ivanovich Panin," *RBS*, 13: 189–205; another work by P. S. Lebedev, *Grafy Nikita i Petr Paniny, razrabotki novieshei russkoi istorii po neizdannym istochnikam* (St. Petersburg, 1863), despite the inclusion of some valuable documents, is more of a political brochure than a scholarly study.

In addition, he was leader of a powerful court party and sponsor of several reform projects. The history of Catherinian Russia can scarcely be complete without a thorough evaluation of the influence of Panin and his party.

This book began with the rather straightforward objective of filling this gap in the historiography, the point being merely to place the contributions of Nikita Panin and his supporters in proper relation to Catherine's overall governing activity. It soon became apparent, however, that the task required considerable rethinking and revision of the political history of the period. For the Panin party had been neglected only in the sense that no one had made a careful inquiry into its influence and actions. It was too important a factor in Russian politics to be passed over in silence, and writers of general histories and topical monographs inevitably offered evaluations of the political role and reform proposals of Panin and his group. Yet lacking sufficient groundwork on Panin himself, authors arrived at judgments based for the most part on pat formulas of how Panin should have reacted to various situations given his social background, position in the state service, personal temperament, and the like. This studied attempt to avoid all the complexities yielded a fairly consistent interpretation of Panin's political activity that has now been accepted with few reservations by Soviet and Western historians alike.

In its general outline the current picture of Nikita Panin in Russian historiography may be summarized as follows. He was a statesman who shared the mentality of the ancient *boiar* aristocracy. During a long stay in Sweden he developed a taste for constitutional monarchy and upon returning to Russia became the leader of a party that hoped to place limitations on tsarist power in the interests of a ruling oligarchy of prominent families, first by forcing Catherine into the position of regent during the minority of her son Paul or, failing that, by using Catherine's initially insecure hold on the throne as a means of exacting her consent to the rule of an Imperial Council on the lines of the Supreme Privy Council, which briefly usurped sovereign power in 1730. When Catherine managed to thwart these designs, Panin turned his attention to the "young court" of the grand duke, where he concentrated not so much on educating Paul as on turning him against his mother, so that he could be used as a focus of opposition to Catherine's policies. Panin expected that

Paul would be able to take over power, or at least gain a considerable share of it, upon his attainment of majority in 1773. When even
this hope failed to materialize, Panin lent his name to the Masonic
movement, which he wished to make a rallying point for disaffected
groups opposed to the government. These positions made Panin, in
current historical jargon, the leader of the "gentry opposition," a
group or party bent on wresting control of government from the monarch.[4]

The persistence of this picture through more than a century of
Russian historiography is in itself something of a curiosity. Its origin
may be traced to the didactic writings of nineteenth-century historians who, for a variety of reasons having little to do with Panin
himself, wanted to show him as an opponent of Catherine.[5] The
interpretation has sustained its force to this day, thanks largely to
the absence of monographic literature on Panin's role in court
politics. At the turn of the century it seemed that a fresh view was
about to emerge as historians began to delve more deeply into
Catherinian Russia,[6] but this development came to an abrupt halt
after the revolution of 1917. Under the Soviets interest shifted from
the elite to questions of economic growth and peasant rebellions.
Instead of giving serious attention to high politics, Soviet scholars
simply took earlier interpretations and wove them into the required
ideological framework. As a result, the old view of Panin's role not
only survived intact; it was further reinforced by a Marxist schema
which, founded in European historical thought, sought evidence of

[4]For a full review of the historiography detailing the emergence and persistence of this
view, see my work entitled "Nikita Panin's Role in Russian Court Politics of the Seventeen
Sixties: A Critique of the Gentry Opposition Thesis" (Ph.D. diss., Yale University, 1969),
pp. 9–65.

[5]Some examples are *Primechaniia k "Histoire philosophique de Russie" par Enneau et Chennechot* (Tobolsk, 1853) by the Decembrist M. A. Fonvizin, who apparently imposed on the
activities of his illustrious forebear, Panin's secretary and collaborator D. I. Fonvizin, his
own hopes for the Decembrist revolt. Lebedev, in *Grafy Paniny*, employed the argument
for Panin's opposition in an effort to spruce up Prince Potemkin's image as a bold defender
of autocracy. Biographers of Paul took the same line to explain their hero's overturn of
many of Catherine's legislative acts. See for example, D. I. Kobeko, *Tsesarevich Pavel
Petrovich 1754–1796* (St. Petersburg, 1882), and E. S. Shumigorskii, *Imperator Pavel I,
zhizn' i tsarstvovanie* (St. Petersburg, 1907).

[6]See especially, N. D. Chechulin, "Proekt Imperatorskogo Soveta," *Zhurnal Ministerstva Narodnogo Prosveshcheniia,* no. 3 (1894), 68–87; and P. N. Miliukov, *Ocherki po istorii
russkoi kul'tury,* part 3, *Natsionalizm i obshchestvennoe mnenie,* II (St. Petersburg, 1913), pp.
246–419 *passim,* and especially 270.

an aristocratic *fronde* in reaction to the centralizing monarchy. Panin now became not only an opponent of Catherine but the leader of a full-fledged "gentry opposition" movement.[7] Although emanating from entirely different schools, the pre-1917 and post-1917 views merged so convincingly that any further investigation of the Panin party seemed entirely unnecessary. The logic and symmetry of the established interpretation constituted sufficient grounds for its acceptance.

The main difficulty with this interpretation is its inclination to view Catherinian politics exclusively in terms of a struggle between a ruler jealous of her autocratic prerogatives and a "liberal" nobiliary opposition eager to usurp imperial authority. This focus has obscured a much more important dimension of the question: the competition among the various patronage groups for influence and position. Given the officials' habit of organizing themselves in informal personal and kinship clientele networks, it is altogether impossible to make sense out of their political behavior without considering the dynamics of such groups. A good example may be found in the reform proposals of the period, a subject that will occupy a great deal of space in this work. Projects for political reform inevitably spoke in terms of bringing greater rationality and legal order to the government. Their ostensible goal was to create efficient

---

[7]M. N. Pokrovskii was the first historian to apply this designation, even while he seemed to vacillate on the issue of Panin's opposition, an indication that he was still to some extent under the influence of the reinterpretations begun in the decades immediately preceding the revolution. *Istoriia Rossii s drevneishikh vremen,* in *Izbrannye proizvedeniia,* (Moscow, 1965), 2: 118, 149. The full development of the thesis culminated with G. A. Gukovskii's work, *Ocherki po istorii russkoi literatury XVIII veka, dvorianskaia fronda v literature 1750-kh—1760-kh godov* (Moscow, 1936), and it is now commonly found in all Soviet and Western works touching on this period. For some examples, see S. B. Okun', *Ocherki istorii SSSR (konets XVIII—pervaia chetvert' XIX veka)* (Leningrad, 1956), p. 52; G. P. Makogonenko, *Denis Fonvizin, tvorcheskii put'* (Moscow, 1961), especially pp. 157–58, 162, 167–68, 171–72, 194–95; K. V. Pigarev, *Tvorchestvo Fonvizina* (Moscow, 1954), pp. 113, 114, 135; S. A. Pokrovskii ed., *Vtoraia polovina XVIII veka,* Vol. 1 of *Iuridicheskie proizvedeniia progressivnykh myslitelei* (Moscow, 1959), pp. 5–14; Georg Sacke, "Katharina II. im Kampf um Thron und Selbstherrschaft," *Archiv für Kulturgeschichte,* 23, no. 2 (1932), 191–216, and other articles; Igor Glasenapp, *Staat, Gesellschaft und Opposition im Zeitalter Katharinas der Grossen* (Munich, 1964), p. 6; James Billington, *The Icon and the Axe* (New York, 1966), pp. 219–20, 223, 230. Some recent Western works have modified this view somewhat, but without entering into a detailed discussion of the question. See, for example, Marc Raeff, *Origins of the Russian Intelligentsia* (New York, 1966), pp. 102–07; Robert E. Jones, *The Emancipation of the Russian Nobility 1762–1785* (Princeton, 1973), pp. 101–8.

administrative and legislative procedures. Yet a close look at their contents and the political battles surrounding their submission makes clear that they were inextricably bound up with traditional patronage contests, and they cannot be properly understood apart from the narrow partisan interests that were at once their chief motivation and a restraint on their effective implementation. The fact is that reform was directed not so much against the sovereign power as against some competing patronage hierarchy vying for influence and position in the central administration. Though admittedly a difficult distinction to make, a definite pattern of such behavior can be established.

Yet this is not the entire story. Reform was seldom divorced from a real aspiration to legal system and rationality. The problem consists of placing this ambition in its proper relationship to the partisan competition at court. By the middle eighteenth century members of the Russian governing elite had come to share an aspiration to systematic government, a result largely of Peter I's efforts to implant legal order in Russian administration. Although Peter failed to establish the substance of legal relations, he created a powerful impetus in that direction. Through ukases and manifestos he projected the values of open and orderly administrative procedure, functional division of responsibility, and hierarchical subordination on the basis of generalized rules and regulations. In the institutions of the senate and central collegia he embodied at least the pretense of rationality and legal system. With these models to look to, the Russian elite began to recognize the new values as superior to the old ways. Western educational institutions, also introduced by Peter, gradually deepened and fortified these values to the point that articulate members of the elite could find nothing to defend in the traditional system of personal relations with the bribery and toadyism that sustained them.[8] Statesmen unquestionably perceived the

[8]For a fuller discussion of this question see my "Bureaucracy and Patronage: The View from an Eighteenth-Century Russian Letter-Writer," in Frederic Cople Jaher, ed., *The Rich, the Well-Born, and the Powerful: Elites and Upper Classes in History* (Urbana, Ill., 1973), pp. 154–78. With regard to this critical view, the stress is on *articulate*. In the rare instances when evidence appears on the attitudes of rank-and-file nobles, as in the cahiers of the Legislative Commission of 1767, the nobles express a preference for the personal or familial nature of authority, although even in this case the assumption seems to be that paternal authority will remove abuses. For a very able discussion of this question, see Wilson Augustine, "Notes Toward a Portrait of the Eighteenth-Century Russian Nobility," *Canadian Slavic Studies*, vol 4, no. 3 (Fall 1970), especially pp. 384–86.

benefits of efficient administration and guarantees of personal security that a truly effective legal order would confer. Without this understanding their reform proposals would not have been taken seriously by either themselves or their opponents (as they most assuredly were). Still, the commitment to legal system was no more than an aspiration. Experience had not yet taught these men to rely on legal relations. More often than not they violated principles of legality even as they pretended to uphold them and instead continued to rely on and protect the patronage organizations, which were the only viable mechanisms for retaining influence and carrying out policy.

Hence, two important dimensions of Catherinian politics have been neglected in the "gentry opposition" thesis formulation: the competition of the court parties, and the relation of this competition to the development of systematic government. These matters deserve more careful study, as they lead to interesting conclusions about the role of fictions in political modernization and the dilemmas such fictions pose for statesmen. More will be said about this problem at the end of this work. But it is worth noting at this point that the Russian officials' maintenance of the pretense of law and system, in the sense that they played out their patronage contests behind a bureaucratic facade, was important over the long run in reinforcing a belief in the efficacy of legal relations. This observation should not conceal from view the fact that the patronage contests themselves were the underlying motive for many of their actions. Nor should this be surprising. It would be wholly contradictory to expect these men to have relied consistently on legal relations to bring about an as yet non-existent legality. The ability of statesmen to act, even the reformer's ability to reform, depended on maintenance of the traditional hierarchies of patronage through which action could be effected. The conflict between the aspiration to legal order and the inescapable need to retain the traditional forms of political action was a real one. Ministers had to cope with it as best they could.

These are the problems with which the book is concerned. The structure is biographical, mainly because the lack of scholarly study on Nikita Panin necessitated a good deal of spadework on his life and made it useful to build the book around stages of his career. The work, however, is not primarily a narrative about Nikita Panin but an analysis of his and his party's political role. Hence, modifica-

tions of the biographical pattern have been introduced here and
there. Within a broad chronological framework each chapter deals
with specific topic areas, carrying them backward and forward as
seems appropriate, the result being something in the nature of the
Russian style of essays (*ocherki*) around a general theme.

2

Nikita Panin's Early Career to 1760

1. Youth and Training

Nikita Panin's family was neither titled nor wealthy. Its origins dated to the Muscovite service class of the sixteenth century. Later Panins liked to trace their ancestry to the Italian family Pagnini, which allegedly emigrated to Muscovy from the Republic of Lucca during the high middle ages. In view of the genealogical skulduggery commonly practiced by Russian nobility, however, claims of foreign origin must be regarded with some skepticism.[1] The first member of the family to appear in historical records was Vasilii Panin, listed as a victim of the campaign against Kazan' in 1530. Then from Ivan IV's time a number of Panins began to figure in the *Razriadnye knigi* (lists of service appointments) where they occupied minor posts as *ryndy*, or court pages, in attendance upon the *tsarevich*. Only in the seventeenth century did Panins attain positions of importance. Nikita Fedorovich Panin was serving as *voevoda* (military governor) at Suzdal' in 1635, and his son became *voevoda* in Koz'modem'iansk.

In Peter the Great's time the family began to rise more rapidly through advantageous marriages with prominent Petrine families. Nikita Panin's father, Ivan Vasil'evich, achieved the rank of colonel in Peter's army by 1712, and he married Prince Alexander Menshikov's niece Agrafena Vasil'evna Everlakova. This association

[1]Most historians have been willing to accept Denis Fonvizin's testimony of the Panins' Italian origin. *FSS*, 2 : 279. The Panins sought confirmation in Italy, and it seems a Pagnini family there was happy to recognize relation to the by-then-renowned Catherinian statesmen. "K rodosloviiu grafov Paninykh," *Russkii Arkhiv* (1876), no. 1, 376. The most thorough investigation, V. V. Sakhanev, "Iz istorii Rossii kontsa XVIII stoletiia (tri neopublikovannykh dokumenta iz istorii roda grafov Paninykh)" *Zapiski russkogo nauchno-issledovatel'skogo ob"edineniia v Prage*, 10, no. 71 (Prague, 1940), however, casts doubt on the Italian heritage. As for the frequent practice of doctoring genealogies to establish a foreign origin, see S. B. Veselovskii, *Issledovaniia po istorii klassa sluzhilykh zemlevladel'tsev* (Moscow, 1969), pp. 7–35.

with the powerful Menshikov clan aided Colonel Panin's career. In 1722 he was named *obershterkrigskommissar*, placing him in the fifth rank on the service hierarchy. Empress Anne promoted him to Senator, and at his death in 1736 he held the rank of Lieutenant-General.

Despite a long and successful career, Ivan Vasil'evich failed to amass great wealth. He was able, nevertheless, to bequeath his children a very respectable 400 serfs, and in more essential ways he provided his family with a rich endowment. True to the spirit and commands of Peter I, he devoted the principal part of his means to the education of his four children. This wise investment paid off handsomely. His daughters Anna and Alexandra gained wide repute for their knowledge and intelligence and had no trouble making excellent matches. Alexandra wed Prince Alexander Borisovich Kurakin, the well-known Petrine diplomat and senator and a relative of Tsar Peter II. Anna married I. I. Nepliuev, another "pupil" of Peter the Great, the renowned builder of Orenburg frontier province and later a prominent senator.[2] These important connections gave Ivan Vasil'evich's two sons, Nikita and Peter, an early entrance to court life. Nikita had as early as 1743 attracted the amorous attention of the empress herself, while his younger brother Peter's marriage to A. A. Tatishcheva in 1748 was celebrated at court with a splendid ceremony bringing together all the leading families of the nation. The empress helped to dress the bride, and the sponsors included the Grand Ducal couple, Chancellor Bestuzhev, Countess Shuvalova, the Kurakins, Vorontsovs, Repnins, Trubetskois, Naryshkins, and several other prominent families.[3] The Panins had arrived as members of the ranking Petrine nobility.

Only a few details of Nikita Ivanovich Panin's early life and education are known. He was born in 1718 in Dantzig and spent his early years in Pernau, where his father served as commandant. During the reign of Empress Anne he began his career in the Im-

[2]Material on the family history from: *FSS*, 2: 279–81; V. I. Buganov, ed., *Razriadnaia kniga 1475–1598* (Moscow, 1966), pp. 228, 236, 244, 246, 260, 313, 459, 469, 478, 493, 503, 504, 513; A. Brikner, ed., *Materialy dlia zhizneopisaniia grafa Nikity Petrovicha Panina*, 7 vols. (St. Petersburg, 1888–1892), Vol. 1, p. 1; *RBS*, 13: 176, 188; E. P. Karnovich, *Zamechatel'nye bogatstva chastnykh lits v Rossii* (St. Petersburg, 1874), p. 337; *Arkhiv Kurakina*, 10 vols. (St. Petersburg, 1890–1902), Vol. 1, pp. 262–63.

[3]V. E. Adadurov to N. I. Panin, 1748, in *Russkii Arkhiv* (1875), no. 3, 370–72.

perial Horse Guards, one of the elite regiments of the capital.[4] Although no information has survived on Panin's formal education, his training was evidently exceptionally advanced for the time. During his later public career colleagues in the diplomatic corps, friends and enemies alike, uniformly praised his learning. His knowledge was by no means limited to political affairs. Throughout his life he took an active interest in the work of the Academy of Sciences and in the growing number of Russian literary talents.[5] His favorite conversation ran to history, manners, and culture.[6] He could with equal ease survey the exploits of Western travelers (Olearius, Weber, and others), trace the history of foreign theater in Russia, or offer an impromptu dissertation on the *Lettres juives, Lettres Persanes, Lettres cabalistiques, Lettres chinoises* and *Lettres russiennes*.[7] Indicative of his early intellectual concerns was the lasting friendship he made during his years in the guards with one of the few young men of the time who could share his interests, V. E. Adadurov, a gifted student at the Academy of Sciences. Adadurov was an assistant to the famous mathematician Euler and the best student of the historian G. F. Müller.[8]

As for Panin's informal political education, it undoubtedly began while he was still a youth. His mother and relatives frequently met at Prince Menshikov's house with Grand Duchess Elizabeth Petrovna and others close to Peter the Great.[9] It was from this source that Panin must have acquired the large fund of personal anecdotes about the famous tsar that he often retold with delight. Peter's life and work obviously made an enormous impression on Panin. The letters, projects, and conversations of his public career were strongly influenced by the Petrine ethic, and even when proposing reforms, Panin always reserved a special respect for Peter's contributions, regarding his own proposals merely as an attempt to refine and

[4]The choice may have been influenced by the fact that Panin's father had participated in the establishment of that regiment. G. N. Leikhtenbergskii, *Istoriia leib gvardii konnogo polka* (Paris, 1938), vol.1, p. 9.

[5]V. A. Bil'basov, *Istoriia Ekateriny II* (Berlin, 1900), Vol. 2, p. 434; *AKV*, 7: 459-60; *FSS*, 2: 97-98; *Arkhiv Kurakina*, vol. 5, xx-xxi.

[6]S. A. Poroshin, *Zapiski* (as pagination of various editions differs, only the date of diary entries will be noted here and hereafter), 28 March and 19 April 1765; *AKV*, 26: 59-60.

[7]Poroshin, *Zapiski*, 1 December 1764, 7 January and 14 September 1765.

[8]"Pis'ma V. E. Adadurova k N. I. Paninu," *Russkii Arkhiv* (1888), no. 3, 178-82.

[9]P. Bartenev, "Predislovie k Zapiskam Poroshina," *Russkii Arkhiv* (1882), 66-67.

perfect the work Peter had begun. Panin seemed to view Russia and
Peter the Great as nearly synonymous entities, as though Russian
history first began with Peter's reforms. Panin's writings contained
a mere scattering of references to Pre-Petrine Russia, and those few
remarks left the distinct impression that he regarded the nation of
that time as something akin to an undifferentiated mass of bar-
barism.

It was scarcely surprising that Panin valued the Petrine reform
era so highly. Despite frequent allusions in the literature to his
aristocratic background, Panin was not associated with the old
aristocracy of Muscovite Russia. His father owed his career to
Peter's system of advancement according to merit. He achieved
success by means of regular promotions through the Petrine service
hierarchy and only late in life reached a position among the general
officers. The family's marital connections, while decidedly advantageous, linked it primarily with the parvenus of the Petrine era. And
although these connections unquestionably aided Nikita Panin's
start in the state service, he too had to work his way up the ranking
hierarchy from the lowest officer grades without jumping any steps.
Hence, in speaking of Panin as an aristocrat, one must keep in mind
that the reference is not to the Muscovite aristocracy of *boiar* families
but to the new Petrine aristocracy of rank.

During Empress Anne's reign Panin was old enough to begin
making political observations on his own. The most celebrated event
of that period was the coup d'état of 1730 when the oligarchs of the
Supreme Privy Council briefly seized control of the government and
limited the empress' autocratic powers. In view of the parallels often
drawn between the actions of the Supreme Privy Council and
Panin's later reform efforts, it would be of great interest to know
what he thought of that abortive revolution from above. Comments
recorded in the Poroshin diary make it clear that Panin, while too
young to participate in the 1730 events, knew well the circumstances
surrounding them.[10] Unfortunately for the historian, the few re-

[10]Poroshin, *Zapiski*, 27 June 1765. Pre-revolutionary scholarship, principally D. A.
Korsakov, *Votsarenie Anny Ioannovny* (Kazan', 1880), P. N. Miliukov, *Iz istorii russkoi
intelligentsii*, 2nd ed. (St. Petersburg, 1903), pp. 1–51; H. Hjärne, "Ryska konstitutionsprojekt år 1730 efter svenska förebilder," *Historisk tidskrift*, 4 (1884), 189–272, has been
superseded by G. A. Protasov's recent studies: "'Konditsii' 1730 g. i ikh prodolzhenie,"
Uchenye zapiski, Tambovskii gosudarstvennyi pedagogicheskii institut, vyp. 15 (1957),
215–30; and "Zapiska Tatischeva o 'proizvol'nom rassuzhdenii' dvorianstva v sobytiiakh

marks he made, though vaguely critical of particular oligarchs, lack sufficient substance to yield conclusions about his attitudes toward the episode. Panin did, however, offer some revealing reflections on one of the oligarchs' best-known opponents, Artemii Volynskii, who himself turned reformer toward the close of Empress Anne's reign.

Volynskii, like Panin, was a Petrine parvenu. His brilliant career began a fast rise after his marriage to Peter I's cousin. He served on a mission to Persia and as governor of Kazan'. By 1736 he had acquired a place in the leading administrative institution in the state, the Cabinet of Ministers. Distressed by the inordinate influence of foreigners in the government and eager to improve the position of the native nobility (as well as to advance his own ambition), Volynskii composed a general reform project, which he hoped to persuade the empress to implement. As it turned out, however, Volynskii's enemies proved more persuasive, and his efforts were rewarded with horrible tortures and execution.[11]

The case is of interest if only because of the similarity between Volynskii's reform ideas and Panin's later projects. Unfortunately, the Volynskii project is not known in detail. At the time of his arrest he managed to destroy most of his papers. The original document was seen only by his so-called "confidants," one of whom modestly hailed the piece as superior to Fénelon's *Telemach*.[12] Judging from a reconstruction of it based upon the record of his investigation, Volynskii aimed at winning a modicum of political rights for the nobility, curbing favoritism and setting limits to the influence of oligarchies.[13] More specifically the investigators reported:

With obvious prejudice and reproach for the past and present

1730 g.," *Problemy istochnikovedeniia*, 11, AN SSSR Institut Istorii (Moscow, 1963), 237–65; for a review of the historiography see my "Perceptions of the Russian Nobility: The Constitutional Crisis of 1730," *Laurentian University Review* (March 1972).

[11]The most thorough background on Volynskii must still be obtained from D. A. Korsakov, "Artemii Petrovich Volynskii," *Drevniaia i novaia Rossiia* (1876), no. 1, 45–60; (1877), no. 1, 84–96, no. 3, 289–302, no. 4, 377–85, no. 5, 23–38, no. 6, 98–114, no. 7, 214–34, no. 8, 277–95, no. 11, 224–54. For the most recent attempt to reconstruct Volynskii's reform project, Iu. V. Got'e, "'Proekt o popravlenii gosudarstvennykh del' Artemiia Petrovicha Volynskogo," *Dela i Dni* (1922), no. 3, 1–31.

[12]V. E. Iakushkin, *Gosudarstvennaia vlast' i proekty gosudarstvennoi reformy v Rossii* (St. Petersburg, 1906), p. 48.

[13]For a general analysis, S. O. Schmidt, "La politique intérieure du Tsarisme au milieu du XVIIIe siècle," *Annales* (1966), 21, no. 1, 101.

administration of the state he began during the previous year [1]739 to write his project, because he observed shortcomings in the governance of state affairs: trials are lengthy, state revenues are not everywhere collected properly, the merchant class suffers great injury in that they are elected as collectors of customs and liquor taxes; if nobles were employed among other chancellery servitors, by their presence more zeal toward affairs could be obtained; there are many incompetents [*neiskusnye*] among the clergy, and they should be improved and the churches staffed with schooled priests.[14]

As a solution to these problems Volynskii proposed to maintain a monarchical form of government, but with broad participation by the nobility. The senate was to be reestablished with the same authority it had in Peter I's time, and in addition to this highest institution there should be a lower house (*nizhnee pravitel'stvo*) representing the middle and lower ranks of servicemen (*shliakhetstvo*). Included as well were proposals for defining the rights and privileges of other estates: the clergy, burghers, and peasants.[15] Hence, sketchy as the details are, Volynskii's project must always be mentioned in connection with the origins of Russian constitutionalism. Its importance in the present discussion is that similar indictments and proposals would be advanced by the Panin party at a later time.

When the investigation of Volynskii was proceeding, Panin was already in his early twenties and apparently had some knowledge of it. He had for some time been following political events at court with attention. His later comments on Empress Anne's reign testify that he knew not only of the intrigues at court but even the details of particular acts of legislation that had since been repealed.[16] With regard to the Volynskii case he may have had an invaluable personal source of information in his brother-in-law Ivan Nepliuev, one of the chief investigators.[17] Possibly, Panin then began to form his own

[14]Got'e, "Proekt Volynskogo," pp. 4–5.

[15]S. Svatikov, *Obshchestvennye dvizheniia v Rossii* (Rostov-on-Don, 1905), p. 18.

[16]Poroshin, *Zapiski,* 25 November 1764, 27 June 1765, 27 November 1765. In addition, anecdotes about leading individuals at Anne's court have been found among Panin's private papers. *Russkii Arkhiv* (1874), 469–74.

[17] S. M. Solov'ev, *Istoriia Rossii s drevneishikh vremen,* 15 vols. (Moscow, 1960–66), Vol. 10, pp. 681–82. However, it is possible that Panin learned the details at a later time, either from G. N. Teplov, who was nearly drawn into Volynskii's circle of "confidants," or from his own reading of the case. Poroshin, *Zapiski,* 15 October 1764.

ideas for reform, and he may have modeled them in part after the proposals of the ill-fated Volynskii. There is no direct evidence to support this surmise, but Panin's later proposals had a great deal in common with Volynskii's, and Panin more than once expressed strong sympathy and admiration for Volynskii's political activity. While freely admitting the well-known seamier aspects of the Petrine statesman's personal life, Panin related that Volynskii possessed "many merits in his public life, was intelligent, very knowledgeable in affairs, expeditious, and a disinterested, faithful son of the Fatherland."[18]

In 1740–41 a turbulent interregnum shook the Russian court for over a year, finally ending in the coup d'état of November 1741, which brought Empress Elizabeth Petrovna to the throne on a wave of Russian patriotism. Although some of Panin's relatives did not fare well through this crisis, he managed to survive without accident and being among the guards regiments that supported Elizabeth's accession he soon after won promotion to the court rank of *kamer-iunker*.[19] It was at this time that Panin first began to play a role in the intrigues at court. The empress, who liked attractive and witty men, eventually took an interest in the young Panin, and for a while he posed a serious threat to the position of the established favorite, A. G. Razumovskii.[20] One circumstance that probably contributed to the worries of the favorite and his entourage was the longstanding ties between Panin and the empress. She had known him since childhood, when he accompanied his mother on visits to the home of Prince Menshikov. It was therefore in Razumovskii's interest to remove Panin from the court. Probably through his efforts, in cooperation with Chancellor A. P. Bestuzhev-Riumin and Vice Chancellor M. L. Vorontsov, Panin obtained in 1747, while still in his twenties, the important post of Russian minister to the Danish court.[21]

[18]Poroshin, *Zapiski*, 15 October 1764.

[19]P. Baranov, *Opis' vysochaishim ukazam i poveleniiam khraniashchimsia v Sankt-Peterburgskom Senatskom Arkhive*, 3, *1740–1762* (St. Petersburg, 1878), 20 March 1747, no. 8790.

[20]Pezold to Count Brühl, 2 March 1743, *SIRIO*, 6: 482; Dalion to Amelot, 9 April 1743, *SIRIO*, 100: 540.

[21]Baranov, *Opis'*, 3, 10 June 1747, no. 9661. Those who prefer a psychological interpretation for Panin's later dislike of favoritism will want to pursue the suggestion that he had to leave court because he fell asleep in the empress' *cabinet de toilette* while waiting to win her charms. Constantin de Grunwald, *Trois siècles de diplomatie russe* (Paris, 1945), p. 91.

His stay in Denmark was brief. After just a few months at his new post, Chancellor Bestuzhev transferred him to Stockholm, where the Russian envoy, Johann Albrecht von Korff, had recently become *persona non grata*.[22] The move signified a major advance in Panin's career; Stockholm was one of the most difficult and sensitive diplomatic missions in the eighteenth century.[23]

2. The Mission in Sweden 1748–1760

Panin arrived in Sweden at an especially trying time. Russia had for some years worked to keep Sweden dependent upon St. Petersburg by blocking the Swedish government's pursuit of an independent foreign policy, including, among other things, Swedish ambitions for renewal of a 1738 alliance with France, an alliance with Frederick II of Prussia, and opening of diplomatic relations with the Ottoman Porte. Russian meddling had, however, provoked a sharp reaction in Swedish politics, and in a tumultuous parliamentary struggle in 1746–47 the anti-Russian forces rose to unchallenged supremacy. This setback was compounded by the danger of a change in the 1720 constitution, a document strongly supported by Russia because of its severe limitation of royal authority. With the reigning King Fredrik in poor health and his heirs, Adolf Fredrik and Lovisa Ulrika, eager to escape the restrictions on royal power, the Russian government feared a sudden change of regime leading to a court coup and major revision of the constitution. As Russian minister, Panin had the unenviable task of trying to block any change by threats and *ultimata* while at the same time working to maintain the Swedish leaders' goodwill and insuring that his court's meddling did not again backfire. By the time he assumed his post the tension in Russo-Swedish relations had reached the point of threatening a major conflict in northern Europe.

Since a precondition for this turmoil may be found in Sweden's form of government, a brief review of that subject will prove useful.

Sweden distinguished itself in the eighteenth century by having

---

[22]Korff was not officially declared *persona non grata*. King Fredrik personally requested Empress Elizabeth to recall Korff, and the Russian government eventually agreed to the request on the condition that the Swedish minister in St. Petersburg, Wulfwenstierna, also be recalled. Malmström, *Sveriges politiska historia*, 6 vols. (Stockholm, 1893–1901), 3, pp. 430–31.

[23]At the same time Panin was promoted to *deistvitel'nyi kamerger*. Baranov, *Opis'*, 3, 5 December 1747, no. 9718; and 31 January 1748, no. 9735.

one of the most severely limited constitutional monarchies in Europe. After Charles XII had exhausted the country with continuous wars in the early years of the century, the Swedes lost their taste for absolutism and forced upon his successors a form of government that left the king as the mere titular head of state. Sovereignty resided in a parliament composed of the four estates: nobles, clergy, burghers, and peasants. The estates *(ständerna)* assembled at a Riksdag once every three years, and special sessions could be called in emergencies. A state council (the *Riksråd*) of sixteen members (plus a governor general for Pomerania) sat permanently and served as the executive. The monarch occupied a seat in council, but he commanded only two votes with the deciding ballot in the case of ties. The monarch likewise had the right of filling vacancies in the council, but this counted for little, as he was obliged to choose a new councillor from a list of three candidates presented by the estates, who had the sole power of dismissing a councillor. The king's power and freedom of movement were in fact so severely restricted that he could not even leave the capital city of Stockholm without being accompanied by a delegation from the state council.

The head of government, the chancellor, was the leader in council. His power depended upon his ability to maintain the council's independence from the estates. This was no mean task. The council differed from a modern cabinet in that it often contained opponents of the chancellor as well as his supporters, and his enemies could always appeal over his head to the sovereign instance, the Riksdag, in order to place limits on the chancellor's authority. Under the strong chancellorship of Arvid Horn (1720–1738) the council was able to maintain a leading position until the late 1730s. But thereafter power devolved more and more to the estates themselves, which exercised it through their committees and party caucuses.[24] With the executive much weakened, Swedish government became increasingly subject to the influence of foreign intrigue and foreign money, or perhaps it would be more accurate to say that bribery

[24]Ludvig Stavenow, "Det adertonde århundradets parlamentarism i Sverige," *Uppsala Universitets Årsskrift* (1923), program 1, 1–31, reviews the Swedish system and compares it with British parliamentary government; also see his *Frihetstiden,* vol. 9 of *Sveriges historia till våra dagar* (Stockholm, 1922). For a more recent review, incorporating several new interpretations, see Sven Ulric Palme, "Vom Absolutismus zum Parliamentarismus in Schweden," *Ständische Vertretungen in Europa im 17. und 18. Jahrhundert,* ed. D. Gerhard (Göttingen, 1969), pp. 368–97.

and corruption spread to much wider circles than would have been the case if the decision-making authority remained in the hands of sixteen senators.[25]

By the time of Panin's arrival in Stockholm this political configuration had been complicated by the emergence of two parties, the Hats and the Caps. Both parties were controlled by nobles and opposed the reestablishment of royal power. Contrary to the assumption frequently found in Russian monographs,[26] Panin's task in Sweden did not concern itself exclusively with preventing the return of absolutism, although that was certainly one object of his mission. His primary responsibility was to help the Cap party gain control of government and remove the influence of the pro-French Hats, whose leaders dared challenge Russian attempts to steer Swedish foreign policy.

The "crisis of the North" that faced Panin in Sweden had been simmering for some time before his arrival. On orders from the Russian court Baron Korff had been collaborating with the opposition Cap party in actions that overstepped the limits of treason. The news of these criminal dealings, coming on top of public threats and blustering by the Russian government, created a sharp reaction in Swedish politics, and the 1746 Riksdag not only fell handily to the pro-French party, but the leadership even went over to the radical wing of the Hats.[27] When information soon after began to leak out that the new Hat leadership, in league with the heirs to the throne, was planning to overthrow the constitution and strengthen royal

[25]It is difficult to establish a neat cause-and-effect relationship here, since even under the absolutism of Charles XI in the late seventeenth century there was a great deal of French money expended in an effort to bring Sweden into an alliance. Palme, "Vom Absolutismus zum Parlamentarismus," pp. 391–92. The whole question of the effects of foreign "bribe" money on Swedish politics is currently under review in a dissertation now in progress by Michael F. Metcalf, "Russia, England and Swedish Party Politics 1762–1766," Stockholm University, 1975.

[26]See, for example, G. A. Gukovskii, *Ocherki po istorii russkoi literatury XVIII veka*, pp. 125–26.

[27]Olof Jägerskiöld, *Den svenska utrikespolitikens historia*, 2:2, *1721–1792* (Stockholm, 1957), p. 170. The victory of the "radical" or "extremist" Hats was, however, qualified to some extent by the actions of the new chancellery president, Carl Gustaf Tessin, who was able to maintain a more moderate course vis-à-vis Russia, despite the protests of the radicals like Nils Palmstierna, Claes Ekeblad, and A. J. von Höpken, who came into the state council in 1746. This split between Tessin and the more radical members of his party has recently been illuminated in a monograph by Arne Remgård, *Carl Gustaf Tessin och 1746–1747 års riksdag* (Lund, 1968).

power to the advantage of the French party, Russian Chancellor Bestuzhev decided to seek a definite change in Swedish politics by outright military force if necessary. The plan was to send Russian troops into Finland, then a part of the Swedish empire, and force the heir apparent, Adolf Fredrik, to renounce his right to the throne. A new election would then be held to insure the succession of a government friendly to Russia. The only problem was that the Cap party had first to make a direct appeal for Russian intervention. It was Panin's job, after he replaced Korff in Stockholm, to persuade the Cap leaders to submit such an appeal. But fearing reprisals in the event of failure, the Caps agreed to no more than sending an antedated request once the Russians had launched the venture.[28] As tensions increased, Panin found his duties more and more distasteful; it gave him little satisfaction to have to encourage Swedes to risk their careers and lives in a desperate gamble. Several of those who cooperated with him suffered political ruin, imprisonment, and exile. One was even executed. It was a demoralizing job and Panin more than once begged to be relieved of it.[29]

Ultimately, military action was avoided. The French party, while remaining firmly in control, eventually decided to drop plans for changing the constitution. Britain and Austria, seeing the danger for peace in the North, prevailed upon Russia to adopt a more moderate course.[30] And finally, Panin himself helped to ease tensions by his cautious handling of the delicate situation and his efforts to soften the most provocative initiatives of his superiors.[31]

In view of Panin's later reputation for caution and indolence, it is interesting to observe the daring and risky enterprises that characterized his embassy in Sweden. His dispatches from Stockholm through

[28]On this entire crisis see: Jägerskiöld, *Utrikespolitikens historia*, pp. 170–78; Olof Jägerskiöld, *Hovet och författningsfrågan 1760–1766* (Uppsala, 1943), pp. 8–10; J. R. Danielsson (-Kalmari), *Die nordische Frage in den Jahren 1746–51* (Helsingfors, 1888), pp. 288–91; and Harald Hjärne's lengthy review of same, "Storpolitiska villobilder från frihetstiden," *Samlade skrifter*, (Stockholm, 1932), 2:292–334; Fritz Arheim, "Beiträge zur Geschichte der nordischen Frage in der zweiten Hälfte des 18 Jahrhunderts," serially in *Deutsche Zeitschrift für Geschichtswissenschaft*, especially vol. 7 (1892); Werner Krummel, *Nikita Ivanovič Panins aussenpolitische Tätigkeit 1747–1758* (Breslau, 1941), pp. 15–38. Sven Ulric Palme is now at work on a review of this entire question.

[29]Panin's dispatch from Stockholm, no. 46, ca. 30 August 1749, *LOII, f.* 36, *op.* 1, *d.* 127.

[30]Jägerskiöld, *Utrikespolitikens historia*, pp. 176–81; also the British dispatches in *SIRIO*, 110, *passim*.

[31]Krummel, *Aussenpolitische Tätigkeit*, pp. 36–38.

the period of the Northern crisis read like a spy thriller. He employed
a network of agents with whom he established secret rendezvous in
the forests outside the capital while pretending to be on hunting
excursions. In 1749 one of his agents, the auditor Hoof, was arrested
by the Swedish authorities and thereby jeopardized Panin's other
agents. For several days he had to hide a badly compromised chancellery official Höök in various houses until he could spirit him across
the border to safety in Denmark. In an admirable display of tolerance, the Russian minister availed himself of the services of a
Catholic priest in this venture.[32] The most difficult days of Panin's
mission in Stockholm came two years later in 1751 with the capture
of his Finnish agent, a certain Wijkmann, and several accomplices.[33]
The French party freely exploited the news of the arrests and
treasonous dealings to arouse the populace against Russia; accusa-
tions even spread that the Russian minister was responsible for a
plague of fires then sweeping the city. For a while Panin was afraid
he might be lynched. To his good fortune, the episode ended a short
time later with the beheading of Wijkmann and imprisonment of
his associates.[34] Since the Northern crisis also subsided about this
time, Panin managed to maintain the goodwill of the Swedish
political leaders, who tactfully placed the blame for the whole affair
on the Russian attaché.

With regard to the remaining nine years of Panin's mission
abroad, there are two common myths that should be set aright. The
first concerns his involvement in Swedish affairs and bears implications for his subsequent activities in Russia. The argument runs that
he acquired a taste for republican government and skill in its operation by his long experience of working against monarchical power in
Sweden. Whether Panin acquired a taste for republicanism must,
of course, be tested on evidence more convincing than the mere
fact of his presence in Sweden for twelve years. On the more verifi-
able point, Panin's efforts were not directed against the monarchy.

[32]Panin's dispatches of 1749, nos. 41, 42, 49, and 58 (11 August-3 November), *LOII,*
f. 36, *op.* 1, *d.* 127; Solov'ev, *Istoriia Rossii,* 12: 80.

[33]Among those arrested Panin mentioned a Finnish pastor and a certain Serenius, who
would seem to be Anders Seréen, imprisoned for a short time in 1751 because of a pam-
phlet he had written. Panin's dispatch for 17 May 1751, no. 21, *LOII, f.* 36, *op.* 1, *d.* 127;
and Malmström, *Sveriges politiska historia,* 4: 16.

[34]Panin's dispatches of 1751, nos. 19, 20, 21, 23, 25, 26, 28, 29, 32, 33, 35, and 37
(3 May-13 September), *LOII, f.* 36, *op.* 1, *d.* 127; Solov'ev, *Istoriia Rossii,* 12: 156.

In fact, after 1751 his work concentrated on reestablishing the authority of the monarchy in Sweden. The principal object was to restore a balance to the political system. The estates had so thoroughly plundered the rights and powers of the crown that by 1756 the king could no longer even refuse to sign the council's decrees. The council simply replaced his signature with a namestamp. To help counter the degradation of monarchical authority, Panin subsidized the party of the court and through the 1750s worked very closely with the royal couple, King Adolf Fredrik and Queen Lovisa Ulrika. Although the King was something of an eccentric and incompetent,[35] Panin placed high hopes on his wife, Lovisa Ulrika, the sister of Frederick II of Prussia and a strong-willed politician in her own right. Under her direction the court party drew up plans to win back some of the powers lost by the crown since the change to parliamentary government in 1719, and Panin may even have been involved in a 1756 plot to which the court party, unsuccessfully as it turned out, attempted to reassert the rights of the monarchy.[36] The object was not, of course, to restore absolutism in Sweden, which would have been inimical to Russia's interests, but merely to create a stable balance among the three elements of government: crown, council, and estates. One must be cautious of drawing unwarranted conclusions from the actions of a minister operating at least broadly within the guidelines set by his court.[37] Yet, with this said, the evidence of Panin's work in Sweden during the 1750s should lay to rest the notion that long experience combatting monarchical power gave him a taste for republicanism. If anything, it indicates his interest in a balanced monarchy à la Montesquieu.[38]

[35]Panin enjoyed describing the king's curious behavior at court receptions. "He would walk around the room not knowing what to say or with whom to start. Sometimes he would talk about the weather, how lovely it was, when outside it was pouring down rain." Poroshin, *Zapiski*, 10 October 1765.

[36]The evidence for Panin's involvement in the coup is tenuous at best, but it is clear that he was very close to the court party at this time. See Jägerskiöld, *Hovet och författningsfrågan*, p. 206; G. Olsson, "Fredrik II och Sveriges författning," *Scandia*, 27, no. 2 (1961), 348–50; and the French envoy Bérenger to Choiseul, 3 September 1762, *SIRIO*, 140: 645. But see also Palme's view that there was no foreign involvement in the coup plans. "Vom Absolutismus zum Parliamentarismus," 390–91.

[37]But in this case Panin may have gone well beyond these guidelines. Instruction from College of Foreign Affairs to N. I. Panin, 1756, *LOII, f.* 36, *op.* 1, *d.* 1072, 93–95.

[38]If this were indeed Panin's position, he was some years ahead of his Swedish hosts, who only in the next decade began to project changes that would bring the executive branch (a combination of king and council) into an effective balance with the unbridled

Another aspect often overlooked was Panin's perception of party politics. It had little in common with the modern definition of that term or even with eighteenth-century Swedish practices. After many frustrating months of trying to regroup the Cap party, which since its formation in the late 1730s had been unable to gain a foothold in the senate, Panin reported that he could "see no better way to form a party than by bribing two or three senators, who would possess the necessary qualities for leading a party and would take upon themselves its formation."[39] In this way he could get some kind of formal party organization with which to work instead of trying to deal with the fragmented, frightened, and powerless Caps.[40] This approach seemed reasonable under the circumstances, but it had little to do with established party politics of the Swedish parliamentary system. It resembled much more closely the *modus operandi* of foreign agents at the Russian court, who tried to achieve their aims not through parties but by buying the cooperation of particular statesmen.

The second myth concerns Panin's relations with his superiors in St. Petersburg. Without exception, historians have pictured Panin as a protégé of Chancellor Bestuzhev-Riumin and as the instrument of his policy. The matter was considerably more complex. Panin was anything but a blind tool of Bestuzhev's policies, and the persistence of this interpretation has not only led historians into unnecessary difficulties but has also obscured some interesting characteristics of Panin's behavior in the system of personal relations governing politics at the Russian court.

In holding to this view, writers have been unable to resolve two major issues of Panin's career history. First, when Bestuzhev lost power to Vice-Chancellor M. L. Vorontsov and I. I. Shuvalov after the outbreak of the Seven Years' War (which exposed the bankruptcy of Bestuzhev's pro-British policy), why was his protégé Panin tolerated at an important diplomatic post for three or four more years? Panin's survival was all the more puzzling inasmuch as one of

---

legislative power. See the discussion of C. F. Scheffer's proposal of 1764 in Jägerskiöld, *Hovet och författningsfrågan*, pp. 155–58, 191, 323, in which the author calls Scheffer's plan the first attempt in Swedish history, and perhaps the first attempt in history generally, to realize Montesquieu's constitutitonal ideals.

[39]Solov'ev, *Istoriia Rossii*, 12: 79–80. On the formation of the Cap party in the 1730s, see the recent dissertation by Göran Nilzén, *Studier i 1730-talets partiväsen*, published in a limited edition (Stockholm, 1971).

[40]Solov'ev, *Istoriia Rossii*, 12: 74–75.

his close friends, V. E. Adadurov, suffered disgrace and exile along with Bestuzhev and others of his clique in 1758.[41] Second, how did Panin manage to receive the much-coveted post of *oberhofmeister* to Grand Duke Paul in 1760 when Bestuzhev's enemies were at the height of their power? In assuming a close link between Panin and Bestuzhev, historians have failed to answer these questions.

If one poses the question in another fashion, however, the explanations appear less difficult. Was Panin in fact beholden to Bestuzhev and his policies? The evidence suggests a more complicated and intriguing picture. Indeed the chancellor helped Panin get his start in the diplomatic service. While in Sweden, Panin often wrote to Bestuzhev about problems connected with his service, and the chancellor responded with fatherly advice and encouragement. Panin always remembered these debts,[42] but at the same time he kept his bets well covered. Like many ambitious young comers in the service, he carefully cultivated personal and family links to other power groups in high government and maintained his visibility with several important patrons. This behavior, so characteristic of aspiring clients in a sociopolitical power structure based on patronage networks,[43] served to shelter the young diplomat against unpredictable fluctuations in court politics. Throughout his service abroad, for example, Panin maintained correct and even amicable relations with Bestuzhev's enemy Vorontsov. Judging from their earliest letters, Vorontsov may in fact have been as important as Bestuzhev in boosting Panin's career in the foreign service.[44] At the same time, Panin quietly built up his connections at the Grand Ducal court of Peter Fedorovich and Catherine. One of his most important contacts there was Adadurov, who had been Catherine's tutor in Russian language and continued to be her friend and con-

[41]About the others who fell with Bestuzhev see Elizabeth's ukase to the senate, 5 April 1759, *SIRIO*, 42:470–71.

[42]Later on when Bestuzhev turned against him in the bitter intrigues of Catherine II's early reign, Panin nevertheless received his petitions and assisted the old man in his family problems. A. P. Bestuzhev-Riumin to N. I. Panin, 26 May 1765, 13 March 1766, *LOII, f.* 36, *op.* 1, *d.* 145, 102–05.

[43]Anthony Leeds, "Brazilian Careers and Social Structure: A Case History and Model," in Dwight Heath and Richard Adams, *Contemporary Cultures and Societies in Latin America* (New York, 1965), pp. 379–404.

[44]*AKV*, 7: 450–87; 26: 56–71. Note especially the first letters from Germany in which Panin writes that the only correspondence he has received has come from Vorontsov; for the informal tone see especially the letter from Stockholm, 14 April 1749, 26: 59–60.

fidant long after the formal instruction was ended.[45] Also, the
British diplomat Charles Hanbury Williams, Catherine's go-between
in her secret correspondence with Stanislaw Poniatowski, spoke to
the grand duchess in glowing terms of Panin's work abroad. As early
as 1756 Catherine was mentioning Panin as a good candidate for a
future foreign minister.[46] Finally, Panin's familial and personal ties
with Empress Elizabeth (through the Kurakins, Everlakovs, and his
own brief stint as favorite), as well as his recognized accomplishments
as minister in Sweden, allowed him a measure of independence from
the intrigues of courtiers.

Certainly, in the execution of his duties after the "diplomatic
reversal" of the middle 1750s, Panin was no more faithful to Bestuzhev's policy than to Vorontsov's. He was clearly acting with a
great deal of personal discretion and formulating a political system
of his own.[47] This rejection of his own court's policies grew out of his
concern for the balance of power in Europe, which he saw endangered by French power. In view of previous French support of Russia's three enemies—Turkey, Poland, and Sweden—France's successful beginning in the colonial war with England caused Panin to
fear for the fate of Russia, should France again become the dominant
power in Europe.[48] In Panin's view it was scarcely the time for Russia to turn against the English-Prussian coalition. This was an
understandable position for the Russian minister in Sweden to
adopt; he had worked for years to stymie the anti-Russian machinations of French agents in the North. Indeed this early recognition of
the threat of French power on the continent no doubt sowed the
seeds of Panin's later foreign policy of the "Northern Accord."[49]
The only change in the meantime was that England's victory over
France in America—the news of which Panin greeted with enthusiasm[50]—reduced the urgency of cementing close relations with the
British.

[45]*Williams Correspondence*, pp. 137, 141, 163, 166–67, 169, 178.

[46]Catherine to Williams, [17 October] 1756, *Williams Correspondence* p. 183.

[47]Krummel, *Aussenpolitische Tätigkeit*, p. 54.

[48]Solov'ev, *Istoriia Rossii*, 12: 425–26.

[49]It was previously believed that a memoir from Baron Korff was the genesis of the
Northern system. The memoir was, however, received after the policy had been formulated. K. Rahbek Schmidt, "Wie ist Panins Plan zu einem Nordischen System entstanden?" *Zeitschrift für Slawistik*, 2, no. 3 (1957), 406–22.

[50]N. I. Panin to A. M. Golitsyn, Stockholm, 16 November 1759, *TsGADA, f.* 1263, *op.*
1, *d.* 2655, 5–6.

Panin's inclination to favor a pro-Prussian orientation for Russian policy at a time when his country was joining the coalition against Frederick II could scarcely have received the approval of either party at the Russian court. Both Bestuzhev's abortive pro-British policy and Vorontsov's pro-French orientation were directed against Prussia. The measure of Panin's independence at this juncture may be seen not only in his dispatches arguing for his own political positions and in the sharp reprimands he received in return,[51] but also in his continued resistance in subsequent years. In willful disregard of a circular letter (10 January 1757) instructing Russian envoys to cease all contact with Prussian representatives in their locations, Panin continued to visit openly with the Prussian minister Solms.[52] Under these circumstances one might well ask again how Panin managed to survive at his post during these critical years, and not only survive but turn up in 1760 with one of the most coveted positions at the Russian court, the guardianship of the Grand Duke Paul.

The answer lies in the complex factional struggle going on at the Russian court in connection with the diplomatic reversal of 1756 and the overthrow of Bestuzhev's system by the Vorontsov and Shuvalov parties. At this juncture Panin's position of independence from Bestuzhev's policies as well as his general political attitudes stood him in good stead. In their effort to remove Bestuzhev the Vorontsovs sent a special commission under the direction of Count Iaguzhinskii to Sweden in 1756. The commission's ostensible task was simply to convey the sympathies of the Russian monarch on the death of the dowager queen. In fact, Iaguzhinskii was also secretly there gathering material to be used in undermining Bestuzhev's position at the head of foreign affairs in St. Petersburg. Bestuzhev himself was sorely deceived by the entire enterprise. He felt certain that the commission, made up in part of clients of Count Shuvalov (whom he regarded as a friend), would act in behalf of the Bestuzhev party. The Chancellor informed Panin in this sense:

I expect that you know even without my telling you that

[51]Solov'ev, *Istoriia Rossii*, 12: 422.

[52]Frederick II warmly acknowledged this gesture from Panin and expressed a forlorn wish that the Russian court might share the same "moderate disposition" toward Prussia. Krummel, *Aussenpolitische Tätigkeit*, p. 54; cf. *Politische Correspondence Friedrichs des Grossen*, 46 vols. (Berlin, 1879–1939), 14: 328–29.

[Iaguzhinskii] is the brother-in-law of His Excellency Iv[an] Iv [anovich] Shuvalov: I recommend and request Your Excellency to show him your goodwill, friendship and every courtesy not only because Ivan Ivanovich is my special friend but even more because when you acquaint him with your own particular needs and requests, on his return I may hope to work in this regard for you with the utmost success.[53]

It soon became apparent to Panin, however, that Iaguzhinskii was there to spy on Bestuzhev and to look into his correspondence with Panin, at which point Panin reaffirmed his wish to steer clear of the factional struggles at the Russian court.[54] What had apparently happened was that the Shuvalovs and Vorontsovs had united to get rid of Bestuzhev and his immediate supporters. The Shuvalovs would also have been happy to include Panin among those destined to share Bestuzhev's disgrace, but two circumstances spared Panin this fate. First, his declared independence of Bestuzhev's system removed him from suspicion as one of the chancellor's close support- ers. Second, and even more important, the Vorontsovs were at this time playing a double game with the Shuvalovs. While gladly accept- ing the Shuvalovs' assistance in replacing Bestuzhev at the leader- ship of foreign affairs, the Vorontsovs were secretly planning a subsequent move against the Shuvalov party's direction of internal affairs. For two years the Shuvalovs and their clients had been forging a new law code that would protect merchant interests from attempts to restrict manufacturing and serf-based enterprise to nobles. While not wanting to harm noble interests, the Shuvalovs meant to strike a balance that would stimulate economic activity generally. This orientation ran counter to the Vorontsovs' desire to enhance the social, political, and economic position of the nobility at the expense of the merchant estate.[55] In the coming fight against the Shuvalov program they wanted to marshal all potential allies who shared their vision of Russia's development along the lines of aristo- cratic predominance. Nikita Panin, a man with personal connections

[53]Solov'ev, *Istoriia Rossii*, 12: 369.

[54]Solov'ev, *Istoriia Rossii*, 12: 371–72.

[55]N. L. Rubinshtein, "Ulozhennaia Kommissiia 1754–1766 gg. i ee proekt novogo ulozheniia 'O sostoianii poddannykh voobsche' (K istorii sotsial'noi politiki 50-kh— nachala 60-kh godov XVIII v.)," *Istoricheskie zapiski*, 38 (1951), 208–52, esp. 237–39, 246, 250.

both to the empress and the grand ducal court, must have looked to them as a valuable support in the eventual struggle. Furthermore, his personal correspondence with Vice-Chancellor Vorontsov over the many years of his embassy abroad had shown him to be sympathetic to the type of program the Vorontsovs wished to initiate. It was no doubt for this reason that Vorontsov kept Panin at his diplomatic post after the disgrace and exile of Bestuzhev's faction in 1758 and then two years later helped to elevate Panin to the position of guardian of Grand Duke Paul.

3. Impressions of the West

There exists a number of letters from Panin to Vice-Chancellor Vorontsov containing observations on the societies and political institutions of the countries he visited. The letters and a few other scattered sources adding to them are interesting for two reasons. Firstly, they shed light on Panin's personal relations with the man who replaced Bestuzhev as grand chancellor. And secondly, they give some idea of Panin's appreciation of European society and government. Inasmuch as historians have credited him with attempting to introduce Western institutions in Russia, his comments during this period take on additional importance.

Although, as with all of Panin's biography, the materials on this question are scanty, it is worth while to note even his superficial observations while traveling in Europe, because they reveal something of his general attitude in comparing Russian and Western life. As one would expect from a Russian traveler of the mid-eighteenth century, his own country fared rather poorly in such comparisons. Like most other expatriates of his generation, Panin remarked very favorably on the level of urban development, external order, and the cleanliness of European cities. Not long after returning from Sweden, for example, he was telling Grand Duke Paul about the journey home and mentioned his stop in the Swedish town of Torneå, a miserable place in his opinion. Paul then asked if it were as bad as the Russian town of Klin. "Well," responded Panin, "if you're going to take our Klin, then of course [Torneå] is better. As yet, Sire, we can't really compare any of these things with what we have. We can only comment on what is over there, whether it is good or bad. In any such comparison we are certainly going to come off the loser."[56]

[56]Poroshin, *Zapiski*, 29 September 1765.

On the way to Denmark Panin passed through northern Germany, and in his letters to Vorontsov he gave the towns there very high marks for orderliness as well as for "the industry of the people and their moderate way of life."[57] As for the Scandinavian capitals, Copenhagen struck him as a great metropolis with a wealthy court and well-developed society life, while Stockholm by contrast appeared as a swollen provincial village, pleasing to the eye but devoid of entertainment and extremely costly.[58] There was one aspect of life in both Scandinavian countries to which Panin never quite adjusted: the weather. Although no votary of the harsh Russian winter, he complained to Vorontsov that several weeks of winter in rain-drenched Copenhagen had made him nostalgic for the bracing eastern frosts of his native land.[59] One thing Panin found particularly surprising was that despite the debilitating weather Scandinavians appeared far more vigorous and healthy than Russians. Rather than seeking the cause of this disparity in the institutions and structure of society—as might be expected from a future political reformer—he came up with the altogether reasonable, though not very illuminating, conclusion that the difference was due to "moderate and healthy foods."[60]

Of greater interest was Panin's opinion of the medicine practiced at the Swedish court, because in commenting on it he delivered an indirect rebuff to his superior in St. Petersburg. When Panin arrived in Sweden the ailing King Fredrik was being treated by alchemists who professed to know the secret of golden tinctures. Panin, whose knowledge of medicine was remarkably advanced for the time, immediately recognized this as a fraud and labeled the practitioners as quacks and charlatans, even though one of them had been recommended by persons in the Russian court, including certainly Chancellor Bestuzhev himself.[61] As Panin must have known, the golden tincture was one of Bestuzhev's prized panaceas; indeed, the formula became known in Russia as Tinctura Tonica Nervina Bestucheffi.[62]

Apart from these observations on the habits of life in Europe,

[57]N. I. Panin to M. L. Vorontsov, 26 September 1747, *AKV*, 26: 56.

[58]N. I. Panin to M. L. Vorontsov, Copenhagen, 3 November 1747; Stockholm, 26 February 1748, and 25 June 1748, *AKV*, 26: 57, 7: 458, 459.

[59]N. I. Panin to M. L. Vorontsov, Copenhagen, 14 November 1747, *AKV*, 26: 57–58.

[60]N. I. Panin to M. L. Vorontsov, Stockholm, 14 April 1749, *AKV*, 26: 59–60.

[61]Panin's dispatches of 1749, nos. 35, 54, 59, *LOII, f.* 36, *op.* 1, *d.* 127.

[62]A. C. Wootton, *Chronicles of Pharmacy*, 2 vols. (London, 1910), Vol. 1, pp. 221–22.

Panin made some comments about trade and commerce. In his letters to Vorontsov he strongly advocated expanding Russian grain trade with Sweden, which may be seen as a foreshadowing of the free trade policies that would later grow under Panin's leadership in foreign affairs.[63] Unfortunately, however, these letters did not contain any statements of general policy that would help trace the evolution of Panin's thinking on the subject.

By far the most illuminating remarks in Panin's correspondence dealt with the social arrangements and the positions of the nobility. Interestingly enough, it was not the Swedish but the Danish nobility that evoked his greatest appreciation. Possibly his favorable reaction owed something to the fact that his stay in Denmark coincided with the brief era of internal harmony that marked Fredrik V's first years on the throne and his happy marriage with Queen Louise.[64] In any case, Panin was very favorably impressed with the Danish court and society, and his comments in this regard must have pleased Count Vorontsov. In an early letter from Copenhagen he praised the arrangements there, emphasizing the importance of rank and personal merit. He observed that there was no sign of the cheap, precipitous advancement of flatterers and favorites, a common occurrence in eighteenth-century Russia and one that troubled established dignitaries like the Vorontsovs. With obvious approval Panin remarked of Denmark:

> a great number of prominent old men, wise, deserved and clothed in various high ranks, who are exceptionally respected by their Majesties, consequently also by all others, are to be seen at court and give an indescribable external majesty to the court; all the more so in that they possess that place [*postup'*] solely according to their deserved ranks, and not according to the importance of the affairs in which they are actually engaged (for many of them are retired), and even less according to other accidental causes [*po pripadkam*; i.e., owing to flattery or favoritism].[65]

[63]*AKV*, 7: 460–72. Panin likewise showed a great interest in the things Russia might receive from Sweden. He was a keen student of Swedish craftsmen and a frequent visitor to the artisans' workshops, which won him the reputation of something of an expert on these matters. Poroshin, *Zapiski*, 30 September 1764.

[64]S. C. Bech, *Danmarks historie*, 9, *Oplysning og Tolerance 1721–1784* (Copenhagen, 1965), pp. 296–302.

[65]N. I. Panin to M. L. Vorontsov, Copenhagen, 12 December 1747, *AKV*, 7: 455.

On the matter of the promotion of young people Panin explained that while personal merit and education were closely examined, nonetheless the proved service and loyalty of one's parents counted heavily. This was apparent, he noted, in the cases of the former first minister of the King's Council and his brother Ober-kammerherr Plesof, Ober-stallmeister Count Larvik and Privy Councillor Count Rantzau. Panin remarked: "Their children and relatives, possessing undisputed merits, are separately distinguished before others in youth with ranks of Kammerherr and Colonel, and certain of them as White Cavaliers and by seats in the high court, where His Majesty himself presides." Panin then pointed out the obvious benefit to the country of such a system:

> The respect which is given without exception to rank occasions each honorable person (which everyone in society ought to be) necessarily to strive for the achievement of it; for he is firmly assured that once having received a prominent rank, under all conditions save for the specific loss of it, he is not subjected to the slightest prejudice.[66]

The immediate objection, Panin continued, would naturally be that those involved in affairs, seeing that others without any duties occupied an equal station, would want to acquire the same leisure. But this did not occur in Denmark, he emphasized, as "the great salaries and royal grants . . . for their labors" did not make such a course attractive. In further support of the system Panin commented that a father could not but be encouraged by the knowledge that his labors and services would also reward his children.[67] More willing and able service could be obtained where there was some promise of it redounding to the benefit of one's offspring.

One may be sure that this concern with the training and qualifications of state servitors was an abiding sentiment with Panin. Ten years later in another letter to Vorontsov, this time concerning the education and promotion of young Russian servicemen, he expressed similar ideas. He congratulated Vorontsov on his scheme for the training of young nobles planning a career in the diplomatic corps. Previously those few who chose the difficult path of achieving rank in civil rather than military service were sent abroad to foreign

[66] *AKV*, 7: 455–56.
[67] *AKV*, 7: 456.

posts to gain experience. Vorontsov proposed to have them serve first in the foreign embassies at home. Panin very much approved the idea, pointing out the great additional burden to a minister with many important duties to have at the same time to train an altogether unqualified young man abroad and, moreover, little benefit was usually derived from it. Nor did the previous system attract the best candidates, since for the most part those who were enthusiasts for such service became so "with the sole intention of being able to spend their youth with great freedom in foreign lands."[68] Here Panin was speaking from painful experience; his own chancellery apprentice A. S. Stakhiev had caused him a great deal of grief.[69]

One final indication of Panin's views may be noted here. A later patron of the arts, sponsor of promising young Russian writers, and original member of the Russian Academy, Panin had a life-long interest in the cultural growth of his native land, and while abroad he maintained regular contact with Russian intellectual life. Naturally, he could count on his friend Adadurov to supply him with books he requested and to send along the latest publications from the Academy of Sciences.[70] But again Vice-Chancellor Vorontsov also helped to supplement his diet of readings. In one letter Panin expressed pleasure at receiving from Vorontsov two works by early representatives of the Enlightenment in Russia, Trediakovskii and Lomonsov. The first was Trediakovskii's well-known *Razgovor mezhdu chuzhestrannym chelovekom i Rossiiskom ob ortografii starinnoi i novoi*, published in September 1748.[71] For the second, Lomonosov's ode on the day of the accession to the throne of Empress Elizabeth, Panin was particularly grateful. He gave it the highest praise, noting that the content and verse were of equal quality.[72] Panin's praise of the author's thoughts takes on special significance when one recalls that

[68]N. I. Panin to M. L. Vorontsov, Stockholm, 19 May 1758, *AKV*, 7: 474–75; for Vorontsov's proposal on bringing capable men into the civil service, *LOII*, *f.* 36, *op.* 1, *d.* 1073.

[69]Panin's dispatch of 1751, no. 51 (13 December), *LOII*, *f.* 36, *op.* 1, *d.* 127. In later years, however, he prided himself on having taken Stakhiev in hand and turned him into an excellent foreign representative. Poroshin, *Zapiski*, 17 October 1764.

[70]V. E. Adadurov to N. I. Panin [n.d., n.p., internal evidence relates to 1747–53], *Russkii Arkhiv* (1888), no. 3, 182.

[71]N. I. Panin to M. L. Vorontsov, Stockholm, November 1748, *AKV*, 7, note by P. B[artenev], 459–60.

[72]Both the date of the letter and Panin's comments leave no doubt that the reference relates to Lomonosov's well-known *Oda na den' vosshestviia na prestol Elizavety Petrovny 1747*.

the two main themes of the work were an enthusiastic approval of Elizabeth's politics of peace (Russia was then being urged to enter the War of Austrian Succession) and a tribute to the empress' support of the Academy of Sciences and the cause of enlightenment in Russia. The causes of peace and enlightenment would be central concerns of Panin's future ministry.

Taken altogether these scattered references to Panin's thoughts and interests during the period of his mission abroad do not allow of any startling conclusions. Their main interest is the reflection of an open and friendly exchange of views between him and Vice-Chancellor Vorontsov. Moreover, one can observe that Panin's attitudes, sketchily though the substantive material reveals them, conformed generally to the style of aristocratic constitutionalism associated with the Vorontsov program. By contrast, there was no evidence to support the frequent assertion that Panin acquired a taste for republican institutions during his tour in Scandinavia. He reserved his most favorable comments for Denmark, an absolutist state in which the nobility played a leading political role. What especially impressed him there was the respect given to prominent families and the security of life, honor, rank, and property afforded by law and custom. These fundamental constitutional guarantees were central concerns of the liberal aristocrats in Russia. Panin left no record of similarly favorable remarks about "republican" Sweden. To the extent that he had anything to write about Swedish institutions he most often expressed fear that they would be overturned by the continuous meddling of the estates. His warmest praise went to spokesmen like the young Baron Wrangel who warned his colleagues in the Riksdag that their heedless violation of civil laws and regulations was threatening to undermine the whole structure of constitutional government. It was probably the misuse of power by the sovereign legislature and not republicanism itself that prompted Panin's concern and disposed him to work toward restoring a measure of royal authority and bringing the political system back into balance. Indicative of his relativistic approach to questions of government was Panin's high estimation of the Swedish political philosopher J. J. Montin, who, in line with Montesquieu, argued that a country's form of government must conform to the attitudes and needs of the people at a particular stage in its development and exhibit a proper balance between freedom and order.[73] By the same token, with regard to the applicability of Swedish models to Russia, it seems highly unlikely that a relativist and diligent student of Montesquieu like Panin would consider such borrowing either possible or desirable. He was even skeptical of the value of many civil regulations Peter the Great had taken over from Sweden. Commenting once on how many Russian laws were borrowed from that source, he noted that they came at a time when the Swedish government was in transition from one regime to another, and even the Swedes were not satisfied with the regulations, "yet we adopted them word for word into a monarchical government, and moreover one that is as vast as ours."[74]

4. The Return to St. Petersburg as Oberhofmeister

Although the foregoing information gives only a very incomplete picture of Panin's early career, it is of great value in clearing up the mystery surrounding his recall from Sweden and his simultaneous appointment as *oberhofmeister* to Grand Duke Paul. This appointment, which marked another major advancement in Panin's personal rise, has baffled all writers on this period. The leading biographer of Catherine the Great, V. A. Bil'basov, reported that Panin's designation to such an important post constituted a riddle to everyone at court, inasmuch as Panin received it "at just the time, 1760, when the Shuvalovs and Vorontsovs, enemies of Panin, were all-powerful."[75] The best explanation Bil'basov could offer was that the appointment occurred through the personal intervention of Empress Elizabeth, one of the arguments being that Elizabeth willingly employed talented men of any party. Werner Krummel, author of a monograph on Panin's activities in Sweden, seconded this opinion and bolstered it with a letter from Peter Panin to

---

[73] Comments on Wrangel and the abuse of legislative power in Panin's dispatches of 1751, nos. 40 and 43 (4 and 25 October), and on Montin's book, identified only as *Meshchanskoi obraz pravleniia*, in dispatch for 1749, no. 65 (9 December), *LOII, f.* 36, *op.* 1, *d.* 127. From Panin's comments it was possible to identify the work as that of Johan Johansson Montin, *Borgelig Regering, til des uprinnelse och art* (Stockholm, 1749). I must thank the staff of the Royal Library in Stockholm for help in identifying this work and for providing a microfilm copy of it.

[74] Poroshin, *Zapiski*, 13 October 1765.

[75] Bil'basov, *Istoriia Ekateriny II*, Vol. 1, p. 434.

Chancellor Vorontsov in which Peter Panin expressed his gratitude for a distinction made him after the battle of Kunersdorf and at the same time mentioned the kindness with which the empress had always treated him and his brother. Krummel accepted the vague allusion as evidence that Empress Elizabeth had been instrumental in obtaining Nikita Panin's appointment to the grand ducal court over the objection of Vorontsov.[76] However, Panin's biographer A. I. Braudo rejected such flimsy evidence. He considered the matter a total mystery:

> [Panin] was altogether unexpectedly named to replace Bekhteev as the tutor of Grand Duke Paul and *oberhofmeister* to His Imperial Highness. In light of the influence which was then enjoyed by Panin's enemies, the appointment of him always seemed incomprehensible and one can scarcely be satisfied with the explanation that "Elizabeth did not like to leave inactive those who had distinguished themselves by their talents."[77]

The date Braudo gave for the appointment, 29 June 1760, likewise revealed how sketchy knowledge of this question was. It is not clear what Braudo was referring to with this date. In any case, Panin was informed of the decision to name him tutor of the grand duke as early as November 1759, at least eight months prior to this reckoning.[78] And he began sending correspondence under his new title as soon as he arrived in St. Petersburg in late spring of 1760.[79]

The assumption responsible for all this difficulty was that Chancellor Vorontsov was Panin's enemy. The notion derived mainly from diplomatic dispatches that associated Panin firmly with the former Chancellor Bestuzhev, and of course about the enmity between Bestuzhev and Vorontsov there was little doubt.[80] So far as it concerned Panin, however, the assumption was entirely unwar-

---

[76]Krummel, *Aussenpolitische Tätigkeit*, p. 57. For the latest example of this opinion see David Griffiths, "The Rise and Fall of the Northern System: Court Politics in the First Half of Catherine II's Reign," *Canadian Slavic Studies*, 4, no. 3 (Fall 1970), p. 550.

[77]"Nikita Ivanovich Panin," *RBS*, 13: 190.

[78]N. I. Panin to M. L. Vorontsov, Stockholm, 23 November 1759, *AKV*, 26: 66–67.

[79]For example, his letter of 13 June 1760 to A. M. Golitsyn identified the sender as "S. E. Mr. de Panin, Gouverneur de S. H. I. Mgr. le Gr. Duc." *TsGADA, f.* 1263, *op.* 1, *d.* 2656.

[80]Bil'basov, *Istoriia Ekateriny II*, Vol. 1, pp. 434–35; Braudo, *RBS*, 13: 189–90; Krummel, *Aussenpolitische Tätigkeit*, pp. 54–55; Herbert Kaplan, *Russia and the Outbreak of the Seven Years' War* (Berkeley, 1968), pp. 36–46 and *passim*.

ranted. As mentioned previously, he was not tied exclusively to Bestuzhev, and his position was certainly not dependent on Bestuzhev's tenure in office. He continued at an important post for some time after Bestuzhev's fall, and when finally recalled at his own repeated requests to return home and repair his family's finances, his recall was considered only temporary.[81] He did not submit his official leave-taking to the Swedish government until long after he reached St. Petersburg and was installed as *oberhofmeister*.[82]

It seems quite clear now that Vorontsov, far from raising any objection to Panin's promotion, was the man who recommended and facilitated it. The regular and amicable correspondence between the two men during Panin's mission abroad provides evidence plausible enough in itself. Nonetheless, much additional evidence exists. Ever since 1755, presumably in connection with the planned move against the Bestuzhev and Shuvalov parties, Vorontsov had been showing special favor to relatives of Panin. Among other things, he arranged for the transfer of Panin's exiled brother-in-law I. I. Nepliuev from Orenburg to a high position in the central government.[83] He also performed a number of favors for Peter Panin. As for the promotion of Nikita Panin in 1760, the letters relating to the subject are altogether explicit. As early as November 1759 Nikita Panin thanked Vorontsov for his representations in regard to the appointment.[84] A few months later, after he had learned more details of the promotion, he turned again to the chancellor with effusive expressions of gratitude:

> The excuses you have made on my behalf to Her Imperial Majesty regarding the delays in my difficult journey, your personal protection in hastening my brother's departure to meet me, and finally your gracious participation in our all-kind Autocratrice's most generous care for me are such beneficent acts on Your

[81]Before learning of his appointment as *oberhofmeister*, Panin understood that he would be returning to Sweden after visiting at home. On 16 November 1759 he wrote to the Russian minister in England, A. M. Golitsyn: "L'Impératrice notre très-gracieuse Souvéraine vient de m'ordonner de venir pour un tems à La Cour, en laissant ici accrédité auprès du Ministère pour le tems de mon absence Mr. de Stachieff Conseiller de Legation." (*TsGADA, f.* 1236. *op.* 1, *d.* 2655, 6).

[82]N. I. Panin to Swedish Chancellor, Peterhof, 2 September 1760, *SRa*, Muscovitica, no. 628.

[83]*AKV*, 4: 105; 25: 216.

[84]*AKV*, 26: 66–67.

Excellency's part that they verily surpass all the power of my words and obligate me eternally to the greatest recognition and gratitude, and truly I feel this obligation most pleasantly to its fullest extent.[85]

Another letter to the chancellor by Peter Panin likewise confirmed Vorontsov's assistance in obtaining his brother's recall from Sweden and "increasing Her Imperial Majesty's favor to him . . . with a generous reward."[86]

The year 1760 marked a major turning point in the fortunes of the Panin family. Just five years earlier the two brothers had been plagued with financial difficulties that threatened to undermine their ambitions for further career advancement. With no war since the early forties Peter had been held at the rank of colonel for some years. Nikita's salary of 6,000 rubles was providing far too little for him to maintain an expensive mission in Stockholm, and his meagre earnings from the family property (1,500 rubles) were an insufficient supplement. For a while he seriously contemplated retiring so as not to insult the imperial service by a display of penury.[87] However, his brother frantically, and wisely as it turned out, admonished him to stay on at whatever cost, as Nikita represented at that time the principal hope for the advancement of "their much eclipsed family." A man of action as well as of words, Peter promised to scrape together some extra money, outlined several additional proposals for increasing their financial resources, and even went so far as to advise his reluctant brother to seek out a wealthy wife to save the situation.[88]

---

[85]N. I. Panin to M. L. Vorontsov, Fredrikshamn, 20 April 1760, *AKV*, 26: 70–71.

[86]P. I. Panin to M. L. Vorontsov, October 1759, *LOII, f.* 36, *op.* 1, *d.* 1087, 217.

[87]N. I. Panin to P. I. Panin, Stockholm, 5 January 1755, *Russkii Arkhiv* (1890), no . 1, pp. 53–56. Panin must have remembered later when he headed Russian foreign affairs, for he allotted the minister to Sweden a salary twice as high as the one he had received. Poroshin, *Zapiski*, 5 November 1765.

[88]After listing a number of possibilities, Peter added: "It remains still to propose to you a most useful means, but I fear that it will be for you the most burdensome of all. Allow me to direct your attention to your merits, character, physical gifts and mature years. Would not all this make a fine catch for worthy fiancées with substantial means? I can assure you from experience that life with a wife is not so terrible as philosophic reflections are wont to represent it, and in married life one's concerns are no different than in other areas of life: i.e., diligent unrelenting and enlightened care must be given in order to obtain a comfortable tranquility. And, of course, your relatives do not regard it as much in their interest that you would leave them as your heirs after your death, but, of

Now matters had taken a dramatic turn for the better. The outbreak of the Seven Year's War provided an arena for Peter Panin's military talents, and he soon brought great honors and a substantial increase in the family's fortunes by participating in brilliant victories over the Prussians. Then a short time later, through the intervention of the new Chancellor Vorontsov, Nikita won promotion to *oberhof-meister*, which in addition to carrying with it payment of his outstanding debts,[89] supplied him with a handsome salary and access to the innermost circles of court. In fact, during the turbulent months preceding Empress Elizabeth's death, a period when intrigues abounded as various factions worked to insure themselves against the changes certain to follow the accession of a new ruler, there was probably no more assured or politically secure position in the Russian government than that of guardian to the heir designate's son.

---

course, desire rather that with your talents you would much to their honor contribute to the renewal of the family and your own glory. If there are no such fiancées where you are, we can find plenty here, if you will only show yourself so inclined." P. I. Panin to N. I. Panin, 4 March 1755, *Russkii Arkhiv* (1890), no. 1, p. 58.

[89]Which amounted to 14,000 rubles. M. Deev to A. R. Vorontsov, 18 July 1760, *AKV*, 31: 45.

3

Preparation for Rule, 1760–1762

1. The Vorontsov Ascendancy

On returning to St. Petersburg after twelve years abroad Nikita Panin found that two major changes affecting high government had occurred. One of these, the takeover of political leadership by the Vorontsov party, will be pursued in some detail in this chapter. About the other change, the breakdown of the domestic administration, a few words should be said at the beginning in order to define the context in which the political struggles of this era played themselves out.

By 1760 the provincial government in Russia was very nearly in a state of paralysis. The Seven Years' War provided the proximate cause, but the explanation lay ultimately in the failure of earlier regimes to expand and modernize the civil bureaucracy. Right through the middle of the eighteenth century Russia had continued to rely on an antiquated territorial administration capable of managing only the most rudimentary governmental functions typical of the previous century. The new burdens imposed by the Petrine reforms, such as periodic census taking, recruiting levies to supply a standing army, and collection of the head tax, could be accomplished only with the participation of the regular army, which came to constitute an indispensable element of the domestic administration. In the provinces the two were often indistinguishable. While this system worked well enough in peacetime, the Seven Years' War quickly exposed its weakness. The removal of the army to the front stripped the country of local government just when it was needed most. Before long the economy was in a slump, the treasury depleted, salaries in arrears, foreign credit evaporating, and peasant disturbances dangerously on the increase.[1]

[1]The principal works on this question are: M. M. Bogoslovskii, *Oblastnaia reforma Petra Velikogo: Provintsiia 1719–1727* (Moscow, 1902); Iu. V. Got'e, *Istoriia oblastnogo upravleniia*

These problems had begun to touch Panin even before his return to Russia. Throughout most of 1759 the Foreign Affairs Collegium had been unable to pay his salary, and when his house in Stockholm burned down that year he had to take out burdensome personal loans just to get a roof over his head.[2] Beyond this, the general problem of administration and governmental reorganization would absorb Panin's attention in this period when he was quietly building his influence in the grand ducal court. There he would develop the two primary objectives of his later ministry: the reestablishment of peace, and the improvement of the state's internal organization.

The second change greeting Panin was the shift in political leadership. Over the past four years the Vorontsovs had successfully managed to dislodge their two most powerful competitors, the parties of A. P. Bestuzhev-Riumin and the Shuvalov brothers. As noted earlier, the Vorontsovs wrested control of foreign affairs from Bestuzhev in the middle fifties and drove him and his supporters into disgrace and exile.[3] Taking over as new Chancellor, M. L. Vorontsov quickly solidified his leadership through direct control of the state council *(Konferentsiia)* and the installation of his own clients in major diplomatic posts.[4] This was the first step in the Vorontsovs' takeover of high government. After toppling Bestuzhev from leadership of foreign affairs, they began another move to capture control of domestic affairs, where the Shuvalov party had held sway for many years. In this area the clash involved important issues of estate privilege.

v Rossii ot Petra I do Ekateriny II, 2 vols. (Moscow, 1913–41); N. N. Firsov, *Petr III i Ekaterina II v pervye gody ee tsarstvovaniia* (Moscow, 1915). See also Catherine's comments in *Sochineniia imperatritsy Ekateriny II*, ed. A. N. Pypin (St. Petersburg, 1907), 12: 499–500, 513–18, 567–68; for a recent discussion see Kerry R. Morrison, "Catherine II's Legislative Commission: An Administrative Interpretation," *Canadian Slavic Studies*, vol. 4, no. 3 (Fall 1970), pp. 467– 68.

[2]N. I. Panin to M. L. Vorontsov, 9 July and 3 September 1759, *AKV*, 26: 509–11, 68–69. As indicated in the previous chapter, the Panin family's economic situation was particularly distressing at this time. With both Nikita and Peter in active service, even the meagre properties they owned could not be managed effectively. Peter had to place what implements and peasants could be employed on a single estate together under the supervision of his wife and release the remaining peasants with passports to find work elsewhere. P. I. Panin to M. L. Vorontsov, October 1759, *LOII, f.* 36, *op.* 1, *d.* 1087, 217–18.

[3]The details of this struggle are recorded by Herbert Kaplan, *Russia and the Outbreak of the Seven Years' War*.

[4]Replacements included A. R. Vorontsov in Vienna, F. M. Voeikov in Poland, and D. M. Golitsyn and P. G. Chernyshev in France. Erik Amburger, *Geschichte der Behördenorganisation Russlands von Peter dem Grossen bis 1917* (Leiden, 1966), pp. 442–51.

The Shuvalovs had been designing and putting into action a program for modernizing the national economy and stimulating productive enterprise. Among other things, they had sponsored the abolition of internal customs duties, encouraged the growth of factories, and introduced state-subsidized credit facilities. In line with this program they were also drafting a new legal code that promised to end government monopolies, open up new avenues for merchant enterprise, and define the privileges of each estate in such a way as to restrict the nobility's rights of serf and factory ownership in the interests of balancing them against similar rights for the merchants.[5] These proposals went directly counter to the desires of the Vorontsovs, who favored the interests of the nobility, especially the upper echelons of metropolitan servicemen, the elite of Russian society. They wanted not only to uphold the nobility's privileges in these matters but even to extend them. Therefore, they set out to undermine the Shuvalovs' power at court, break their control over domestic affairs, and turn government policy in the direction they desired. By 1760 they succeeded in achieving these ends.

The victory of the Vorontsov party can be followed in the personnel changes that took place in the leading policy bodies. Of first importance was the Governing Senate. The Shuvalovs' two most powerful adherents there, General-Procurator N. Iu. Trubetskoi and the second in charge Ober-Procurator, A. I. Glebov, were eased out and replaced by members of the Vorontsov faction. A close collaborator of the Vorontsovs, Prince Ia. P. Shakhovskoi, took over the position of general-procurator, while I. G. Chernyshev assumed the ober-procuratorship. At the same time several new senators and presidents of collegia were named, giving added strength to the new leadership. Among these were the chancellor's brother R. L. Vorontsov, and two relatives of the new procurators, M. I. Shakhovskoi and P. G. Chernyshev.[6] These changes effectively shifted the balance in the senate, depriving the Shuvalovs of their patronage. Not only were they no longer able to pass decisions through the powerful institutions, they could not even beg positions for their minor clients.[7]

[5]S. O. Schmidt, "La politique intérieure du Tsarisme au milieu du XVIIIe siècle," *Annales*, vol. 21, no. 1 (Jan.-Feb. 1966), 103; Rubinshtein, "Ulozhennaia Kommissiia," pp. 208–52.

[6]*IPS*, 2: 147, 153; Rubinshtein, "Ulozhennaia Kommissiia," p. 217–19.

[7]Ia. P. Shakhovskoi, *Zapiski kniazia Iakova Petrovicha Shakhovskogo pisannye im samin*, 2 (Moscow, 1810), pp. 55–71.

No less significant were the changes that took place in the Law Commission. This was the body that had, under Peter Shuvalov's direction, been working out the new legal code so odious to the Vorontsovs. Consequently, the shift in power at court signaled major alterations here as well. All three men responsible for drafting the articles on estate privileges (A. I. Glebov, F. H. Strube de Piermont, and I. Vikhliaev) were promptly dismissed and replaced by Vorontsov appointees. And, of course, the main spirit behind the legal reform, Peter Shuvalov, also had to step down. His name now disappeared from senate papers referring to the Law Commission, and henceforth business was conducted by representatives of the victorious party, R. L. Vorontsov and Ia. P. Shakhovskoi.[8]

Nikita Panin's appointment as *oberhofmeister* must be counted as another of the Vorontsovs' successes. Although Panin gave only qualified support to the Vorontsov party and was cutting out an independent base of authority in the grand ducal court, he was a staunch opponent of the Shuvalovs and all they stood for.[9] Add all these changes together and one can see how thoroughly the Vorontsovs dominated the political institutions of the day. To the state council, which they had controlled since 1756, they now added the Senate, the Law Commission, several administrative collegia, as well as the court of Grand Duke Paul. The only point of uncertainty remained the first grand ducal court of Peter Fedorovich, where men of the Shuvalov party, Glebov and D. V. Volkov, still had great influence. But this exception was crucial, for it was only a matter of time before the ailing Empress Elizabeth would die and Peter Fedorovich would succeed to the throne.

In the meantime, the Vorontsovs did what they could to turn back the Shuvalov reform program and advance the interests of the nobility. Of primary concern was the question of service obligations to the state. Since Peter the Great's time nobles had been lobbying for reduction of the period of obligatory service as well as for a clear definition of their amenities and privileges. It is not sur-

[8]Named to the Commission by recommendation of R. L. Vorontsov and Shakovskoi were: Eropkin, Sievers, Den, and Kvashin-Samarin. Rubinshtein, "Ulozhennaia Kommissiia," p. 225.

[9]Paul's first tutor, F. D. Bekhteev, was a Vorontsov client (*RBS*, 3: 3–4) but too little distinguished to assume the office of *oberhofmeister*. The most likely candidate seemed to be Ivan Shuvalov, the favorite, a highly educated man and friend of the French philosophers. By closing out Shuvalov, Panin's appointment aided the Vorontsovs.

prising, therefore, that among the Vorontsov papers from this time one finds a project entitled "Points for consideration in freeing the nobility." Apart from its significance in laying the foundation for the famous Manifesto of 1762 declaring the nobility's freedom from state service, the document was most remarkable for revealing the strong aristocratic bent of its author, M. L. Vorontsov. For example, the project suggested that a distinction might be made between the ancient, especially titled, nobility and new members of the class. At the same time, however, the author stressed the need of special privileges based on rank: that noble servitors retiring in the highest ranks should receive special quarters in cities and fortresses and be accompanied in travel by military detachments. Another article raised the question of entailing estates of prominent families and designating them for all time as duchies, counties, or baronies. In this connection it was advised that the Heraldry Office should determine the lineage and age of princely and noble families.[10] Although the aristocratic tendency of the project was obvious enough, the author nevertheless seemed to confuse issues of rank and lineage. This confusion was typical of men reared in the Petrine system. So strongly imbued were they with the notions of service and rank precedence that they carried these concepts into their speculation on a purely aristocratic order. It will be recalled that the same synthesis appeared in Nikita Panin's observations on the Danish nobility, in which he emphasized the importance of both birth and qualifications in selecting young men for state service. Apparently, these two ideas did not conflict in the minds of eighteenth-century Russian statesmen. As will be shown in due course, this may also have reflected an attempt to revive certain practices of the ancient Muscovite *boiarstvo*, which very successfully united the two concepts of family and meritorious service.

More readily discernible in the Vorontsov program was the defense of the interests of the nobility as a whole against the pretensions of other estates. A number of substantive changes made in the Law Commission's draft code during the Vorontsov ascendancy produced a striking reversal of the policies developed under Peter Shuvalov's leadership. The new members of the commission repudiated the previous efforts at establishing a balance between the economic interests of nobility and merchants and instead altered the

[10]See the full project in *AKV*, 4: 518–19.

old draft in such a way as to circumscribe merchant access to the nation's productive resources. The nobility was granted not only a full monopoly over all metallurgical enterprise and receivership of all metalworks then held by non-nobles. The new draft likewise forbade any but nobles to hold serfs, the country's principal source of labor, and ordered that serfs then owned by other classes of people be sold (to nobles) within one year. Finally, an article in the Shuvalov draft prohibiting monopolies harmful to the merchants disappeared entirely from the code worked out under Vorontsov's direction. Only in the case of regulation of trade within towns did the new commission retain articles favorable to the merchantry. Understandably, representatives of the merchantry bitterly contested these changes. They pointed out that the proposed code expressed a degree of hostility to their interests that would lead one to believe the merchantry "was altogether unnecessary to the state."[11]

Soviet historians have characterized these moves as a "feudal reaction."[12] And so they would appear if one evaluates them in a Western context. In the autocracy of eighteenth-century Russia, however, the Vorontsov program exhibited elements of innovation as well as reaction. The Russian nobility had not previously enjoyed special rights and privileges setting it apart from the rest of the unenserfed populace. Like other social groups, its position was defined by its obligations and duties in state service. Now after fifty years of contact with the West, families like the Vorontsovs, which had obtained superior education, risen through the Petrine ranking system, and distinguished themselves in state service, wanted to protect their acquired status from the challenge of newcomers to their own ranks and from the economic competition of other estates. To borrow Marc Raeff's words, they "aimed at transforming the upper stratum of the Russian nobility into a genuine estate *(Stand)* in the Western sense, with intangible rights and privileges, access to membership almost exclusively by birthright, and implying (without requiring it) that its members accept public responsibilities, deriving from their cultural and economic leadership."[13] However reactionary these ideas may appear by Western standards, they were altogether new to eighteenth-century Russia and represented the first step toward de-

[11]Rubinshtein, "Ulozhennaia Kommissiia," pp. 237–46.
[12]Rubinshtein, "Ulozhennaia Kommissiia," pp. 237–38.
[13]Raeff, *Origins,* p. 103.

fining the rights of any group vis-à-vis state power. Moreover, in this case the selfish estate-centered demands were mitigated somewhat by retention of the Petrine service ethic, implying a reciprocal moral responsibility on the part of the privileged group.

In their short period of ascendancy, the Vorontsovs initiated two essential elements of this program by working first of all to obtain the release of nobles from obligatory state service and in that connection to define the special privileges of the highest ranking members of the estate. Second, through changes in the proposed law code, they endeavored to create favorable conditions for the growth of enterprise among the nobility, particularly among its wealthier members, who were in a position to obtain and exploit monopolies granted by the state. The third element in this program, the transformation of the autocracy into a *Rechtstaat*, would not be taken up until Catherine II's reign. This concept, whose purpose was to place the autocratic power within an immutable legal framework guaranteed by the participation of leading families in the policymaking and administrative institutions, would be sponsored not by the Vorontsovs but by Nikita Panin and his supporters, to whom the mantle of the aristocratic party passed after the reign of Peter III.

2. Catherine under Panin's Tutelage

The breakdown of state administration and change in political leadership that Panin found on his return from Sweden did not pose any immediate problems for him. The post of *oberhofmeister* furnished him with an enviable measure of financial and political security. The office carried a respectable salary and living quarters in the finest house in town, the imperial palace. A regular staff attended to the needs of the grand ducal court, a separate budget covered incidental costs, and of course, the social life and cultural resources of the court were available to the *oberhofmeister* and his staff. Equally important in this period of instability at court was the personal security attached to the position of guardian of the young heir. People commonly associated the welfare of the grand duke with the position of the man charged to care for his well-being and instruction. The arbitrary removal of a respected guardian could produce as much concern and apprehension as the fall of a minister of state. Consequently, Panin's office sheltered him somewhat from the intrigues of court parties. Well aware of this advantage, Panin refused to accept

any rank but *oberhofmeister* right up to Paul's majority in 1773, although his duties after 1763 entitled him to a higher service rank.[14]
Even while Empress Elizabeth was alive, the Shuvalovs, in what
was probably an effort to outflank the Vorontsovs, tried unsuccessfully to persuade Panin to relinquish his post in favor of becoming
vice-chancellor, an office carrying a much better salary.[15] Beyond
the attractive financial increment, however, the vice-chancellorship
offered only the dubious opportunity of bearing responsibility for a
war policy certain to be overturned as soon as Peter Fedorovich
succeeded to the throne. Panin prudently opted to stay on as guardian of Paul and await the outcome of the political turmoil expected
to follow Elizabeth's death.

Another advantage of Panin's new office was the access it afforded
to Grand Duchess Catherine, later Catherine II. As guardian to her
son, Panin was in daily contact with the grand duchess, and their
long period of collaboration, which was to have such important
consequences for Russian history, began soon after his return to St.
Petersburg.

The basis for their cooperation had been laid still earlier. Contrary
to the impression conveyed by Panin's biographer,[16] political links
had formed between them even while Panin was on his mission
abroad, and their correspondence, although indirect, touched on
questions serious enough to demonstrate a high degree of mutual
trust and esteem. Although difficult to pinpoint exactly, their communication on political affairs probably first began through the
mediation of their mutual friend V. E. Adadurov.[17] Chancellor
Bestuzhev likewise introduced Catherine to Panin's ideas and
activities and facilitated their correspondence by sharing with her
extracts from Panin's diplomatic dispatches. It is even possible that
Panin wrote directly to the grand duchess, as she occasionally
forwarded his letters to a secret correspondent, the British ambas-

[14]He never forgot the primacy of his position with Paul, remarking that his importance
would last only so long as his bed remained in the palace. Braudo, "N. I. Panin," *RBS*,
13: 195; Bil'basov, *Istoriia Ekateriny II*, 1: 436.

[15]Poroshin, *Zapiski*, 5 August 1765.

[16]Braudo, "N. I. Panin," *RBS*, 13: 190; Bil'basov shared this view, *Istoriia Ekateriny II*,
1: 435.

[17]See chapter 2, note 41. They probably knew one another even earlier, as Catherine
came to Russia in 1744 and Panin did not leave court until 1747, but it is unlikely that
they shared political interests at that time. See also Poroshin, *Zapiski*, 1 October 1764.

sador Williams.[18] Thanks to these contacts, as early as 1756 Catherine knew Panin well enough to say that she had "for some time past seen a future Vice-Chancellor in Panin."[19]

Nor was Panin for his part in ignorance of the grand duchess' flattering speculation about his career. Hearing of it through the Russian minister in London, A. M. Golitsyn, he modestly replied:

> At this time I do not even dream of any such thing, nor do I feel the slightest temptation to such a daring ambition. There are, my gracious lord, persons in our country of incomparably greater merits and talent than I, and my complete satisfaction and happiness I place in the opportunity of punctually fulfilling their directives.[20]

Hence, long before his return to St. Petersburg, Panin knew of Catherine's hopes for him and, if only indirectly, had managed to communicate to her his opinions on important political questions. Therefore, once back in the capital and at a post placing him in immediate contact with the grand duchess, he soon came to act as her unofficial personal adviser, a position left vacant since the arrests of Bestuzhev and Adadurov.[21] For Catherine's part, she found in Panin a man with an enviable independent position at court, wide knowledge and experience, and above all, a person in whose discretion and confidence she could put complete trust.

The degree of candor and confidence characterizing their relations may be judged by the following story, which Catherine recorded in a memorandum about the last days of Empress Elizabeth's life. It involved the delicate question of excluding Peter Fedorovich from the succession. The favorite Ivan Shuvalov, who with good reason feared the accession of Peter, went to Panin and asked what he thought of sending Peter and Catherine away and arranging the succession instead for their son Paul, then six years of age. Or, alternately, would it be possible to send only Peter away and keep Paul

[18] Although they may first have come to Adadurov or Bestuzhev. Catherine to Williams [27 August] 1756 (NS) and Williams to Catherine [16 October] 1756 (NS), *Williams Correspondence*, pp. 91, 180–81.

[19] Catherine to Williams [17 October] 1756 (NS), *Williams Correspondence*, p. 183.

[20] N. I. Panin to A. M. Golitsyn, Stockholm, 23 July 1758, *TsGADA, f.* 1263, *op.* 1, *d.* 2654, 18.

[21] *Despatches Buckingham*, 1: 66; Petsschauer, "The Education and Development of an Enlightened Absolutist" (Ph.D. diss., New York University, 1969), p. 394.

and his mother? Without some such arrangement, Shuvalov argued, Peter would succeed, and in his hands Russia would be brought to ruin. Panin's response, as reported by Catherine, was that "what had been established by oaths for twenty years could not now be altered without internecine strife." However, Panin went immediately to Catherine and informed her of the conversation, adding his own opinion "that if the empress, on her sick bed, were presented with the plan of leaving mother and son and sending away the father, it was quite likely that she would agree to it."[22] While it would be of interest to know which of these two opinions truly reflected Panin's view at the time, the story is most important for the light it sheds on Catherine's confidential relation to Panin. Shortly after his return to the capital they were discussing, if not already conspiring on, the most crucial political question of the time.

Although additional information about their discussions is limited and indirect, Catherine's writings from this period contain some traces that suggest their collaboration in thinking through important issues. In fact, it was in this period of Panin's tutelage that historians have found Catherine's earliest notes on theoretical questions of politics.[23] The book prompting these notes was F. H. Strube de Piermont's *Lettres russiennes,* an impassioned critique of Montesquieu's *Esprit des lois.*[24] The work appeared in St. Petersburg about the time of Panin's return to the capital, and one may be sure that he and Catherine, both enthusiasts for the writings of Montesquieu, spent time analyzing and comparing notes on Strube's attempt to destroy their mentor.

Strube de Piermont was one of the first professors of Russian law. Educated at Halle under Christian Thomasius, he had come to Russia in the 1730s as secretary to the Duke of Courland. Shortly thereafter he was appointed to the Academy of Sciences, where he taught jurisprudence and politics, and in the following decade he made an original attempt, unsuccessful as it turned out, to put together a "Brief Guide to Russian Laws."[25] In the 1750s he emerged

[22]Catherine, *Sochineniia,* 12: 513–14.

[23]Pypin, "Ekaterina II i Montesk'e," *Vestnik Evropy,* vol. 38, no. 5 (1903), p. 283.

[24]Inexplicably, P. P. Pekarskii described the work as an attack on Montesquieu's *Lettres persanes,* with which it had no common ground other than the similarity of titles. *Istoriia Akademii Nauk* (St. Petersburg, 1870), 1: 687.

[25]The Academy gave him a special stipend to carry on the work but withdrew it a few years later when it was discovered that instead of compiling a synopsis of Russian laws,

as an adherent of the Shuvalov party in the Law Commission, where he served as an exponent of that party's brand of statist development and participated in drafting the first, or Shuvalov, version of the code. As a student of the cameralist school of statecraft and an ardent patriot for his newfound home in Russia, Strube was particularly annoyed by what he regarded as Montesquieu's contemptuous attitude toward Russian political institutions. As early as 1756 he began setting the record straight with regard to specific distortions he discovered in the Frenchman's writings.[26] His full-scale attack on the *Esprit des lois* appeared in his *Lettres russiennes* of 1760.

While the book corrected a large number of factual errors that had crept into Montesquieu's work, Strube's main point was to counter Montesquieu's designation of Russia as a despotism. As a result, *Lettres russiennes* bore characteristics of a propaganda piece defending the Russian government from unfavorable foreign evaluation. This effort led Strube into making statements of the most dubious kind, including assertions of the beneficence and moderation of Peter the Great's laws, and remarks that Russians enjoyed civil liberties as extensive as those found in European monarchies, in short, that Russia was in fact a constitutional monarchy of the European type, pure and simple.[27] He also defended serfdom as fully compatible with monarchical order and went on to assert that it was actually a very useful institution. Yet Strube was no ordinary propagandist. An erudite jurist, he was able to win a number of points against his opponent. His criticisms of Montesquieu's methods of inquiry and analytical categories were often cogent. One could scarcely disagree that Montesquieu employed rather simplistic and fuzzy terminological definitions in categorizing particular states, or that in speaking of virtue and honor as the bases of government in republics and monarchies the French philosopher was merely representing, so far as these vague terms had any meaning at all, qualities necessary to good governance in all states. With equal good sense Strube attacked Montesquieu's device of denying absolute princes any humane

---

Strube was simply recopying ukases in extenso. This seems to be an early case of grantsmanship abuse. Pekarskii, *Istoriia Akademii Nauk*, 1: 681–83.

[26] See his *Slovo o nachale i peremenakh rossiiskikh zakonov* . . . , trans. S. Naryshkin (St. Petersburg, 1756), in which he criticizes Montesquieu's statements about Russian commerce. Also Pypin, "Ekaterina i Montesk'e," p. 288. For Strube's full biography, see Pekarskii, *Istoriia Akademii Nauk*, 1: 671–89.

[27] Strube, *Lettres russiennes* (St. Petersburg, 1760), pp. 194–210, 245–70.

impulses while attaching such feelings exclusively to constitutional monarchs.[28]

But with regard to the most fundamental definitions and distinctions Strube's arrows landed very wide of the mark. To take only one of the most important examples, he answered Montesquieu's insistence on separating the administration of justice from the executive power with the assertion that the question was merely one of convenience.[29] In this assertion, so typical of the cameralist approach to statecraft, Strube revealed his ignorance of the central point of Montesquieu's writing. The idea that men were endowed with fundamental rights that had to be protected from unbridled governmental power, a notion central to the Anglo-French Enlightenment, was lost on a man like Strube who came out of the milieu of the German Aufklärung, which stressed man's duty to the community and state. For the same reason he had difficulty apprehending the Frenchman's idea of estates. In reference to Montesquieu's requirement that a monarchical power be based on the mediative powers of the various estates, Strube argued the absurd proposition that the etymological similarity of Russian and European words for nobility proved that Russia fulfilled this requirement. Moreover, he baldly asserted, the Russian nobility had never been plundered of its rights and prerogatives. Finally, in answer to Montesquieu's denial of the existence of a third estate in Russia, Strube obtusely asserted that Russian cities were teeming with workers and merchants.[30] These observations, questionable enough in themselves, only demonstrated the enormous gulf that separated the two men's understandings of political institutions.

Fortunately for historians, Strube's critique, however maladroit, provoked Catherine's intense interest and led her to produce notes containing valuable clues to her thinking at this time. As might be expected from one who later hailed the *Esprit des lois* as the Bible of sovereigns, Catherine reacted unfavorably to Strube's attack. "The purpose is bad. The dispute scholastic. The beginning of the book boring. The middle very weak. The end passable," she jotted in the front leaf. Then in numerous marginal notes she launched into a running discourse with the author, sometimes expressing astonish-

---

[28]*Lettres russiennes*, pp. 127–30, 146–51, 165–68, 173–82.
[29]*Lettres russiennes*, pp. 136–38.
[30]*Lettres russiennes*, pp. 221–33.

ment at his audacity to attack Montesquieu, at other times disgust
with his defense of slavery. Typical was her comment on the argument for serfdom. "An ancient Greek or Roman would have said
that this book is the opprobrium of the human spirit, a praise of
slavery! And why then doesn't the author sell himself into slavery?"[31]

But Catherine's curiosity also prompted her to probe the substantive issues. She showed particular interest in just those questions
that were then occupying the aristocratic party in the Law Commission. For example, Strube asserted that Russian sovereigns distinguished the nobility from the third estate by means of special prerogatives. Catherine was suspicious. She wanted to know of what these
prerogatives consisted. Strube spoke of the nobility never having been
plundered of its rights. Catherine demanded to know what these
rights were. And where Strube described the third estate by noting
the existence of Russian cities teeming with workers, Catherine
simply exclaimed in disbelief: "Morbleu! ce sont donc des serfs ou
des affranchis ou des déserteurs."[32] Obviously, Strube's refutation
satisfied her with neither its arguments nor its information. In a
summation at the end of the book, she rejected the author's defense
of Russia as a true monarchy and then added in accord with Montesquieu that despotism seemed to be the only form of government
appropriate to such a vast empire. Russians could, therefore, only
pray that their sovereigns would be reasonable and enlightened.[33]

The degree to which Catherine's association with Panin at this
time contributed to her critique and rejection of Strube's work cannot be measured. It is known that Panin shared this criticism of the
book, having remarked that after "Strube had said all he had to say,
Montesquieu still remained Montesquieu"[34]—that is, Russia was still
a despotism. Beyond this, one is left with conjecture. Still, the facts
that Catherine first began making notes on political questions about
the time of her close association with Panin and that their opinions
on the basic issues coincided do suggest a certain amount of influence
from his side. In this connection it is also interesting to note that
Catherine's opinion on the central issue of Strube's book changed
after she became *tsaritsa* and was less under Panin's influence. Not

[31]Catherine, *Sochineniia*, 12: 663–74.
[32]Catherine, *Sochineniia*, 12: 672.
[33]Catherine, *Sochineniia*, 12: 674.
[34]Poroshin, *Zapiski*, 7 January 1765.

wishing to recognize a despot in herself, she too began to defend Russia as a monarchy, and as time went on she sounded more and more like Strube, whom she here accused of having "neither talent, knowledge, nor experience."[35] In contrast, her adviser Panin continued to view Russia as a despotism. For reasons that will become clear, he could not accept Catherine's reforms as having established the rule of law.

Additional evidence of Catherine's interest in the theoretical side of politics may be found in her notebooks from this period. This source also reflects a remarkable identity of views between Catherine and Panin. Turn again, for example, to the question that had so exercised the Law Commission and captured Catherine's attention in Strube's book: the matter of the nobility's rights and obligations. Catherine's notes on this issue included the following:

> According to the law of Peter the Great. . . every nobleman should be subject to military service, but the law should determine the period of service and allow a man to relinquish it at the age of forty or forty-five, or even earlier. Otherwise the land and the family suffer from neglect and the nation suffers with them.

And on maintaining the aristocracy:

> I must admit that though free of prejudice and of a philosophical turn of mind, I have a great inclination to respect families of ancient descent. I suffer when I see them reduced to poverty and long to reestablish them in their former condition. It would be possible to restore their lustre by bestowing rank and decorations on the head of the family so long as he can claim some quality, and by granting him pensions and even land, according to necessity and position, on condition that they should only be passed on to the eldest son and remain inalienable.[36]

These comments, which bear some similarity to the aristocratic program proposed by the Vorontsovs, reveal even more the influence

[35]Catherine, *Sockineniia*, 12: 671.

[36]Catherine, *Sochineniia*, 12: 614–16; translation borrowed in part from *The Memoirs of Catherine the Great*, ed. Dominique Maroger (New York, 1961), pp. 299–308. It should be noted that these "Miscellaneous Notes," as presented by Maroger, are incomplete and in some instances misnumbered.

of Panin's qualified version of that program. As will be shown in more detail later, Panin wished to introduce modifications in the Petrine service system, small changes that, without prejudicing the rewards of a service career or restricting unduly the enterprise of other estates, would permit the leading families to maintain their wealth and status and not fall into economic ruin through onerous life-long service and the tradition of subdividing estates equally among heirs. On the question of property division Catherine's notes also reflected Panin's desire to restore certain elements of Peter I's legislation concerning the nobility, in this case Peter's effort to preserve the inheritance of leading families by entailing estates. While not wishing to return completely to the unenforceable single inheritance law of 1714 or to introduce duchies and baronies on the Vorontsov model, he hoped the government could introduce changes that would dilute the most corrosive effects of the current system by showing special care for families that had distinguished themselves in meritorious service to the state.

But the view of the nobility that Catherine and Panin were developing required more than the mere preservation of elite families. They wished to create an aristocracy that would be free to engage in economic enterprise and be secure in the property and rewards derived from enterprise and inheritance. In recent decades, however, court favorites had turned the Petrine reward structure into an instrument of their personal caprices and power ambitions. So long as this condition continued, flattery and obsequiousness would remain the principal means of advancement, and honest men would be discouraged from engaging in useful undertakings. Therefore, the monarch also had a duty to establish conditions within which an aristocracy of merit could thrive and to recognize and reward special achievement. As Catherine noted:

> I want the laws obeyed, but I want no slaves. My general aim is to create happiness without all the whimsicality, eccentricity, and tyranny which destroy it.
>
> Never grant favors that are not asked for personally, unless you yourself recognize the need to do it without being pushed to it by others; it is necessary that one be obliged to you and not to your favorites.
>
> He who does not esteem merit has none himself. He who

fails to seek merit and to uncover it is unworthy and incapable of ruling.[37]

Creating a structure within which these desiderata could be accomplished required a long period of peace and a legal framework in which men would be free of arbitrary changes in the law and secure in their possessions. Catherine also recorded advice on this matter.

> Peace is necessary to this vast empire; we need population, not devastation; we need to populate our great spaces as much as possible.
>
> One should beware of introducing a law and then revoking it: it only reveals your imprudence and weakness and shatters the nation's confidence in you.
>
> The state, whose laws must be sacred to a monarch, for they remain forever while subjects and kings disappear, has every interest in keeping strictly to the laws. (Memoirs of Christina, Queen of Sweden, vol. II.)
>
> Political liberty in relation to the citizen consists of the security in which he finds himself under the protection of the law, which causes one citizen not to fear the other.[38]

These comments and others recorded by Catherine during this period show that she had been reading widely in the literature on political theory and consciously preparing herself to play a leading role in government. Moreover, the notes, which all dated from the time she was directly under Panin's influence, indicate that she shared his convictions about Russia's need to end an aggressive foreign policy and concentrate on peaceful development at home. They show, too, both her understanding of the relationship of a consistent body of law to the motivation of the citizenry and her desire to implement such concepts. As for Panin's influence, although the points mentioned above were among his favorite ideas, one can finally only speculate on the degree to which he was responsible for their appearance in Catherine's notebook. What her notes do show, however, is that Panin's and Catherine's thinking ran along the same lines during this period, and considering the special place he occupied in her confi-

[37]Catherine, *Sochineniia*, 12: 615–17.
[38]Catherine, *Sochineniia*, 12: 607–08, 610, 615; Bil'basov, *Istoriia Ekateriny II*, 2: 139.

dence it seems safe to assume that the comments faithfully reflected at least some of the content of their discussions and the reading Panin recommended to her.

3. The Private Journals of the Sumarokov and Kheraskov Circles

In an altogether new development for Russia, at about this time a number of popular journals began to appear, giving expression publicly to the very ideas Catherine and Panin were discussing privately. The editors and contributors to the journals gathered in two circles, one in St. Petersburg and after 1760 another at Moscow University. The leading representative of the St. Petersburg group was the famous poet and dramaturge A. P. Sumarokov. In 1759 he published the journal *Industrious Bee*, which was explicitly oriented toward the grand ducal court and toward Catherine in particular. Risking the anger of Elizabeth's court, where Catherine was then in disfavor, Sumarokov dedicated his new journal to the grand duchess. He called Catherine "Minerva,"[39] and with even greater daring, considering Elizabeth's abhorrence at hearing any beauty praised save her own, began the dedication with the following words: "In mind and beauty, and in graciousness a goddess, Oh enlightened Grand Duchess . . . ."[40] Two more journals of a similar orientation appeared in these years. The first, *Idle Time* (1759–60), a product of the St. Petersburg Cadet Corps, also owed much to Sumarokov's influence. In fact, he became a regular contributor to it after his own journal closed down. For the most part, however, the writers came from a younger generation, cadets and teachers of the Corps. A number of them later joined Nikita Panin's staff or assisted in Catherine's reform efforts,[41] demonstrating yet another link between these young journalists and the opposition group surrounding Catherine. In Moscow the same spirit was expressed by a poet and Moscow University official, M. M. Kheraskov, who with a number of students published the journal *Useful Entertainment* (1760–62) and

[39]A. V. Zapadov, ed., *Istoriia russkoi zhurnalistiki XVIII–XIX vekov* (Moscow, 1963), p. 33.

[40]P. N. Berkov, *Istoriia russkoi zhurnalistiki XVIII veka* (Moscow, 1952), p. 117.

[41]Berkov, *Istoriia zhurnalistiki*, p. 127. Among others were A. M. Belosel'skii, later Russian ambassador in Saxony, and S. A. Poroshin, whom Panin engaged to teach Paul. For more detail on this group, see D. D. Shampai, "Ob izdateliakh pervogo chastnogo zhurnala (Po materialam arkhiva kadetskogo korpusa)," *XVIII vek* (Moscow, 1935), pp. 377–85.

several other titles during the 1760s. In this group the young writer
Denis Fonvizin got his start. Later he became Nikita Panin's secretary and chief spokesman for the Panin party.

These journalists represented a new breed in Russian literary life.
Unlike the court poets of the 1730s and 1740s, hired to produce odes
for ceremonial occasions, the new writers maintained a greater
independence from the government and court; they wished to establish a new cultural hegemony based upon social acceptance rather
than on court subsidies. They had a mission. Their approach was
uncompromisingly didactic. Their journals aimed at educating the
uncultured Russian nobleman to abandon vice and embrace the
virtuous life, to strive for moral perfection. Filled with optimism for
the improvement of mankind through education, they expected to
uplift their compatriots by explaining how much happier they
would be if they would but follow the path of goodness. To this end
they filled the pages of their journals with translations and more
or less original reworkings of the moral rationalism of Racine, Fénelon, and the Stoic philosophers of antiquity.[42]

There was certainly nothing radical about all this. Sumarokov,
Kheraskov, and their associates were all convinced monarchists.
As one historian summarized it:

> In the world-view of the Kheraskov group the universe is ruled
> by order and hierarchy which have nothing to do with man's
> own will. Since man is only a transitory guest in this world facing
> the prospect of certain death, the best way in which he can live
> out this life is in conformity with the existing order of things.
> Our reason, freed from unruly passions, shows us how.[43]

Hence, the object was not to seek a more perfect political and social
order but rather to improve the moral quality of the ruler and the
political elite. As innocuous as this idea appeared on the surface, it
nevertheless implied a serious criticism of the current regime of

[42]The fullest treatment may be found in G. A. Gukovskii, *Ocherki po istorii russkoi literatury XVIII veka* pp. 32–41; also Solov'ev, *Istoriia Rossii*, 13:569; on connections of the Stoic
writings to early Masonic activity, G. V. Vernadskii, *Russkoe masonstvo v tsarstvovanie Ekateriny II* (Petrograd, 1917), pp. 100–01. The most recent discussions are in Berkov, *Istoriia
zhurnalistiki*, pp. 115–16, and Walter Gleason, "Cultural Value Changes Among Certain
Russian Writers, 1759–1772" (Ph.D. diss., University of Chicago, 1973).

[43]In-Ho Lee Ryu, "Freemasonry under Catherine the Great: A Reinterpretation"
(Ph. D. diss., Harvard University, 1967), p. 54.

Empress Elizabeth, with its undisguised rule of favorites and rampant corruption. Included among the moralistic offerings of the journals, particularly Sumarokov's, were poorly disguised satires on the extravagance at court, favoritism, bribery, graft, and other vices. Moreover, the strong orientation of these writers toward the grand ducal court and especially toward Catherine showed that they placed their hopes for improvement in a new and more virtuous ruler.

In the *Industrious Bee* Sumarokov left a picture of what he regarded as the ideal sociopolitical order. His article was entitled "A Dream of the Happy Society," and it sketched the outlines of a commonwealth that bore a close resemblance to the ideas Catherine and Panin had been discussing. In Sumarokov's opinion, the happy society depended first of all upon the greatness of its ruler and "his chosen *pomeshchiks*." They are all enlightened men akin to the Stoic philosophers, over whom passion has no control. Their rule is based upon reason, and the monarch, an exemplar of all virtues, thinks only of the welfare of his people, which he never confuses with his own personal interests. Religion, too, has an important, albeit carefully circumscribed, role in the happy society. It constitutes the "foundation of national well-being." The much respected priests share the enlightenment of the ruling group, yet in their wisdom they never meddle in the secular affairs of state, matters best left to the ruler and his aristocrats. At the head of government Sumarokov finds a state council. Although he unfortunately says nothing of how it is constituted, he does mention that the council possesses legislative functions and is not intended to be used for the private affairs of its members—a jab at the cabinets of Elizabeth's government, notorious for their corruption. Legislation in the happy society is, of course, based on natural law. As a consequence, Sumarokov exclaims in a brief fit of egalitarianism, "there are neither nobles nor commoners, but people are preferred according to ranks given them on their merits; a peasant's son has as much right to be a great lord as does the son of the first aristocrat." Finally, on the question of justice the author quips: "in the happy society it is dispensed in exactly the opposite manner as prevails in the real life of the dreamer."[44]

A similar independent critical position found expression in the

---

[44]A. P. Sumarokov, "Son—schastlivoe obshchestvo," in I. V. Malyshev, ed., *N. I. Novikov i ego sovremenniki, Izbrannye sochineniia* (Moscow, 1961), pp. 354–57.

Moscow journal *Useful Entertainment*. As in Sumarokov's short-lived publication, this second journal employed irony as a vehicle for its criticism of Elizabeth's reign. One example was Kheraskov's poem "To the Muse of Satire:"

> I don't see the slightest failing in anyone.
> Here everyone stands on his merits:
> Judges swear that there is no injustice in the courts;
> And their alleged robbery of everyone is probably just a lie,
> They devote their lives to God and have nothing much to
>   hide.
> Fathers know how to educate their sons,
> And grownups don't know the meaning of squandering their
>   goods.
> Our lawyers being honest men never would deceive
> And husbands are as true to wives as Adam was to Eve.[45]

A singular feature of *Useful Entertainment*, possibly related to the participation of Moscow University students, was its anti-war sympathies. The journal warmly applauded the accession of Peter III in expectation of his ending the unpopular Seven Years' War. Soon after, with these hopes fulfilled, Kheraskov produced an "Idyll on the Conclusion of Peace 1762 April 29th" in celebration of the emperor's action. Yet despite these positions, *Useful Entertainment* was less actively political and openly hostile to Elizabeth's government than was Sumarokov's *Industrious Bee*. The primary objective of the Moscow journal was to define a nobiliary culture independent of either bourgeois culture or the lavish glitter of the court. Accompanying this, of course, went the desire to uplift the still boorish members of the nobility to an appreciation of these new cultural norms.[46]

---

[45]Quoted in Berkov, *Istoriia zhurnalistiki*, p. 130.

[46]Berkov has designated the following poem (*Istoriia zhurnalistiki*, p. 137) as the credo of the Kheraskov group:

With pompous glory	Do love one another
My soul is not yearning,	The law us intones,
Nor write I my story	To serve a dear brother
Poisoned evil aburning . . .	Will soften our moans . . .
Enough suffering have we	I work to praise goodness
Without further enmity,	What my verses reflect,
Minds do not levy	For this I hold highest
A tax on stupidity.	As a source of respect.

But before this movement could gain momentum, the death of Empress Elizabeth intervened, producing much uncertainty as to the future course of government. Since the program of these moralist ideologues implied direction from above, it depended ultimately on the succession of political leadership sympathetic to it. For the time being, then, the young journalists would have to leave the principal field of action to their political counterparts, Catherine and Nikita Panin. For if their ideal of an enlightened elite ruling through rational order and hierarchical system was to be realized, Catherine and Panin would have to get into a position to implement it. But before this possibility could be considered, they all had to face the challenge of a much different model of political organization advanced by Peter III.

4. Peter III's Reign

Peter III's accession on December 25, 1761 brought an end to the period of political education and philosophic speculation. While the young writers and possibly Catherine herself may at first have believed that the new reign would bring the grand duchess' influence forward, it soon became obvious that she and all those associated with her and Grand Duke Paul would instead have to turn their attention to the serious business of political and personal survival.

Peter's government moved swiftly to win the support of major social groups. As one of his first acts the new emperor reduced the hated salt tax imposed during the previous regime. In other popular moves he abolished the Secret Chancellery and granted religious freedom to the Old Believers, who had suffered persecution under Elizabeth's rule. Even the merchant class obtained benefits, as members of the Shuvalov party returned to positions of influence. A. I. Glebov replaced Shakhovskoi as General-Procurator of the Senate, and D. V. Volkov became the emperor's private secretary. M. L. Vorontsov managed to retain his post as grand chancellor, thanks no doubt to the fact that his niece was Peter's mistress, but the family's influence was nevertheless much reduced.[47] Aside from Peter's German relatives, who formed his immediate entourage, Glebov and Volkov now exercised the leading influence on government policy. And they soon put into action the economic program of the

---

[47]M. L. Vorontsov wrote to his nephew complaining that his niece, the favorite, was unable to secure the family's position during Peter III's reign. Rubinshtein, "Ulozhennaia Kommissiia," p. 250.

Shuvalov party by abolishing government monopolies and maintaining restrictive tariff rates.[48]

These men were also responsible for Peter's famous decree granting the nobility freedom from obligatory service. Originally, of course, this measure had been worked out by the Vorontsovs, who attached to it a whole series of social and economic privileges as well as distinctions between upper and lower ranks of nobility. Peter's decree emasculated this entire aristocratic program while retaining the item with the broadest potential appeal, freedom from service. The measure was an immediate success. Elated and grateful, large numbers of nobles took advantage of the law to request leave to return to their estates.[49]

The only significant social group to suffer from Peter's policies was the clergy. Not only did the government initiate a wholesale confiscation of church property, but Peter heaped insult upon injury with his disparaging comments about Russian religion. But this exception was not crucial. Other things being equal, the government could easily have survived the churchmen's impotent rage.

In fact, these early successes could have assured Peter a long tenure as ruler had he not simultaneously launched a head-on attack against the most powerful interests in the court and high administration. What he failed to understand was that the arena of active politics in Russia defined a very narrow circle. It seldom extended beyond members of the imperial family and their favorites, the guards regiments of the capital, and the leading noble families represented in the Governing Senate. The poorly organized social estates possessed no mechanism for exerting political influence. They simply accepted as legitimate whatever could be agreed upon by the court parties, the senate and the guards.[50] Yet it was precisely these latter groups that Peter's policies were driving into desperate insecurity.

Firstly, having taken up with a mistress, the emperor openly

[48]Rubinshtein, "Ulozhennaia Kommissiia," pp. 219, 250.

[49]See Marc Raeff's discussion in "Domestic Policies of Peter III," 75: 1291–94, 1301–02; also Firsov, *Petr III i Ekaterina II,* pp. 19–20; and A. Romanovich-Slavatinskii, *Dvorianstvo v Rossii ot nachala XVIII v. do otmeny krepostnogo prava,* 2nd ed. (Kiev, 1912), pp. 195–96, cited below in chapter 5, note 4.

[50]Even those who had at one time occupied powerful positions in government lost their political standing altogether once they left the court. For some interesting observations on this aspect of Russian politics see the British envoy's report from 20 July 1768, *SIRIO,* 12: 336–38.

talked of divorcing his wife, Catherine, and removing her son Paul
from the line of succession.[51] This plan directly threatened Catherine
and the coterie of young officers in her favor. It likewise represented
a serious challenge to Nikita Panin and the growing number of re-
form-minded men in government and society who looked to him and
the grand ducal court as the potential source of a new enlightened
aristocratic order in government.[52] Secondly, Peter went out of his
way to criticize and humiliate the guards of the capital. He abolished
the Life Guard altogether and replaced it with his own troops
brought from Holstein. The other Russian regiments were outfitted
in Prussian uniforms and threatened with front-line duty in the war
Peter planned to wage against Denmark.[53] Finally, and perhaps most
importantly, the emperor quickly alienated the influential dignitaries
of the senate with his steady erosion of the institutional prerogatives
they had acquired through the first half of the century.

By the end of Elizabeth's reign it had become accepted practice
in Russian government for the senate and its subordinate institutions
independently to dispose of the routine business of administration
with the autocrat intervening personally only in special cases. Peter
dramatically reversed this trend and threatened to develop a police
power unencumbered by the prerogatives of established institutions.
First, the senate lost its control over the processing of petitions and
the review of promotions in lower administrative offices, two extremely important powers in a government that functioned through
favor and patronage more often than by bureaucratic regulations.
A short time later the police administration was removed from
senate supervision and placed in the hands of one of the emperor's
personal favorites. Then in June 1762, only weeks before his overthrow, Peter delivered a final blow to the power and prestige of the
senate. He strictly prohibited it from issuing any decrees having the
force of law or even to receive reports on affairs not directly concerned with its current activity without the prior approval of the
sovereign.[54]

[51]E. R. Dashkova, *Memoirs of the Princess Daschkaw, Lady of Honour to Catherine II*, ed.
W. Bradford, 2 vols (London, 1840), 1: 38. This section is missing in the French text
published in *AKV*, 21.
[52]Raeff, "Domestic Policies of Peter III," p. 1292. In fact, one of Panin's closest associates, Grigorii Teplov, was arrested in March. Posse to Chancellery President, 5 March
1762, *SRa*, Muscovitica no. 307.
[53]Firsov, *Petr III i Ekaterina II*, pp. 28–32.
[54]Raeff, "Domestic Policies of Peter III," pp. 1307–08.

It should be understood that these changes amounted to much more than a redefinition of administrative procedures. They represented something in the nature of a constitutional revolution. The senate was not a bureaucratic office in the usual sense. It was the seat of the leading noble families in the country and represented the interests of the entire elite of servicemen. However impotent it may have been to challenge particular decisions of the monarch on any question, the senate could and did serve as a watchdog for the nobility's interests. Thus, a direct attack on its powers represented a challenge to the political power of the nobility as a whole.

Peter's actions soon left no doubt that he intended to establish a highly centralized regime in which a small camarilla of his personal (and in this case mostly foreign) favorites would rule through professional bureaucratic offices uninhibited by the established institutions representing the interests of the noble elite. This program reawakened fears of a return to the dark days of Empress Anne's reign, when a clique of German Baltic favorites lorded it over the Russian nobility and subjected even the most prominent families to humiliation, confiscation, torture, and exile. In the context of such fears even the much-heralded grant of freedom from obligatory service lost a great deal of its luster. For it could be read as yet another measure to remove the nobility from active participation in government.[55]

Oddly enough, Peter seemed oblivious to the fear and hostility simmering around him. He directly threatened Catherine and Panin and yet, to the dismay of his counselors, refused to give serious attention to reports of plots forming around Catherine and in the grand ducal court. He whittled away at the powers of the senate with utter disregard for the resentment these measures provoked among the leading families represented there.[56] Most ominously, he humiliated the guards without really drawing their teeth. The natural result of such a reckless policy was the formation of a powerful conspiracy among the threatened parties that toppled Peter from power on 28 June 1762, after just six months of rule.

[55]Raeff, "Domestic Policies of Peter III," p. 1309.

[56]Chancellor Vorontsov, with tears in his eyes, told the Danish ambassador of the great discontent and stated that Peter was the only one who was either unaware or indifferent to it. A few days earlier members of the court and government had made a futile appeal to the emperor to avoid a war with Denmark. Haxthausen to Bernstorff, 31 May and 10 June 1762, *DRa,* Russland A III, no. 80.

The coup d'etat was swift and bloodless. Organized by Catherine with the backing of Panin, Hetman Razumovskii, and several other dignitaries, it was carried out by the guards regiments under the leadership of the five Orlov brothers, one of whom, Grigorii Orlov, was Catherine's lover at the time. To the disappointment of some dignitaries, the guards immediately proclaimed Catherine the new ruler and led her to the Kazan' Cathedral, where church leaders happily sanctified the proceedings. Peter, who was staying at the suburban palace of Oranienbaum, attempted some futile gestures of resistance and then weakly submitted to abdication and imprisonment.

5. Panin's Role in the Conspiracy

Panin's reasons for adhering to the conspiracy were obvious enough. His career and personal security bound him to the fate of his charge, the grand duke. Once Peter made it clear that he intended to remove Paul from the succession, Panin had every reason to oppose such a plan with whatever means were necessary. But in addition to his concern for his career, Panin was a would-be statesman and reformer. If Peter's regime menaced him personally, it threatened as well the values and programs he wished to see implemented for the improvement of his estate and nation. Panin saw no hope of such programs being approved by Peter's government. First of all, to a man of Panin's sentiments the entire style of the regime was simply revolting. The depth of this revulsion may easily be gauged by Panin's description of the emperor and his court:

> [Peter's] favorites were fools or traitors. He indulged himself with them in the most dissolute debauchery of drunkenness. His mistress, Mlle. Woronzow, was ugly, stupid, annoying, [and] offensive. Peter believed it was fashionable to have a mistress. He spoke only German, and wished that everyone knew that language. Russian he spoke but rarely and always poorly. He wanted to change everything and to remodel everything. Holstein, however tiny it was in comparison with the vast empire of Russia, seemed to him larger, richer and more worthy of his affection. All minds, except those which were as depraved as Peter's, were therefore alienated from him; no one was satisfied

with him; they wanted another sovereign no matter what trouble it could bring.[57]

Particularly distressing for a refined diplomat like Panin was the barracksroom tone of the regime. When Peter, who delighted in granting military ranks, promoted him to General of Infantry, "Panin quietly declared that if no other means could be found of escaping an honour of which he was so extremely unworthy, he was resolved on immediately deserting into Sweden."[58] As for Peter's foreign policy, the very thought of his leading the country, already exhausted by six years of war, into new battles over a worthless territory in far-off Denmark so upset Panin that he threw off his usual caution. In the weeks preceding Peter's fall he entered into secret, possibly treasonous, communication with Danish representatives in Russia in order to keep them informed of changes at the court possibly affecting the outbreak of war against their country.[59] If anything, Peter's domestic policies were even greater anathema than his war plans. His effort to establish a personal regime above the controlling influence of the established nobiliary institutions represented the very tyranny that Panin hoped to see forever removed from Russian government. As he wrote shortly after Peter's overthrow: "What loyal and reasonable son of the fatherland can recall without emotion the manner in which the former Emperor Peter III ascended the throne? And does not such an unfortunate situation belong rather to those times when not only was there no established government, but not even written laws?"[60]

While Panin's reasons for entering the conspiracy were clear enough, the precise nature and extent of his participation have remained somewhat of a mystery. The two prevailing interpretations run to opposite and equally misleading extremes. The first, which

[57]A. F. Asseburg, *Denkwürdigkeiten* (Berlin, 1842), 316–17.

[58]Dashkova, *Memoirs*, 45–46; The Swedish ambassador observed at about the same time that Panin wished to resume his post in Sweden, Posse to Chancellery President, 1 January 1762, *SRa*, Muscovitica, no. 307. Panin's protest must have been effective, as he soon received the equivalent civil rank of active privy councillor. Baranov, *Opis'*, 3, 6 April 1762, no. 12, 109.

[59]Haxthausen to Bernstorff, 10 June 1762, *DRa*, Russland A III, no. 80. For further comments on the particularly well-informed position of the Danish secretary Schumacher, see Bil'basov, *Istoriia Ekateriny II*, 1: 119–120n.

[60]*SIRIO*, 7: 210.

owes its origin to the almost universally cited source on the events of the coup, Princess Dashkova's *Memoirs,* strongly downplays Panin's role (as, in fact, everyone else's except that of the authoress herself). To give but one illustration, according to Dashkova's account not only Panin but even the Orlov brothers were prime bunglers who, if left to their own counsel, would have done more to hinder the revolution than to forward it.[61] In sharp contrast, the second interpretation gives Panin principal credit for organizing and carrying out the coup d'etat. In this view Catherine was altogether dependent on Panin and therefore had reluctantly to entertain his proposals for reform after the successful overthrow.[62] Since an understanding of Panin's subsequent relations with Catherine hinges in some measure on the interpretation of his activity during the coup d'etat, the subject is worth pursuing in detail.

Fortunately, there exists a valuable and much neglected source that throws light on Panin's role in the conspiracy. The document is Panin's own retelling of the events in which he participated. Known as "Mémoire sur le detrônement de Pierre III,"[63] it was preserved among the papers of Baron von Asseburg, a Danish diplomat who had first become Panin's friend when they served together in Stockholm and who was, at Panin's request, later appointed Danish minister at St. Petersburg after Panin took charge of foreign affairs in Russia.[64] The information contained in this

[61]Dashkova's list of her contributions left no doubt that without her there could have been no revolution. She delivered orders to keep the guards tranquil; at the arrest of Passek (the event that touched off the coup), she sent Orlov to learn the cause; she gave the Orlovs orders to fetch Catherine from Peterhof; she had to order them a second time an hour later because of their hesitation; she had the foresight to prepare a carriage for Catherine's escape; she had to remind Catherine that Peter III might try to oppose the revolution. *Memoirs,* 1: 74–83.

[62]For a review of the historiography on this side of the question see my article "Catherine II's Instruction to the Commission on Laws: An Attack on Gentry Liberals?" *Slavonic and East European Review,* vol. 50, no. 118 (January 1972), pp. 10–28.

[63]A. F. Asseburg, *Denkwürdigkeiten,* pp. 315–22.

[64]N. I. Panin to A. M. Golitsyn, Stockholm, 24 July 1759, *TsGADA, f.* 1263, *op.* 1, *d.* 2655, 1; Asseburg, *Denkwürdigkeiten,* 408n; the appointment of Asseburg was recommended soon after the coup d'etat by the then Danish envoy Haxthausen, 2 July 1762, *DRa,* Russland A III, no. 80; Panin's personal request was sent through the Prussian ambassador Solms and included several enticements, among which was the following: "[Panin] begs your pardon for the climate of his country. It is harsh and often disagreeable and our friend is too honest to tell you otherwise, but he believes that you should already be hardened to it in view of your experience in neighboring countries, and in return he offers you pretty women and pretty girls to distract you and make you forget

account from Asseburg's papers came directly from Nikita Panin and represented Panin's own words dictated to Asseburg. [65]

According to this source, Panin was in the conspiracy from the beginning. [66] He was responsible for drawing into the plot such prominent figures as Hetman K. G. Razumovskii and General M. N. Volkonskii, a circumstance that other sources, including Dashkova, agreed on. Moreover, Panin's account gave the exact date of these men's adherence to the consipracy, a point that lends further credence to the report.

When the event touching off the revolution occured—the arrest of one of the conspirators—Panin was visiting with Princess Dashkova. This may explain how she knew a number of credible circumstances surrounding the initiation of the action. But according to Panin's account, it was he and not the princess who give orders to set the project in motion. After instructing the Orlovs and alerting Razumovskii and Volkonskii of the decision to launch the coup d'etat, Panin returned to the Summer Palace to be with the grand duke, as he wished to avoid arousing the suspicions of those in attendance there. The following morning Panin brought Paul to the Cathedral of Kazan' where Catherine's elevation was solemnized. Then they all paraded to the Winter Palace, where the new empress had a manifesto announcing the reign drawn up, and in the meantime, received oaths of allegiance from the senate, Holy Synod, and the people.

With her position in the capital secure Catherine mounted an

---

in nice heated rooms whatever bad weather might be going on outside." *Denkwürdigkeiten*, pp. 409–10.

[65]A number of circumstances speak for the authenticity of the source. First, Panin had a close, confidential relationship with Asseburg. Second, the account was penned during Asseburg's embassy in Russia, when he was in frequent personal contact with Panin. Third, the story focused consistently on Panin's activities during the days of the coup d'etat and retold in detail events that only Panin could have known thoroughly. Finally, Asseburg apparently did not tamper with or alter the original text, since what additional information he supplied was set aside in marginal notes. For discussions of the memoir, see Bil'basov, *Istoriia Ekateriny II*, 2: 473–74; and Maikov's introduction to the translation, "Rasskaz N. I. Panina o vosshestvii Ekateriny II," *Russkii Arkhiv*, (1879), no. 1, p. 363.

[66]Panin gave the date as four weeks prior to the coup d'etat. Asseburg, *Denkwürdigkeiten*, p. 321. He was probably referring to the formation at that time of a definite plan of action. Catherine indicated (in a letter to Poniatowski, *Sochineniia*, 12) that persons had been in touch with her for six months; she may, however, have been alluding to informal plans or, given the context of the remark, attempting to minimize Dashkova's exaggerated claims. Nevertheless, it is likely, considering Panin's objections to Catherine's elevation to empress, that she excluded him from discussions concerning the question of who was to succeed.

expedition the next day to apprehend Peter III, who had been
staying at the suburban palace of Oranienbaum. According to his
own account, Panin accompanied the expedition, leaving the grand
duke and responsibility for the capital city in the hands of the senate
under the direction of his brother-in-law Senator Nepliuev, and he
gave that body orders to report every half hour on events in the capital.[67] En route to Oranienbaum the expedition received news that
Peter had set out by boat for Kronstadt naval base. It was feared that
the emperor, finding the island fortress closed to him (Admiral
Talyzin had already secured it for Catherine), might then proceed
by water to St. Petersburg and take the city. A decision was immediately made to send Panin with an escort of guards to head off such
an attempt. As it turned out the precaution was unnecessary; Panin
soon learned that Peter had returned from Kronstadt to Oranienbaum. The capital was tranquil. By the time Panin rejoined the
expedition, Peter had dispatched a formal letter of abdication and
agreed to give himself up at the nearby palace of Peterhof. Finally,
Catherine entrusted Panin with the arrangements for Peter's arrest.
Panin personally supervised the signing of the official abdication
papers and handled the details of the fallen emperor's internment.[68]

The account seemed an accurate rendering of the details of Panin's
participation. Where it suffered the fault was less an exaggeration of
his role than a failure to describe the full context. Nevertheless, one
striking omission distorted the record. On the issue of greatest concern to Panin at the time, the objective of the conspiracy, he was
altogether silent. His differences with Catherine on this matter were

[67]I. I. Nepliuev, "Zapiski," *Russkii Arkhiv*, (1871), no. 1, p. 681.

[68]Panin regarded this duty as one of the most unpleasant of his entire career. Peter
presented a pitiful sight. He tried to take Panin's hand and kiss it; his mistress, E. R.
Vorontsova, fell on her knees and begged to stay with her master. The scene well deserved
Frederick II's often-quoted remark that Peter let himself be overthrown like a baby. The
Prussian monarch's first judgment was, however, less accurate. Panin related that when
General Chernyshev brought Frederick the news of the dethronement, the king said to
him: "Je suis sûr que ce Prince ne vit plus; il est mort l'épée à la main." Asseburg, *Denk-
würdigkeiten*, p. 322n.

Panin's chagrin at the emperor's debasement could scarcely have derived from any
personal sympathy for Peter. He had none. Peter had earlier humiliated and threatened
him. While Panin was attending Empress Elizabeth, already in a coma on her deathbed,
Peter became angered at Panin's refusal to listen to his boasting about a war against
Denmark. Pointing to the dying empress, Peter menaced: "Attends un peu, bientôt je te
déboucherai les oreilles pour t'apprendre à mieux écouter." Asseburg, *Denkwürdigkeiten*,
p. 316.

fundamental. While agreeing on the necessity of removing Peter, he desired the succession to fall not to Catherine but to her son, Paul.

Panin could find no grounds for recognizing Catherine as the legitimate sovereign, and he was perfectly frank with her on this point. As she wrote to her former lover Stanislaw Poniatowski, "Panin wanted the declaration to be made in favor of my son, but everyone else was against it."[69] The story could scarcely have been fabricated, as Catherine was continually at pains to convey the impression that her elevation came about by popular acclaim and with the relieved approval of all classes and important personages. Another close associate of Panin, Princess Dashkova, likewise gave this description of his position. According to her, Panin's opinion was that "the empress could not be brought forward as having any right to the throne, except as regent during the minority of her son."[70] Panin himself, while naturally omitting any mention in a written memoir, let his views on this question be known to relatives and trusted friends.[71]

As he saw it, legitimacy was the central issue. However attractive Catherine may have appeared as a substitute for Peter III, she had no legal claim to the Russian crown through either blood or imperial

[69]Catherine to Poniatowski, 2 August 1762, *Sochineniia*, 12, p. 548.

[70]Dashkova, *Memoirs*, 1: 60; some people believed Catherine had promised Panin to do no more than serve as regent, an allegation that she vigorously denied. Catherine to Suvorov, 31 May 1763, *SIRIO*, 7: 293.

[71]Particularly revealing was a letter by his nephew, Nikita Petrovich Panin, who served for a time as foreign minister under Paul. In his youth Nikita Petrovich was attached to the grand ducal court under his uncle's direction, and most likely his information about the coup d'etat came directly from conversations with Nikita Ivanovich. In this letter to Paul's wife, Mariia Fedorovna, Nikita Petrovich attempted to justify his own involvement in the overthrow of Paul by comparing that event with the coup d'etat of 1762. "I risked my life in order to bring the state out of the abyss. My deceased uncle and my second father, whose memory Y[our] I[mperial] M[ajesty] still honors, planned a regime to save the Empire. He wanted to be able to entrust it to the spouse of the reigning sovereign, flattering himself that she would place the scepter in the hands of the legitimate heir when he had come of age." Nikita Petrovich went on to say that Mariia Fedorovna had esteemed his uncle for what he did in Paul's behalf, yet when he was placed "in the same circumstances" he became the "object of your hate." N. P. Panin to Mariia Fedorovna (Autumn 1801 ?), *Tsentral'nyi Gosudarstvennyi Istoricheskii Arkhiv Leningrad, f.* 651, *d.* 1134. (I am indebted to Richard Warner for this reference.) Caspar von Saldern's version differs slightly from the others but confirms Panin's desire to give Catherine only a share in rule. Saldern, *Histoire de la vie de Pierre III*, p. 66; Panin's opinion was well known to the foreign envoys in St. Petersburg. See, for example, Shirley to Weymouth, 28 February 1768, *SIRIO*, 12: 327–28, and Bérenger to Choiseul, 2 July 1762, *SIRIO* 140: 9; also F. N. Golitsyn, "Zapiski," *Russkii Arkhiv*, (1874), no. 1, p. 1282.

designation. There were at least two living princes whose rights preceded Catherine's: her son, Paul, and Emperor Ivan VI, who had been interned at the beginning of Elizabeth's reign. Catherine's elevation therefore constituted a usurpation. This violation of an orderly succession process troubled Panin with good reason, and not merely because he stood to gain personally from the succession of Paul. He understood that the absence of an orderly legal succession had left the eighteenth century a legacy of rule by powerful favorites, palace coups, and peasant disturbances fomented by pretenders. The accession of Catherine, a German princess with neither hereditary nor legal title, could only give rise to continued difficulties of the same nature. For in a real sense her elevation represented a more flagrant breach of the traditional succession system than any other that had occurred in the eighteenth century.[72]

Of course, the question arises as to why he and Catherine continued to cooperate *after* she ignored his wishes and had herself declared empress. For Panin's part the answers were fairly obvious. Although disappointed at seeing Paul bypassed, he was nevertheless deeply committed to the original purpose of overthrowing Peter III. Once this was accomplished, his own security depended on preserving the new arrangements.[73] Moreover, his hopes of bringing reforms into Russian government would be altogether lost if he were to oppose the new regime.

On Catherine's side, although undoubtedly displeased with Panin's stand, she also desperately needed his continued support. To the extent that she had any claim to rule it was as a defender of the legitimate rights of her young son. Had Panin, Paul's widely respected guardian, been pushed out or had he even withdrawn his support of the new regime, it would have undermined public confidence in the enterprise. Furthermore, Panin was the only experienced minister among the inner circle of conspirators. Catherine could rely upon the Orlov brothers and guards officers to provide the necessary muscle for the overthrow, but they were of no help in managing the delicate political details, composing government manifestos, and advising on relations with foreign courts. These tasks required states-

[72]Firsov, *Petr III i Ekaterina II*, p. 67.

[73]Catherine could also have used on him the argument with which she later chided Princess Dashkova. "If it is a crime for me to have this place I occupy (for I realize that I have never had any right to it either by birth or anything else), then you share with me in this crime." See Dashkova's letter to her brother, 1793, in *Russkii Arkhiv*, (1884), no. 1, p. 271.

manship, and Panin was the one man among her supporters who could provide it. Thus, from the first day of the revolution Catherine entrusted him with the most important political affairs. He acted as her intermediary with both the Governing Senate and the key military fortress of Kronstadt[74] and arranged for his brother to assume command of the army at the Prussian front.[75] He took charge of the arrest of Peter III and handled arrangements with the fallen emperor's family and Holstein guards, all of whom were being sent back to Kiel in Germany.[76] For all practical purposes, he functioned as the chancellor of state; even the nominal Grand-Chancellor Vorontsov had to work through Panin in his dealings with the new empress.[77]

The most convincing illustration of Panin's special position may be seen in Catherine's actions at the time of Peter III's death. Just six days after the revolution, officers guarding the emperor at Ropsha strangled him in a drunken brawl. One of their number, Aleksei Orlov, sent Catherine a panicky note confessing the crime. On receiving the fateful note, Catherine immediately withdrew to her private chambers taking with her only Panin and one or two others.[78] During the consultations they worked out an explanation of the tragedy and at the same time entrusted Panin with yet another delicate assignment to cover Catherine's embarrassment at this untimely death. He was to make an appeal in the senate requesting that the senators dissuade the empress, for reasons of health, from taking part in the funeral ceremonies for Peter III.[79] Truly, Panin was, as the English envoy Keith reported, "the person that takes the most upon him," an opinion seconded by other foreign representatives in St. Petersburg.[80]

[74]I. L. Talyzin to N. I. Panin, 29 July [sic] 1762, *Perevorot 1762 g.* (Moscow, 1908), p. 3. The date given here must be a printing error, as the content of the letter relates clearly to June 29.

[75]*SIRIO*, 7: 102–03.

[76]Haxthausen to Bernstorff, 19 July 1762, *DRa*, Russland A III, no. 80.

[77]M. L. Vorontsov to A. R. Vorontsov, 12 July 1762, *AKV*, 31: 171.

[78]Posse to Chancellery President, 9 July 1762, *SRa*, Muscovitica, no. 308; Bil'basov, *Istoriia Ekateriny II*, 2: 130; the French envoy reported that Catherine was very worried about Panin's reaction and did everything in her power to persuade him that she had nothing to do with the horrible act. Bérenger to Praslin, 26 December 1763. *SIRIO*, 140: 304.

[79]Solov'ev, *Istoriia Rossii*, 143: 115.

[80]Keith to Grenville, 21 July 1762, *Despatches Buckingham*, 1: 61: "Monsieur de Panin est . . . le ministre qui l'emporte sur tous et qui seul proprement fait ici les affaires," was Haxthausen's opinion. 23 July 1762, *DRa*, Russland A III, no. 80; similar statements are

Whatever differences Panin and Catherine had over her right to the succession—and they were considerable—the two managed to close ranks and work together through the ensuing crisis. Panin had little choice but to go along with the *fait accompli* of Catherine's elevation and attempt to influence subsequent events in a direction favorable to his ideas. As for Catherine, she needed the support of all factions at court, but during the first weeks in particular she needed Panin's experience and judgment. And he did not disappoint her. A short time later she wrote to Poniatowski declaring that Panin was "the most skillful, most intelligent, and most zealous person at my court."[81]

6. The Promise of New Directions

Catherine and Panin moved quickly to right the political errors that had led Peter III to ruin. On the day following the coup Catherine turned over care of her son and the capital city to the senate during her absence on the expedition to Peterhof.[82] This act, more symbolic than substantive, demonstrated her intention of reestablishing the prestige of the senate. It was followed within a few days with a full restoration of the senate's previous powers. On July 2 that body regained the authority to render decisions having the force of law so long as the decisions did not alter present law and were made by a quorum of at least four senators. The power of reviewing petitions was restored on July 30.[83] The guards and others actively participating in the revolution received generous financial rewards, and measures were taken to return the regiments to the organization and status they had enjoyed during Elizabeth's reign.[84] Additionally, Catherine suspended the confiscation of church properties, further reduced the price of salt by ten kopecks, and, of course, immediately called off Peter's planned campaign against Denmark.

Beyond these initial steps to reward supporters and pacify potential

---

found in the Swedish dispatches. Posse to Chancellery President, 5 July 1762, *SRa*, Muscovitica, no. 308.

[81]Catherine, *Sochineniia*, 12: 559.

[82]*SIRIO*, 7: 101; Koliupanov cites this move as evidence that Catherine, rather than Elizabeth, was first to restore the Petrine senate to its original authority, "Ocherk vnutrennogo upravleniia v Rossii pri Imperatritse Ekaterine II," *Russkaia mysl'*, (February 1883), no. 2, p. 65.

[83]*LOII, f.* 36, *op.* 1, *d.* 132, 2–3. Raeff, "Domestic Policies of Peter III," p. 1308, gives additional references on the act of July 2.

[84]*LOII, f.* 36, *op.* 1, *d.* 132, 3; list of rewards in *SIRIO*, 7: 108–19.

sources of opposition there were broader issues to be considered. The legacy of administrative disorganization and government by favorites left over from Elizabeth's reign and the Seven Years' War demanded immediate attention. There were those within the government like Panin who counted on Catherine to make good her promises to introduce legal relations into the governing process. At the same time, the aspiring young leaders of social opinion, the young men of the Sumarokov and Kheraskov groups, looked to the new ruler to fulfill their hopes for a legal order based upon reason and moral enlightenment.

In anticipation of these desires Catherine published a manifesto on July 6 setting out the aims of the new regime. The document, composed by Nikita Panin and his associate, Grigorii Teplov,[85] enunciated the fundamental principles of the reform Panin planned to submit forthwith. The main points were summed up in the final paragraph of the manifesto.

> We graciously assure all our faithful subjects that We shall unceasingly implore the assistance of God in helping us to maintain Our Orthodox Law, to strengthen and defend the beloved fatherland, to preserve justice and extirpate evil and wrong-doing, and also to fortify us in all goodness. As it is Our sincere and honest wish to demonstrate [this desire] by actions . . . We do here most solemnly promise, by Our Imperial word, to promulgate such state laws according to which the government of Our beloved fatherland would carry on its activity within its power and proper bounds, so that in the future every state office [*mesto*] would possess its limits and laws for the observance of good order in everything and by this [means] [We] hope to preserve the unity of the Empire and Our Autocratic power, which has through misfortune been somewhat undermined, and to bring zealous sons of the fatherland out of despondency and offense.[86]

The manifesto outlined the basic program of the Panin group and its supporters among the young journalists of St. Petersburg and Moscow. As the document indicated, their objectives were to fore-

[85] The Danish ambassador Haxthausen, who was in Panin's special confidence at this time, reported that Teplov wrote the manifesto and "Monsieur de Panin l'a corrigé et y donné la dernière main," 19 July 1762, *DRa*, Russland A III, no. 80.

[86] Full text of the manifesto reproduced in Bil'basov, *Istoriia Ekateriny II*, 2: 84–91.

stall the renewal of government by favorites, establish legal procedures in government, and guard against the intervention of special
directives in the administrative and judicial offices. With the introduction of effective checks against arbitrary rule the citizens would
regain confidence in government and "zealous sons of the fatherland" could once again expect to receive their just rewards.

In the following weeks Panin and Teplov sat down to compose
a detailed reform project by which these principles could be implemented. Success of the reform seemed assured, and by the end of the
year hopes were running very high for its realization. A new era of
rational enlightenment free from the tyranny and insecurity that had
plagued the nobility during the first half of the century appeared at
hand. Panin told his friend the Prussian ambassador Solms that "the
time had passed when the intrigues of ministers could determine the
actions of the government." And in Moscow, where Catherine went
for the official coronation, the men of the Kheraskov circle expressed
their enthusiasm in a much more vivid fashion. They treated the
public to a street masquerade hailing "Minerva Triumphant." A
great parade of giants, dwarfs, and allegorical animals portraying
various vices trooped by singing the "Chorus of the Depraved
World," while "a contrasting picture of Utopia ruled by the 'Triumphant Minerva' . . . depicted the new reign of virtue and learning heralded by the enthronement of Catherine."[87] It remained,
however, to see whether Catherine was as enthusiastic about reform
as were her spirited reformers.

[87]Ryu, "Freemasonry," p. 63. There is a contemporary account of the masquerade
quoted in B. V. Varneke, *History of the Russian Theatre,* trans. B. Brasol (New York, 1951),
p. 74.

4

The Imperial Council Project

1. The New Regime's Commitment to Reform

The new government immediately turned its attention to domestic reform. A short time after the coup d'etat Panin told the French ambassador Breteuil of the urgent need to concentrate all efforts on the home front. Foreign affairs would have to take a back seat while Russia "occupied herself for many years solely with the general reestablishment of all sections of her internal administration which is in such a state of disorder as to demand prompt remedies."[1] Above all, Breteuil reported, "Panin deplored the deterioration and frightful disorganization" that had spread throughout the government during the last two reigns, and "regarding himself as a reformer, he gladly devotes much of his conversation to this kind of problem."[2]

Peter III's reign, in particular, had exposed all the abuses of autocratic power, and, as Panin understood it, the first priority of the new government had to be to insure that such excesses would not recur. In a few short months Peter had nearly destroyed the authority of the Governing Senate while at the same time neglecting the advice of his leading statesmen to institute a legally established council at the top of government. Under the circumstances such a body was urgently needed to coordinate policy and act as a control on autocratic caprice. During the early 1760s Chancellor Vorontsov had three times attempted to gain approval for a council that he hoped would restore order to the decision making process.[3] While these proposals

[1] Breteuil to Choiseul, 9 October 1762, *SIRIO*, 140: 87.

[2] Breteuil to Choiseul, 29 November 1762, and Breteuil to Praslin, 20 December 1762, *SIRIO*, 140: 116, 136.

[3] Vorontsov wrote to P. I. Shuvalov about this problem just before Peter ascended the throne, arguing the need for continuing the Conference and putting it in order. *AKV*, 32: 45; for his other proposals, see *AKV*, 25: 251–54; also P. N. Danevskii, *Istoriia obrazovaniia gosudarstvennogo soveta v Rossii* (St. Petersburg, 1859), appendix 4. For a discussion of this problem, see V.G. Shcheglov, *Gosudarstvennyi sovet v Rossii* (St. Petersburg, 1892), pp. 647–50.

were of a general nature, at the same time another very detailed council project appeared. Probably worked out by Count B. C. Münnich with the cooperation of Nikita Panin,[4] this "Plan for a newly established council at court" called for a state council divided into four departments (War, Admiralty, Domestic, and Foreign Affairs), each under the direction of a state secretary. Its proposed membership included representatives of all the leading political factions and clearly reflected the desire of the native elite to regain their lost influence on government affairs. Peter, however, rejected these efforts to regulate and channel his autocratic power. The council he finally set up just before his overthrow showed that he was in no mood to compromise his prerogatives; he restricted its membership to a small circle of personal favorites.[5]

Catherine's reign would see an end to such arbitrary use of power, Panin assured Breteuil. He noted that he had discussed this matter at great length with the empress and they had come to certain understandings. While explaining to her that it would not be in her interests to seem to alter her despotic authority, he was nevertheless convinced that "she had no intention of using a power whose abuse and injustice she recognized." Catherine understood that Russia no longer lived in a time when men would accept blind and abject submission to autocratic rule. Moreover, the special circumstances of her elevation "demanded that she justify the Russians' choice by granting the nation general advantages which another [ruler] would not have conferred; it was with such marks of gratitude that the peace and glory of her reign would be associated." Finally, said Panin, she had an obligation to protect the honor and security of those who had helped her achieve the throne. This meant building guarantees against "the illegal investigations and punishments that up to now have been the lot of every Russian at one time or another."[6]

---

[4]The "Plan" is described briefly in Shcheglov, *Gosudarstvennyi sovet,* pp. 650–51. My attribution of it to Münnich and Panin is based upon two considerations: 1. the very close resemblance of its main features to the reform projects later proposed by these two statesmen, and 2. the inclusion in its proposed membership of the two leading figures of the Panin party, Nikita Panin and B. A. Kurakin. In the absence of direct evidence this attribution must be regarded as tentative. On Münnich's later project ("Ebauche pour donner une idée de la forme du gouvernment de Russie") and its relation to Panin's reform, see my article "The 'Memoirs' of Count Münnich," *Slavic Review,* vol. 30, no. 4 (December 1971), pp. 843–52.

[5]*PSZ,* 15, no. 11538.

[6]Breteuil to Praslin, 23 February 1763, *SIRIO,* 140: 162.

In fact, Catherine had already entrusted Panin with the task of designing a reform of central government.[7] He was to ascertain the causes of incessant turmoil in Russia's central administration and propose changes that would fulfill Catherine's promise "to enact state laws by which the government . . . would carry on its activity within its power and proper bounds, so that in the future every state office would possess its limits and laws for the observance of good order."[8] Panin began the task by surveying the legislation of previous regimes. He wanted to know above all why Peter the Great's attempts to implant legal order had failed to take root. These inquiries led him to the conclusion that the problem lay with the incompleteness of Peter's reform program. Deficiencies that may have gone unnoticed at the time or been compensated by the energy of that unusual monarch had allowed others after his death to abuse and distort the organization he shaped.

The short life, burdened by difficulties and wars, of the Great Peter, the creator and legislator of the Russian Empire, did not allow him to complete the civil and political establishment; his successors on the Russian throne, viewing the mere foundations laid by him as if they were the forms of government, endeavored to take care of the defects they noticed by various temporary regulations and decrees. In the absence of a firm foundation in the state, however, and lacking the force of permanence, the latter either lapsed of themselves as times changed, or fell under control of accidental favorites. Hence, at times even the highest institutions were preserved in name only, while the entire state was governed by ignorant individuals and their pleasure apart from institutions.[9]

In short, since Peter's time, "government business was run more by the personal power of individuals than by the authority of state

[7]Many writers dispute the implication that Catherine requested the reform from Panin. Their arguments seem to be based on Catherine's later rejection of part of the project. Internal evidence and the circumstances of the reform's appearance leave little doubt, however, that the empress solicited it, whatever she may have thought of the results of Panin's work. For a discussion see N. D. Chechulin, "Proekt Imperatorskogo Soveta," pp. 79–80.

[8]As expressed in her manifesto of July 6. See above, Chapter 3, section 6.

[9]*SIRIO*, 7: 210; here and elsewhere translations of Panin's project and memorandum are borrowed with some emendations from Marc Raeff, ed., *Plans for Political Reform in Imperial Russia, 1730–1905* (Englewood Cliffs, N. J., 1966), pp. 54–68.

institutions." Panin's remedy to this problem appeared in his "Project for Imperial Council and division of the Senate into departments," which he presented to Catherine within a month of her accession. The project's provisions can best be understood when viewed together with a memorandum the author offered in support of the reform.

2. Panin's Analysis of Central Government Disorder

Preliminary to his reform project Panin thought it necessary to examine the conditions that had permitted the corruption of Peter's work and the supremacy of personal power over legal order. He therefore submitted a lengthy memorandum critically reviewing the practices of previous eighteenth-century administrations. The memorandum dissected each institution, exposed the failings of particular monarchs, excoriated ministers, and heaped mountainous abuse on court favorites—in short, it was as much an indictment as a review. Little escaped his critical eye as he nudged forward his own proposals for setting the whole sorry game aright.

Since the purpose of the memorandum was to justify the need for a general policymaking body to advise the monarch on legislation, the author set out first of all to explain why the present political institutions were incapable of performing such a function. After outlining the main sections of government, he immediately focused on the Governing Senate as coordinator of these various administrative branches. Some persons still believed the solution to disorder in the central state lay in reestablishing the senate according to Peter I's legislation, and Panin wanted to make clear that this approach could not possibly produce the desired results. The senate, he wrote, was "like a center toward which everything converges," and in consequence it staggered along under an enormous volume of work. In addition to supervising the entire state administration, it was called upon to unify and regulate the law. In conception the senate possessed a quasi-legislative function, a kind of judicial review. Its instructions allowed it, in the absence of a systematic legal code, to act as judge of the applicability of various conflicting statutes and regulations that had accumulated through time. But owing to its size, structure, and dilettantism, Panin went on, it could at best preside passively over its subordinate bureaus and offices. Their activities were quite beyond its ability to regulate and control. Well it was that the senate did not attempt control; the effort would more likely paralyze than facilitate administration. Under such conditions the various items of state business were handled through the collegia and bureaus without any special regard for their general applicability but only with a concern for whether they fit into the established procedures of the office. The senate could not correct this defect because it was bound to act in accordance with the decrees regulating the procedures of the offices below it. "The natural and necessary consequence of this [state of affairs] is that every senator and judge has no other aim than to render decisions provided for by the decrees and to submit a report on whatever is in doubt."[10]

It was rare indeed, Panin continued, to find a senator who would be willing to go beyond his prescribed duties and consider the general usefulness of a decision. Instead senators simply arrived at their offices expecting the secretaries to provide them with enough information on existing law to render some sort of decision.

> Naturally, such an official does not even spend an hour a day in examining the laws, decrees, and business personally, and in evaluating the good or harm that might come from them. And thus a senator, or any other official, arrives at meetings like a guest to a dinner who not only does not yet know the food's taste, but not even the dishes which he will be served.[11]

While this was a regrettable situation, Panin did not expect a great deal more from officials. Superior personnel were hard to find in any government. The chief difficulty was structural. The senate and its bureaus had more than they could handle simply supervising the administration and could not provide that concern for general policy so necessary to the smooth transaction of state business. They could only preside over the existing governmental organization, not actively direct it or mold it to a positive purpose.

Instead this important task, the "genuine overall concern for the whole state," had to be found in the person of the sovereign. The autocrat's power of legislation made this altogether obvious. "But he cannot translate this [power] into useful action except by intelligently

[10]*SIRIO,* 7: 203.
[11]*SIRIO,* 7: 203.

apportioning it among a small number of persons specially selected for this purpose." Here was Panin's central proposal. General policy should be articulated through a state council of trusted dignitaries.

No other body could perform this function successfully, Panin argued. He had already shown the senate's inappropriateness. Now he warned against the use of bureaucratic offices for this task. Some former monarchs had indeed made the mistake of relying upon collegial presidents or procurators to provide general coordination. In Panin's view, this approach only succeeded in corrupting the offices in question and unbalancing their relations with other institutions. Presidents of collegia were essentially competitive. Being separately responsible for a wide variety of affairs which they usually carried out with reference to their own particular regulations, they frequently engaged in undermining one another to the detriment of general policy considerations. In the exceptional case where a collegial president took a wider view of his office, he could do so only by going beyond the confines of his authority and thereby disrupting the orderly hierarchy of decision making.[12] As for the office of general procurator, it was equally inappropriate to the task. This "eye of the sovereign," as Peter the Great called the general procurator, was supposed to limit himself to "overseeing the regular flow of business and the accurate application of the laws in the Senate,"[13] and not to provide recommendations on general policy or legislation. One of the most serious obstacles to good government in the past, Panin remarked, arose from the arbitrary enlargement of the competence of that office. He explained how this had happened with the first general procurator, P. I. Iaguzhinskii, and then turned to the particularly notorious case of Prince N. Iu. Trubetskoi.

> If we take the reign of Empress Elizabeth in the first period of office Prince Trubetskoi was general procurator by virtue of court favor, as an accidental personage [sluchainyi chelovek];

[12]Although Panin did not specify any cases, an excellent example of what he was referring to may be seen in the War Collegium under Count Münnich's presidency. While Münnich had Empress Anne's favor, his collegium could reject senate orders, bypass the senate and Cabinet of Ministers in recommending promotions to the highest ranks, and even make dispositions in foreign policy without consulting the Foreign Affairs Collegium. What was normally a third level office had suddenly ascended to the apex of the government hierarchy. *PSZ*, 8, nos. 5920, 6155, 6178, 6299, and on the abolition of these privileges, no. 6911. Discussed in Shcheglov, *Gosudarstvennyi sovet*, pp. 624–25.

[13]*SIRIO*, 7: 204.

consequently, he did not enforce the laws in good order, but could and did everything and, we daresay, arbitrarily corrupted everything; in the later period he himself became the toady of favorites and minions [*pripadochnye liudi*].[14]

Given the absence of a separate legislative body to coordinate general state policy and the influence of personal favoritism, Panin believed that bureaucratic offices could not resist the pressure to expand and abuse their powers.

The next section of the memorandum took up the question of previous councils, the Supreme Privy Council, the Cabinet of Ministers, and others. What was wrong with them? Why did they not provide a satisfactory solution to the problem of general policy coordination? Panin had answers to these questions as well. As he saw it, the ingredients necessary for the success of such a body included permanence, a membership identified by rank and function, and a legally defined competence and relationship to other institutions. Otherwise favorites would continue to bend any such body to their own purposes. Only one of these councils, Empress Anne's Cabinet of Ministers, had to some extent satisfied these conditions, and Panin had good words for that institution. It was a legally established body and its members bore ranks which distinguished them from minions who might exercise power without occupying a responsible position. It at least partially closed the gap between the senate and the monarch, making it more difficult for favorites to step in and rule in the monarch's name. But it lacked permanence. With the change of regime matters again degenerated rapidly.

When Empress Elizabeth abolished the Cabinet of Ministers and relied upon a personal cabinet with no legal relation to the administrative hierarchy, an enormous void opened between the top administrative offices and the sovereign. Court favorites composing this personal cabinet jumped into the breech and started issuing orders in the empress' name. They turned the regular administration to their own partisan purposes, which naturally meant enriching themselves at state expense and appropriating an increased number of offices and patronage to provide for one or another personal clique.

Capricious favorites abused the cabinet, corrupting the form and good order of government; from everywhere business was

[14]*SIRIO*, 7: 204.

transferred to the cabinet, and the cabinet's prejudiced decrees
and orders resulted in matters never being settled. . . . [The
favorites] created their own governmental procedures and ruled
through them; illegally and without cause they intervened in
matters concerning inheritances and the splitting up of individual private properties they had put under seal; they confiscated
from one and gave to the other. [They] set no limit to their
aspirations and designs, while governmental matters remained
unattended; everything was thrown into confusion; the most
important duties and offices were transformed into ranks and
rewards for favorites and flatterers; favor and seniority became
everywhere the basis for assignments; nothing was left to talent
and merit. Arbitrarily and by means of court intrigue everyone
was grabbing and taking possession of the section of government he expected to be of greatest convenience in defeating his
rival or for combining with others against a third.[15]

Panin saw nothing in the current organization of government
that furnished an effective guard against these abuses. The Governing Senate, to take the most obvious example, stood helpless before
the arbitrary authority of the favorites and their personal cliques.
Since orders from the cabinet came down under imperial seal, the
senate had no choice but to act upon them.[16] Moreover, the senate
itself was composed of warring cliques and factions tied to various
patronage groups and powerful individuals. Therefore, the orders of
favorites met no unified resistance in the senate and simply worked
their way through and around it to the advantage of one or another
faction.

Finally Panin turned his attention to the Seven Years' War. In
light of his known opposition to the war, it was scarcely surprising to

[15]*SIRIO*, 7: 206.

[16]In these comments I have extrapolated some from Panin's own arguments. It should
be mentioned as well that Panin had a tendency to exaggerate the importance of the
cabinet. To be sure, it could and did send imperial orders to lower offices (see, for example,
PSZ, 11, no. 8584), but this was more the exception than the rule and did not affect the
dominance of the senate, which Elizabeth had reestablished in accordance with Peter
I's legislation. In fact, the senate even won the right to elect its own members, a prerogative that much enhanced its position as a representative of the leading families of the
nation. Later, after 1756, the Conference began to infringe upon the senate's preemi-
nence, but even then the senate continued to cling to its former position. A vigorous expression of this conflict may be found in a Conference report of 1760 in *LOII, f.* 36, *op.* 1,
d. 1072, 87–88. For another example and discussion of the foregoing, see Shcheglov, *Gosudarstvennyi sovet*, pp. 634–45; *IPS*, 2: 37–143.

find him lacking sympathy with those who had begun and prosecuted it. He remarked, for example, that the only rules of government during Elizabeth's reign were "of a kind that sacrificed the state's domestic prosperity for the sake of foreign affairs which . . . precipitated a war."[17]

What disturbed Panin most was that the war provided the favorites with one more opportunity to create havoc in the central administration. On the pretext of having to establish a central coordinating body to bring together all branches of the state administration for the prosecution of the war, they managed to usurp full powers from the monarch.

> A Conference, an unheard-of monster, was set up. Nothing was provided in it, and consequently, everything was left to irresponsibility; and having wrested from the Sovereign a law to the effect that edicts signed by the Conference would compel execution everywhere, they [the favorites] cut off the Monarch from all business of state and, consequently, also from all knowledge of their activities.[18]

This system, while boasting a legally instituted state council (the Conference), did nothing to correct the abuses inherent in the former unofficial cabinet. There was again a failure to maintain a recognized correspondence between official position and responsible authority. The fiction of rational order merely substituted for its substance, concealing the real power of influential individuals and cliques. These conditions, Panin bitterly observed, permitted a mere Conference secretary, D. V. Volkov, "to perform the functions of a prime minister under the pretext of administering a bureaucratic order that did not exist."[19] Volkov decided what affairs were to be dealt with, and he ordered ministers to do his will on the arrogant presumption that he was acting in the name of the sovereign. His and the favorites' whims and caprices ruled the state administration. "Nor could it be otherwise," Panin concluded, "when the spheres of government were not separated in the highest institution of the state and when none was anybody's particular concern."[20]

[17]*SIRIO*, 7: 206.

[18]*SIRIO*, 7: 207.

[19]*SIRIO*, 7: 207.

[20]*SIRIO*, 7: 207; one has to agree with V. V. Fursenko that Panin's and, for that matter, Catherine's view of the Conference was somewhat biased and impassioned, and that the men of Catherine's entourage, Panin above all, often adopted a light tone toward

This final statement announced his principal reform objectives: separation of governmental functions and their assignment to responsible ministers. Neither of these aims could be satisfied by establishing another "non-legal" council like those of previous reigns. Such a council, by allowing individuals to avoid responsibility for their decisions, simply served as a cover for continued disorder. In fact, it was precisely because each previous council had become associated with a particular individual's arbitrary power that it had to be replaced in the next regime;[21] whereas an official council, Panin was quick to add, furnished the monarch with many advantages. In the past favorites had used the administration at their pleasure while at the same time they "tried particularly hard to blame on the monarch's own arbitrariness everything they themselves did in [an underhand] manner."[22] Why were they able to do this? The reason was obvious. "A person entrusted with the business of a secret and basically unofficial institution may consider himself not subject to the judgment of the public [*publika*] and not responsible to it, and consequently free from all obligations toward the monarch and the state."

Elizabeth's reign and were quick to pillory the statesmen of that time. Yet Fursenko admits farther on that there was little sympathy among those statesmen for the collegial principle, and in running their various agencies they avoided calling councils or conferences as much as possible and strove toward a monocratic form of administration. "Konferentsii i konsiliumy v tsarstvovanie imperatritsy Elizavety Petrovny," *Zhurnal Ministerstva Narodnogo Prosvescheniia*, 45 (June 1913), 388–89, 403–04.

[21]Historians have for the most part accepted Panin's evaluation of the failings of central government organization in this period. The mixture of legislative, judicial and executive powers in both the senate and the various councils opened the way to any powerful faction to dominate all areas of government from a single institutional locus. So long as a group or family had the backing of the sovereign, they could quite arbitrarily arrogate to themselves all the functions of governance and employ special prerogatives to inhibit the action of other institutions with their equally diffuse and poorly defined powers. The same argument was advanced to explain the frequent changes in the names of councils (Cabinet, Supreme Privy Council, Conference, etc.). A new designation was necessitated by the loss of authority each council suffered as it expanded and abused its powers. Closely connected with this was the fact that each council became associated with the authority of a particular powerful individual or familial clique, and the fall of those persons discredited the institution and rendered it less useful to successors. Shcheglov, *Gosudarstvennyi sovet*, pp. 513–14; *IPS*, 2: 30–35; S. P. Pokrovskii, *Ministerskaia vlast' v Rossii* (Isaroslavl' 1906), pp. lx–lxix; I. I. Ditiatin, "Verkhovnaia vlast' v Rossii XVIII stoletiia," *Stat'i po istorii russkogo prava* (St. Petersburg, 1895), pp. 591–631; A. Liutsh, "Russkii absoliutizm XVIII veka," *Itogi XVIII Veka v Rossii* (Moscow, 1910), pp. 116–26.

[22]*SIRIO*, 7: 205.

The flatterers, however, say to the sovereign: "But you have your cabinet—command through it." This is a dangerous distinction! Do not all governmental institutions belong equally to the autocratic monarch if the whole state is his? The only difference is that when the monarch's business comes from these governmental institutions the public ascribes every surprise and error to the sovereign's ministers who, as officials, have a special obligation to prevent these [mistakes] from happening; and the ministers cannot arrogantly shift the burden onto the monarch, for by virtue of their rank and office they are obliged to render account of their behavior not only to their sovereign but also to the public.[23]

Here was the principle of responsible ministers announcing its debut on the stage of autocracy. To be sure, Panin's memorandum dressed it in a somewhat deceptive garb. It revealed far too little to clarify how this concept could be fitted into the autocratic form of government, which lacked the means for subjecting ministers to public review. Panin would attempt to resolve this difficulty in his reform project.

Equally important in this regard was the separation of responsibilities by function in the council. "Can a private proprietor manage his household," Panin asked, "if he does not first subdivide and organize it on an orderly basis?" Or better yet, look at the craftsmen —Panin was a great fancier of artisans—"how will an able manufacturer set up his factory if he assigns his master craftsmen to various machines and tasks on the basis of his liking of them, rather than according to their skill? Our master cobbler does not confuse the worker with the apprentice and hires each for the appropriate task." To these examples he opposed the proverb then current that "provided there is favor, anyone can manage anything." That happened most of the time, Panin complained, and as a consequence "affairs fall behind, and the intrigues of factions are in full swing."[24]

In concluding the memorandum, with an eye toward those very factions, he issued the following warning:

I should in all humility remark to Your Imperial Majesty

[23]*SIRIO*, 7: 205–06.
[24]*SIRIO*, 7: 207–08.

that, as she knows, there are among us persons to whom such a new organization of the government would be undesirable because of private interest known only to them. For this reason Your Imperial Majesty should not consider this business completed for the good of the people merely by giving her consent to this or some other project; it will require Your Imperial Majesty's care and firmness, so that Your Majesty's Council will acquire immediately its proper form and may be brought into action; indeed, in the beginning, most gracious Lady, there is almost no possible doubt that these persons will endeavor to find difficulties in the establishment or, as a last resort, will try to shape it the way they themselves would wish. In such a case, it is immeasurably more useful to establish [the form] now, rather than, as has been the case in the past, to allow the corruption of what has already been established.[25]

Appropriately enough, the memorandum's conclusion brought Panin back to the very problem his reform project promised to solve: to those irresponsible people who would mold the government into an instrument to serve their self-interest.

3. The Imperial Council Reform

Together with the memorandum Panin submitted his specific proposals in the form of an imperial decree for official promulgation. The decree has become known in the historical literature as the Imperial Council Project. It contained Panin's remedy for the abuses listed in the memorandum, and naturally he was eager to see it implemented. Therefore, he skillfully worded the preamble to remind Catherine of her earlier commitment to reform and bind her to it. After briefly cataloging the failings of earlier administrations, the project continued: "That is why, at the very moment of Our accession to the throne, We have assumed before God and Our people the imperial obligation . . . that We shall correct the defects of administration of our Empire mentioned above and remedy the harm that on occasion stems from them; in short, to secure on an indestructible basis the forms and procedures by which—under imperial autocratic power—the state will always be governed; all this We solemnly promised to our beloved subjects in the lengthy manifesto of July

[25]*SIRIO*, 7: 209.

6 of this year." Then, as if to bolster the case beyond refutation, Panin threw the weight of Peter I's authority into the balance. "We have based ourselves," the preamble continued, "particularly on those words of the Spiritual Regulations . . . of the *Sovereign Lord*, Peter the Great, in which this glorious and wise ruler says: the power of monarchs is autocratic, God Himself commands to obey them for conscience's sake; and [the monarchs] have their counselors not only to learn the truth better, but also so that disobedient men may not slanderously say that the monarch has commanded such and such by force and out of caprice, rather than [guided] by justice and truth."[26]

Clothed with this formidable authority, Panin proceeded directly to his specific reform proposals. The outlines were already clear from his arguments in the memorandum. Article I announced the establishment of an Imperial Council of six to eight members. They were to be called imperial councilors, and among their number would be state secretaries for foreign affairs, internal affairs, war, and navy. Article II of the project provided that these "secretary-councilors" were to be chosen from members of the administrative collegia dealing with the respective affairs. Other key articles were as follows:

> III. Although . . . the above mentioned state secretaries are counted among the number of those same imperial councilors, nevertheless capable men from outside the Council may also be employed as state secretaries. But in such a case, the prescribed number of former imperial councilors, not including these [additional] secretaries, should remain.
>
> IV. All matters which on the basis of statutes and by virtue of our autocratic monarchic power fall within Our concern and decision—such as reports submitted to Us outside the Senate, opinions, projects, all petitions addressed to Us, complete information on all the various aspects constituting the state's welfare—in short, everything that is to serve the autocrat personally in his efforts at increasing and improving the state is to be [taken up] in the Council as if it were by Us personally.
>
> V. . . . .all matters coming to Us as Sovereign ought to be

[26]*SIRIO*, 7: 210–11; the quote is from Peter I's Spiritual Regulation of 1721, one of his most famous didactic decrees. Italics are in original decree. The book is now available in English translation, *The Spiritual Regulation of Peter the Great*, trans. and ed. Alexander V. Mullen (Seattle, 1972).

distributed according to their character among the state
secretaries; and the latter shall review them in their departments, work them out, clarify them to Us in Council, and
dispose of them according to Our [i.e., the sovereign's] decisions
and orders.

X. Every new enactment, law, decision, manifesto, charter,
and letter patent which sovereigns sign themselves must be
countersigned by the state secretary in whose department it
was prepared, so that the public may know to what department
it pertains.

XI. From the above it may be seen that nothing may issue
from the Imperial Council except over the monarch's own
signature.[27]

The reform project provided a council, duly established in law,
to advise the monarch on legislation. As an advisory body, it apparently posed little threat to the autocrat's authority. The monarch
would determine its membership. And unlike Empress Anne's
Cabinet of Ministers and Empress Elizabeth's Conference, in which
the members by unanimous assent could issue orders possessing the
same authority as an imperial decree, no orders could issue from this
new council except over the monarch's personal signature.

All this seemed harmless enough. But there were several important points that Panin neglected to clarify. One of these, article
X, bore directly on the sovereign's legislative power in stating that
"every new enactment . . . which sovereigns themselves sign must
be countersigned by the state secretary in whose department it was
prepared." The article failed to explain whether the signing by
the state secretary was obligatory on receipt of a law signed by the
monarch. Could the responsible state secretary, for example, refuse
to countersign a decree of the monarch and would such a refusal
invalidate the decree? In other words, was there built in here an
attempt at a *droit de remontrance* like that enjoyed by the French
parlements of the eighteenth century?

At first glance, Panin's aim would appear more modest. His
overriding concern, as expressed in the memorandum, was to lay
responsibility for laws squarely on the shoulders of some legally
appointed official holding a post whose powers, competence, and

[27]*SIRIO*, 7: 211–14.

relationship to other organs of the state administration was determined by statute, so that those who formulated policy and drew up laws could no longer evade their obligation to render account of their actions. Those making public policy had for too long hidden behind the skirts of the monarch. They preferred to work from positions with no legally defined place in the administrative hierarchy. They preferred to govern through the name of the monarch and to influence policy without occupying an office of corresponding responsibility. It was high time, Panin was saying, that these men should be made to sign laws falling within the competence of their office. But even this interpretation implied some restriction of the monarch's autocratic authority. The restriction becomes clear when article X is viewed within the context of the council itself. The novel aspect of Panin's Imperial Council was its official and permanent status. Having a legally defined and recognized relation to the rest of the state administration it would, if properly employed, establish a place through which all decisions of state would have to pass and thus delimit the channels by which the imperial power could be articulated. It could prevent decrees from taking a circuitous route through the hand of favorites who in the past had moved into the gap separating the monarch from the executive institutions. In other words, the very existence of a legally established state council implied a certain process or procedure to which the monarch was expected to conform when enacting legislation. The additional rule requiring a state secretary to countersign each new law served to reinforce the procedure and restrain tsarist power within the prescribed limits. Hence, even with the understanding that the state secretary's signature was obligatory, the rule nevertheless obliged the sovereign to submit each decree to the council in order to obtain the signature. By the very necessity of this process, a law would become explicitly something more than the arbitrary will of the monarch.[28]

[28]There was as yet no procedural definition of law in Russia, an expression of the monarch's will in any form being in itself binding. Despite Peter I's prescription that no law was to have force unless expressed in writing and signed by the emperor (*zaruchen*), simple verbal commands continued to be regarded as law until Catherine II's reign. She tried to improve this situation. Without depriving verbal commands of legal force, she declared them binding only when announced through the senators, general procurator, or the first three collegial presidents (War, Admiralty, and Foreign Affairs). They could not, however, be considered valid for cases involving deprivation of life, honor, and property, or the exchange of monetary sums over 10,000 rubles, awards of villages, or ranks above colonel. For a discussion, see Ditiatin, *Stat'i po istorii russkogo prava*, pp. 629–30.

But the countersigning provision carried still greater implications for another feature of the reform project: the call for responsible ministers. This concept was making its first appearance in Russian political thought and was by far the most interesting and daring aspect of Panin's project. Every decision had to be countersigned by a state secretary, Article X read, "so that the public may know to what department it pertains." Although the article itself left the issue rather vague, the forceful argument for responsible ministers in the accompanying memorandum showed clearly what Panin was driving at. Ministers "by virtue of their rank and office," he wrote there, "are obliged to render account of their behavior not only to their sovereign but also to the public."

This formulation immediately raises a number of difficult questions. That ministers were responsible to the sovereign was understood and scarcely bore any relation to the nature of government institutions. But what about the public? Whom did Panin intend here? To whom would responsible ministers render account? It was unlikely that he employed the term in a juridical sense to define a class or estate (*soslovie*). More precise concepts were available. It was equally unlikely that he understood by this term an "opinion publique," for this notion presupposed independent organs of public expression, which had scarcely emerged at the time. Nor did the word itself provide any hints. The Latin loanword *publika* carried only the vague meaning of upper classes, high society, or simply society.[29] Panin may have had the metropolitan nobility in mind here. But, of course, there existed no representative institutions through which the nobility or any other group could exercise a review of ministerial responsibility. In view of these difficulties, one is

[29]Judging from English and French etymological dictionaries this was one of the meanings in use at that time in Western Europe as well. As for Russian, A. Preobrazhenskii, *Etimologicheskii slovar' russkogo iazyka* (Moscow, 1910–1914), 2, indicates the word as a borrowing in Peter I's time, evidently from Polish. V. Dal', *Tolkovyi slovar' zhivogo velikoruskogo iazyka* (St. Petersburg, 1882), 3: 535, gives for the nineteenth-century usage "obshchestvo, krome cherni, prostogo naroda." Earlier usage was, however, more restricted. As the archaic variant the Academy of Sciences' *Slovar' sovremennogo russkogo literaturnogo iazyka* (Moscow, 1961), 11: 1646, gives "people from the privileged ranks of society (in contradistinction to the simple folk.)." Then as an example a passage is cited from the memoirs of S. T. Aksakov, who was born in the late eighteenth century. Further evidence of this restricted usage for the eighteenth century comes from S. M. Linde, *Slownik jezyka polskiego* (Lwów, 1858), 4: 716–17, which gives the meaning from *Monitor Warszawski* (1764–1784) as "wielki świat, bywanie na świecie; . . . grosse Welt."

tempted to write off the whole issue as mere window dressing to embellish the council proposal with one of the ideas of good government favored by the Enlightenment philosophers so popular with Catherine. In fact, the one historian who took note of the concept in Panin's project treated it in this offhand manner.[30]

A closer look, however, reveals a serious purpose behind the proposal. The repeated references to this matter in both the memorandum and the reform project were anything but stylistic embellishments. Although obviously unwilling to spell out the full implications of his case, Panin was clearly trying to implant a new practice in Russian government. And he was going about it in much the same way as the British parliamentarians who a century earlier had begun groping their way toward this principle.

In struggling for this idea the British found that they had to elucidate three items: 1) the denial that the monarch could do wrong, 2) the identification of the minister responsible for a particular policy or malfeasance, and 3) this minister's accountability to parliament.[31] It required a long battle to win acceptance of these axioms and ministerial responsibility did not become a part of English government until late in the eighteenth century.[32] Without going into that story, one can see in Panin's proposals an attempt, however hesitating and subtly stated, to introduce these same ideas into Russian government.

Consider the first proposition, "the monarch can do no wrong." It ran through the entire memorandum. Here again, however, Panin expressed himself mainly by implication. He took care to lay blame for abuses on favorites and ministers, never hinting, even where the facts spoke clearly, that a monarch bore responsibility. Still in one instance he addressed the issue more directly. He wrote: "A monarch who is always trusted and loved cannot be suspected by the people that, on his own (without the perfidious advice of others), he will prefer what is harmful to what is good."[33] The second issue, the identification of a minister responsible for a particular fault, he tried to cover by the rule on countersigning decrees. Of course, this method

[30]S. P. Pokrovskii, *Ministerskaia vlast'*, pp. lxviii–lxix.

[31]Clayton Roberts, "The Growth of Ministerial Responsibility to Parliament in Later Stuart England," *Journal of Modern History*, vol. 28, no. 3 (September 1956), pp. 216–17.

[32]F. G. Marcham, *A Constitutional History of Modern England 1485 to the Present* (New York, 1960), pp. 209–17, reviews the main stages in establishing this principle.

[33]*SIRIO*, 7: 206.

in no way assured one of finding the real culprit. As the British had learned, it was difficult in any government, no matter how well regulated, to locate the adviser or generator of a policy if the monarch was willing to conceal and protect him. The minister signing the decree often had nothing to do with its genesis, and his signature placed him under a moral rather than a legal obligation. In the final analysis, its effectiveness depended on the minister valuing his reputation with the nation higher than his reputation with his sovereign. Then there remained the third, and in the Russian context seemingly insurmountable, problem of making a minister accountable to some legal body other than the monarch. Aside from indicating a minister's general moral responsibility to the nation—an idea adopted in German constitutional theory in the next century[34]—did Panin have anything more specific in mind?

An answer to this question may be hidden in Article III of the reform project. This article treated the appointment of new members to the council and ordained that while monarchs had the option of seating additional state secretaries, they could not in so doing reduce the existing council membership.[35] The intent, it seems clear, was to insure the council's permanence by restraining the monarch from precipitously overhauling the membership or stacking it with enough additional state secretaries to override the regular members. Although here as elsewhere Panin avoided the delicate question of sovereign power, the article certainly implied a prohibition on the

[34]The German concept of *Verantwortlichkeit* implied two things: juridical or legal responsibility for an act, and general moral or historical responsibility. It was not necessary, in the view of German liberals, that legal responsibility actually lead to impeachment, but that the principle be established that no one, including the king's minister, could set himself above the law. The constitution of the North German Federation in 1867 gave truly constitutional government in the German view because, on the one hand, it provided a genuine division of responsibility between monarchical and parliamentary institutions and, on the other, because government business was to be conducted by a constitutionally responsible chancellor rather than by court favorites of a diffuse council of bureaucrats. See Otto Pflanze, "Juridical and Political Responsibility in Nineteenth-Century Germany," in L. Krieger and F. Stern, eds., *The Responsibility of Power: Historical Essays in Honor of Hajo Holborn* (Garden City, N. Y., 1967), pp. 162–82, and Fritz Hartung, "Verantwortliche Regierung, Kabinette, und Nebenregierungen im Konstitutionellen Preussen, 1848–1918," *Forschungen zur Brandenburgischen und preussischen Geschichte*, 44 (1932), pp. 1–45, as cited in Gordon Mork, "The German Constitution of 1866/71: Pseudo-Constitutional Absolutism?" (presented to Duquesne History Forum, October 1971).

[35]Raeff left this article out of his partial translation in *Plans for Political Reform*, evidently regarding it as merely procedural and of little importance. It seems to me to be a basic key to interpreting the whole project.

monarch's withdrawal of councilors once appointed. Yet as every government required some means of removing officials adjudged criminal or incompetent, the article also assumed the existence of some other body qualified to act in this capacity, a body which would be the representative of the public mentioned in the reform project. While Panin did not name this body in the project itself, he was more candid in his conversations with the French ambassador Breteuil. The information recorded by Breteuil may be given some credence, since he visited frequently with Panin and exhibited an exceptional knowledge of many other details of the reform proposal. On the point in question he expressed himself without the slightest qualification. "M. Panin," he wrote, "on giving the empress his plan for reform and for the new arrangements to reestablish order in all areas of the domestic administration, had proposed that the Council of State, once created, would be immutable and that the members chosen by the empress could never be removed at her pleasure. According to his view, in cases of malfeasance they could only be judged and deprived of their office by a full assembly of the Senate."[36] If Breteuil's information can be believed, Panin's intention was to allow the senate to act as representatives of the public.

Now it is easier to see what Panin was aiming at. His reform project called for the establishment of a permanent Imperial Council with a legally defined relationship to the monarch on the one side and the leading administrative bodies on the other. All legislation and other affairs requiring the monarch's decision were to pass through the council for discussion, and before becoming law a decision had to bear both the monarch's signature and that of a state secretary. This arrangement would certainly help to exclude the interference of court favorites without official position, and to some extent it would expose a minister's actions to public view. It would also, however, constrain the autocratic monarch's exercise of power within well-defined channels and admonish her to act responsibly in relation to established government institutions. Beyond this, the provision for life tenure of councilors and their

[36]Breteuil to Praslin, 3 February 1763, *SIRIO*, 140: 151; V. Vodovozov, *Ocherki iz russkoi istorii XVIII-ogo veka* (St. Petersburg, 1882), p. 245, without substantiating the point or discussing it any further, mentioned that Panin wanted to put the senate on almost the same level as the sovereign. Vodovozov seems to have hit on something very important; had Panin's scheme for ministerial review been implemented it would indeed have transferred prerogatives of the sovereign to the senate.

possible review by the senate opened the way for an evolution into truly responsible ministries—but with one important catch. Ministers would not be accountable to the public under any definition of that term. They would be accountable to the most purely aristocratic body in the Russian Empire, the Governing Senate. If Panin was hoping to plant the seeds of constitutional order with his project, his ambition at this time extended no farther than to a narrowly aristocratic variety of constitutionalism.

4. The Division of the Senate into Departments

A second section on the division of the senate into departments concluded Panin's reform project. It called for an expansion of the senate's membership and its division into six discrete departments, each handling particular categories of government business. The First Department, which was to be under the supervision of the general procurator of the senate, answered for internal political affairs. The remaining five departments, each having an ober procurator for supervision, dealt respectively with the following areas: appeals, petitions, and heraldry; mines, trades, manufactures, and the Chief Magistrate; affairs of collegia of justice and patrimonies; military and naval matters; and affairs concerning non-Russian areas of the empire.[37]

According to Article V of this second part of the reform project, each department could decide cases coming before it by unanimous vote of the five departmental members, and the decision would carry the authority of the entire senate. Cases on which opinions divided went, however, to a general assembly of all departments, where majority vote would obtain. As in the past, matters to which no existing law applied or whose disposition remained unclear had to be referred to the sovereign for final decision.

As was clear from Panin's memorandum, in drawing up the reform he aimed at separating judicial and legislative responsibility in high government. The object in regard to the senate started with a recognition of that institution's inability to carry out its manifold and undifferentiated functions. Instead of demanding more of it than

---

[37]*SIRIO*, 7: 214–16; this proposal was not new to Russian government. Empress Anne had for a time divided the senate into five departments to deal with an accumulation of cases overloading the general assembly of senators, *PSZ*, 8, no. 5570 (1 June 1730), and Shcheglov, *Gosudarstvennyi sovet*, pp. 611–12.

was reasonable, Panin wished to turn it into an efficient judicial and supervisory organ operating according to a rational functional division of labor. This change would enable it more rapidly to dispose of the backlog of undecided business and handle an increased caseload without breaking down. This advantage, he remarked, everyone could understand.

But he added another more compelling reason for the change, a reason he could be sure would appeal to Catherine, whose hold on the throne was menaced from the very first days by ambitious and dissatisfied lower officers. Panin pointed out that his reform would combat this danger.

> For over thirty years we have experienced palace revolutions, and the more their force is spread among commoners, the more daring, safe, and feasible they become. Among Your Imperial Majesty's wise measures to cope with a situation fraught with danger for the future, attention should be paid to the fact that by increasing the number of senators greater respect will be shown to the government, and the Senate in turn will thereby be constrained to the order of the state.[38]

The enlargement of the senate would indeed contribute to the monarch's security by building increased support for the new regime. This measure would also serve Panin's plan for reordering the channels of state power. The senate would be enlarged, divided into departments, and "constrained" to a purely judicial and administrative role. Legislation and general policy would be the sole prerogative of the Imperial Council.

The two sections of the reform project were integrally related. The effectiveness of one section depended upon the implementation of the other. The institution of the one or the other separately would undermine the entire scheme. To divide the senate into departments and increase the number of senators without at the same time creating the Imperial Council would simply weaken the senate, diminishing its ability to guard the interests of the established families against the depredations of court favorites.[39] By the same token, to create the

[38]*SIRIO*, 7: 208–09.

[39]The French envoy Bérenger made some very keen observations to this effect later on when Catherine decided to divide the senate without also erecting the Imperial Council. "Ce corps [senate] n'a plus de consistance: c'était le seul tribunal de la nation qui put opposer une barrière aux entreprises du trône. Aujourd'hui ses membres, épars dans

Imperial Council without reducing the senate and circumscribing its activities would amount to placing two high government bodies with similar functions in competition with one another. This arrangement would do little to improve the efficiency of government. It was this integral relation between the two parts of the reform that prompted Panin to press for the establishment of the whole project immediately, before other persons could have time "to shape it the way they themselves would wish." For Panin, the unity of the reform was a basic condition for its implementation. He even intimated to the French ambassador that were the project to be corrupted he would prefer to scuttle it rather than see it implemented in a distorted form.[40]

5. Foreign Influences

A final question arises with regard to the influence of Swedish ideas on Panin's reform. Nearly every historian of this period has attributed the Imperial Council project to "republican" influences that Panin acquired in Sweden.[41] Catherine herself seems to have made an innuendo to this effect,[42] and later writers regarded this as more or less sufficient evidence in support of their assertions. The only other evidence adduced was Panin's long residence in Sweden at a time the government was dominated by a powerful state

---

plusieurs branches d'administration, n'ont plus de fonctions communes. Ils ont perdu toute l'unité qui faisait toute leur force. Les Sénateurs sont devenus des commis isolés qui ne pourront désormais s'assembler pour délibérer en concert sur un même objet que sous le bon plaisir de la Despote. Le bien public, la prompte expédition des affaires ont été le prétexte plausible de cette innovation. Les Russes n'en ont senti la consequence qu'après coup; ils voient à présent que leurs chaînes ont été resserrées." Bérenger to Praslin, 5 March 1764, *SIRIO*, 140: 330–31. One wonders if Panin was not here again the instigator of the French envoy's reflections.

[40]Breteuil to Praslin, 23 February 1763, *SIRIO*, 140: 162–63.

[41]Among many others, see Shcheglov, *Gosudarstvennyi sovet*, 653; D. A. Korsakov, *Iz zhizni russkikh deiatelei XVIII veka* (Kazan', 1891), pp. 383–84; V. E. Iakushkin, *Gosudarstvennaia vlast'*, p. 49; V. O. Kliuchevskii, *Kurs russkoi istorii*, 5 (Moscow, 1937), p. 18.

[42]In a secret memorandum to Prince Viazemskii (1764) that included evaluations of various senators, she wrote; "Another [senator (unnamed)] thinks that because he has spent a long time in this or that country everything everywhere should be established according to the policy of his favorite country, and that everything else without exception deserves his criticisms irrespective of the fact that the internal dispositions are based on the morals of the nation." From "Sobstvennoruchnoe nastavlenie Ekateriny II kniaziu Viazemskomu pri vstuplenie im v dolzhnost' general-prokurora," February 1764, *SIRIO*, 7: 346. Although it seems likely that this remark referred to Panin, there is no direct evidence to support such a surmise.

council, and his occasional disagreements with Catherine. From this meager scrap historians have built some rather grand theories about Panin's desire to usurp tsarist power and run the government by means of an oligarchic Imperial Council.[43]

It should be said at the outset that the influence of Swedish models on eighteenth-century Russian government has received a great deal of emphasis in historical literature. In several instances, however, well-grounded research by recent scholars has shown this influence to be much exaggerated. Even in regard to the first half of the century in which borrowing of specific Swedish laws has been fairly well documented, many questions remain as to the ultimate impact of such borrowing on the thinking of Russian statesmen and the reforms they implemented.[44] In the case of Panin's Imperial Council project no direct evidence of Swedish influence has been found. As indicated earlier, there was nothing in the record to suggest that Panin himself was especially fond of the Swedish system of government.[45]

As a matter of fact, the Imperial Council and its supposed model in Sweden differed in many fundamental respects. The Swedish *Riksråd* of the eighteenth century exercised not only legislative functions but also control over the military and judiciary, matters not under the authority of Panin's council. The Swedish council was composed of sixteen members, more than twice the number proposed by Panin, and most significantly, *Riksråd* members received appointment not by the king but by a committee of the first three estates of the realm. According to the constitution of 1719–1720 the king had to rule with the majority in council. Only in the case of a seven-to-nine split could he side with the minority.[46] Moreover, the Swedish council could place stringent controls on the king's freedom of movement within his own country. All in all, there was very little

[43]See above, chapter 1.

[44]On Peter's reforms see H. Hjärne, "Svenska reformer i tsar Peters välde," *Ur det förgångna* (Stockholm, 1912), pp. 123–31; E. Puttkamer, "Einflüsse schwedischen Rechts auf die Reformen Peters des Grossen," *Zeitschrift für ausländisches öffentliches Recht und Völkerrecht*, 19 (1958), pp. 369–84; on the "Konditsii" of 1730, also attributed to Swedish influence, see the qualifications by W. Recke, "Die Verfassungspläne der russischen Oligarchen im Jahre 1730," *Zeitschrift für Osteuropäische Geschichte*, 2 (1911–1912), p. 37; and G. A. Protasov, " 'Konditsii' 1730 g. i ikh prodolzhenie," *Uchenye zapiski*, Tambovskii gosudarstvennyi pedogogicheskii institut, vyp. 4 (1957), pp. 215–30.

[45]See chapter 2, section 3.

[46]"Riksråd," *Svensk uppslagsbok*, 24 (Malmö, 1952), pp. 159–64.

comparison between the *Riksråd*'s powers and those Panin proposed for the Imperial Council.

It would be going too far, however, to assert that Swedish practices and Western ideas of government in general had no part in Panin's reform project. Certain aspects of council-constitutionalism in Sweden bore a close resemblance to the Russian reformer's ideas. The question of countersigning orders came up, for example, in the 1723 Swedish parliament in much the same form Panin later posed it in Russia. Delegates were concerned about the integrity of foreign policy leadership and asked whether "Sweden's foreign policy was to be run hereafter by legal and responsible instances or would the king with the aid of non-responsible advisers be able to exercise a decisive but uncontrolled influence." They decided that in the future all orders would be countersigned by a particular state secretary, "who thus answered for their agreement with the protocols."[47] This was an important link in developing a system of responsible ministers in Sweden, because the estates exercised control by reviewing protocols of the council's meetings. Obviously Panin, who also worried about the secret thieves of monarchical power, was angling to establish the same sort of relationship in Russia between the council and the senate. But one must be careful in attributing this idea solely to Swedish influence. Such practices were common in other well-regulated governments, most prominently in Great Britain.[48] Many political tracts of the age, including Montesquieu's *Esprit des lois*, discussed the same ideas. They had even been tried briefly in Russia during the reign of Empress Anne.[49] There was no reason to believe that Swedish practice more than any of these other examples was responsible for their appearance in Panin's project.

The most illuminating comparison in Swedish history came from a much earlier period, the late sixteenth-century attempt by Erik

[47]Jägerskiöld, *Utrikespolitikens historia*, pp. 24–25, 50. The practice of countersigning decrees went back further in Swedish history. In the seventeenth century it had led to secretary power more often than to responsibility, at least until the chancellor was given strong supervisory powers at mid-century. Stellan Dahlgren, "Kansler och kungamakt vid tronskiftet 1654," *Scandia*, 26 (1960), pp. 108–09, 142.

[48]Debates and discussions of the British system were readily available in writings of the period. C. Roberts, "Growth of Ministerial Responsibility," pp. 229–30 and elsewhere.

[49]A reform made evidently under A. P. Volynskii's influence. Liutsh, "Russkii absoliutizm," p. 179; Speranskii, *Plan*, p. 256.

Sparre and Hogenskild Bielke to bring Swedish government under enlightened aristocratic rule. Like Panin, they too were protesting the lack of ordered governance and making a plea for efficiency and modern administrative practice. "Sparre wanted an administration which should be properly articulated, specialized, regularly paid, and above all national, as opposed to the domestic, cameral, *ad hoc* methods which had been good enough [in the past]."[50] Like Panin, these men were endeavoring to bring the monarchy within the rule of law, and they hoped to do it by asserting the constitutional prerogatives of a state council dominated by aristocratic families. In both cases the reformers left themselves open to the criticism that their program was nothing but a scheme to advance the interests of a narrow circle of leading families. This interpretation scarcely told the whole story, but there was an element of truth to it. In the Swedish example it was a question of an old aristocracy that was losing economic ground as the system of fief-holding passed away and was replaced by more modern methods of reward distribution. "Erik Sparre and his associates hoped to find, in the revenue-assignments and wages which were now the return for government service, some compensation for the fiefs which were no longer given to them; and hence they demanded a monopoly of high office."[51]

Much the same analysis may be applied to Panin's reform, although in the Russian case it concerned a new aristocracy of rank and merit. The ostensible purpose of the Imperial Council reform was to regulate government business, assign specific functions to responsible officials, and achieve a properly articulated administration. But in practice it meant closing out the unworthy, excluding from high office all those who had not proved themselves by birth, experience, and rank. Since Peter I's time it seemed that the great landed estates and lucrative salaries that were the rewards of high office had gone principally to favorites and time-servers. Only during the brief ascendancy of the Vorontsovs, Shakhovskois, and their associates had the ranking families been able to reassert their leadership, but they had again been shaken severely by Peter III's attempt at personal rule. Hence, Panin's reform, modern and enlightened

---

[50]Michael Roberts, *Essays in Swedish History* (Minneapolis, Minn., 1968), p. 21; for more detail on Sparre's ideas see Kerstin Strömberg-Back, *Lagen, rätten, läran. Politisk och kyrklig debatt i Sverige under Johan III's tid* (Lund, 1963).

[51]M. Roberts, *Essays in Swedish History*, p. 39.

though it was in conception, aimed above all at consolidating the gains made by the leading dignitaries of Elizabeth's reign and securing a monopoly of high office to the families of the new Petrine aristocracy who had proved themselves by education, loyal service, and achievement of high rank. This scheme naturally posed a direct threat to the young upstarts who had played such an important part in carrying through Catherine's conspiracy. The ensuing struggle between them and the Panin-led aristocrats would finally settle the fate of the Imperial Council project.

5

Court Parties and the Defeat of Council Reform

1. Catherine's View of the Political Structure

Catherine ascended the Russian throne as a usurper and, implicitly if not directly, a regicide. She owed her accession to neither testamentary devolution, blood ties, nor even, as some historians have suggested, following her own lead, to the desires of the whole Russian nation. A princess of the politically insignificant German territory of Anhalt-Zerbst, she had come to Russia in 1744 to marry a legitimate heir to the Russian throne, Peter of Holstein-Gottorp. In sixteen years of marriage she bore Peter but one son of questionable fatherhood. Through this son, Paul Petrovich, she held her sole legal right to participate in a regency council once Peter III was overthrown. But Catherine was not to be bounded by such considerations. Intelligent, ambitious, and long determined to rule supreme either through her husband or on her own, she turned to advantage a favorable conjuncture of discontent among the guards regiments, the clergy, and the aristocratic administrators of the senatorial elite, swiftly occupied the capital and had herself proclaimed empress. To the united action of these groups she owed her throne. This fact explains much of the political history of Catherine's reign.

Few foreign observers gave Catherine's rule much chance of success. With two legitimate claimants on hand, her son Paul and the deposed Tsar Ivan VI, as well as the ghost of her murdered husband, Peter III, astir among the discontented peasantry, the possibility of another overturn lingered for several years after Catherine's coup d'etat.[1] Only political skill, occasional ruthlessness,

[1] There were, in fact, several conspiracies discovered in the first years of her reign, justifying Panin's warning (cited in chapter 4 above) of the increasing tendency toward such acts as well as Firsov's observation that the greatest danger came in the beginning from adventurers like Catherine herself. Firsov, *Petr III i Ekaterina II*, p. 71; reports on some of these conspiracies may be found in Barsukov, "Batiushkov i Opochinin," *Drev-*

and a certain degree of good fortune carried her through these dangerous years.

By 1762 Catherine was no longer the naive German girl who had come to Russia to marry the heir to the tsarist throne. In nearly two decades at court she had acquired considerable personal and intellectual maturity through extensive reading, a trying marriage, and the handling of many practical administrative details connected with her husband's duties as Duke of Holstein. She had also observed politics at the Russian court and mastered its intricacies. She had participated in two major political crises that tested her mettle, resiliency, and calm calculation in the face of near disaster. The first of these was an abortive conspiracy to hinder Empress Elizabeth's prosecution of the Prussian war. Catherine was the only participant to escape the empress' wrath and survive with her position intact.[2] Then in the period just prior to Elizabeth's death, Catherine again went to work, carefully selecting her friends from the most important points of power in the government and guards. At the same time she meticulously observed the rituals of court and church to convey the image of a respectful servant of Russian interests and a dutiful daughter of the Orthodox Church. This attention to detail served her well when the second crisis came, the overthrow of her husband, Peter. It would also serve her in maintaining the throne acquired through this act of violence.

One of the lessons she learned from Elizabeth's reign was the degree to which the sovereign's power depended upon the action of court parties and their subordinate hierarchies. Her own involvement in the court intrigue during the Seven Year's War exemplified the point. As noted, she joined in a conspiracy to hamper the war effort and encouraged a passive strategy by the army command. Although ultimately unsuccessful, the intrigue helped to stall decisive action for a time and thereby confound the war party at court. It also gave Catherine a measure of the limits of tsarist power. She could observe firsthand that the policies of the ruler stood at the mercy of clashing party interests in the high administration, interests strongly in-

niaia i novaia Rossiia, vol. 3(1878), pp. 287–309; E. P. Kovalevskii, *Graf Bludov i ego vremia* (St. Petersburg, 1866), appendices; Bil'basov, *Istoriia Ekateriny II*, 2: 326–405; and Saldern, *Vie de Pierre III*, p. 130. In the last third of the century there were at least twenty-three pretenders taking the name of Peter III. *Istoriia SSR*, 3 (Moscow, 1967), p. 465.

[2]Petsschauer, "Education and Development," pp. 342–88; Bil'basov, *Istoriia Ekateriny II*, 1: 360–89.

fluenced by foreign intrigue and money as well as by considerations of domestic patronage in a still largely patrimonial bureaucracy. As one historian wrote of this period, "the life and activity of the Russian state was not determined by the extent of the empress' authority recognized as absolute, but by the resultant force of all those influences which refracted her autocratic will."[3]

The second lesson she learned from this time was that the power of the parties, when it did not come directly from tsarist favor, rested on their position in the state service. Unlike the situation in some European monarchies where dignitaries in retirement could be seen at court and exert an influence, in Russia a minister or favorite who left service and retired to the provinces, either voluntarily or through disgrace, lost status and as a consequence also his power to act.[4] The precipitous loss of influence and subsequent physical removal of Bestuzhev and his circle in 1758 made a deep impression on Catherine. The utter impotence of her former friends once they had fallen into disgrace left her painfully isolated during the years that followed.[5] When she herself became empress, she certainly understood that imposing disgrace could be a powerful weapon against her enemies. But there was another side to the question. After the Bestuzhev party fell, Empress Elizabeth became entirely dependent upon the remaining party led by the new Chancellor Vorontsov and his associates. With no substantial opposition to check them, they ran the government at their pleasure, controlled the flow of information to the empress, and implemented or stalled her decisions as suited their interests.

---

[3]Shchepkin, *Russko-avstriiskii soiuz vo vremia semiletnei voiny 1746–1758 gg.* (St. Petersburg, 1902), p. 698. Also compare Prince Shakhovskoi's comments on this problem in his *Zapiski*, 1, pp. 36–37.

[4]The British envoy Shirley, speaking six years later of how "no revolution can be brought about in such a country as Russia except at court," remarked: "If those who are absent from the Court could have the smallest hope of succeeding, there is a long time that the Empress would have been obliged either to descend from the Throne, or to confine the Orloffs to their estates, but out of sight of the Court nothing can be attempted. As soon as a person in place retires to Moscow, or to his estate, he is looked upon in this country as a man out of favor, and loses his credit immediately. I am sorry to be obliged to say, that the Russians have not yet shown themselves capable of any real or personal attachment for those who have served their country with distinction." Shirley to Weymouth, 20 July 1768, *SIRIO*, 12: 336–38. Other foreigners observed the same phenomenon. Romanovich-Slavatinskii, *Dvorianstvo*, p. 19. These comments echo Panin's wistful observations of the much different situation at the Danish court. See above, chapter 2.

[5]Catherine, *Sochineniia*, 12:406–33.

Catherine fully understood the imperatives of court politics when she came to the throne. Throughout the early years of her reign she was keenly aware of the obstacles confronting the articulation of her power. To uphold a balance of opposing parties was to invite constant bickering, delays, and confusion in the execution of policy. But the alternative was even less palatable. To permit a single party full power would risk its leading her around as it pleased, manipulating her authority for its own partisan purposes, and possibly even disposing of her altogether.[6] Hence, when Catherine ascended the throne in June 1762 her first concern was to maintain a balance among the factions that had sponsored the coup d'etat.

2. Political Alignments at Court

A new arrangement of political forces emerged with Catherine's accession. Two government changes within the previous six months had removed the leading families of recent times from contention for influence in the new regime. The powers of Elizabeth's reign, the Vorontsovs, the Shuvalovs, and the Holstein family of Peter III, could now only hope to escape with the material gains of their period of ascendancy intact. All had at one time or another opposed Catherine's ambitions and thereby forfeited credit with the new government. Of the leading political actors of the two preceding reigns only a handful managed to survive the first years of Catherine's reign with positions comparable to those held earlier. One of these was the venerable Count B. C. Münnich. He had come to Russia during Peter the Great's time and taken charge of Peter's waterways projects. After 1730 he rose rapidly, becoming president of the War Collegium and leading military figure in Empress Anne's government. Following her death and the overthrow of the favorite Biron, Münnich seized control of the government, assumed the title of Prime Minister, and for a short time acted as the effective arbiter of national policy. Sent into exile for all of Elizabeth's reign, he was finally pardoned and recalled by Peter III, whom he served loyally as a personal adviser, even standing by the hapless tsar during

[6]She had a very real fear of becoming dependent upon one group, as she explained once in a letter to Baron Grimm (August 1776): "I have always been greatly inclined to be led by people who know the business better than I. Only they had better not cause me to suspect they wish to own me. In that case I run away showing them a clear pair of heels." "Novootkrytye pis'ma . . . baronu Grimmu," *Russkii Arkhiv*, (1878), no. 3, p. 33.

Catherine's coup d'etat. With Catherine's victory assured, however, Münnich wisely submitted and ingratiated himself with the new ruler. She gave him charge once again of important engineering projects and received him warmly at court.[7] Finally, although not in the inner circles of power, Münnich would manage to play one more winning hand in the game of court politics.[8]

Others who were able to recoup their fallen fortunes included the powerful Conference Secretary Dmitrii Volkov. After a brief exile as governor of Orenburg he was recalled and given a responsible position in the central government, president of the Manufactures Collegium. He also acted as personal adviser to Catherine in some of her later reforms.[9] Hetman Razumovskii and Prince M. N. Volkonskii, among the earliest dignitaries to join Catherine's conspiracy, managed to retain some degree of influence. However, Razumovskii's credit fell sharply in 1764 when he tried to make the Ukrainian Hetmanate hereditary in his family.[10] Volkonskii, who harbored no such ambitions, held the empress' favor and ended up in the powerful and trusted position of Moscow Governor-General. Likewise, A. P. Mel'gunov, chief of the St. Petersburg Corps of Cadets and much favored by Peter III because of his fluent command of German, regained his credit with the new regime after a brief period of exile. He returned in 1764 to head the Commission on Commerce and later became a widely respected governor-general.[11] But Münnich, Volkov, Volkonskii and Mel'gunov were exceptions. The rest of the men who served Elizabeth and Peter III in the highest policy-making positions were soon either phased out or downgraded. Catherine's victory in the court struggle shifted the centers of political influence toward new men and produced new party alignments.

One group began to form around the Orlov brothers. The leading figure was Grigorii Grigor'evich Orlov, an officer in the artillery corps and Catherine's lover at the time of the coup d'etat. He and four brothers—Ivan, Aleksei, Fedor, and Vladimir—constituted by

[7]The most recent biography is Francis Ley, *Le Maréchal de Münnich et la Russie au XVIIIᵉ siècle* (Paris, 1959).

[8]See below, section 4.

[9]S. A. Rudakov, "Dmitrii Vasil'evich Volkov. Materialy k ego biografii," *Russkaia Starina* (1874), pp. 478–96.

[10]Shirley to Weymouth, 20 July 1768, *SIRIO*, 12: 339–40.

[11]L. Trefolev, "Aleksei Petrovich Mel'gunov, general-gubernator Ekaterininskikh vremen," *Russkii Arkhiv* (1865), pp. 931–78.

themselves a considerable party. All men of energy and daring, strategically located in St. Petersburg as officers of the guards and cadets, they organized the muscle for Catherine's coup d'etat, and, aside from Catherine herself, undertook the greatest risks. Catherine looked upon them as her personal saviors and was very much in their debt. Since the Orlovs—tall, handsome, daring—were much admired by the young officers of the capital, Catherine had every reason to reward them richly and elevate them to important positions. If dissatisfied, they could always be dangerous. But Catherine's attachment to them, above all to Grigorii, went much deeper than compelling political expediency. It was an affair of the heart. Save for her later romance with G. A. Potemkin, Catherine's attachment to Grigorii Orlov was her only lasting love affair. He stayed with her for ten years after the coup d'etat, and then it was he and not Catherine who broke trust, a rejection that threw her into dismay and confusion for several months. Nevertheless, she released him with many favors and great wealth and maintained her affection for him to the end of her life.[12]

While the Orlovs obviously occupied a critical position in the guards and had the favor of the new empress, they possessed few allies among the dignitaries in high government. The five young brothers were the first of their family to enter the world of court politics. Although descended of an old *dvorianstvo* family from the Novgorod area, they could claim no illustrious forbears. The earliest information on the family survives only from the time of their grandfather, Ivan Ivanovich, who died in 1693. His son Grigorii Ivanovich Orlov served in nearly all of Peter the Great's wars and managed to work his way to major-general rank, eventually becoming governor of Novgorod in 1742, a position of merely regional importance and influence. At age fifty-three Grigorii Ivanovich made a second marriage to the sixteen-year-old daughter of a Muscovite aristocratic family, the Zinov'evs, a not uncommon arrangement between rising members of the Petrine service class and failing aristocratic families of the previous period, which in certain respects enhanced the status of both families. From this marriage issued the five Orlov brothers. Their father's service connections gained them entrance to the

---

[12]Barsukov's 130-page monograph on G. G. Orlov in his *Rasskazy iz russkoi istorii XVIII veka* (St. Petersburg, 1885) is the most thorough treatment of the family available; however, it is dated and heavily reliant on a single source, Prussian diplomatic dispatches.

military academy and metropolitan guards regiments. Another favorable relationship provided their entree to court. A cousin, Anis'ia Nikitishna Protasova (née Orlova), through her marriage to Senator S. F. Protasov, had access there and could introduce the young Orlovs to the best society of St. Petersburg. It was probably through this connection that Grigorii Grigor'evich managed, after a brief participation in the Seven Years' War, to become personal adjutant to one of the most powerful men of Elizabeth's court, P. I. Shuvalov. From this point Orlov's skills as a daring Don Juan provided him all the recognition he needed. A reckless involvement with Shuvalov's mistress, which led to a falling out with his superior, inadvertently led him into the bedchamber of Grand Duchess Catherine, who had for some years been seeking out love matches to compensate for her husband's neglect.[13] Hence, after the coup d'etat Grigorii Orlov was unquestionably the man at court closest to the new empress.[14] But beyond this personal association with Catherine and his strong following among the guards officers, Orlov possessed few political assets. He had no training in the conduct of government or experience in court politics and political intrigue. Nor could he count on support from the powerful families represented in the senate and high government.

The return of former Chancellor A. P. Bestuzhev-Riumin soon after the coup d'etat promised to correct the Orlovs' deficiencies. Bestuzhev had fallen victim to an intrigue by the Vorontsovs and Shuvalovs in 1758, been stripped of his ranks and offices, and sent into exile. Catherine, whom he had earlier befriended, now recalled him, restored his former ranks and privileges, and appointed him senior member of the proposed Imperial Council. But despite the empress' personal favor, Bestuzhev very soon realized that he was as much an outsider in the current court politics as were the Orlovs. At age seventy-nine he was the most experienced statesman at the Russian court. His career had begun in the diplomatic service as early as 1713. He had been Russian minister in Denmark for many years, cabinet minister under Empress Anne, vice-chancellor and then chancellor for Empress Elizabeth. By 1762, however, Bestuzhev's old friends had long since passed from the political scene,

[13]Barsukov, *Rasskazy*, pp. 63–75.
[14]She had given birth to his son, the later Count A. G. Bobrinskii, on 11 April 1762. Bil'bsaov, *Istoriia Ekateriny II*, 1: 464 and note.

and he had no hope of finding allies among the dignitaries now in high office. Most of them had contributed to his disgrace four years earlier. Consequently, he turned instead to the young men raised to prominence through Catherine's coup d'etat. Like them, he was entirely dependent upon Catherine's personal favor. And the Orlovs, being the most ambitious and well placed of these newcomers, were for their part delighted to take advantage of the skillful old courtier's assistance.

More typical of the adherents to the Orlov group was Master of Ordnance A. N. Vil'boa (Villebois), the son of a recent immigrant. His father had left the French navy in 1696 to join Peter I's service and through a successful career of fifty-one years had risen to the rank of rear admiral.[15] The son served for a time as *kamer-iunker* at the grand ducal court of Catherine and Peter Fedorovich until removed for political reasons.[16] When Peter came to power he remembered Vil'boa's earlier services and promoted him to master of ordnance, an important post recently left vacant by P. I. Shuvalov's death. Quickly sizing up the situation at court, Vil'boa decided to cast his lot with Catherine and the Orlovs in their conspiracy. The plotters most urgently needed money to bribe the soldiers, and that was one commodity the ordnance command could supply abundantly. Accordingly, Vil'boa arranged for Grigorii Orlov's promotion to captain and appointment as paymaster of the artillery corps,[17] thus placing him in an excellent position to work for the success of the revolution. This move tied Vil'boa's fate closely to the Orlovs and the new empress. Like other men not related to the established senatorial families, he naturally gravitated to the Bestuzhev-Orlov party after the coup d'etat.

The second court party took shape under the leadership of Nikita Panin. Its locus was in the grand ducal court of the young heir Paul, where Panin ruled with little interference from Catherine or her courtiers. The Panin group was not opposed to Catherine's coup d'etat. Its most prominent adherents had helped to organize and carry through the conspiracy, and they were certainly relieved to be rid of Peter III's threat to the integrity of the central government institutions. Yet they were also miffed at the hasty elevation of

[15]"Kontr-admiral N. P. Vil'boa," *Russkii Arkhiv* (1867), pp. 1188–1203.
[16]Catherine, *Sochineniia,* 12: 51, 104.
[17]Bil'basov, *Istoriia Ekateriny II,* 1: 433.

Catherine, the by-passing of Grand Duke Paul's succession rights, and especially the role of the Orlovs in pressing ahead with the immediate settlement in favor of Catherine without consulting other participants in the conspiracy. No doubt, most disturbing of all was to find Grigorii Orlov just after the coup swaggering at court and playing at being an important government minister.[18]

The leading figures of the Panin party were separated from the Orlovs and other young men of the guard by age, temperament, and experience. A generation older than the Orlovs, the leaders of the Panin group had been in government service for years, some since the time of Peter I, and believed that they had earned the right to rule through their proved ability and loyalty. Most of them had come up through the ranks and like Panin had put in time at each position on the ranking hierarchy. They resented the young men who wanted to move directly into the highest positions of responsibility without first having demonstrated their merits by years of service in less exalted posts.[19] Moreover, the dignitaries of the Panin group had participated in the coup d'etat not so much from a sense of personal loyalty to Catherine, the primary motivation for the Orlovs and their friends, as from broader political and institutional purposes. They acted less in the desire to put Catherine on the throne than to remove Peter III. In fact, Nikita Panin explicitly opposed Catherine's accession and hoped that she would serve merely as regent during the minority of her son. The officials primarily sought to preserve the central government institutions from the depredations of Peter III's reforms and to pull Russia back from the brink of a foolhardy military adventure against Denmark; Peter's actions threatened to destroy the authority of the Governing Senate and remove all institutional restraints on his arbitrary exercise of power. It was precisely in the senate and other leading administrative bodies of the empire, where positions were monopolized by the leading families, that these older officials saw

---

[18]Dashkova, *Mémoires* in *AKV*, 21: 80.

[19]See, for example, Shakhovskoi's reaction, in writing that in the Semenovskii regiment he served time at each rank, "private, corporal, quartermaster-sergeant, and sergeant, . . . not as afterward when many young nobles got promoted through the non-commissioned ranks while sitting at home, only to enter service when they reached a commissioned officer rank." *Zapiski*, 1: 3; or Nikita Panin's own comments in Poroshin, *Zapiski*, 26 September 1764 and 20 August 1765. Also Romanovich-Slavatinskii, *Dvorianstvo*, pp. 428–29.

an effective guarantee for their continued security, retention of their wealth and status, their last line of defense against autocratic caprice. They had spent twenty years building the authority and independence of these institutions and were loath to see them destroyed by a new ruler. They wished rather to extend the authority of these institutions, regularize their functions, and define their relationship to the sovereign in such a way as to reduce the charismatic, personal, and ultimately capricious aspect of autocracy. In addition to providing greater personal security, these changes would affirm the bureaucratic service hierarchy rather than imperial favoritism as the main upward route to political power.

Closest to Nikita Panin personally was his brother Peter Ivanovich Panin. At the time of the coup d'etat Peter was in his early forties and had already distinguished himself as a brilliant field commander in the Seven Years' War. His leadership in the victories at Gross-Jägersdorf, Zorndorf, and Kunersdorf won him honors and recognition from Elizabeth's court. Absent from the capital at the time of the coup d'etat, Peter Panin was not directly involved in the conspiracy to overthrow Peter III. But he was drawn in almost immediately afterward. Catherine named him commander of the Russian forces in the field and entrusted him with the removal of the army from the war.[20] A short time later Peter joined several others as new appointees to the Governing Senate and took an active role in government affairs through the 1760s.[21] This younger Panin brother differed markedly in temperament from Nikita Ivanovich. Having spent his entire career in the military, he showed none of the subtlety and refinement of his diplomat brother. In dealing with equals or superiors he was straightforward and rather tactlessly candid; with subordinates he could be haughty and occasionally even cruel. A stern disciplinarian, he was reportedly not well liked by his troops and his officers but respected for his military skill and boldness.

It was above all his honesty and incorruptibility that set him apart from most of his contemporaries. He carried these virtues to the extreme. He was not afraid to oppose Catherine's policies and

[20]SIRIO, 7: 102–03.

[21]Biographical material from RBS, 13: 219–21; P. A. Geisman and A. N. Dubovskoi, Graf Petr Ivanovich Panin (1721–1789), passim: G. R. Derzhavin, Sobranie sochinenii, 7 vols. (St. Petersburg, 1864–72), 6: 580–81.

actions, either in council or in public, and was a particularly bitter critic of her favoritism toward the Orlovs. On one occasion in the 1760s when Catherine offered him the ribbon of St. Andrew he refused to accept it because the same decoration was being given to one of the creatures of the Orlovs. He said that under the circumstances the decoration "had become a joke," and he would have nothing to do with it.[22] In the early years of her reign Catherine brushed aside these criticisms and seemed to value Peter Panin's frankness. She once told Count Stroganov: "You know that I am no great admirer of Peter Panin, yet I have to do justice to his mind and character. Here is one instance. . . . I brought the Senate a draft ukaz. At its reading all the senators unanimously approved it; Panin alone, lowering his eyes, maintained silence. I asked his opinion. With firmness and thorough analysis he presented me with all its weak points and disadvantages. I was persuaded by his opinion and had to agree with him. The draft was rejected."[23] Later, however, Catherine showed less tolerance for such opposition and her relations with Peter Panin deteriorated. Despite his important services during the first Turkish War, she promoted others ahead of him and drove the proud man into retirement.[24] His continued criticism led her to brand him a "liar" and "slanderer."[25]

This later personal hostility between Catherine and Peter Panin has seriously colored interpretations of Catherine's relations with the entire Panin party. Peter Panin was rather exceptional, however, and his break with the empress reflected the clash of two obstinate personalities at least as much as a disagreement over substantive issues. While the party's concern with favoritism, merit, responsible division of authority, service and the rest were unquestionably at the bottom of Peter Panin's fight with Catherine, in his case they took on a distinctly personal character not typical of the Panin group as a whole.[26]

[22]Bausset to Praslin, 21 October 1765, *SIRIO,* 140: 552.

[23]P.A. Viazemskii, *Fon-vizin* (St. Petersburg, 1848), pp. 90–91.

[24]There was even a memoir produced (by Prince M. M. Shcherbatov?) about this injustice to Peter Panin: "Zapiska o ne shchastlivom prodolzhenii sluzhby generala Grafa Panina v sravenenii ego sverstnikov," which Geisman reportedly received from Princess S. A. Shcherbatova and reproduced in an appendix to his *Graf Petr Ivanovich Panin,* pp. 115–19.

[25]For the background to these comments see John T. Alexander, *Autocratic Politics in a National Crisis* (Bloomington, Ind., 1969), especially chapter 8, pp. 146–70.

[26]See, for example, Pigarev's evaluation, *Tvorchestvo Fonvizina,* p. 114; and Shchebal'-

The man who worked closest with Nikita Panin in a practical way in the months following Catherine's takeover was Grigorii Teplov. At age forty-six he was one year Panin's senior but without comparable family status or esteem among the nobility. The son of a Novgorodian smelter, Teplov managed to get a good education in one of the schools started during Peter's time by Feofan Prokopovich, archbishop of Novgorod.[27] Later he became a student at the St. Petersburg Academy of Sciences and in Elizabeth's reign was given charge of the education of Kirill Razumovskii, the young brother of the favorite. When Kirill became president of the Academy of Sciences in 1746, Teplov, as assessor, took over the day-to-day management of the institution and joined battle with such leading figures of the day as Trediakovskii, Lomonosov and G. F. Müller in the incessant squabbles of the academy. In 1750 he followed his pupil, now Ukrainian Hetman, to the Ukraine, where again he conducted the practical business of administration in Razumovskii's name. Peter III's accession brought Teplov his first taste of serious trouble.[28] Arrested and held for a time under suspicion, he went to Panin after his release and attached himself to the conspiracy against Peter.[29] He and Panin, being the best educated and most experienced statesmen among the conspirators, were responsible for drawing up the principal decrees connected with Catherine's elevation, and they carried out the most important affairs of state in the first months after the coup.[30] One object of their collaboration was, of course, the Imperial Council project.

The elder statesmen of the Panin group included most prominently N. I. Panin's brother-in-law Ivan Ivanovich Nepliuev and Count B. C. Münnich. Active in Russian politics since Peter the Great's time, both Nepliuev and Münnich were a generation older than the Panin brothers and had reached the height of power and influence under Empress Anne. Both had been in exile during the

---

skii, "Perepiska Ekateriny Vtoroi s gr. N. I. Paninym," *Russkii Vestnik*, 45 (1865), p. 759, both of whom take exception to the usual view of Panin's hostility toward Catherine.

[27]His father was a smelter at the archepiscopal house (Hence the surname Teplov). Romanovich-Slavatinskii, *Dvorianstvo*, p. 13; information following on his biography from *RBS*, 20: 471–76; Brokgaus-Efron, *Entsiklopedicheskii slovar'* (1901 ed.), 32: 924.

[28]He had, however, nearly become implicated in the Volynskii affair in 1740 and luckily escaped the net of arrests. *RBS*, 20: 471.

[29]Poroshin, *Zapiski*, 26 July 1765.

[30]*SIRIO*, 7: 105–107; Bérenger to Choiseul, 12 July 1762, *SIRIO*, 140: 27.

1740s and 1750s, although thanks to M. L. Vorontsov's intervention Nepliuev had returned to court in the final years of Elizabeth's reign.[31] Despite their long absence from affairs, these men added to the Panin group's prestige by lending it the reverence of age and a personal link to Peter the Great, advantages which in every sense matched those Bestuzhev's backing afforded the Orlovs. Even in some more practical ways Nepliuev and Münnich were able to advance the Panins' fortunes.

Other adherents to the Panin party were found among the two brothers' relatives. Through their sister's marriage to the Petrine diplomat, A. B. Kurakin, they drew support from that numerous aristocratic clan. Their nephew, B. A. Kurakin, although only twenty-nine years old at the time of Catherine's coup, was the leading member of his family, a highly educated and gifted administrator, a senator, lieutenant-general, and specialist on commercial affairs. Until his untimely death just two years later in 1764, he worked closely with the Panins from his positions as president of the State Revenue and Economic Collegia and chairman of the Commission on Commerce. After Kurakin's death the Panins administered his estate and took over the rearing of his two sons, who would eventually form the nucleus of the younger generation of their court party.[32] They also saw to it that Kurakin's position in commercial affairs was filled by A. P. Mel'gunov, a man who would carry forward his predecessor's plans for Russia's economic development. A second important participant from the Kurakin side was N. V. Repnin, the husband of the Panins' niece Natal'ia Kurakina and the representative of another family of ancient lineage. Like his brother-in-law B. A. Kurakin, Repnin was in his late twenties at the time of the coup d'etat and had already achieved high ranks. He won honor and advancement as an officer in the Seven Year's War, and then after Catherine's rise was appointed Russian minister in Prussia. The Panins could also count on support from their mother's clan, the Everlakovs. This branch of the family, which boasted direct links to the family of Tsaritsa Natal'ia Naryshkina, the Menshikovs, Rumiantsevs, and Eropkins, was headed up by the Panins' cousin Nikolai Leont'ev. The two most prominent figures in this period were

[31]See above, chapter 2.
[32]Poroshin, *Zapiski,* 28 November 1764; *Arkhiv Kurakina,* 5: 229–61; and below, chapter 8.

Leont'ev's brother-in-law P. A. Rumiantsev, later field marshal and good friend of the Panins, and a son-in-law, General Eropkin, a senator and head of the Moscow Salt Office.[33]

Finally, there were some holdovers from the former Vorontsov party who joined the Panins in preference to Bestuzhev and the young men around the Orlovs. Chancellor Vorontsov himself was among this group, although he had lost much of his influence and was now at least as dependent on Nikita Panin as helpful to him. More useful was the incorruptible Prince Ia. P. Shakhovskoi, the former procurator-general who by timely retirement had escaped the taint of participating in Peter III's government. An old comrade of Panin during their days in the Horse Guards, Shakhovskoi was a strong proponent of legal principle and objective standards in state service, and he shared Panin's criticism of the abuses personal power had caused in previous administrations. He went straight to Panin after the coup d'etat and as a senator worked closely with him, co-operating in reform schemes and playing a major role in the move to secularize church properties.[34] Panin also kept on some of Vorontsov's less exalted protégés like Baron Bilistein[35] and the chancellor's nephew A. R. Vorontsov. More difficult to define were Panin's relations with the chancellor's niece, Princess E. R. Dashkova (née Vorontsova), the nineteen-year-old adventuress who suffered from the delusion of having single-handedly organized and carried through the coup d'etat in Catherine's behalf. Nikita Panin enjoyed a special relationship with her. He protected her and acted as con-ciliator in several squabbles Dashkova had with Catherine, quarrels prompted no doubt by the former's inordinate boasting and com-plaints about not having been sufficiently rewarded for her partici-pation in the revolution. Whether Panin's motivation in helping Dashkova was political or personal has, however, remained some-what of a mystery. Stories about his personal attachment ranged from the implausible suggestion that she was his daughter by a youthful liason[36] to the more likely hypothesis that she was his

[33]On Leont'ev family connections, see "Iz bumag N. I. Panina (1771)," *Russkii Arkhiv*, (1878), no. 3, p. 426; P. I. Panin to N. I. Panin, 4 August 1763, *Russkii Arkhiv*, (1888), no. 2, pp. 86–88.

[34]Shakhovskoi, *Zapiski*, 1: 4, 180–83, 186–94, 206; 2: 60–87, 199–200, 204–06, 214–16; V. Korsakova, "Iakov Petrovich Shakhovskoi," *RBS*, 22: 590–99.

[35]Edmund Heier, *L.N. Nicolay and His Contemporaries* (The Hague, 1965), p. 153.

[36]That is, with R. L. Vorontsov's wife Marfa Ivanovna Surmina, one of Empress

mistress.[37] Panin seemed to have a weakness for Vorontsov women, as evidenced by his later liason with Anna Mikhailovna Stroganova (née Vorontsova). But political considerations may also have played a role. His protection would help cement the alliance with the Vorontsov family. Possibly more decisive, Dashkova was an outspoken critic of the Orlov influence at court, and as such she on occasion served as a focal point for disaffected nobles who retired to Moscow to grumble against the government. In part through her influence this "Moscow opposition" looked to the Panins as their champions.[38] The Panins also added to their group a number of personal friends, A. I. Bibikov,[39] Caspar von Saldern,[40] Ivan Chernyshev,[41] and others.

Two other families in high government chose to adhere to neither side in the competition for political dominance. The first, the three Chernyshevs, all held leading government posts in the 1760s. One brother, Ivan, head of the Admiralty Collegium, joined

Elizabeth's close friends. Possibly Panin did know her when he was a gentleman of the bedchamber *(kamer-iunker)* in the early forties. Madame Shuvalova was one of her enemies, and perhaps this was where Panin's dislike for the Shuvalovs originated. *AKV*, 5: 9–10. On the Vorontsov family background, see Riabinin, "Biografiia gr. S. R. Vorontsova," *Russkii Arkhiv*, (1879), p. 59; and Humphreys, "The Vorontsov Family: Russian Nobility in a Century of Change" (Ph.D. diss., University of Pennsylvania, 1969), who seriously discusses the question of Panin's fatherhood. See especially pp. 41–42.

[37]Dashkova vehemently denied this suggestion in her memoirs, *AKV*, 21: 43–44. It almost seemed as if "the lady doth protest too much;" her uncle twice wrote to her brother about this matter saying it was "not to [Panin's] credit that he passionately loved and revered Dashkova." On another occasion, complaining of receiving no reply to his letters to Panin, the chancellor suggested that the reason was Dashkova, to whom Panin "blindly makes himself a slave." M. L. Vorontsov to A. R. Vorontsov, 8 December 1763 and 9 March 1764, *AKV*, 31: 260, 272 respectively. Dashkova's precise known relationship to Panin was as granddaughter-in-law to Panin's aunt. "Iz bumag," *Russkii Arkhiv*, (1878), no. 3, p. 426.

[38]Dashkova may, for example, have been the moving spirit behind the Moscow journal *Innocent Exercises*, published in the early months of 1763. The journal, in which I. F. Bogdanovich also played an important part, differed form Kheraskov's journal in that it showed no support for Catherine's regime, and hence it figures as one of the early signs of the Moscow opposition. Berkov, *Istoriia russkoi zhurnalistiki*, pp. 144–45, rejects the common assumption of Dashkova's backing of the journal on grounds of her participation in the coup d'etat. But her break with Catherine occurred shortly thereafter, and they were on particularly unfriendly terms at the time this journal appeared.

[39]A. A. Bibikov, *Zapiski o zhizni i sluzhbe A. I. Bibikova* (St. Petersburg, 1865), vol. 2, p. 5; *AKV*, 33, appendix, p. 22.

[40]On Saldern, see *Arkhiv Kurakina*, 5: 261; and Otto Brandt, *Caspar von Saldern und die nordeuropäische Politik* (Kiel, 1932).

[41]"Ivan Grigor'evich Chernyshev" *RBS*, 22: 319–20.

with the Panin group during the early years of the decade. But the other two, Senator Peter Chernyshev and War Collegium Vice-President Zakhar Chernyshev,[42] refused to commit themselves in the court struggle. Instead they played a waiting game. Trying to avoid the intrigues of either party, they more often than not shifted their support with the fortunes of the battle; at any moment they could be found backing the party that seemed to have the upper hand. This tactic did nothing to enhance their influence over policy, but it worked well enough to keep them in office.

The second "non-aligned" family, the Golitsyns, descended from the Lithuanian Grand Prince Gedymin, boasted an ancient aristo-cratic lineage and had long served in leading government posts. They could recall recent forebears like V. V. Golitsyn, the lover of Tsarevna Sof'ia and director of national policy during her regency, or D. M. Golitsyn, the leading statesman of the Supreme Privy Council and author of the "Conditions" limiting autocratic power for a brief time at the beginning of Empress Anne's reign.[43] In those days the family could count many sons among the top civil and military administrators. By Catherine's reign, however, their in-fluence had waned considerably. The senior family member, A. M. Golitsyn, occupied the office of vice-chancellor, and two relatives held important diplomatic posts at Paris and Vienna. But they were, all three, generally observed to be mere functionaries whose opinions carried little authority,[44] and they seemed to recognize that their interests were best served by staying aloof from the court infighting.

[42]Their father, Grigorii Petrovich Chernyshev, collaborated with Peter the Great in the reform era and was able to open excellent careers to his sons. The eldest, Peter Grigor' evich (1712–1773), did long service at top diplomatic posts in Europe, then returned to Russia in 1762 to become a senator. Zakhar (1722–1784) studied in Vienna, then served as *kamer-iunker* at the grand ducal court of Catherine and Peter Fedorovich during Eliza-beth's reign. Despite some trouble he ran into by circumventing orders in favor of a patron (for which he was broken to the ranks), he managed to win back his honor by distinguished service in the Seven Years' War and rose to vice-president of the War Col-legium in 1763. Ivan (1726–1797) also was educated abroad and spent time in the diplomatic corps. Biographical information from *RBS*, 22: 314–30.

[43]The long-held view of D. M. Golitsyn's authorship of the "Conditions" has recently been disputed by G. A. Protasov, "'Konditstii' 1730 g. i ikh prodolzhenie," *Uchenye zapiski*, Tambovskii gosudarstvennyi pedagogicheskii institut, vyp 15 (1957) pp. 215–31, who attributes them to V. L. Dolgorukii. In any event, Golitsyn was the outstanding leader of the Supreme Privy Council.

[44]D. A. Golitsyn and D. M. Golitsyn respectively. Amburger, *Behördenorganization*, pp. 450, 477.

Various circumstances combined to keep the members of these two families in office. Sometimes a particular individual possessed a needed talent not available from the members of the established court parties. In other cases the empress sought to hold down certain posts with non-partisan officials who could act as a check on her other ministers or simply fill a space that, if allocated to one of the competing parties, might tip the balance too far to one side. Most importantly, perhaps, she favored these families with high position in order to guarantee the loyalty of their numerous relations and swing the support of their clans behind the new government.[45]

The presence of these two families did not substantially affect the rivalry between the Bestuzhev-Orlov and Panin court parties, who alone occupied the arena of policy development and execution.[46] One should not, however, mistake these parties for tightly disciplined groups with well-defined ideological programs. They may more accurately be described as the product of personal alliances among friends and relatives sharing certain general attitudes and interests and held together by patronage networks reaching across institutional lines and down into the bureaucracy. The groups often exhibited a high degree of internal cohesion, but this was based not so much on policy as on the strength of kinship ties or considerations of patronage. A good case in point was the adherence of the Vorontsovs to the Panin party.

One issue sharply divided the Bestuzhev and Panin parties: the question of Russia's foreign policy orientation. Bestuzhev argued uncompromisingly for a return to his former pro-Austrian alliance system directed against Prussia. Chancellor Vorontsov likewise favored a pro-Austrian policy, including, if possible, the adherence of France as well. In contrast, Panin stood for his own system of the

[45]See, for example, the French consul's remarks on the Golitsyns. In noting that Panin uses Saldern as his main associate in foreign affairs, he wrote that Vice-Chancellor Golitsyn has no more influence than Panin wishes to give him "de sorte que le Vice-Chancelier ne paraît occuper cette place que pour être en opposition de M. Panin et en lui servant de contrepoids; c'est en même temps envers la Souveraine un garant de la fidélité de sa nombreuse famille." Rossignol to the King, 4 November 1765, *SIRIO*, 140: 566–67.

[46]A fact well known by the most observant of the foreign envoys. Breteuil probably described it most accurately: "La Cour de la Czarine . . . est divisée en deux partis: Panin & Bestoujeff, dans lesquels les deux chanceliers, Woronzow et Galitzin sont à celui de Panin qu'à celui de Bestoujeff qui est protégé et soutenu par le favori Orloff." Breteuil to Choiseul, 28 October 1762, *SIRIO*, 140: 103–04.

"Northern Accord," which would put Russia in close alliance with Prussia and Denmark and counter the power of the Hapsburg-Bourbon system to the south. If policy questions were by themselves decisive, one should expect to find Vorontsov siding with Bestuzhev against Panin. As late as August 1762 Vorontsov was strongly recommending that Catherine continue the defensive alliance with Austria, because "Russian interests and the interests of the Vienna court were united by nature itself."[47] Yet with Bestuzhev's return and the sharpening of the court struggle in early 1763, Vorontsov turned right around and cooperated with Panin in negotiating an alliance with Prussia.[48] For this complete about-face there can be one explanation. The power struggle between Vorontsov and Bestuzhev during the Seven Years' War had left in its wake a personal animosity that no agreement on policy could possibly resolve. Vorontsov had nothing at all to hope for from Bestuzhev. A Bestuzhev victory in the court struggle would not only end any chance of Vorontsov's retaining favor with the empress, it might even bring disgrace and exile. Moreover, Chancellor Vorontsov had more persons than himself to consider. Other members of his family were then holding positions in the diplomatic corps and government. Bestuzhev would not be likely to maintain them in those positions if he got control,[49] whereas a Panin victory would place at the head of affairs a potential friend who had previous debts to the chancellor, a warm interest in certain female members of the Vorontsov family, and above all, a common desire to prevent the rise of the ambitious young men who surrounded Bestuzhev.[50]

This rough breakdown of political alignments at the Russian

[47]The comments were included in a point-by-point reply to Catherine's questions on Russia's position in ending the Seven Years' War. *TsGADA, f.* 1261, *op.* 1, *d.* 259, 3.

[48]He promised Ambassador Solms that he would delay his planned leave of absence until Panin could overcome Bestuzhev's resistance and negotiate a treaty with Prussia. Solms' dispatch quoted in Solov'ev, *Istoriia Rossii,* 13: 259–60.

[49]For example, Vorontsov made a special point of warning his nephew, then Russian minister at the Hague, about Bestuzhev's letters. M. L. Vorontsov to A. R. Vorontsov, 13 March 1763, *AKV,* 5: 119.

[50]And, in fact, Panin did many favors for the family in subsequent years. In regard to handling affairs after the death of Prince Dashkov, *GBL,* Barsk, VXIa, 24, 30; examples concerning other members of the Vorontsov clan in serveral letters in *AKV,* 31: 260, 308–09, 381, 385, and 32: 93; also Humphreys, "The Vorontsov Family," p. 42. N. Panin played a major part at the funeral of Chancellor Vorontsov in 1767, from which, incidentally, the Orlovs were conspicuously absent. S. R. Vorontsov to A. R. Voronstov, 19 February 1767, *AKV,* 32: 97–99.

court formed the context in which the Imperial Council project appeared. Party conflict was in no sense incidental to the reform. It was the very heart of the whole issue. The reform project served as a weapon in the court struggle. The battle for influence and position prompted the project in the first place, and the push and pull of party interests ultimately decided the fate of the reform program. The project's consideration and the accompanying actions of the court parties during the first two years of Catherine's reign make this very clear.

3. Opposition to Reform

The Imperial Council project was under serious consideration from the first month of Catherine's reign into February of the following year.[51] During this period the empress several times demonstrated her intention to establish the council. At the time of Bestuzhev's return from exile (31 August 1762) she issued a decree reinstating him in his former ranks and honors and then added: "We moreover grant him [the position of] first imperial councilor of the new Imperial Council being instituted at Our court."[52] Behind the scenes indications were equally favorable. Catherine once or twice sent the draft back to Panin for minor emendations, all the while proceeding as if the reform were a certainty.[53] Foreign diplomats were fully informed of the impending change and described it to their home governments in some detail. The Prussian envoy Solms,

[51]Little effort has been devoted to dating the Panin project. Svatikov, *Obshchestvennye dvizheniia*, p. 21, argued that it was composed in cooperation with Princess Dashkova sometime before Catherine's elevation. However, he irresponsibly cited in support of this contention sources that had nothing at all to say about the matter. Aside from Dashkova's cooperation (doubtful at best), Svatikov may have had a speculative point, as Panin seems to have begun his project in Peter III's reign in response to other proposals being offered then. In any case, the first mention of his work came from a French dispatch of 16 July 1762. "Je crois . . . qu'il [Bestuzhev] sera membre d'un Conseil d'Etat que l'Impératrice se propose d'établir." Bérenger to Choiseul, *SIRIO*, 140: 30. This was confirmed by the Dane Haxthausen a few days later, *DRa*, TKUA, Russland A III, no. 80.

[52]In *Sanktpeterburgskie vedomosti*, 3 September 1762, no. 71; words about the council were, however, deleted from the official ukase, published in *PSZ*, 16: no. 11659. The editors must have struck this section because the council was not finally established until after Bestuzhev's death. The archival copy of the ukase in Catherine's own hand showed no correction or deletion of this sentence. *SIRIO*, 7: 141–43.

[53]The requested changes amounted merely to deleting the word "barbarous" in reference to their ancestors and altering the titles of state secretaries. Bil'basov, *Istoriia Ekateriny II*, 2: 155–56.

Panin's close friend, already had a complete analysis of the reasons for the reform. The Danes knew the precise composition of the new council.[54] The Saxon representative Prasse could report with almost uncanny accuracy the date the reform decree was to be signed into law, which he placed in late December or early January.[55] Indeed, on December 28 Catherine put her signature to the decree prepared by Panin and was on the verge of announcing it to the nation. But at the last moment she hesitated, explaining in somewhat vague terms that its implementation would have to be delayed for a few days.[56] A few days stretched into more than a month, and it became clear that Catherine had decided to defer the reform indefinitely. Instead, in early February she assembled the proposed members of the council and appointed them to an altogether different body, a temporary commission to discuss the question of the nobility's freedom from state service.[57] Obviously, weighty considerations had intervened to change Catherine's attitude toward the council reform. Foremost among these considerations was the resistance of the anti-Panin faction at court.

From the very beginning the young men of the Bestuzhev-Orlov party had resented Panin's influence at least as much as he disapproved of their pretensions to leadership. They did not intend to

[54]Solms to King, 29 December 1762, *SIRIO*, 22: 16–17; Haxthausen to Bernstorff, 30 July 1762, *DRa*, TKUA, Russland A III, no. 80.

[55]Dresden Archive, vol. 7, no. 98, cited in Bil'basov, *Istoriia Ekateriny II*, 2: 158n.

[56]She wrote to Panin: "Il faut laisser les arrangements jusqu'après le nouvel an et à la première séance du Sénat, j'apporterai moi même la pièce en question signée le 28 Décembre; il m'est impossible de faire autrement." *Chteniia*, vol. 2, pt. 2, p. 140; on 6 January 1763 Solms reported in reference to the council reform that "l'arrangement est déjà tout fait et va bientôt être mis en execution." *SIRIO*, 22: 21; "The establishment of a State Council at Court will be announced to the people soon," M. L. Vorontsov wrote to A. R. Vorontsov on 16 January 1763, *AKV*, 5: 113–14. These reports, among others, refute the commonly held notion that consideration of the project ended on 28 December.

[57]The commission, empowered on 11 February, had the exact composition proposed for the council: A. P. Bestuzhev-Riumin, K. G. Razumovskii, M. L. Vorontsov, Ia. P. Shakhovskoi, N. I. Panin, Z. G. Chernyshev, M. N. Volkonskii, and G. G. Orlov. Compare the two membership lists in *SIRIO*, 7: 201, 232. The only difference was the assignment of secretary of the commission going to G. N. Teplov instead of seemingly more appropriate persons like General Procurator Glebov or Petitionsmaster I. I. Kozlov. Chechulin ("Proekt Imperatorskogo Soveta," p. 83) puzzled over this last appointment and could not understand why Kozlov in particular did not receive the job, as his office would seem to be essential to the matter in question. It appears likely that the choice was a concession to the Panin party to help ease the disappointment of losing the council reform.

stand idly by while he pushed through a scheme to restrict the empress' discretion in employing personal favorites. But how did they manage to turn Catherine against a reform plan to which she was apparently so firmly committed? The principal clue to this question lay in four commentaries on the council project. Catherine herself solicited the commentaries in order to sound the reactions of various advisers to the reform proposal. In view of her weak hold on the throne in these early months of her reign, she was especially sensitive to the recommendations and criticisms contained in the commentaries.

One of the four commentaries seems to have been authored by a member of the Vorontsov family. It wholeheartedly supported the proposal for instituting an Imperial Council and merely raised a few questions about formal aspects of the reform decree. The author recommended that the number of councilors not be precisely defined, as the monarch might later wish to expand or diminish the size of the council. He further advised deleting sections of the project relating to the duties of state secretaries in order to avoid disputes and misunderstandings on the part of other administrative offices. These sections should be left to a separate document setting out the rules of procedure. Finally, he wanted to put aside the reform of the senate altogether, leaving this question for the senate itself to decide.[58] None of these criticisms went to the heart of the issue, and thus the Vorontsov commentary must be regarded as favoring the basic purpose of the reform.[59]

The remaining three commentaries, however, contained more or less clearly stated warnings about the dangers of instituting the reform project. One of these, possibly written by A. P. Bestuzhev-Riumin, recommended a whole series of emendations and deletions of the reform decree in order to render it "more intelligible to simple and unlettered people."[60] The sense of this author's remarks was

[58]"Doklad imperatritse Ekaterine Vtoroi ob uchrezhdenii Soveta," 7 February 1763, *AKV*, 26: 1–4.

[59]On the assumption that this commentary came from M. L. Vorontsov, there is further evidence of his support in a letter to his nephew on 16 January. "Here, thank goodness, everything is going well and Her Majesty, to everyone's surprise, is working tirelessly on the administrative affairs of state, for the better execution of which a State Council at Court will soon be announced to the people. Pray God, that for the glory of Her Majesty and good of the state this new institution will come into being." *AKV*, 5: 113–14.

[60]This is the editor's view, based on a somewhat obscure marginal reference. *SIRIO*,

that the public might misunderstand the intention of the reform and might think that the council was more powerful than the monarch wished to make it. Among other things, this commentary advised the elimination of transcripts of council debates and the deletion of any reference to the senate's power of making representations to the monarch, "because there could thus be made public some restriction of Your Majesty's autocratic authority."[61]

Still more cautious in its approach to the project was the third commentary, submitted by an altogether unknown author. This writer first suggested that the council be named not the Imperial Council but the Supreme Privy Council. He followed this advice with the reminder that Empress Anne, who had not stood in direct line of succession *(pri izbranii ne po krovi)*, had encountered great difficulties in connection with her accession; therefore, it would be necessary, the commentator continued, to watch "with an unsleeping eye so that the autocratic power should not slip from [the monarch's] hands like a bridle rein."[62] This remark constituted another veiled warning against implementing the reform.[63] The author meant for Catherine, who like Empress Anne had ascended the throne outside the direct line of succession, to draw the obvious conclusions: the reform proposed by Panin endangered the autocratic power and threatened the establishment of oligarchic rule like that of the notorious Supreme Privy Council.[64]

But if these commentaries were not warning enough, the final one

---

7: 217n. Shcheglov disagrees and argues that M. R. [sic] Vorontsov authored it, the evidence being one point of similarity with M. L. Vorontsov's project submitted to Peter III. *Gosudarstvennyi sovet,* p. 659. Both efforts at attribution lack sufficient grounds for acceptance.

[61]"Zamechaniia neizvestnogo na manifest ob uchrezhdenii imperatorskogo soveta i razdelenie Senata na departamenty," *SIRIO,* 7: 217–19.

[62]"Zapiska pri predstavlenii zamechanii na manifest ob uchrezhdenii soveta i razdelenii senata na departamenty," *SIRIO,* 7: 220–21.

[63]Contrary to the surmise by Shcheglov, *Gosudarstvennyi sovet,* p. 664, that this writer was a friend of Panin unwittingly defending him with poor arguments.

[64]N. D. Chechulin, it seems, missed the point somewhat when he remarked that these first three commentaries limited themselves to the purely external aspects of the project. "Proekt Imperatorskogo Soveta," p. 81. Strictly speaking, his remark was accurate. But the two latter commentaries bore an unequivocal message: it would be dangerous to establish the council in the precise form Panin recommended. The second writer (Bestuzhev?) saw the possibility of misunderstandings arising that might react unfavorably upon the autocrat. The third author as much as said outright that the reform would lead to an oligarchic takeover.

submitted by General A. N. Vil'boa left no doubt whatsoever that some observers, in this case the Orlov party, considered the council project nothing less than a covert attempt to snatch supreme power from the monarch. Eschewing any resort to subtlety, Vil'boa spoke directly to the issue:

> I know not who the author of this lengthy project is; it would however seem to me that although he wishes to appear to be defending the monarchy, he is much more inclined in his own way toward an aristocratic government. A binding and legally established Imperial Council with members of importance (especially if they possessed as well sufficient arrogance, ambition, and wit) would be able in time to grow very conveniently into co-rulers. At least if there is a design for such an edifice, then this Imperial Council is certainly the first step [erste Anlage] toward it; and such an outcome would bring unmistakable ruin to the power and greatness of the Russian Empire.[65]

Instead of a council, which "the prudence and spirit of the empress" would have no need for, Vil'boa recommended that Catherine's private cabinet be divided into departments designed to handle different categories of business. Personal secretaries, he argued, could arrange various affairs to the empress' convenience, thus removing the danger of undue authority falling into the hands of a council.[66]

Vil'boa's response, and in a subtler way the two preceding commentaries as well, typified the attitudes of the young parvenus associated with the Orlovs. Wedded to imperial favor, they needed above all to retain the informal governing mechanisms of the past as the best guarantee of their continued influence and advancement. They knew very well what Panin's project was aiming at. The reform spoke eloquently of ordering government procedures, asserting the authority of legal institutions over personal power, and creating a more efficient administration. But in the context of court politics

[65]In concluding Vil'boa reiterated his warning: "A Russian monarch would of necessity require unrestricted power. An Imperial Council, on the other hand, would bring the subjects too close to the sovereign, and the former would ultimately wish to share the power of the latter." Entire commentary in K. L. Blum, *Ein Russischer Staatsmann: Denkwürdigkeiten des Grafen J. J. Sievers* (Leipzig, 1857), 1: 144–46.

[66]For futher evidence of the Orlovs' resistance to a council in the form proposed by Panin, see Breteuil to Praslin, 23 February 1763, *SIRIO*, 140: 162.

the reform could have, so far as these men could see it, one unmistakable objective. It was meant to wall off the influence of the opposing court party led by Bestuzhev and the Orlovs, gather all government business into a single body where the established dignitaries by virtue of rank, experience and expertise would occupy a majority of seats, and thus destroy any institutional *point d'appui* for the young favorites.[67] In other words, as seen by contemporaries the exchange between the author of the reform project and the commentators who warned against it was not so much a debate about what form of government would be most useful for Russia; it was a debate about which court party should win a controlling influence on policy and a monopoly of high office.

The commentaries placed Catherine in a very difficult position. As much as she may have agreed with Panin's criticisms of the disorder in Russian government before she became empress, she now had to weigh the political consequences of putting an end to it in the way Panin proposed. Some of her most ardent supporters resented the reform and feared, not without reason, that it would severely inhibit their ability to influence government business. Although one doubts that they persuaded her of Panin's desire to usurp the imperial power,[68] they certainly told her that the reform would generate sufficient hostility to render its implementation dangerous. She had to take this opposition seriously; at this early stage of her reign she could not afford to alienate any sizable group of supporters, least of all the men who had mobilized the palace guards for the revolution. Her interests lay most clearly in maintaining a balance between the court parties and acting as arbiter of their conflicts. If, as the commentaries inferred, the reform would shift the balance in favor of the Panin-led aristocrats, then indeed Catherine would not only have to contend with the resentment of the Orlovs and their friends but

[67]While the project was still under serious consideration Orlov tried the ploy of expanding its membership and stacking it with his own people. He had Prince Volkonskii added, for example, and with less success endeavored to replace Chernyshev with his friend Vil'boa as state secretary for war. Breteuil to Praslin, 3 February 1763, *SIRIO*, 7: 151.

[68]Catherine occupied a much different position from that of Empress Anne. She knew Panin and his relatively weak position much better than Anne had known the oligarchs of 1730. Moreover, Catherine had already been declared empress and was not accepting the gift of a throne on certain conditions or even facing an already established council with well defined prerogatives dating from before her accession.

she would also become dependent upon a single faction which might or might not cooperate effectively in executing her policies. With these considerations in mind, she finally decided to allow the council project to lapse and diverted her advisers' attention to the specific problem of working out a solution to the question of the nobility's freedom from service. Perhaps to ease Panin's disappointment she also kept the matter of senate reform on the docket referring it for further study and development.[69]

4. *The Bestuzhev-Orlov Faction Ascendant, Summer 1763*

The struggle between the Bestuzhev-Orlov and Panin groups did not cease with the shelving of the Imperial Council project. It continued in see-saw fashion throughout the summer and fall of 1763 until a specific foreign policy issue emerged that could not be handled in the midst of party strife. At that point, in the interests of establishing a consistent line of policy, Catherine finally had to end her balancing act and resolve in favor of a single party. The details of this struggle reveal the dynamics of politics in an autocratic state and point up the problems of reform in such a context.

The defeat of the Imperial Council reform marked the opening phase of the battle. This represented a setback for Panin and a corresponding victory for the Bestuzhev-Orlov party. It also brought the dispute, previously muted, out into the open. A week before the decision to abandon the council project, Catherine began giving Bestuzhev particular notice at court, and Bestuzhev himself let the British ambassador know that he was no longer on good terms with Panin.[70] By the following month it was clear to most foreign envoys that Panin had suffered a loss of credit. Solms reported that Panin was being slighted and that the empress now "listened to Bestuzhev as much as to any other minister."[71] Buckingham recorded the same story but still gave Panin a small edge.

> The foreign ministers seem all equally ignorant where to find the real Minister. Panin has the first sight, after the Empress, of all the foreign correspondence, which from him is carried to Bestuzhev. They thwart each other and everybody else; they

[69]Liutsh, "Russkii absoliutizm," p. 189.
[70]Buckingham to Halifax, 3 February 1763, *Despatches Buckingham,* 1: 222.
[71]Solms to Frederick II, 31 March 1763, *SIRIO,* 22: 49.

have each of them weight enough to keep her Imperial Majesty undecided, but neither of them sufficient to bring her to a determination. It is said that she has a better opinion of Bestuzhev's abilities and information, but that she esteems Panin as the honester and more unbiassed man.[72]

Buckingham further asserted that Panin was leaning toward the French interest. Since he repeated this charge several times in subsequent dispatches often *en clair* rather than in cypher, it indicated that he was trying to resolve the court dispute himself by exposing Panin's alleged double-play to the empress.[73] It is difficult, however, to tell if such innuendos did Panin any harm. In any case, he was having to contend with much more threatening blows from his opponents on the homefront.

Emboldened by their victory in the council dispute, Bestuzhev and the Orlovs made a desperate attempt to secure the final defeat of the Panins by pressuring Catherine into a marriage with Grigorii Orlov. Apparently with her acquiescence Bestuzhev began sounding the reactions of various court officials toward the marriage plan.[74] This daring move, the seriousness with which many at court regarded it (nearly a dozen highly placed persons, believing the marriage to be Catherine's wish, agreed to support it), and especially the fact that Bestuzhev had now taken the lead in this and other affairs all combined to throw Panin into a mood of despondency.[75] He confided to his friend Solms that he considered himself set aside. Solms reported:

> He acknowledged to me that he was no longer consulted as he had been in the beginning and that the empress listened more willingly to the opinions of Count Bestuzhev than to his, and since he sees that he is no longer so necessary, he would in the future limit his attentions to the education of the grand duke as

[72]Buckingham to Halifax, 5 March 1763, *Despatches Buckingham*, 2: 16.

[73]Diplomats often left *en clair* parts of their dispatches they wanted the court of their residence to read. Göran Behre, "Postspionaget under 1700-talet," *Scandia*, 29 (1963), pp. 292–94; A. Brückner, "Vskrytie chuzhikh pisem i depseh pri Ekaterine II," *Russkaia Starina* (1873), pp. 75–78; Adolph Beer, Ed., *Joseph II und Graf Ludwig Cobenzl* (Vienna, 1901), 1: 81, 97.

[74]Marriage plan reviewed in Barsukov, *Rasskazy*, pp. 87–89; Bil'basov, *Istoriia Ekateriny II*, 2: 275–96.

[75]Bil'basov, *Istoriia Ekateriny II*, 2: 283–84 and notes.

the principal object with which he has been entrusted. Your Majesty will be aware that these are the resolutions of an offended man.[76]

Panin's statement probably expressed only a temporary pique, but it revealed the marked change that had occurred in his relations with Catherine.

Panin maintained enough presence of mind, however, to mobilize resistance to the marriage plan. Chancellor Vorontsov, Hetman Razumovskii, and Grigorii Teplov, among others, joined him in counseling Catherine against the move.[77] Before long the whole business seeped out to the public, and Panin became the focal point for a wider opposition. People repeated his alleged assertion that "a Mrs. Orlov would never be Empress of All Russia."[78] His name also became linked with a conspiracy discovered among the guards regiments. An investigation of *kamer-iunker* F. A. Khitrovo disclosed conversations of some guards officers to the effect that they would overthrow Catherine and murder Orlov if the marriage plan went ahead.[79] Khitrovo further claimed to know that Catherine had signed an agreement with Panin prior to the coup d'etat promising that she would only assume the position of regent during Paul's minority.[80] This apparently unfounded rumor incensed Catherine and naturally did nothing to improve her relations with Panin. Nevertheless, the Khitrovo affair and subsequent investigations revealed the depth of public resentment toward the Orlovs' ambitions,

[76]Solms to Frederick II, 15 May 1763, *SIRIO*, 22: 63–64; Buckingham, too, had noted that Panin recently suffered the empress' displeasure, which he thought to have resulted from Panin's objections in the senate to some of Catherine's favorite programs. Buckingham to Halifax, 30 April 1763, *Despatches Buckingham*, 2: 29–30.

[77]See the Dutch envoy Meinertzhagen's dispatch, 15 July 1763, Kleinschmidt, "Vom Tode Peters III bis zum Tode Iwans VI. Gesandtschaftsberichte aus dem Haager Reichsarchive," *Russische Revue*, 23: 549; Breteuil to Praslin, 18 May 1763, *SIRIO*, 140: 193–94; on Teplov, *RBS*, 20: 474.

[78]Knorring, "Ekaterininskaia zakonodatel'naia komissii," *Sbornik state i posviashchenny i P. N. Miliukovu* (Prague, 1929), p. 331.

[79]Details of investigation in *Osmnadtsatyi Vek*, 1: 77; and Bil'basov, *Istoriia Ekateriny II*, 2: 295–96, 713–36.

[80]Strangely enough, a relative of the Panins, Nadezhda Andreevna Panina (née Ladyzhenskaia), married to Collegial Councilor Vasilii Alekseevich Panin, seems to have profited from this affair, as she was among those who reported Khitrovo's disaffection and threats. Karabanov, "Freiliny russkogo dvora v XVIII i XIX stoletiiakh," *Russkaia Starina* (October 1871), pp. 379–80.

the widespread concern for the position of the young heir Paul, and support for Panin's opposition to the marriage plan. These disclosures convinced Catherine of the danger of pursuing the marriage plan, and she put a stop to any further discussion of it.

The damage had been done, however, and the summer of 1763 was a turbulent time for the Russian court. Diplomats reported the guards regiments in a continuous state of turmoil. The Khitrovo affair spawned a number of further investigations of disloyalty. For the first time since the previous autumn foreign envoys expressed the view that Catherine might at any moment fall victim to a coup d'etat. Troubled echoes of the marriage plan reverberated for several months. As late as October Grigorii Orlov received a package from Moscow accompanied by a blank letter and containing beneath multiple wrappings a "large empty cheese filled with horse dung and stabbed through the center by a truncheon." The allusion of terror was unmistakable.[81] But the marriage plan was not the only source of discontent. Catherine's innovations in the military (changing of officers and shifting regiments around), the secularization of church property, and other reforms unsettled people and caused many to complain that "she had taken the scepter from her husband merely to glory in his reforms."[82]

The disorder in the lower echelons was mirrored at the top. While Catherine herself decried the party split in government and the harm it was causing,[83] she nonetheless continued to vacillate, still fearful of deciding in favor of one or the other party. This situation compelled the foreign representatives to expend a great deal of energy simply trying to find someone with whom to do business. They complained of not knowing which minister, if any, possessed the monarch's confidence. Chancellor Vorontsov had already made plans to go abroad on leave. Vice-Chancellor Golitsyn, who managed the routine conferences with ambassadors, was regarded as a mere cypher. And between the two apparent heirs to

[81]Bérenger to Praslin, 8 November 1763, *SIRIO*, 140: 267.

[82]Solms to Frederick II, 7 June 1763, *SIRIO*, XXII, 22: 73–74. For troubles concerning secularization, see V. S. Ikonnikov, "Arsenii Matseevich, istoriko-biograficheskii ocherk," *Russkaia Starina* (1879) 24: 731–52; 25: 1–34, 577–608; 26: 1–34, 177–98; and A. Zav'ialov, *Vopros o tserkovnykh imeniiakh pri Ekaterine II* (St. Petersburg, 1900).

[83]In an order to the senate of June 4, 1763, *PSZ*, 16, no. 11845, also reported in Büsching's *Magazin für die Neue Historie und Geographie*, 7 (Hamburg, 1774), pp. 247–48.

leadership, Panin and Bestuzhev, no one could reckon for sure which had Catherine's trust.[84]

The tide still seemed to be running against Panin. In the middle of July Solms got word that Panin had resolved to retire from all his offices. It was, of course, possible that Panin had become so disturbed with the deterioration of his position and the disruption in the country that he truly considered retirement. More likely, if indeed there was any substance at all to the report, it represented a threat rather than a serious resolution.[85] In any case, the very fact that such a story could circulate testified again that Panin's influence had considerably diminished. But July saw the full ebb of Panin's fortunes. Thereafter his influence increased steadily until late October when, despite Bestuzhev's last minute attempts to subvert him, Panin won full and undisputed control of affairs. The process is a great deal easier to trace than to explain, but it would seem to have been connected rather closely to the approaching Polish succession crisis.

5. The Polish Succession and Panin's Takeover, October 1763

It must be kept in mind that since Catherine's elevation to the throne Russian foreign policy had been in a state of flux and uncertainty. None of the foreign courts, and not even the Russian ministers abroad, had any clear idea what course Russian policy would take. From 1756 Russia, as an ally of Austria, France, Saxony, and Sweden, had been locked in a major conflict with Prussia. When Peter III mounted the throne, he immediately repudiated this policy, allied himself with the Prussian king, and ordered Russian troops to turn against their erstwhile brothers-in-arms, the Austrians. At the same time, for purely personal reasons, Peter prepared to attack Denmark. But before either of these two projects had pro-

---

[84]Buckingham to Halifax, 20 June, 11 August, and same to Yorke, 20 August 1763, *Despatches Buckingham*, 2: 43, 56–57, 64 respectively; Posse to Chancellery President, 20 June, 27 June, 11 July, 25 July, and Jahnke to same, 5 August 1763, *SRa*, Muscovitica 309, nos, 42, 44, 48, 52, and 55 respectively; Solms to Frederick II, 20 June, 24 June, 1 July, 22 July, 25 July 1763, *SIRIO*, 22: 79–84, 94–95, 96 respectively.

[85]Solms wisely expressed doubt about the report: "On m'a voulu assurer positivement que ce ministre (le comte de Panin) était resolu de se retirer tout-à-fait de la cour et des affaires; j'ai peine à y ajouter foi si tôt. Il aimera toujours à conserver la place de gouverneur auprès du Prince Paul." 8 July 1763, *SIRIO*, 22: 85–86.

gressed very far, Catherine overthrew her husband and suspended all Russian military activities.

Catherine's first move in the international arena was to abandon the hostile plans against Denmark and reestablish amicable relations with that country. But for the time being she left the far more important question of Russia's relation to the Central European powers undecided; she went only so far as to remove Russia from the Seven Years' War and attempt to maintain correct relations with the belligerents, showing no particular preference for either side.

During this period the battle developed at court between a pro-Austrian faction led by Bestuzhev-Riumin and a pro-Prussian faction led by Nikita Panin. Until mid-summer 1763 Catherine had been able to avoid committing herself to either faction. By then, with the death of the old and sickly Polish king imminent, she had to act to secure a reliable ally who would support a Russian candidate for the Polish throne. Prussia appeared the most willing to cooperate. Austria was firmly committed to the continuation of the Saxon dynasty in Poland, whereas a native Pole, especially if he were Catherine's former lover Stanislaw Poniatowski, would be much more easily controlled by the Russians. This resolution also appealed to Frederick II. Prussia had no fondness for Saxony; nor could Frederick possibly have relished the prospect of a Polish king indebted to Austria for his election to the throne.

With these considerations in mind Catherine instructed Panin to move toward an alliance with Prussia. This decision had an immediate effect on the court struggle between Panin and Bestuzhev.

One of the first signs of change came at the end of July. Bestuzhev sent a polite invitation to Solms and tried to effect a rapprochement with the Prussian ambassador. Previously he had avoided seeing Solms altogether and even refused to admit him to his home.[86] The unexpected *volte-face* on Bestuzhev's part reflected Catherine's decision to open negotiations for a treaty with Prussia and revealed the fact that she had entrusted the job to Panin. Bestuzhev, with his strongly anti-Prussian and pro-Austrian policy, found himself in trouble and no doubt thought he had best start mending fences on the Prussian side.

Subsequent dispatches by the foreign representatives would give

[86]Solms to Frederick 29 July 1763, *SIRIO*, 22: 97–100.

added support to this hypothesis. The Swedish envoy Jahnke learned that Panin was advising the empress on Swedish affairs in a manner that would answer to the requirements of his Northern System, and Catherine, the diplomat reported, intended to act on Panin's recommendations.[87] Buckingham, too, noticed the change. Late in July he had his first conference in some time with Panin, and afterwards notified the British envoy at the Hague of Panin's rising favor. A few days later he wrote home that Panin might soon become first minister. He even got Bestuzhev to admit that "Panin had lately gained ground."[88] About the same time Solms informed his court that Panin's star had been rising.[89]

There were other signs of Panin's growing favor with Catherine at this time. She turned over to him the general direction of the St. Petersburg wall upholstery (shpalernaia) manufacture which, though not valuable monetarily, greatly interested the empress as an example of Russian skilled craftsmanship, and she wished it expanded to serve the "glory and advantage of her subjects."[90]

An even more significant indication of Panin's rising favor was the announcement in early September that Princess Dashkova would be allowed to return to court. Dashkova had incurred Catherine's anger earlier in the year and had been ordered to retire to Moscow. Panin, who naturally had a personal interest in Dashkova's return, was said to have mediated the reconciliation with Catherine.[91] And indeed when she arrived at St. Petersburg in the last days of November Panin excused himself from a dinner engagement with the

[87]Jahnke to Chancellery President, 9 September 1763, SRa, Muscovitica 339, no. 65; see also the Prussian dispatches in which a clear outline of Panin's Northern System was discernible by the end of August. Solms to Frederick II, 8, 12, and 29 August 1763, SIRIO, 22: 103–16.

[88]Buckingham to Halifax, 20 August; to Yorke, 20 August; to Halifax, 22 August and 9 September 1763, Despatches Buckingham, 2: 63–72.

[89]"Il parait depuis quelque temps, que le credit du premier [Panin] commence à reprendre." Solms to Frederick II, 9 September 1763, SIRIO, 22: 118.

[90]Ukase to N. I. Panin, July 1763, GBL, f. Pan IV, d. 1, 51; this manufactory had been subsidized originally by Peter I and was evidently of some importance to the eighteenth-century court. The factory established in 1718 with five French masters, two dyers, and four Russian apprentices was not to produce tapestries for sale but exclusively for the tsarist house. Ocherki istorii SSSR, period feodalizma, v pervoi chetverti XVIII v. (Moscow, 1954), p. 101; the staff, grown to 117 by 1763, was further enlarged under Panin's directorship to 181. AKV, 5: 477–78.

[91]Jahnke to Chancellery President, 12 September 1763, SRa, Muscovitica 339, no. 66.

British ambassador in order, as it turned out, to visit the princess.[92]

By August Panin had persuaded Catherine to conclude an alliance with Prussia, and, in the bargain, won the job of negotiating it. Chancellor Vorontsov, having stayed on until this matter was established according to Panin's and ambassador Solms' wishes, was now free to depart for Western Europe.[93] The negotiations proceeded in strictest secrecy; Catherine allowed neither Bestuzhev nor the Orlovs a part in them.

Then in early October the battle seemed to sharpen appreciably. As the balance of influence tilted heavily in Panin's favor, Bestuzhev evidently made a play to prevent him from gaining full control over affairs. Bestuzhev's principal object would seem to have been to block the conclusion of the Prussian treaty. Such an inference emerged very clearly from Solms' dispatch of 4 October, in which he was undoubtedly transmitting Panin's own evaluation of the situation, as Panin was the interlocutor for the remainder of the dispatch. Solms reported:

> Those who are interested in maintaining the old confusion or in opposing the successful completion of an affair have found a *cheval de bataille* of which they make use on every occasion; they cause the Empress to fear that with this or that action which she proposes to take she could displease the nation. This fear of losing her subjects' affection, which has taken root, makes her hesitant to act and has taught her that with time she might become dependent upon one party that would lead her around as they found convenient for their particular interests.[94]

The "affair" would refer, of course, to the Prussian treaty, and naturally Solms and Panin would be upset over any delay in its conclusion. As for the rest of the report, it recalled strikingly the same problems that contributed to the abandonment of the Imperial Council. The references to those who opposed the establishment of any new arrangements and wished to maintain the former disorder echoed Panin's warnings in his memorandum on the council project. The attempts to worry Catherine about losing the affection of her subjects called to mind the objections in the commentaries on the

[92]Buckingham to Sandwich, 28 November 1763, *Despatches Buckingham*, 2: 117.
[93]Solms to Frederick II, 8 August 1763, *SIRIO*, 22: 103–05.
[94]Solms to Frederick II, 4 October 1763, *SIRIO*, 22: 125–26.

project. Panin's complaints to Solms about such hindrances indicated that Bestuzhev and his associates were not ready to give up control without a fight.

Just two days after the sending of this dispatch news of the Polish king's death reached St. Petersburg, and the fight between Bestuzhev and Panin suddenly shifted into another arena, a new council established especially to discuss problems involved in the Polish succession crisis.

According to the first protocol of this "October conference," the membership comprised A. P. Bestuzhev-Riumin, Vice-Chancellor Golitsyn, N. I. Panin, Prince Ia. P. Shakhovskoi, I. I. Nepliuev, and Adam Olsuf'ev.[95] There were persons at the Russian court who either expected or feared that this body would be much more than an ad hoc commission. The diplomats received information from unnamed sources to the effect that the October conference would occupy a position similar to the Conference of Empress Elizabeth's reign. The Swedish envoy Jahnke considered the new body a regular state institution. The British minister called it a "Supreme Council" and reported that the senate and collegia were to be subordinated to its directives.[96] And the Prussian Solms even described in some detail the position the conference was to occupy.

> It will be, so to speak, the "milieu" between the person of the Empress and the Senate. All affairs of importance, be they external or those of the country, will go there for the final decision, and Her Majesty will preside in person. This new council, which is supposed to assemble three times a week in the Cabinet of the sovereign, had its first meeting last week.[97]

This sounded like the Imperial Council suddenly resurrected from the ashes. But something was wrong. Instead of rejoicing at this unexpected victory for his reform, Panin was complaining bitterly. He told Solms that he might be turned out at any moment. He pleaded for Frederick II's intercession with the empress to stave off the ruin of the system he had worked so hard to erect.[98] Apparently,

[95]*SIRIO*, 51: 5.

[96]Jahnke to Chancellery President, 7 October 1763, *SRa*, Muscovitica 339, no. 73; Buckingham to Sandwich, 10 October 1763, *Despatches Buckingham*, 2: 88.

[97]Solms to Frederick II, 10 October 1763, *SIRIO*, 22: 138–39.

[98]Solms to Frederick II, 17 October 1763, *SIRIO*, 22: 140–41; Frederick responded in

the October conference was working to thwart Panin's policies rather than to further them.

The October Conference was then not Panin's idea at all. It was not modeled on the Imperial Council project. The protocol described it as an ad hoc body specifically intended for discussion of the Polish succession question; it was to have no permanent and legally defined relation to other government institutions.[99] Moreover, Panin regarded the conference as a positive hindrance, a move sponsored by "those who are interested in maintaining the former confusion or in opposing the successful completion of an affair." Conceivably, Bestuzhev stood behind the conference idea, playing on Catherine's fear of falling under the influence of a single party. Or, what amounted to the same thing in the court struggle, Catherine herself called the assembly in a final effort to bring Bestuzhev to support the policy she had already worked out with Panin. Catherine was still vacillating. She refused to end the balancing act between the two parties.

At this critical point Panin marshalled all his forces for the battle. He first got his nephew (by marriage) Prince N. V. Repnin appointed as plenipotentiary minister in Warsaw.[100] This gave him control over information coming from that quarter. Then he submitted a lengthy memorandum warning Catherine that if she wanted to place Stanislaw Poniatowski on the Polish throne she would have to act with speed and firmness. Any hesitation would open the way for increased Austrian and French influence in Warsaw. Without mentioning Bestuzhev's name or the pro-Austrian party at the Russian court, but clearly pointing to them, Panin predicted that France and Austria would, in attempting to create difficulties for Catherine's choice, "increase the number of every intrigue here for the embarrassment of Your Majesty's intentions."[101] Finally, his friend Count B. C. Münnich went to work on a proposal that from all indications was planned as a direct counter to the October Conference and the pro-Austrian party at court. Borrowing directly from Panin's Imperial Council project, Münnich argued that in setting up a council the empress should not repeat the mistake of earlier monarchs by

accord with Panin's wishes, 3 November 1763, no. 14825, *Politische Correspondenz Friedrichs des Grossen*, 23: 183–84.

[99]*SIRIO*, 51: 5.

[100]*SIRIO*, 5: 130n.

[101]N. I. Panin to Catherine II [October 1763], *GBL, f.* Pan II, *d.* 10, no. 345.

establishing an ad hoc, temporary commission; she should insist on a regular state institution juridically integrated with other sections of government and divided along functional lines. Münnich further added his own opinion that the first task of such a council should be the establishment of a Russian policy friendly to Prussia. In effect Münnich's project constituted a brief for all of Panin's favorite ideas, and it seems likely that Panin brought him in at this juncture as the one man who could match Bestuzhev's long record of faithful service to the tsarist family.[102]

In the last analysis, all these efforts proved unnecessary. If Catherine had any hopes of weaning Bestuzhev away from his pro-Austrian sympathies she was sorely deceived. He showed no desire to bend and acted as his own worst enemy. Refusing even to attend the first meeting of the conference, he sent his views in writing to the empress, expressing an adamant opposition to the elevation of a Piast on the Polish throne.[103] The British ambassador was told that Bestuzhev pushed his zeal for the Austrian candidate so far as to "disgust" the empress.[104] A few days after this report Catherine finally decided to abolish the conference and work through Panin alone. She appointed him "senior member" *(starshii chlen)* of the Foreign Affairs Collegium and gave him full control over the direction of foreign policy.[105] As a result, Bestuzhev faded rapidly from the scene. He no longer consulted with foreign envoys, and he played no part in the decisions of court. In fact, Panin had so far convinced the empress of the need for secrecy on the question of the Prussian treaty that he could confidently assure Solms that Bestuzhev and the Orlovs would read about it in the newspapers.[106] A few months later Bestuzhev was disgraced and sent into retirement on his estates.

[102]Münnich's project, which was later published as *Ebauche pour donner une idée de la forme du Gouvernement de l'empire de Russie* (Copenhagen, 1774), and its relation to the court struggle is detailed in my article, "The 'Memoirs' of Count Münnich," *Slavic Review*, 30: 4 (December 1971), pp. 843–52.

[103]Bérenger to Praslin, 21 October 1763, *SIRIO*, 140: 252.

[104]Buckingham to Sandwich, 21 October 1763, *Despatches Buckingham*, 2: 95.

[105]Solms reported Panin's appointment in a dispatch of 28 October. *SIRIO*, 22: 143–145; Jahnke gave even more detailed information on the same date: "Vice Chancellor Prince Golitsyn told me yesterday during the usual conference that he was to inform me that Her Majesty the empress had appointed Herr Oberhofmeister, Senator, and Privy Councilor Panin as first member of the State Collegium of Foreign Affairs, and henceforth I could take all business to Herr Panin in the same manner as to him the vice chancellor." *SRa*, Muscovitica 339, no. 79.

[106]Solms to Frederick II, 21 October 1763, *SIRIO*, 22: 146; on the secrecy of the nego-

6. Council Reform and Court Struggle

The pattern that emerges from this exposition of various council projects and counter-proposals, their timing, and finally their relation to personal rivalries at court throws light on an underlying motivation for council reform throughout the century. While having the important long-term effect of asserting the primacy of objective legal standards over personalism, the reform projects also had an immediate purpose as weapons in the battles between personal and familial groups vying for power. Council proposals invariably came from out-groups and appeared at times when the balance between factions representing official position and personal favoritism was unstable. Men enjoying the full confidence of the monarch, those in undisputed control of affairs, never sponsored such reforms. A few examples will illustrate the point.

The first council of the eighteenth century, the Supreme Privy Council (1727–1730), represented a move by Petrine dignitaries to check the arbitrary power that Prince Menshikov had acquired through Catherine I's favor after Peter the Great's death in 1725. By establishing the Supreme Privy Council, they forced Menshikov to allow them back into the decision-making process.[107] In 1747 M. L. Vorontsov tried the same tactic against Chancellor Bestuzhev, begging the empress to reaffirm collegial decision-making after the chancellor subverted it and acted on his own outside the Foreign Affairs Collegium.[108] Nine years later, as power began to slip from Bestuzhev's hands, he himself resorted to this weapon. When his policies ceased to please Elizabeth and she turned the conduct of affairs over to his opponents, Bestuzhev countered by pressing for the institution of a special state council or conference. Since the chancellor could scarcely be excluded from such a body, he could be

tiations, see also Bérenger to Praslin, 13 December 1763, *SIRIO*, 140: 285.

[107]See the discussion in S. M. Seredonin, *Istoricheskii obzor deiatel'nosti Komiteta Ministrov* (St. Petersburg, 1902), 1: 1–4.

[108]Solov'ev, *Istoriia Rossii*, 11: 480; the statesmen of this era understood the tactic perfectly well, as is evidenced by the Marquis de La Chetardie's letter of January 1744 concerning another attempt to undermine Bestuzhev's personal power. "We, Mardefeld, Brümmer, Lestocq, General Rumiantsev, Procurator-General Prince Trubetskoi, their associates, and I agreed to try and win the chancellorship for General Rumiantsev, who, as head of the collegium, would have the power to restrain Bestuzhev. If, however, this design does not succeed, it will be necessary . . . to arrange a council or cabinet with a sufficient number of members that Bestuzhev could not control them." Solov'ev, *Istoriia Rossii*, 11: 265.

sure of regaining the voice he had lost to his enemies.[109] Again in October 1763, when Bestuzhev was losing power to Panin, a similar conference emerged, and it may be surmised that Bestuzhev stood behind this move too, using it as a device to prevent Panin's dominance.

Another example fitting this pattern was M. L. Vorontsov's proposal for a state council during Peter III's reign. As grand-chancellor Vorontsov ostensibly bore responsibility for policy. Yet he had almost no say in its formulation. Peter abolished the Conference of Empress Elizabeth and ruled with the advice of a small circle of friends, including his uncle Prince George of Holstein, Prince Peter August Fredrick of Holstein-Beck, Count Münnich, and even the Prussian ambassador Baron Goltz—but not the emperor's own grand-chancellor. Vorontsov twice attempted to alter this situation by proposing reorganizations of the central government. Both plans called for the creation of a central coordinating body or council in which the chancellor would play a leading role. The nature of the proposals left little doubt that they were designed to regain Vorontsov the voice in policy formulation he had lost after Elizabeth's death.[110]

Nikita Panin's Imperial Council project exhibited a similar motivation. Although he was regularly consulted in the weeks following the coup d'etat, there was no guarantee that he and his party would be retained. He had alienated many of the young men in Catherine's entourage by his expressed desire to elevate Paul. The upstarts of the Orlov group resented Panin's influence and were eager to exclude his party from preferment. Moreover, Bestuzhev was returning from exile and would surely use his considerable skill in court intrigue to isolate and dispose of anyone bold enough to challenge his leadership. Under the circumstances, the best way for Panin to secure the position of the established dignitaries of his party was to win Catherine's approval of a permanent state council that would legitimize their authority and protect them from subversion by imperial favorites.

This motivation becomes clearer if one looks at Panin's response to council proposals not of his own making. First there was the

---

[109]See discussion in Kaplan, *Russia and the Outbreak*, pp. 40–41; also my article "Nikita Panin's Imperial Council," pp. 458–59.

[110]*AKV*, 25: 251–54; *LOII, f.* 36, *op.* 1, *d.* 1073, 251–53, 376–79.

October Conference of 1763, established to discuss the Polish succession crisis and, moreover, established just as Panin was winning control over policy. Although it lasted only a short time, Panin decried it as a threat and complained to Solms of the obstacles being thrown in his path. Once he defeated this last bid from Bestuzhev's party and won unchallenged control, he seemed to lose interest in his original council idea. If, as historians contend, Panin wished to force a legally established permanent council on Catherine, this was the time to do it. She had committed herself to his policies and disposed of the two ministers, Bestuzhev and Vorontsov, who could have replaced him. But as senior minister enjoying the full backing of autocratic authority, he had little need of a council to bolster his position. Such an institution would only allow his enemies back into the corridors of power.

A good indication of Panin's attitude toward a council that would dilute his control emerged at a later time in connection with the outbreak of war against Turkey in 1768. For more than five years he and Catherine had managed Russian foreign affairs unaided by any special commissions, and Panin had maintained Catherine's trust throughout this period. Where attempts were made to discredit him, the empress put an immediate halt to the intrigues.[111] The outbreak of the Turkish war, however, raised doubts about the wisdom of his policies. He had based his pro-Prussian system, which left Russia poorly protected in the south, on the assumption that war could be avoided in that area. Now Catherine was ready to listen to his critics. Upon receiving news of the diplomatic breach with Turkey, she decided to establish a new conference and sent the following note to Panin: "I request you to tell me in conscience whom you think best to place in the council of which we spoke. Write [a list] now at least as a first draft."[112] So again Panin had the opportunity to propose a council. But he was not pleased with the prospect. It could have but one effect: to remove responsibility from his hands and share it out among other persons, including his enemies. Not surprisingly, he attempted to block or at least delay the institution of a regular council. In his answer to Catherine he wrote:

[111]Catherine to N. I. Panin, 23 November 1763, *Chteniia,* vol. 2, pt. 2, p. 3; Solov'ev, *Istoriia Rossii,* 13: 512; Catherine to A. M. Golitsyn, rec'd. 9 August 1765, *AKV,* 28: 34.
[112]*SIRIO,* 10: 302.

I am obliged to tell Your Majesty straightforwardly that it is altogether impossible suddenly in the space of a day to establish a permanent council or conference for conducting and dispatching affairs, and, in truth, this is not necessary during the first year and can even cause difficulties considering the lack of time, for on such a basis many days can pass in [arranging] mere procedural dispositions regarding questions of how business is to be conducted and dispatched.[113]

Instead, Panin asked that a mere ad hoc committee be set up, without special provisions or procedures, as had been done under past monarchs when faced with extraordinary events. An informal body would not require a separate chancellery office or functional division of authority among the members, thus leaving leadership to the Foreign Affairs Collegium, which Panin headed and had staffed exclusively with his own clients.

This explanation of the partisan motivation for council proposals is not meant to detract from the positive contributions of political reformers like Panin but rather to emphasize another often neglected aspect of the question, namely, how the informal organizations of personal patronage groups and the nature of elite competition placed enormous obstacles in the way of reform. If implemented, the type of council Panin proposed in 1762 would have moved Russia in the direction of constitutional government and legal relations. It promised to introduce if not a separation of powers at least a potential for development toward it by dividing responsibilities between a central policy body for drafting legislation and a senate primarily concerned with handling judicial matters. Both bodies would operate through well-defined channels and procedures. Moreover, the council membership would in some degree depend on senate review, which afforded a measure of stability and permanence. This set-up would have served to uphold the nobility's rights of life, property, and honor by protecting them from the arbitrary caprice of autocrat and favorite. These principles were important in contributing to the long-term development of legal consciousness and constitutionalism in Russia, and more will be said about them later in this study, as Panin toward the end of his life returned to his

[113]Solov'ev, *Istoriia Rossii*, 14: 281.

critique of arbitrary power and developed a fullscale constitutional program. But it is important to note in any discussion of this matter that commitment to reform of a legal nature was always secondary to the immediate power interests of the competing political factions.

The chief difficulty for constitutional reform was the structure of political organization, the personal and familial clientele networks that formed the basis for political action. Even the Panin group, while urging the empress to move Russia toward a *Rechtstaat,* was itself operating out of this most tenacious and traditional of Russian political formations. Nor could it be otherwise. In the absence of legal system the ability of statesmen and administrators to act, even the reformers' ability to reform, depended on the maintenance of the traditional clientele networks through which action could be effected. It was perfectly natural for party leaders to wish to change this system when they were out of power and subject to the action of a competing clientele. But once having obtained power themselves, their only hope of holding it and carrying through their policies lay in monopolizing as many offices as possible for their clients and pushing aside all competing groups—in other words, by giving maximum reinforcement to the traditional patronage system.

6

The Panin Party in Power

This chapter takes up two themes. First, the process by which the Panin party reached its preeminent position must be traced in greater detail than heretofore. The Panins did not defeat their rivals solely because of a fortuitous turn in foreign policy. They provided guidance and support for Catherine on a whole range of critical issues from secularization of church property to commercial policy and administrative reform. Since the established interpretation of this period posits a two-way struggle between the empress and her leading party,[1] it is worth emphasizing the large degree of cooperation that characterized their work in the 1760s. Catherine's agreement with the Panin group on domestic policy was as important as the Polish succession crisis in her decision to favor the Panins over the Bestuzhev-Orlov group.

The second theme will consider Catherine's response to her growing dependence on the Panin party. As the empress increasingly came to rely upon the Panins' direction, she took measures to prevent this single party from dominating all the channels of power and thus inhibiting her own prerogatives. She strove to insure that Nikita Panin would be her minister and not her master. Therefore, without displacing Panin's leadership, she built up checks against his party's power. Her methods provide an instructive example of the controls an autocrat may employ in a political system based on clientele networks. This theme, which finds its clearest expression in the senate reforms of 1763–64, demonstrates that effective autocratic rule, as understood and exercised by Catherine, did not involve an assault on the chief court party mediating her will. Rather it implied the ability to maintain the loyalty and cohesion of her leading court party while simultaneously insuring the existence of competing groups that could act as a check on the Panin's monopoly of power.

[1] For a review of the historiography see my article "Catherine II's Instruction to the Commission on Laws."

The approach suggested here will make it possible to evaluate the nature of the Panins' cooperation with the empress as well as her methods of dealing with clientele groups. In addition, developments in this period will bring the Panin party's ideas on government and society into sharper focus and form the background for a more systematic treatment of their views to be presented in subsequent chapters.

1. Secularization and Administrative Reform

One of the first issues on which the new government had to take action was the secularization of church property. Peter III's precipitous order to secularize all church lands was the immediate source of concern, but the matter had also troubled previous rulers. Ever since Peter I the government had toyed with the idea of taking over the administration of church lands, in part because of the revenue they yielded, in part because of disturbances among ecclesiastical peasants. Complaints and rebellions by the peasants reached alarming proportions during the last years of Elizabeth's reign, and the government finally decided that the church administration could no longer cope with the situation. By this time pressures for change were also coming from landlords on estates adjoining the church lands, as they feared the disturbances might spill over onto their own domains.[2]

Although resolved to intervene in this matter, Elizabeth's government was absorbed in a war. Definite action had to await Peter III's accession. Wasting no time, the new emperor ordered the immediate transfer of all church peasants to state jurisdiction with a simple one-ruble quit-rent obligation. This hasty solution not only failed to answer the complex problems of support for church responsibilities (some, like caring for disabled veterans imposed by the state itself), but also spurred rumors that the emperor was about to extend the same advantage to proprietary serfs.[3] The latter circumstance helps explain why Peter III's name became a popular rallying symbol among peasant insurgents in subsequent years.

After taking the throne, Catherine faced an unpalatable choice. Confirmation of Peter III's secularization decree would alienate

---

[2]V.I. Semevskii, *Krest'iane v tsarstvovanie imperatritsy Ekateriny II* (St. Petersburg, 1901), 2: 220–37; P.K. Alefirenko, *Krest'ianskoe dvizhenie i krest'ianskii vopros v Rossii v 30–50-kh godakh XVIII veka* (Moscow, 1958), pp. 187–214.

[3]Semevskii, *Krest'iane*, 2: 238–39.

leading churchmen whose support she needed to legitimize her seizure of power. Yet to rescind the decree would invite renewed and embittered resistance from the church peasants, whose discontent now more than ever threatened to kindle disturbances on surrounding lands and thus undermine Catherine's support with the landed nobility. Faced with these difficult alternatives, the empress tried to finesse the issue. On the advice apparently of A. P. Bestuzhev-Riumin, she repealed Peter's decree on August 12, 1762, and returned the peasants to their hated ecclesiastical lords. Simultaneously Catherine stressed that the action was only temporary, "until a future improved institution" could be established for the peasants.[4]

As might be expected, the peasants placed little faith in such promises and responded with stubborn, passive resistance. Their refusal to perform work services for the ecclesiastical authorities or to pay their customary dues occasioned repeated intervention by the secular powers and further exacerbated tensions.

Although Catherine was following Bestuzhev's advice in the early weeks, it was unlikely that she intended to leave the peasants under church jurisdiction indefinitely. Her pious predecessor Elizabeth had already decided against the eccelsiastical authorities. A student of the encyclopedists like Catherine could scarcely do less, and the renewed disturbances on church estates must have stiffened her resolve to carry through reforms in this area. If the Panins needed a wedge to act against Bestuzhev, this situation offered them an excellent prospect. They fully supported reintroducing secularization, and they evidently prevailed upon the empress to choose one of their clients, Prince Ia. P. Shakhovskoi, as her chief adviser on the problem. A former ober-procurator of the Holy Synod, Shakhovskoi was thoroughly familiar with the church administration and had long favored secularization.[5] Together with Nikita Panin he worked out the details of a new, full-scale secularization, which Catherine adopted and carried out in a series of measures beginning in 1763 and completed by the decree of February 26, 1764.[6]

[4]Bestuzhev submitted a recommendation for repeal shortly before the decision was taken. Semevskii, *Krest'iane*, 2: 238; *PSZ*, 16: no. 11643.

[5]He had fought for it under Elizabeth as one of several means to ease a government financial crisis. S.M. Troitskii, *Finansovaia politika russkogo absoliutizma v XVIII veke* (Moscow, 1966), pp. 79–81.

[6]Shakhovskoi, *Zapiski*, 1: xix, 2: 204–206; Semevskii, *Krest'iane*, 2: 239–55, especially 254; *PSZ*, 16: no. 12060.

It is important to observe how this issue got caught up in the party dispute at court. Bestuzhev, committed to a pro-church stand in 1762, maintained his position throughout the following year. Despite Catherine's decision to secularize, he took up the defense of Rostov archbishop Arsenii Matseevich, the most vehement critic of the policy.[7] Since it is difficult to believe that Bestuzhev's opposition arose as a matter of principle, the explanation of his behavior may well lie in his struggle against the Panin party. At precisely this time (summer 1763), Bestuzhev was exerting all his energy to arrange Catherine's marriage to Grigorii Orlov, a move which, if successful, would have delivered the *coup de grace* to the Panin party.[8] As the marriage plan could scarcely succeed without the cooperation of church leaders, Bestuzhev had no choice but to stand with them in the dispute over church lands. By the same token, the Panin party had every reason to encourage secularization. By hindering the marriage plan it would curtail the Bestuzhev-Orlov bid for influence and further enforce Catherine's dependence on the Panin group.

But the issue should not be viewed solely in terms of political infighting. The reasons for secularization were in themselves compelling and urgent. The government had to deal with the mounting threat of peasant rebellions. It also desperately needed the revenue from church lands to expand the provincial administration.[9] To the Enlightenment mind, moreover, independent ecclesiastical domains represented a medieval relic, inappropriate to a well-regulated state. The Panins probably had little difficulty convincing Catherine of these points. Both in a generational and intellectual sense they stood closer to Catherine than did either Bestuzhev or the Orlovs. She needed and valued the Panins' advice, because of all the factions at court they could best appreciate her aspirations for reform. Accordingly, she not only carried through secularization in the form recommended by Shakhovskoi and Nikita Panin, but also placed another Panin client, Boris Kurakin, at the head of the Economic Collegium, the institution responsible for administering the former church peasants.[10] And after Kurakin's untimely death in 1764,

---

[7]Semevskii, *Krest'iane*, 2: 238; Bil'basov, *Istoriia Ekateriny II*, 2; 266–68.

[8]Chapter 5, section 3 above.

[9]Chechulin, *Ocherki po finansov* (St. Petersburg, 1906), p. 71, and *IPS*, 2: 387, as cited in Morrison, "Catherine II's Legislative Commission," p. 472. Firsov, *Petr III i Ekaterina II*, pp. 76–78.

[10]*PSZ*, 16: no. 11814; Amburger, *Behördenorganisation*, p. 110. The Panins were Kura-

Peter Panin took over his job temporarily and worked to rationalize and streamline the administration in this sector of government.[11]

This tendency to bring areas of administrative autonomy within direct state control characterized other recommendations of the Panin party during this period. One example was the abolition of the Ukrainian Hetmanate, a move worked out by G.N. Teplov and Nikita Panin. There seemed to be some fear that the present Hetman, Kirill Razumovskii, was cutting out an independent territorial base and wished to make the Hetmanate hereditary in his family.[12] Before such ambitions could become dangerous, Catherine and Panin acted to draw the Ukraine into the regular sphere of Russian administration.[13] In later years this policy continued with moves to bring the Baltic Provinces, Zaporozhie, the Ukraine to an even further degree, and other areas in line with the rest of the empire's administrative system.

Here the Panins supported the established bureaucratic tradition in ordering the relations of local government. Despite proposals made at this time for infusing a greater class element into provincial administration,[14] the Panin brothers showed no inclination to place increased responsibility for local affairs in the hands of elected officials. In designing an administrative structure for the newly-opened southern province of New Russia, the two brothers followed a highly centralized model. The administration was to consist of two sections, a military department responsible to the War Collegium, and a civil department subordinate to the senate, although this second section, too, took on a military aspect. Got'e has suggested that this structure arose from the high number of military personnel residing in the province and its exposed position on the Turkish fron-

kin's uncles and guardians of his children and estates after his death a short time later. *GBL,f.* Pan. XV, 38–46, 49, and Pan. XV, no. 3, 351–73.

[11]Reform measures described in *SIRIO*, 28:106–10; presidency of the collegium then went to yet another Panin relative, S. V. Gagarin; see Amburger, *Behördenorganisation*, p. 110.

[12]Shirley to Weymouth, 20 July 1768, *SIRIO*, 12:339–40.

[13]Solov'ev, *Istoriia Rossii*, 13:340–41; documents in *SIRIO*, 7: 359–60, 375–91. For Panin's role, Catherine to N. I. Panin, in *Chteniia*, vol. 2, pt. 2, pp. 68–70, and Catherine to Olsuf'ev, 17 February 1764, *Russkii Arkhiv* (1863), pp. 184–85.

[14]See project by Ia. P. Shakhovskoi, discussed in Got'e, *Istoriia oblastnogo upravleniia*, 2:165–70, and A. P. Bestuzhev-Riumin's proposals submitted to the Commission on Noble Freedom, in A. N. Kulomzin, ed., "Pervyi pristup v tsarstvovanie Ekateriny II k sostavleniiu Vysochaishei Gramoty dvorianstvu rossiiskomu," in N. Kalachov, *Materialy dlia istorii russkogo dvorianstva*, vol. 2 (St. Petersburg, 1885), pp. 31–32.

tier. It is interesting, however, that the administration of Slobodsko-Ukraina, worked out soon after by Peter Panin, A. V. Olsuf'ev, and Ia. P. Shakhovskoi, likewise witnessed no attempt to introduce local elective office. Only as an afterthought and a result of the especially complex local property arrangements did they allow a small measure of participation by previously existing elective Cossack commissars.[15] These cases might still be considered exceptional, were it not known from other evidence, in particular Nikita Panin's recommendations to the Commission on Noble Freedom, that he preferred bureaucratic organization over the concept of elective participation at the local level.[16] For Catherine's part, she supported the bureaucratic approach right through the 1760s. Only after the Legislative Commission did she appear to develop second thoughts, and in 1772 she began the shift toward election of local officials, which bulked large in her provincial reform of 1775.[17]

2. Commercial Policy

In the reform of commercial policy the Panin party also exerted a predominant influence. This area demanded immediate attention; when Catherine took over in 1762 the economy was on the brink of collapse. Although the Shuvalov regime of Elizabeth's time had made significant advances in the abolition of internal tariffs and establishment of credit facilities, it had likewise initiated a number of ill-conceived experiments in taxation and monetary policy. Another factor contributing to the decline was Peter Shuvalov's penchant for distributing state enterprises and monopoly rights to his clients, who through mismanagement and exploitation for immediate gain helped to throw the economy into a tailspin. Finally, the financial burden imposed by the long war with Prussia proved to be more than the country could bear.[18] At the time of Catherine's accession, the treasury was depleted and payment to the army many months in

[15]Got'e, *Istoriia oblastnogo upravleniia*, 2: 251–53.

[16]Kulomzin, "Pervyi pristup," especially p. 36; this is also the burden of the final majority report of the Panin-led Commission on Noble Freedom, included in this source.

[17]Got'e, *Istoriia oblastnogo upravleniia*, 2: 254–59.

[18]Firsov argues that the war came to an end not only due to Peter III's admiration for Frederick II: financial collapse made any other choice impossible, as evidenced by Catherine's reaffirmation of Peter's peace. *Petr III i Ekaterina II*, pp. 72–73. Russia was not an exception in this regard. The war disrupted the financial administration of all participating countries. Troitskii, *Finansovaia politika*, pp. 30–33.

arrears, foreign credit had evaporated, and state debt was piling up at an alarming rate.[19]

Nikita Panin took a special interest in the problem. He told the French ministers at St. Petersburg that he planned to devote his time principally to questions of commerce. In discussions with Breteuil, he continually returned to the subject, emphasizing the need for a long period of peace to give Russia time to establish its economy and administration on a firm footing.[20] About the same time, he began outlining the basic elements of his Northern Accord foreign policy, a program he believed would produce a stable balance in Europe and the maximum commercial advantage to Russia. As he saw it, the country needed a conservative policy; it was already too large and too thinly populated to derive any benefit from further territorial acquisition. All efforts now had to be placed on consolidating previous gains and developing the untapped resources of the nation. This meant concentrating on commerce and manufacture.[21]

Catherine shared this view, and her agreement with Panin on this matter undoubtedly contributed to the decision in favor of his foreign policy program. In addition, she moved quickly to establish a special commission on commerce that would supervise Russia's economic growth. Panin was among the first persons she called upon for advice. In a note from 1763 she told him: "It is my intention to establish a commission for looking into commerce, with the additional job of examining all state revenues and, in a word, everything that concerns finances. I want you to give me your opinion, what you think would serve as an instruction for my commission."[22] By some oversight historians have failed to identify Panin's response to this request. Without realizing it, however, they have had his reply

[19]So much so that Nikita Panin ordered a strict limitation on expenditures for the coronation, dispensing with certain parades, fireworks, and the distribution of vodka. See his note to Nepliuev, 16 September 1762, in *Russkii Arkhiv* (1884), no. 1, 253–54.

[20]Breteuil to Choiseul, 1 September, 9 and 28 October, and 29 November 1762, *SIRIO*, 140: 66–67, 87–88, 104, and 116.

[21]Bérenger to Choiseul, 31 July, 6 August, 9 October, 29 November, and 20 December 1762, *SIRIO*, 140: 33–35, 87, 114, 136. Solms to Frederick II, 29 December 1762, *SIRIO*, 22: 16–17. He expressed this idea even more firmly in later reports. G. Esipov, "Fridrikh II i graf Panin," in *Beseda*, no. 1 (1871), p. 276. Poroshin, *Zapiski*, 18 September 1765. These reports also confirm the view of K. Rahbek Schmidt that Panin and not Baron Korf first designed the Northern System. "Wie ist Panins Plan zu einem Nordischen System entstanden?" *Zeitschrift für Slawistik* (1957), vol. 2, no. 3, 406–22.

[22]Note in *Chteniia*, vol. 2, pt. 2, 140.

available for some time. N. N. Firsov published the contents of an
"anonymous memoir" from this period, which corresponded in
every detail to the assignment given to Panin. The document came
from a state official specifically empowered to advise on the creation
of a commerce commission. It reproduced Panin's prose style and
mode of discourse as well as several specific policy recommendations
and points of view familiar from his other writings. Moreover, the
memoir in question formed the basis of a later, final commission
instruction penned by G. N. Teplov.[23] Panin and Teplov worked
very closely during this period, and their discussions most frequently
concerned commercial affairs.[24] There can be little doubt, therefore,
that the memoir found by Firsov was Panin's reply to the empress'
request. He either wrote it himself and later turned it over to Teplov
for drafting the final instruction, or likely as not, he collaborated with
Tepolv on the original memoir. In any case, the piece reflected the
views of Nikita Panin and his closest aides.

In a characterization reminiscent of his critique of the political
administration, Panin began the memoir by depicting the economy.
"What did Your Majesty find upon ascending the throne?" he
asked.

> Revenue sources were exhausted and in the greatest disorder;
> the treasury was plundered and stripped of a large part of its
> most reliable income; various revenue sources without any
> reason were handed over to private persons; administration was
> weak; *there was no direct commerce with foreign nations and no pro-
> vision for carrying wares in Russian bottoms;* domestic trade every-
> where [labored] under restraints; manufactures instead of
> being improved languished in their former backwardness;
> currency of a single denomination varied in worth. The Com-
> merce Collegium and Magistracy were staffed by ignoramuses;
> and finally there was a nobility burdened by useless luxury, and
> a people suffering from oppression and poverty for lack of trades
> or the ability to perform crafts.[25]

[23]Firsov, *Pravitel'stvo i obshchestvo v ikh otnosheniiakh k vneshnei torgovle Rossii v tsarstvoranie imperatritsy Ekateriny II* (Kazan', 1902), pp. 52–56.

[24]See the many instances recorded in Poroshin, *Zapiski*, 15 April, 2 and 6 September, 21 October, and 21 December 1765. Panin also served as liaison between commerce commission and Catherine. *SIRIO*, 42: 303, 368–69.

[25]Firsov, *Pravitel'stvo i obshchestvo*, pp. 4–5. Italics in original.

This "sorry state of affairs," according to the author, arose from a number of causes, chief among which were "the neglect of certain rulers, the cupidity and avarice of ministers, and an insufficient knowledge of our true revenues." In consequence, the government had continually issued laws and orders that contradicted one another and flew in the face of common sense; they aimed at serving some temporary private interest, not at establishing a consistent policy.[26] Panin then praised the empress' intention to correct this miserable situation and offered a series of "points" which would serve as a guide to the commission she planned to establish. Since these points corresponded in most respects to those in Teplov's subsequent instruction, the two documents may be evaluated together.

The policies advised by Panin and Teplov smacked strongly of the German cameralist stances then in vogue.[27] The authors placed special emphasis on Russia's wealth in raw materials and agricultural products. The first were much in demand abroad and could provide lucrative exports. The second, if properly encouraged and developed, would serve to increase the empire's sparse population. One of the best ways to encourage agricultural production, Panin noted, was to allow farmers to gain an honorable living as free as possible from external restraints.[28] Both writers strongly supported a free internal market and urged abolition of all remaining restraints on domestic commerce, such as tolls, customs, and inspections. They also spoke out against monopolies and restrictions on exports, although they favored turning certain foreign options, especially the eastern trade, over to private companies composed of artisans, merchants, nobles, and even foreigners.[29] These ideas were not entirely new. The Vorontsov brothers and Dmitrii Volkov had made such proposals toward the end of Elizabeth's reign in an unsuccessful effort to roll back the mercantilist policies of the previous half century.[30] The Panin-Teplov memoirs were, however, the first guidelines of this nature to form the basic instruction of an official

[26]Firsov, *Pravitel'stvo i obshchestvo*, p. 5.

[27]Although Firsov identifies them somewhat inaccurately as physiocratism, *Pravitel'stvo i obshchestvo*, p. 53.

[28]From "anonymous" project. Firsov, *Pravitel'stvo i obshchestvo*, p. 53.

[29]From Teplov project. Firsov, *Pravitel'stvo i obshchestvo*, p. 57; Teplov project also reviewed by Shpilevskii in *Beseda* (1872), no. 1, 154–68, who, however, erroneously ascribes it to Lomonosov. See Firsov's note, *idem*, p. 56.

[30]Troitskii, *Finansovaia politika*, pp. 86–97.

government commerce commission, and in this sense their "liberal" program marked an altogether new departure.

Nevertheless, the authors stopped far short of advocating unrestricted trade or salutary neglect. They left considerable latitude to state intervention and supervision. One might expect this from men who were above all government servitors. But there was more to it. Russian conditions offered compelling reasons for state tutelage. Panin's lugubrious depiction of the economy indicated his awareness of the enormous disadvantages Russia had to overcome in order to compete favorably with more developed nations. Only careful government supervision, protection, and positive contributions could compensate for these deficiencies. Panin particularly advised the construction of an adequate infrastructure of roads and waterways to facilitate domestic exchange and access to port cities.[31] Teplov focused on the poor condition of foreign trade, noting especially the lack of a merchant fleet and the inadequacy of financial instruments such as banks and stable currency. "Up to this time," he wrote, "Russian merchants have been nothing but hirelings, or better, carters for foreign merchants."[32] They could not transcend this position without government subsidies and guidance.

The two writers placed their most important qualifications of the free trade program in the area of foreign commerce. Panin insisted specifically on strong government backing of Russian merchants abroad and strict reciprocity in dealings with other nations.[33] Both men likewise recommended high tariffs and even outright exclusion of some imports when the government saw a need to protect domestic industry or restrict consumption of luxury items.[34] In essence, Panin and Teplov argued for an eclectic policy. They wanted to introduce

[31]Firsov, Pravitel'stvo i obshchestvo, p. 53.

[32]Firsov, Pravitel'stvo i obshchestvo, p. 57.

[33]On reciprocity, Firsov, Pravitel'stvo i obshchestvo, p. 55; in practice Panin went even further, demanding favored treatment (at least from Russia's ally Prussia) with the argument that Russian merchants deserved special consideration because of their previous undeveloped position in foreign trade. See his note to Solms, 24 July 1766, SIRIO, 67: 34–36; further comments on this question in his rescript to Golitsyn in Vienna, 30 June 1766, SIRIO, 67: 8–9. Efforts to improve Russia's position also included the establishment of a special commerce school, another enterprise in which Panin and Teplov were closely involved. SIRIO, 13: 279.

[34]Firsov, Pravitel'stvo i obshchestvo, pp. 57–58; Panin's comment to Bérenger repeats this view, Bérenger to Choiseul, 6 August 1762, SIRIO, 140: 34–35. Admittedly fragmentary evidence from the state council during the 1770s, however, shows Panin advising a lower tariff for the eastern trade and attempting to hold the line on raising barriers to the west due to established reciprocal agreements. AGS, 1: 629–30, 673–74.

a broad measure of free trade while allowing for government subsidies and protection in special cases. They also wished to maintain
close bureaucratic supervision of all aspects of the economy.

In several respects this program paralleled demands then being
made by the merchantry. Soviet experts have noted this fact and
argued that the similarity arose quite naturally from the exceptional
economic position of the wealthy court nobles. Their production was
tied much more closely to the market than was the predominantly
natural economy of less well-to-do nobles. As a result, the wealthy
aristocrats formed an alliance with the bourgeoisie.[35] This interpretation, while quite accurately recognizing the gulf between the
interests of the court nobility and the rank and file, misreads the
main emphasis of the project writers. To be sure, neither the Panin
proposals nor the quite different policies pursued by Shuvalov gave
much consideration to the desires of the rank-and-file nobility. They
chiefly sought to increase the productivity and wealth of the country,
and it was scarcely surprising therefore that they concentrated on
those elements that produced for the market. Certainly this approach
coincided with the interests of the wealthy merchants. The project
writers even encouraged joint ventures between nobles and merchants. But the main concern of these state officials was not an alliance with the merchantry; rather they wanted to stimulate a spirit of
enterprise on the part of all those who could take advantage of it.
This would enhance the power of the state, in which their primary
identity and allegiance lay. Furthermore, they wanted to make the
nobility useful to themselves and to the state by directing them toward greater enterprise; that is, creating a "noblesse commerçante,"
to borrow the title of a tract that especially interested some members
of the Panin group.[36] Panin once chided Count A.S. Stroganov, for
example, by comparing his family with the wealthy Ural industrial-
ists, the Demidovs. The Stroganovs would have been much better
off, Panin admonished, had they imitated the Demidovs instead of
dissipating their fortune in chasing after ranks and court honors.[37]
The idea was that the nobility, which had access to the knowledge,

[35]Troitskii, *Finansovaia politika*, pp. 95–97; Schmidt, "La politique interieure du Tsarisme," pp. 95–110.

[36]Nikita Panin's secretary, D. I. Fonvizin, translated the German jurist Justi's work of
this title into Russian during the mid-sixties. *FSS*, 2: 117–186; for discussion see Makogonenko, *Fonvizin*, pp. 39–47, where the author unconvincingly credits this act as a mani-
festation of opposition toward Catherine.

[37]Poroshin, *Zapiski*, 11 November 1764.

resources, and leisure required for enterprise, had an obligation to apply themselves to this task. Shuvalov seemed to think he could best encourage such enterprise by turning over large factories and monopoly rights to particular individuals. Panin preferred to create the necessary framework of transportation, credit facilities, open markets, and stable currency that would encourage the nobility to develop commercial interests voluntarily.

Despite the opposition of some members of the commerce commission, the empress gave the Panin-Teplov program her full support, another example of the Panin party's influence in this period. She repeated the program's fundamental principles a couple of years later in her *Instruction* to the Legislative Commission and followed this modified free trade policy through most of her reign. While the question of whether this policy had appealed to her earlier or had won her approval as a result of the Panin party's arguments must remain speculative, once again the proposals of Panin and his collaborators had proved determining. In this field, too, Catherine chose to honor a Panin client, Grigorii Teplov, with the highest trust and turn over to him the management of her special commission on commerce.[38]

3. Serf Reform

The treatment of peasant serfs affords still another illustration of the community of views between Catherine and the Panins. In this area, however, the Panins were somewhat less successful in getting their policies implemented. In 1763 Peter Panin undertook an investigation of peasant flights in the western borderlands, where the problem was reaching crisis proportions. His report identified the chief causes for the mass desertions into Poland as brutal recruitment procedures, the sale of peasants apart from their families, and especially, the unrestricted power of landlords over their serfs. These observations led him to advise strict regulation of serf-landlord relations, including tough laws against abusive serfowners, prohibition on sale of recruits and individual peasants apart from their families, a maximum of two rubles quit-rent and a limitation of labor dues.[39] Although less evidence is available on Nikita Panin's views, he too

[38]Firsov, *Pravitel'stvo i obshchestvo*, pp. 58–85.

[39]Solov'ev, *Istoriia Rossii*, 13: 228–30; V.I. Semevskii, *Krest'ianskii vopros v Rossii v XVIII i pervoi polovine XIX veka*, 2 vols. (St. Petersburg, 1888), 1: 22–23.

clearly sympathized with the plight of peasant runaways. One of his most unpleasant duties as envoy to Sweden was to arrange for the return of Russian fugitives, and he later admitted to friends that he had tried so far as possible to circumvent his instructions in that regard.[40] He expressed these same sentiments at another time in a letter to the Ukrainian Governor-General P.A. Rumiantsev. He told him not to return Polish refugees, as "the law of humanity, superior to all others, gave people the right to seek a tranquil existence in a place of their choosing," and it was not for others to deprive them of this advantage or to disturb "their innocent settlement by chasing them from place to place."[41]

The Panins were not, of course, opponents of the serf system as such, nor could they have been in an age when few Russians bothered to question even the abuses of the system. They were mainly concerned about the brutalities and excesses of serfdom and feared that, if permitted to go unchecked, these abuses would undermine the position of the nobility and strength of the regime. Like Catherine, they seemed to prefer moral suasion and force of example as means to improve the situation. Peter Panin, for instance, volunteered strenuous personal efforts to convince one recalcitrant landlord to treat his peasants more humanely.[42] When Nikita Panin had the opportunity of disposing of a relative's estate after the owner died intestate, he liberated many of the bonded servants and provided well for the others.[43]

Still there was an important difference between Catherine and the Panins concerning their willingness to apply legal remedies. Although the empress raised the question of limiting serfdom in her *Instruction* and even hinted at eventual liberation, she quickly withdrew these suggestions at the first sign of resistance. The Panins, however, continued to favor government regulation, believing that abusive landlords provoked peasant resistance and menaced the good

[40]He reasoned that "man was given the whole surface of the earth to live on, and each person should naturally be able to choose where it was best for him to live." Poroshin, *Zapiski*, 21 December 1764; Pigarev, *Tvorchestvo Fonvizina*, p. 138.

[41]*GPB, f.* 563, *op.* 1, 27–28.

[42]Without much success, it seems, as the landlord, N.M. Leont'ev, was murdered by his peasants a few years later, in 1769. Semevskii, "Volneniia krepostnykh krest'ian pri Ekaterine II 1762–1789," *Russkaia Starina* (1877), nos. 1–4, 199; as Leont'ev was a relative of the Panins, a question remains as to whether this action was indicative of their attitudes.

[43]S. S. Apraksin to A. B. Kurakin, 27 January 1772, *Arkhiv Kurakina*, 6: 326.

order of the state. In their view, landlords who tormented their peasants forfeited their right to be treated as nobles. This dignity implied a code of honor, which if breached, deprived the noble of special consideration. Peter Panin's recommendations for government regulation were somewhat vitiated, it is true, by his accompanying admonition that they be kept secret, that is communicated only to the responsible local officials and not announced in a public ukase—a precaution dictated by the fear of raising peasant hopes unreasonably. He nevertheless again spoke up a few years later at the Legislative Commission for a moderate limitation of the landlord's power, despite the majority of noble deputies' strongly expressed opposition to such proposals.[44] This stand demonstrated the lengths to which the Panins were prepared to go to achieve a stable, well-regulated state order.

These instances of agreement between the empress and the Panin party indicate both the general tenor of reform pursued by the new regime and the large measure of Panin participation in defining its direction. The Panins were cooperating with Catherine on a whole range of policy decisions, domestic as well as foreign, and she clearly valued their advice and support. They shared with her the desire to stimulate the productive capacity of the economy and to expand and rationalize government processes, among other things, by bringing areas of administrative autonomy within direct state control. Commercial policy likewise followed lines recommended by the Panins, including chiefly the lifting of trade barriers and encouragement of private initiative. Their effort to temper the abuses of serfdom clearly proved less successful—but not because Catherine disagreed with them. Judging from her *Instruction*, she fully endorsed such views in principle, and in the early years of her reign, no doubt with the Panins' support, she resisted pressures from landlords to remove the last remaining legal protections for serfs.[45]

The difficulty Catherine faced was that while the enlightened officials of the capital might applaud government intervention in serf-landlord relations, the vast majority of provincial nobles shuddered at such interference. Not until the Legislative Commission of 1767 was she to discover the full depth of the ordinary nobleman's

[44]*RBS*, 13: 220–21.

[45]Beliavskii, *Krest'ianskii vopros v Rossii nakanune vosstaniia E.I. Pugacheva* (Moscow, 1965), pp. 92–93.

antagonism to serf reform. Yet even before that time she seemed to perceive the gulf separating the westernized metropolitan officials from the rank-and-file nobility. She knew that she badly needed experienced officials like the Panins. She knew too, however, that their views did not always reflect the outlook of the majority of the nobility. This understanding, which showed itself most clearly in the case of the Commission on Noble Freedom, reminded Catherine that she had to maintain a check on her leading ministers.

4. Commission on Noble Freedom

Catherine convened the Commission on Noble Freedom early in February 1763. This was another case of settling an affair initiated by Peter III, who had declared the nobility's freedom from obligatory state service nearly a year earlier. The matter had remained in limbo since Catherine's accession in June 1762, and she was evidently feeling some pressure to define the new government's position. Prior to forming the commission she wrote to Panin that "There is some murmuring among the nobility about the failure to confirm their freedom, and we shouldn't forget to begin some action [*pristup sdelat'*] on that matter."[46] In forming the commission Catherine, interestingly enough, drew its membership from the list proposed for the stillborn Imperial Council, a sign that she may have found it convenient to set up the noble freedom commission at this time to divert attention from the languishing council project.[47] In this single move, she was able to demonstrate her intention to act positively on the question of noble freedom while also engaging the energies of the proposed council membership in a forum that would be less likely to inhibit her own prerogatives.

The political motivation for calling the commission may, however, have undermined its work. Catherine's desire to win the cooperation of the Panin party, which dominated the commission, apparently conflicted with her ideas about a satisfactory solution to the problem of freedom for the nobility, a circumstance reflected in the ambiguous wording of her charge to the commission:

> Former Emperor Peter III gave freedom to the Russian nobility. But as the act restricted this freedom in certain respects

[46]*SIRIO*, 7: 233; also published in *Chteniia*, vol. 2, pt. 2, 74.
[47]Compare the membership lists in *SIRIO*, 7: 201, 232.

> even more greatly than the welfare of the country and Our
> service may now require, given both the altered position of the
> government and breeding of noble youth, We order you . . .
> in gathering at Our court to examine this act and take counsel
> among yourselves about perfecting its content, such that by
> special state legislation the Russian nobility might receive for
> its posterity a new pledge of Our royal favor. In order that a
> reasonable policy would serve as the basis of all this, in arrang-
> ing the rights of noble freedom one should institute articles
> which would for the most part encourage [the nobles'] ambition
> in a direction useful to Our service and Our beloved country.[48]

Catherine seemed to have in mind an extension of privileges and
liberties that would serve as an inducement for nobles to enter service
or otherwise contribute to the well-being of the state. This view of the
matter depended, however, on the assumption that increased freedom
and privilege would indeed produce this result, an assumption that,
as will be seen in due course, Catherine did not share.

The commissioners for reasons of their own took Catherine's words
at face value. Within five weeks they returned a report fully in accord with the assumption expressed in her order, and they prefaced it
with a detailed rationale defending that assumption. The report
began by admitting the need in earlier times for the enforced obligations of service and education introduced by Peter I. The low level of
culture and lack of ambition characteristic of the nobility in those
days unquestionably justified such measures. Peter had to meet the
challenge of foreign invasion, and he could only do so "by using
naked force to compel into service those who through lack of knowledge and schooling did not have an intrinsic ambition for it and had
not yet sensed that service gives birth to ambition and ambition
leads to service." Instead, "they evaded service and hid themselves
in their homes and villages, preferring their age-old tranquility to an
honored name."[49]

[48]*SIRIO*, 7: 232–33; protocol (*idem*, p. 233) repeats these points, reemphasizing the
desire to increase liberties of the estate. Contemporaries viewed the calling of the commission as a repeal of Peter III's law, according to Romanovich-Slavatinskii, who, however, disagrees and argues that Catherine truly wished to extend noble freedoms. *Dvorianstvo*, p. 197. As will be seen, neither view was quite accurate.

[49]Kulomzin, "Pervyi pristup," p. 39. The final report of the commission in a variant
corrected by Catherine may be found in *SIRIO*, 7: 238–66; all citations here are taken
from Kulomzin's later publication of the original report, which includes as well some
protocols and minority opinions of the commission.

But this situation no longer existed, the report went on. Peter I's great labors and wise legislative measures thoroughly regenerated morals and instilled the nobility with a desire to serve. Naturally, there were still a few nobles "living in poverty and isolation" who did not yet share in this great awakening. But their numbers were so small as to be unworthy of consideration, and "in time they will undoubtedly follow the example of those bred in the noble spirit and be encouraged by the rights Your Imperial Majesty will grant to the entire nobility." As for the rest, they showed no inclination to return to their former lethargy; indeed there were not sufficient places to accommodate all those seeking to enter service. "In a word," the commissioners concluded, "there is simply no comparison between the current nobility and that which used to hide from service for several years not only in the villages but even in the capital cities and called it their ruin."[50]

Accordingly, the commissioners advised that no restriction whatsoever be placed on noble freedom. Personal ambition and self-esteem alone would be sufficient inducement to service. They then gave this idea practical expression in a proposed statute of 21 articles, which included the following points:[51] restrictions on entry into the nobility through the Table of Ranks, equalization of rewards for civil and military service, distinction in honors between serving and nonserving nobles, the right to serve or not to serve, right to service abroad or permanent emigration, rights of nobles in temporary or permanent residence abroad, freedom from corporal punishment and confiscation of property, right to counsel in criminal cases, establishment of *fideicommissium* and right to adopt heirs.

Judging from the motivating sections of these articles and from Nikita Panin's separate clarifications, the commission sought to combine greater stability, exclusiveness, and corporate unity in their estate with increased incentives to participation in the civil bureaucracy. This direction may be seen in Panin's proposal for modifying the Table of Ranks. The Table now set the level at which a man could receive hereditary nobility at the 14th rank in the military and 8th rank in the civil bureaucracy. In Panin's view, Peter I had instituted these standards under urgent pressure to build a modern standing army. Now that the need for military talent was

[50]Kulomzin, "Pervyi pristup," pp. 39–40.
[51]Summarized here from Kulomzin, "Pervyi pristup," pp. 46–71; certain items will be discussed separately below.

less pressing, the government should rectify this imbalance and upgrade the entire system. Life nobility should be granted to those in either the civil or military hierarchies who attained the 8th or 9th rank, and hereditary nobility be reserved for those who reached the 7th rank.[52] Ostensibly, this measure aimed at improving the civil administration by equalizing rewards for civil and military service, and undoubtedly it would have modified the tendency, quite strong in Russia until Paul's time, for able young men to seek their careers in the military.[53]

But another effect of the measure would be to stem the tide of new entrants into the nobility and thereby stabilize the composition of the estate. This proposal revealed the extent to which Panin's idea of merit was tied to the idea of family, heredity, and a kind of caste exclusiveness. Although this notion probably owed much to Panin's observations of western nobility, it also compared in certain respects to the old Russian *boiar* concept of *mestnichestvo* (at least before its corruption in the seventeenth century); that is, the belief that the proved merit of a man's forebears entitled him to special consideration for the most responsible posts in government.[54]

Upward mobility being but one source of instability in the elite, the Commission on Noble Freedom offered correctives for the no less troublesome phenomenon of steady impoverishment of noble families through the custom of dividing estates equally among all heirs.[55]

[52]This proposal appears in Panin's separate personal commentary to the commission, which was incorporated into the final report in a slightly modified form. Kulomzin, "Prevyi pristup," p. 37, for Panin's commentary. It is interesting to observe the difference between Panin's view and that of the conservative thinker Prince M. M. Shcherbatov, who used a somewhat similar argument for change; i.e., that Peter I's laws were products of special circumstances that no longer applied. Shcherbatov's solution was, however, to end entry via the Table of Ranks altogether and allow ennoblement solely through a particular grant of the tsar. Panin wanted to retain the bureaucratic merit principle but within a more limited scope. For discussion of Shcherbatov's ideas, see I.I. Ditiatin, *Ekaterininskaia kommissiia 1767 g.*, (Rostov on Don, 1905), pp. 68–69.

[53]Romanovich-Slavatinskii, *Dvorianstvo*, p. 134.

[54]Veselovskii, *Issledovaniia po istorii klassa sluzhilykh zemlevladel'tsev*, especially pp. 472–79.

[55]Romanovich-Slavatinskii argues that the lack of desire for *majorat* in Russia was because Russian nobles were a serving, not a landowning estate, and therefore had very little attachment to the family estate. In support, he cites several examples of an anecdotal nature; one is Vasil'chikov's comment that "Russian nobles would sit in Paris clubs loudly declaiming on aristocracy and its rights, while at home they sold off their estates around Moscow and St. Petersburg with the memorabilia, archives and portraits, having no sense of their value. It is difficult to find an estate around Moscow and St. Petersburg that remained in the family of its founder—rarely do they last three generations." *Dvori-*

While the commissioners specifically rejected a Vorontsov proposal to establish principalities, baronies and counties,[56] they did advise introducing the right of *fideicommissium* as practiced in Austria: the right of primogeniture combined with sequestration or guardianship. The commission members argued that this measure would act as a beneficial restraint on profligacy and encourage a moderate style of life, "for the wealth of each person will be limited, and his credit will therefore also remain within bounds." But quite clearly such a statute would chiefly serve to solidify the position of the established court families and especially to protect them from the vagaries of political fortune that might at any time lead to their arrest, confiscation of property, and destitution for their dependents. Not surprisingly, the discussion of this statute most emphatically stressed the guarantees adhering to property. "The assembly considers that an estate confirmed in this way [through *fideicommissium*] to a family or an heir should in no case be subject to confiscation or be taken in payment of debts public or private."[57]

To bolster its case the commission included a survey of the rights of Livonian nobles as they existed under their former Swedish absolutist kings and currently under the Russian autocracy. The commissioners offered the example as a case study in the benefits of noble freedom. They pointed out that Baltic nobles, without the slightest compulsion, provided their sons with an excellent education and sent them into service in greater numbers than the government could possibly want or need. The survey further described the different educational and service routes pursued by Livonian nobles, some in the military, others in the civil service. Naturally, the top positions were reserved for sons of prominent and wealthy families

---

anstvo v Rossii, pp. 166–67. This explanation has been given some support recently in Raeff, *Origins*. But Michael Confino has challenged Raeff's thesis in a critique, "Histoire et psychologie: A propos de la noblesse russe," in *Annales E. S. C.* vol. 22, no. 6, pp. 1163–1205, which, while confirming the extraordinary social mobility within the leading estate, raises serious questions about the lack of attachment to the land as a basis for it.

[56] Judging from the report on this proposal by Robert Jones, "The Russian Gentry and the Provincial Reform of 1775" (Ph.D. diss., Cornell University, 1968), pp. 94–95, which he found in the Soviet archives, it appears to be identical with or very similar to the document published in *AKV*, 4: 518–19, which Rubinshtein relates to Elizabeth's legislative commission during the early 1760s. The Vorontsov proposals were discussed by the Commission on Noble Freedom on 5 March 1763. *SIRIO*, 7: 238 n. See above, Chapter 3; also Rubinshtein, "Ulozhennaia Komissiia," pp. 250–51.

[57] Kulomzin, "Pervyi pristup," pp. 65–69.

that could furnish the educational and foreign travel opportunities required for high office. Also to capture important posts like that of resident, minister, or *Oberlandrichter* demanded considerable solicitation, patronage, and gifts *(podarki)*. This was as it should be, the commission implied. Poorer nobles could not hope for such positions. They properly found their place among the clerks and chancery officials.

Given the Livonian nobility's eagerness and preparation for service there were naturally not enough positions to go around. But this was no matter for concern. Non-serving nobles likewise made contributions to the well-being of society. They engaged in private economy, established factories, mills, and mines and thereby spread the knowledge of trades and provided subsistence for many people. They enriched the country while enriching themselves. The commission then underlined its belief that the reason for all this diligence on the part of Livonian nobles was the special privileges and freedoms they enjoyed as an estate. The explicit conclusion was that if similar rights and prerogatives were granted to the Russian nobility, the same beneficial results would naturally ensue.[58]

The commission report gave Catherine all that she seemed to ask for. It included the extension of noble privilege alluded to in her directive. It also demonstrated how this broadening of rights would contribute to the welfare of the state and provide inducements to service. Yet Catherine showed no enthusiasm for the report. She held it for several months and then on 11 October returned it to the commission for further study. This time the commissioners firmly resisted her suggestion on grounds that they possessed insufficient knowledge of her intentions to proceed productively. As they saw it, the proper procedure would be for Catherine first of all to define the freedoms she wished to grant and then the commission could undertake to draw up a set of appropriate laws. "Otherwise, if the laws are written up in accordance with the articles presented in the report and Your Majesty should subsequently wish to alter or eliminate certain articles, the laws already composed will not only lose their coherence, but all of them will in large measure be left subject to change and hence the time spent in composing them will have been

[58]Kulomzin, "Pervyi pristup," section on Livonian nobility, pp. 41–44, commission view of comparability, pp. 44–46.

THE PANIN PARTY IN POWER

wasted."[59] To this objection Catherine evidently had no reply, and she left the matter in abeyance for another twenty-two years before instituting the Charter of Nobility.

Catherine's reasons for rejecting the commission report, though not stated explicitly, were plainly revealed in her marginal notes. She mocked the commissioners' glowing portrayal of the Russian nobility. Where they spoke of the advantages of foreign travel and study in the service of foreign governments, Catherine noted "as in Paris hanging around at theatricals and houses of ill-fame." Where they suggested preparatory service in "many armies" abroad as the best possible military school, Catherine simply jotted "vagabond."[60] She directed her most forceful criticism, however, against the validity of comparisons between the Baltic and Russian nobilities. The commission report implied throughout that because the opportunities for education were now comparable in both areas (a doubtful assertion in itself),[61] one could draw similar conclusions about the response of nobles in Russia to laws such as existed in the Baltic Provinces. Catherine immediately skewered this naive proposition. "Everywhere," she noted, "you speak of schooling, nowhere of mores, which are more necessary than schooling."[62] One principle Catherine had thoroughly mastered from her reading of Montesquieu and other jurists was that laws must derive from the mores of a nation. She knew well enough that the Russian nobility's attitude toward service and personal enterprise compared poorly with that of their German counterparts. She knew, too, that the number of Russian nobles "living in poverty and isolation" and not yet enlightened enough to wish to serve and be useful was much greater than the commission admitted. Consequently, she must have feared that implementation of the com-

[59]*SIRIO*, 7: 265–66.

[60]Kulomzin, "Pervyi pristup," pp. 52–53.

[61]See, for example, Romanovich-Slavatinskii's comments on illiteracy among the Russian nobility. *Dvorianstvo*, p. 175. The commission may have had a point with respect to the desire for education, which seemed to be well implanted. The Freedom of Nobility decree of 1762 insisted upon nobles educating their children "under pain of Our anger," and provided that all those with less than 1000 serfs should enter the Noble Cadet Corps, where they would receive an education befitting a nobleman (*PSZ*, 15: no. 11444, section 7). A short time later I. I. Shuvalov, director of the Corps, reported that there were not enough places for all applicants. Many had to be sent directly into various types of service. *Dvorianstvo*, pp. 194–95.

[62]Kulomzin, "Pervyi pristup," p. 44.

mission's guidelines might lead sooner to a degeneration of the nobility than to a flourishing spirit of enterprise.

Catherine had really been looking for some solution to the problem of the entire nobility's relation to state service. The men of the commission framed a document that answered their own needs as the elite of serving nobles. The provisions they outlined for study abroad and service in foreign armies would benefit families in the top stratum of noble officialdom, the dignitaries or *sanovniki* as they were called, who alone could take advantage of such opportunities. The guarantees against administrative trial, confiscation of property, and right to emigrate, which figured prominently in the report, spoke to the needs of the leading officials who might fall victim to a court coup or sudden shift in policy. Panin might have believed, as he told the French minister Breteuil, that "illegal investigations and punishments have up to now been the lot of every Russian at one time or another,"[63] but he was undoubtedly thinking first of all of his fellow dignitaries who had fallen one after another in previous reigns.

Finally, it should be mentioned that the Panin-led majority on the commission did not escape a vigorous minority challenge. Count Bestuzhev-Riumin again set himself in opposition to the Panin party and mapped out a position possibly designed to attract support from the middle and lesser ranks of nobility. He took a firm stand against any government regulation of serf-landlord relations, and he argued for the participation of locally elected nobles in provincial administration.[64] Both proposals conflicted with the Panins' views and were set aside by the majority. But in stating them, Bestuzhev accurately anticipated two importunate demands of the rank and file nobility that were to find expression in the Legislative Commission of 1767. That experience would be enough to give Catherine pause and turn her subsequently from the Panin party's views in the direction of satisfying these desires with her major reforms of the 1770s and 1780s.

Catherine already seemed to sense the danger of relying exclusively on the views of the *sanovniki* dominating the Commission on Noble Freedom for a policy suitable to the entire nobility. She decided against enunciating a general policy on noble freedom at this time and shelved the commission report until 1785, when some of its recommendations were retrieved for use in the Charter of Nobility.

[63]Breteuil to Praslin, 23 February 1763, *SIRIO*, 140: 162.
[64]Kulomzin, "Pervyi pristup," pp. 30–32.

Meanwhile, the senate several times confirmed the decree of Peter III,[65] an action sufficient to quiet fears that obligatory service would be reintroduced.

5. Senate and Procuracy Reforms

Another task given to the Commission on Noble Freedom led immediately to an important reform. In addition to its primary work, the empress had asked the commission to study the second part of Panin's Imperial Council project, the section recommending a division of the senate. As early as December 1763 Catherine decided to implement this reform. She did so apparently with the commission's support, as the change conformed in most respects to Panin's original proposal. The senate was split into six departments serving different functional areas, and two departments were relocated in Moscow. The law carried this principle even further in calling for a similar departmentalization of several other central government agencies.[66] Panin certainly also had a hand in this expanded application; he led the commission deliberations, and his brother later recommended the same kind of functional division in other institutions.[67]

The senate reform, nevertheless, produced a situation at variance with Panin's original intentions. In dividing the senate without at the same time establishing a coordinating body like the Imperial Council Catherine reduced the senate's influence on policy.[68] Moreover, the form in which Catherine implemented the change circumscribed the discretionary scope allowed in Panin's plan. She followed Panin in directing that decisions made unanimously by a single department bear the full weight of senate ukases (article IV). But when it came to disputed issues, which Panin had wanted settled by a majority vote of the combined senate, Catherine hesitated. Without fully clarifying the matter, she implied that in these cases too, there had

[65]*PSZ*, nos. 12610, 12731, 13087.

[66]Departmentalization had previously been introduced under Empress Anne but only as preparatory commissions; decisions were still made by the entire senate forming a single department. Shcheglov, *Gosudarstvennyi sovet*, p. 677. Other agencies thus departmentalized included the Justice, Estates, and Revision collegia. *PSZ*, 16: no. 11989.

[67]"Raport Imperatritse Ekaterine II generala i senatora P. Panina, ot 20 ianvaria 1765 goda," *SIRIO*, 28: 106–13.

[68]Shcheglov, *Gosudarstvennyi sovet*, p. 678; see also Bérenger's comments on this matter in a dispatch to Praslin, 5 March 1764, *SIRIO*, 140: 330–31.

to be general agreement before a decision could take effect.[69] The result was to diminish the senate's discretion and give it the aspect of a bureaucratic arm of the autocratic power. It may be recalled that only a year earlier, when Panin first submitted his reform, he particularly dreaded this outcome, insisted on the integrity of the projected changes in the senate and council, and even vowed to sabotage the whole scheme if his views were not upheld.[70] But that threat came from a man battling for political survival. His victory over the opposing party had changed the picture considerably. As leading minister he no longer had any use for a council, and predictably he raised no opposition to the reform being carried through.

Catherine was, however, becoming aware of her increasing dependence on a single court faction, and she followed the senate reform with a personnel change that did not work to the Panin party's advantage. She appointed Prince A. A. Viazemskii, a man attached to neither of the leading parties, as general-procurator of that body.[71] The move was altogether consistent with her past efforts to keep control of the clientele hierarchies. From the very earliest days of the reign she had balanced off prominent groups in the senate with new appointees of her own choosing. In addition, she had placed two trusted agents, the kamer-iunkers F. G. Orlov and V. V. Vsevolozhskii, in "permanent attendance in the Senate" as a check on the activities of that institution.[72] The same purpose evidently now motivated her to rearrange the senate leadership following the reform of December 1763.

[69]Article V of the reform decree read: "If for a particular affair there is no precise law, or not all the senators confirm the same opinion, in such a case the general-procurator should present the entire affair along with the senators' opinions and his own evaluation in a report to Us for examination." *PSZ*, 16: 11989.

[70]See above, chapter 4, section 4.

[71]Viazemskii was from an old but not especially distinguished family. His father was a naval lieutenant, he himself a graduate of the Serpukhovskii cadet corps, which he left in 1747 as an ensign. His career advanced rapidly, and in 1763 he came to Catherine's attention through his report on conditions at the Ural factories, where as special commissioner he had accomplished two important tasks: the settling of a dispute between factory owners and insurrectionary peasants, and an economic study of the Ural mining industry. Soon after his return from this mission, Catherine appointed him general procurator. *Entsiklopedicheskii slovar'* (Brokgauz-Efron), 7: (1892), p. 718; A. Veidemeier, *Dvor i zamechatel'nye liudi v Rossii* (St. Petersburg, 1846), p. 201.

[72]The new "non-party" appointees included N. P. Sheremet'ev, Baron N. A. Korf, M. K. Skavronskii, and A. I. Ushakov. V. A. Petrova, "Politicheskaia bor'ba vokrug senatskoi reformy 1763 goda," *Vestnik Leningradskogo Universiteta*, vyp. 2, no. 8 (1967), p. 60.

The general-procurator's office was a pivotal point of control in high government, all the more so now that the senate division greatly enhanced the office's power. Much of the discretionary authority lost to the senate as a whole devolved upon this single official. Not only did he retain supervision of the entire procuracy at all levels of government; he also chaired the First Department of the Senate, supervised the five ober-procurators in the other departments, and exercised extensive initiative power in the conduct of business. He decided when general assemblies of the senate would be convened, what cases would be discussed, and whether these cases should go to the sovereign for final decision.[73]

At the time of Viazemskii's appointment Catherine wrote him a "most Secret Instruction," a memoir that has spawned conflicting interpretations. The document reveals much about the relationship between the imperial power and the court parties.

Catherine opened the memoir by explaining her lack of confidence in the previous general-procurator, A. I. Glebov. He had been too attached to Peter Shuvalov, she said, and had fully imbibed his principles, which "while not very good for society, were sufficiently profitable for these men themselves." Since that time Glebov had further proved his abilities as an extortionist and generally had "a greater inclination to the dark side of affairs than to the light."[74]

She implied that her reasons for choosing Viazemskii were related to his unattached position, and she demanded his utmost candor and loyalty, reminding him that his sole support would be her personal protection. So long as he carried out his duties faithfully, she would not sacrifice him to the interests of a particular party. Then she told him what to expect in his dealings with the senate:

> You will find two parties, but a reasoned policy on my part requires that neither be respected in the least; deal with them firmly and they will disappear more quickly. I have watched them with an unsleeping eye and employed these people according to their ability for one or another matter. Both parties will now attempt to win you to their side. In the one you will

[73]*PSZ*, 16: no. 11989; see Veretennikov, "Iz istorii instituta prokuratury nachala Ekaterininskogo tsarstvovaniia," in *Russkii istoricheskii zhurnal*, no. 5 (1918), pp. 86–100, for background and consequences of this reform, which in time allowed the general-procurator to grow into a prime minister for domestic affairs.

[74]Both quotes from Catherine's memoir, *SIRIO*, 7: 345–46.

find honest men, although without great foresight; in the other, I think, their views extend much farther but it is not clear that they are always for the best purposes. Some people think that because they have spent a long time in this or that country, the politics of their favorite country ought to be instituted everywhere, and everything else without exception merits their criticism, despite the fact that everywhere the internal dispositions are based upon the mores of a nation.[75]

This passage has frequently been identified as a direct attack on Panin and his Imperial Council project. Clarification of this important issue must, however, be preceded by a full review of the document, as the context of these remarks tells much about their meaning.

In the next section, for example, Catherine launched a critique of administrative disorder, many points of which she lifted directly out of Panin's Imperial Council project. "Through the neglect of some of my predecessors and even more through the partiality of their favorites," she wrote, "all state offices and the Senate itself have exceeded their bounds in various cases. The Senate was established for the execution of prescribed laws, yet it often promulgated laws, distributed ranks, honors, money, villages, in a word, nearly everything, and restricted other judicial offices in [the exercise of] their laws and prerogatives.[76] I even had occasion to hear in the Senate that they wished to censure one collegium for the mere reason that it had dared to present its opinion to the Senate."[77] The abject dependence of the subordinate officials on the powerful men above, Catherine continued, had caused such servility in the lower offices that they had completely forgotten the regulations by which they were to make representations against senate ukases not in conformity with the law. The empress remarked sadly that "the slavishness of persons working in these [lower] offices is indescribable, and no good can be expected from them so long as this evil is not stamped out."[78]

[75]*SIRIO*, 7: 346.

[76]Panin's interest in improving this aspect of affairs had not diminished since 1762. The subject came up in discussions at the grand ducal court. Poroshin reported N. Panin and P. G. Chernyshev talking about "abuses here in granting ranks, about the bureaucratic order and the like." The grand duke then said to Panin: "It seems to me that no one describes the neglect of state interest and the disorganized administration as well as you do it." Poroshin, *Zapiski*, 7 November 1764.

[77]*SIRIO*, 7: 347.

[78]*SIRIO*, 7: 347.

Panin's solution to this problem was, of course, much different. While strongly in favor of improving the quality of lower officials, he wished to define the senate's sphere of competence more precisely and remove the influence of imperial favorites at the top. But Catherine was not concerned about favorites. She chose them herself. She worried more about the corrupting influence of the mediating patronage hierarchies in the senate and wished to encourage the lower offices to act as a control on them. The next passage quite clearly expressed her apprehension that the autocratic power might be corrupted by the senate's overly broad exercise of authority:

The Senate, having once exceeded its bounds, now has difficulty conforming to the proper order. Perhaps, the former examples tempt the pride of certain members; however, so long as I am alive, we shall remain as duty prescribes. The Russian Empire is so vast that any other form of government, except an autocratic ruler, is harmful to it, as all other [forms] are slower in executive dispatch and possess an abundance of various passions all tending to a splintering of authority and power; unlike a single ruler, having all means for ending any harm and considering the general welfare as his own, all others, in the words of the Evangelist, are hirelings.[79]

Despite the desire of many writers to see this affirmation of autocracy as an attack on Nikita Panin and the Imperial Council project, the explanation of Catherine's words appeared much closer to hand, in the memoir itself and the events with which it was most immediately concerned.

In addition to these general comments, the memoir to Viazemskii dealt with a number of specific policy questions then on the senate docket. Catherine devoted a large part of the memoir to just such questions. One was the issue of increasing the amount of silver coin in circulation. In her words, this was "extremely delicate" and "most secret material" which had to be decided without partisan considerations. In fact, five of the memoir's nine sections treated similar matters of a purely financial or administrative nature.[80] They all related to the burning issues being discussed in the senate, issues that in-

[79]*SIRIO*, 7: 347.

[80]Besides the monetary issue, she spoke of organizing the chancery, systematizing law, reforming the liquor and salt monopolies, and refurbishing provincial administration. *SIRIO*, 7: 347–48.

volved the personal interests of many leading members of that body.

One was the case of the English merchant Gome to whom Peter Shuvalov had granted rights to exploit crown timber lands on conditions very unfavorable to the state treasury. Catherine had already asked Nikita Panin to investigate this scandal and report on Gome's enterprises, but she must have doubted that the senate under Glebov's leadership would render an unbiased judgment in the affair. A second question involved the "Copper Bank" established in 1758 with a capitalization of two million rubles to be lent to nobles and merchants. Four persons, M. L. Vorontsov, P. I. Shuvalov, S. P. Iaguzhinskii and A. I. Glebov, had each borrowed over 200,000 rubles, while Gome was obliged to the tune of over 350,000. In other words, these five men had helped themselves to nearly three-quarters of the bank's capital and taken it on very easy terms. They themselves or their clients all sat in the senate. Finally, there was a need for immediate reform of the liquor and salt monopolies, which were imposing a heavy burden on consumers. Here again Glebov, P. S. Sumarokov, the Vorontsovs, and the Shuvalovs all had large vested interests.[81]

Viazemskii would have to deal with these important matters as soon as he took office, and Catherine designed her memoir primarily to apprise him of the difficulties he was likely to encounter in arriving at impartial judgments. Her immediate aim was to clean out the remnants of Shuvalov influence from the senate. This was her reason for removing Glebov in the first place. He was so deeply compromised by graft and influence peddling that no useful reform could be expected from him. Catherine had explained the general problem very well. Powerful interest groups had taken over the senate and so thoroughly controlled or intimidated the subordinate officials that no effective check operated from those levels. Neglect by her predecessors had allowed these groups to entrench themselves and manipulate the state machine for their own private advantage. In short, she was telling Viazemskii that she had no intention of seeing crucial financial and monetary business decided by familial and personal patronage groups, as had occurred during Shuvalov's time and had led to the present serious budget deficit. Unlike her predecessors, she

---

[81]Catherine had, in fact, already found it necessary to order Sumarokov removed from senate discussions of the liquor monopoly due to his especially compromised position in that regard. *SIRIO*, 7: 235–37; for review of all these cases, see *IPS*, 2: 353–55.

meant to have a strong procuracy that could turn these decisions to the benefit of the state rather than to private interests.

But what about the view that Catherine intended the memoir as an attack on the Panin party? She spoke of a party whose ideas might be harmful to the state. She even mentioned that some persons sought to introduce foreign institutions into Russia. Then she felt compelled to state the reasons for a single autocratic authority. Was this not, after all, an answer to Panin's council reform?

This interpretation, while plausible enough on the surface, raises more questions than it answers. If Catherine wished to argue the need of autocracy for the benefit of Panin and his supporters, why did she confine her statements to a "most secret" instruction to Viazemskii? Or, conversely, given the thoroughly confidential nature of her instruction, what reason would she have to cloak this important issue in ambiguous allusion? She certainly did not hesitate to mention Glebov directly and categorize his many abuses. She also went into some detail on specific policy questions. There was no reason for her to avoid mentioning political opposition from the Panins, if the problem were on her mind.

But politics as such was not the question. Neither Catherine nor the clientele groups with which she had to contend viewed the action of parties as political. They were informal groupings cemented by familial and personal ties, or made up of office cliques, with established economic or institutional interests, which they jealously defended from penetration above and below. Catherine warned Viazemskii of one in particular:

> The most difficult thing of all for you will be governing the Senate chancellery without being deceived. You will see this more clearly in the following example: the French Cardinal Richelieu, that wise minister, used to say that it was less difficult for him to rule the state and persuade Europe to his views than to govern the royal antechamber, because all the court idlers were against him and hindered his great plans by their base intrigues. But you have one means not available to Richelieu— to discharge mercilessly all doubtful and suspicious persons.[82]

No one would suggest from this statement that the senate chancellery constituted a political party. It was simply another interest group,

[82]*SIRIO*, 7: 348.

like the parties Catherine perceived in the senate, but one that, through the power of the procurator, she could master and use as a check on the patronage groups of the senate.

Seen from this point of view, Catherine's advice applied to the Panin party as well as to all others. She may well have had Panin in mind when referring to the desire of some people to introduce foreign institutions. But she was probably not thinking so much of the Imperial Council project, which Panin had long since abandoned, as of the more recent report of the Commission on Noble Freedom, whose provisions Catherine specifically rejected as alien and inappropriate to Russian conditions. Beyond this one allusion there was little in the memoir to suggest that the empress intended it as an attack on the Panin party. In fact, by looking again at the broad context of events, one can see that Catherine's relation to the Panins at this time was much more complex than has usually been interpreted.

Catherine's primary aim was to remove the Shuvalov influence from the senate. She was doing this, moreover, on the basis of a plan worked out by Nikita Panin.[83] Her instruction to Viazemskii repeated many of Panin's criticisms of the neglect that had allowed favorites to enrich themselves at government expense. Catherine had even entrusted Panin with investigating and cleaning up the financial mess surrounding the Gome affair. It seems perfectly clear that Catherine and Panin were cooperating in this reform, not using it as a battleground. The Panin party's influence was at a high point during this period. Nikita Panin was the unchallenged leader of foreign affairs. In domestic matters all secret business had recently come under his control.[84] Catherine had placed supervision over the grand duke and the entire "young court" exclusively in his hands.[85] He and his clients led all the most important reform commissions. Their influence in all these areas had not grown because they desired to usurp power from the sovereign, but because Catherine sorely needed and relied upon them to help establish the new regime, weed out the former patronage networks, and formulate new policies.

[83]This is clear enough from the reforms themselves, but it might be added that not long before making them she wrote to her secretary Elagin: "Please get from Glebov the council project written by Panin, which I gave him in Moscow . . . I have spoken to you several times about this, and I recall clearly that I gave it to him, I don't know for what purpose. I cannot get it back from him, and I have great need of it." *SIRIO*, 7: 339.

[84]This ukase was evidently deleted from the *PSZ*, but see Catherine's reference to it in *SIRIO*, 7: 349.

[85]For more on this matter see below, chapter 8.

Even so, Catherine always feared becoming overly dependent on a single court party. She realized that to keep the autocratic power firmly in her own hands she had to balance off the clientele groups in the central administration. The Panins presented a special danger in this regard precisely because their ideas corresponded so closely to Catherine's own plans. Moreover, they were hermost skillful ministers and the men least susceptible to corruption. Because she needed them, she had to be especially careful to bring into play a counterweight to their growing influence. In this view, Catherine's instruction to Viazemskii told very little about her relations with the Panins. Inspired in large part by Nikita Panin's own ideas, the instruction dealt principally with current policy decisions. However, the change in the person and power of the general-procurator told a great deal. It far surpassed in significance anything the instruction had to say about the Panin party. The key was Catherine's decision to exclude a Panin client from this important post, a decision that obviously surprised and chagrined Nikita Panin, who described Viazemskii's appointment as the product of undeserved "fortuna."[86] Indeed, the empress purposely chose a mediocrity with little to recommend him besides his independence from the court parties,[87] and she more or less encouraged him to build up a following of his own in the senate chancellery that would be able to force business through the established interest groups.

In short, the usual picture of a two-way struggle between Catherine and the Panin party scarcely provides an adequate explanation of the politics of this period. Tensions ran in several directions at once, and their configuration had changed considerably since the Panin victory in the court struggle of 1762–63. To begin with, Panin was no longer so concerned about maintaining the senate as a guarantee of the dignitaries at the top. This was only important so long as the principal challenge came from the upstarts in Catherine's immediate entourage. But now that Panin was confident of his leading position and responsible for government action, he and Catherine had to work together to stabilize their regime and establish new policy directions. One of the first objectives was to phase out the power

[86]Poroshin, *Zapiski*, 17 November 1765.
[87]This judgment of Viazemskii's abilities was generally shared by all who had occassion to deal with him. For a typical evaluation see the Prussian minister Görtz's comments, G. N. Leikhtenbergskii, ed., "Iz zapisok fon Gertsa," in *Vestnik Obshchestva Revnitelei Istorii* (1914), 1: 28–30.

groupings left over from previous reigns, in particular to remove what was left of the Shuvalov influence in the senate. It was not surprising, therefore, that Panin fully cooperated in ridding the senate of opposing interest groups and bureaucratizing it for greater efficiency. In fact, as Panin's influence mounted, he and his brother even discussed the desirability of introducing military discipline into the civil bureaucracy.[88] These were the fancies of men in power, men who felt an urgent need to get things done.

For Catherine's part, she willingly relied upon the Panin party during this period for both reform ideas and policy implementation. She had no intention of attacking the party or disturbing its cohesion. To do so would risk destroying the most competent executive organization at her disposal, and she sorely needed it to help remove the previous interest groups from key positions of power. But at the same time, she guarded against all these posts falling to the Panins and their clients. She made certain that at a minimum the powerful agency of the procuracy remained in different hands to serve as a check on the actions of her chief minister and his supporters. The measure of her political skill lay in the ability to retain the loyalty and cooperation of the Panins while she carefully limited the scope of their growing influence.

[88]Poroshin, *Zapiski*, 6 December 1765.

7

The Legislative Commission, War, and Decline
of the Panin Influence

Two events, the Legislative Commission of 1767–68 and the outbreak of war with Turkey toward the end of 1768, combined to break the dominance of the Panin party in Russian politics. In quite different ways these events affected the empress' confidence in the Panin leadership and prompted her to limit further the Panins' discretion in setting domestic and foreign policy. These issues will form the central concern of this chapter. But before this break occurred there was a period of increasing cooperation between Catherine and the Panin party. It is necessary to review this era of collaboration from 1764 to 1768 in order to place the Panins' contributions in proper perspective and to question again the widely accepted notion of an underlying conflict in their relations with Catherine throughout the 1760s, a conflict that supposedly found expression in all of Catherine's political activity.[1]

1. The Mirovich Affair

A good example of their collaboration was the handling of the Mirovich affair, an abortive coup d'etat that occurred in the summer

---

[1]This view is firmly established in recent historiography, especially in Marxist works, but it has influenced other writers as well. The chief contributions may be found in Georg Sacke, "Zur Charakteristik der gesetzgebenden Kommission Katharina II. von Russland," pp. 161–91; idem, "Katharina II. im Kampf um Thron und Selbstherrschaft," *Archiv für Kulturgeschichte,* vol. 23, no. 2 (1932), pp. 191–216; idem, "Adel und Bürgertum in der gesetzgebenden Kommission Katharina II. von Russland," *Jahrbücher für Geschichte Osteuropas,* 3 (1938), pp. 408–17; G. A. Gukovskii. *Ocherki po istorii russkoi literatury XVIII veka*; S. A. Pokrovskii, *Iuridicheskie proizvedeniia progressivnykh myslitelei,* 1, pp. 5–14; G. P. Makogonenko, *Denis Fonvizin,* pp. 157–58, 162, 167–68, 171–72, 194–95; K. V. Pigarev, *Tvorchestvo Fonvizina,* pp. 113, 114, 135; P. N. Berkov, *Istoriia russkoi zhurnalistiki,* pp. 158–59, 332; S. B. Okun', *Ocherki istorii SSSR,* p. 52; James Billington, *The Icon and the Axe,* pp. 219–20, 223, 230; Igor Glasenapp, *Staat, Gesellschaft und Opposition,* p. 6. For a review of this question see my article "Catherine II's Instruction to the Commission on Laws."

of 1764.[2] The matter was exceptionally critical, because it involved the murder of the former emperor Ivan VI Antonovich. It will be recalled that Ivan VI, while still a small child, became emperor of Russia in 1740 upon the death of Empress Anne. The following year Elizabeth overthrew the regency council led by Andrei Osterman and Ivan's parents, and after ascending the throne she exiled Ivan and his family to the far north. In 1744 Ivan was taken from his parents and spent the remainder of his life in prison, first in Kholmogory and then from 1756 in Schlüsselburg fortress not far from St. Petersburg.

The legitimate claims of Ivan VI, who had reached twenty-two years of age by the time of Catherine's elevation, presented a very delicate problem for the new empress. Her predecessors, Elizabeth and Peter III, had naturally made special provisions for Ivan's internment and supervision. Yet those two rulers possessed legitimate rights of their own and had much less to fear from Ivan's existence than did Catherine, a foreigner and usurper. Any pretender posed a serious threat to her tenure. Accordingly, in Catherine's case extreme care had to be exercised in regard to the imprisoned ex-emperor, and she turned this responsibility over to Nikita Panin.

Despite many precautions,[3] an attempt was made to liberate Ivan and establish him on the throne. On July 4, 1764, a lieutenant of the Smolensk regiment, V. Ia. Mirovich, occupied Schlüsselburg fortress with a guard detachment under his command and tried to force Ivan's release at gunpoint. The incident lasted only a short time, since the jailers hastily carried out a standing order to kill Ivan if a rescue threatened. They flung the corpse before the rebels, and Mirovich, seeing the hopelessness of his cause, gave himself up to the fort's commandant.

The Mirovich plot and Ivan's death took place while Catherine was away from the capital on a visit to the Baltic Provinces, and for some time prior to her departure for Livonia a rumor had circulated, both within Russia and abroad, that the Panins planned to carry out a coup d'etat in favor of Paul during her absence. So if there was any stress in Catherine's relations with the Panin party it should have

[2]Fortunately, a thorough documentary record has survived and is published in great detail in Bil'basov, *Istoriia Ekateriny II*, 2, appendices.

[3]The complex secret arrangements for Ivan's internment are described in my article "Catherine II's Instruction to the Commission on Laws," pp. 18–22 and notes.

shown up in this period. But this alleged threat did nothing to shake Catherine's confidence in Panin and his supporters. According to the Prussian envoy, the empress rejected the rumor "with indignation,"[4] and despite continual disturbances among the guards for several weeks prior to her departure, she refused to change her plans for the Livonian trip. Just two days before she left, a mutiny broke out in one regiment; Catherine was undaunted, departed on schedule, and turned the inquiry into the mutiny over to Nikita Panin.[5] During her absence Panin stayed at Tsarskoe Selo with the grand duke and continued to maintain supervision over him and Ivan VI. Senator Nepliuev, Panin's brother-in-law and one of his closest supporters, was given charge of the capital city.[6]

The Panin party likewise played an important role in all the events that led up to and followed the murder of Ivan VI. Nikita Panin had drawn up and signed the instructions authorizing the killing of Ivan in the event an attempt to free him could not be repulsed. The same instructions prohibited the admittance of a doctor to the prisoner in case of serious illness, while they allowed for the visit of a priest if the prisoner lay dying. Judging from these instructions and Panin's regular correspondence with Ivan's jailers, there is little doubt that he expected a speedy resolution of Ivan's internment, either through a natural death unaided by a physician or, in the worst case, through rapid fulfillment of the murder authorization should an attempt at liberation be made.[7]

[4]The rumor reached Prussia (according to Esipov, directly from its originator Bestuzhev), and Frederick II warned Panin about it. Panin reported Catherine's reaction through Ambassador Solms, who wrote: "Panin dankt für den avis des Königs d'une révolte, qui se tramait actuellement en Russie, die Sache anlangend, sagte Panin, die Kaiserin habe schon vor einigen Monaten die Nachricht erhalten, dass er, Panin, nebst dem Hetman tramait une conspiration pour culbuter l'Impératrice et pour mettre le Grand-Duc Paul sur le trône, qui devait éclater pendant qu'elle serait absente en Livonie. Die Kaiserin habe die Grossmuth gehabt, diesen avis mit indignation zurückzuweisen . . . (Bestuscheff stecke dahinter)." Solms to Frederick II, 17 April 1764, *SIRIO*, 22: 247; also Esipov, "Fridrikh II i graf Panin," p. 273.

[5]Solms to Frederick II, 18 May and 22 June 1764, *SIRIO*, 22: 253–54, 261–62; Düben to Chancellery President, 23 and 30 March, 14 and 28 May 1764, *SRa*, Muscovitica 343, nos. 14, 15, 24, 27; Buckingham to Sandwich, 11 May and 18 June 1764 (NS), *Despatches Buckingham*, 2: 182, 192–93; Bérenger to Praslin, 29 May 1764, *SIRIO*, 140: 371.

[6]Solms to Frederick II, 22 June 1764, *SIRIO*, 22: 262; Bil'basov, *Istoriia Ekateriny II*, 2: 383; Nepliuev, "Zapiski," *Russkii Arkhiv* (1871), no. 1, 679–80.

[7]See two letters from N. I. Panin to Ivan's guards Vlas'ev and Chekin in Bil'basov, *Istoriia Ekateriny II*, 2: 346–47, and the instructions, pp. 737–45. Panin was, of course, carrying out the will of the empress. No one was more apprehensive about Ivan's presence

Other members of the Panin party managed the arrangements and explanations that became necessary as a result of Ivan's death. Nepliuev had charge of St. Petersburg and saw to it that the capital remained tranquil during the crisis. After the news of Ivan's death arrived, Catherine went into consultation with Peter Panin, who had accompanied her to the Baltic Provinces.[8] Later she appointed him to the committee investigating Mirovich.[9] And as far as Nikita Panin's handling of the affair was concerned, Catherine could not have been more pleased:

> Ivan Ivanovich [Nepliuev] tells me of your concern over whether or not I am satisfied with the measures you have taken concerning the Schlüsselburg affair—and although I hope you have already seen in my letters my satisfaction with all the measures you have taken, still hearing the above I want to repeat that I am not only very satisfied but I recognize that it could not have been done better than you have done, for which I am very grateful.[10]

Panin's services in this matter extended even to the point of fabricating the story of Ivan's insanity, a falsehood evidently intended to lessen the shock of the news of his death.[11]

While the Mirovich case provides strong evidence against the notion of a conflict between the empress and Panin in this period, the

---

or more relieved at his death than was Catherine. Upon receiving the news of his death, she exclaimed involuntarily: "God's hand works in wonderful and mysterious ways!" *Idem*, p. 381.

[8]Catherine to N. I. Panin, *Chteniia*, vol. 2, pt. 2, 154.

[9]Geisman and Dubovskoi, *Graf Petr Ivanovich Panin*, p. 26.

[10]Catherine to N. I. Panin, 22 July 1764, *Chteniia*, vol. 2, pt. 2, p. 8.

[11]There exists no reliable evidence of Ivan's insanity and much evidence to the contrary, even from Panin himself. See, for example, Article II of his instructions to Vlas'ev and Chekin in Bil'basov, *Istoriia Ekateriny II*, 2: 741–42; also Bil'basov's analysis of the problem, "Attestat bezumiia," *idem*, pp. 522–39. Contrary, however, to Bil'basov's assertion that Panin was covering Catherine in mentioning Ivan's insanity to the British ambassador (Buckingham to Sandwich, 3 August 1764 (NS), *Despatches Buckingham*, 2: 212; Bil'basov, *op. cit.*, p. 538), the fabrication came originally from Panin himself, as is abundantly clear from his corrections to this end of a circular letter explaining Ivan's death. Original and corrected version of "Tsirkuliarnoe pis'mo ot deistvitel'nogo tainogo sovetnika Panina ko vsem zdeshnim, pri inostrannykh dvorakh obetaiushchimsia Ministram," *GBL, f.* Pan. II, *d.* 11. The final version is published along with a letter from Panin to Catherine, explaining that he chose this form of announcing Ivan's death so as not to prevent the empress from making further public explanations of her own. *Russkii Arkhiv* (1871), no. 9, 1421–24.

objection may still be brought that Panin had as much stake as Catherine in the removal of Ivan Antonovich. If, as many writers have argued, Panin's power ambitions rested on the hope of Paul's succession, any action on behalf of another pretender menaced his own plans. Paul could only succeed through inheritance from his father and mother, whose elevations cut across the prior rights of Ivan VI. Catherine may then have reckoned on Panin's faithful service in the Mirovich affair and purposely employed him in it. But against this objection, it is possible to place much additional evidence of the strong agreement and cooperation between Catherine and Panin.

2. Expansion of Panin's Responsibilities

This evidence may be seen principally in the steady expansion of Panin's duties during the mid 1760s. His responsibility for foreign affairs has been well documented by several studies. It is worth adding that Catherine not only accepted his general policy system of the Northern Accord;[12] she also relied on his guidance in specific problems in this area, gave him the last word on the dispatch of instructions, and praised the calm, measured approach to affairs he had taught her.[13] Panin's exclusive control over the care and education of the grand duke is likewise well known and will be treated at length in a later chapter.

His duties covered many other matters as well. He continued to sit on all important commissions, directed several state enterprises, handled senate business, and participated together with Prince Viazemskii as the sole ministers privy to all secret business.[14] His concerns extended to educational endeavors. He made arrangements for the training of Russian physicians abroad, the hiring of foreign teachers in the Russian service, and worked with I.I. Betskoi on the establishment of the Moscow Foundling Home.[15] In the central gov-

---

[12]In ordering Vice-Chancellor Golitsyn to turn over all the former chancellor's papers to Panin, Catherine told him that "Panin alone has a complete knowledge of the system I have established . . . the interest of the Empire requires that [policy] direction remain in the hands of M. Panin." Catherine to A. M. Golitsyn, rec'd. 9 August 1765, *AKV*, 28: 34.

[13]Among many such examples, see the letters in *Chteniia,* vol. 2, pt. 2, pp. 124, 125; and *SIRIO,* 7: 399.

[14]*Chteniia,* vol. 2, pt. 2, pp. 9, 66.

[15]Solms to Frederick II, 17 June 1765, *SIRIO,* 22: 381–82; A. Tereshchenko, *Opyt*

ernment, in addition to his responsibilities as foreign minister, he assisted I. G. Cheryshev in managing the Admiralty Collegium and consulted on matters of trade and commerce.[16] At the same time his brother served on the important committees supervising the land survey, factories and assigned peasants, and the construction of Baltiiskii Port, and played a leading role in military affairs,[17] while Nikita Panin himself had an important say in appointments to high military posts. Catherine even consulted with him before naming her favorite Grigorii Orlov to general artillery master; on Panin's advice she made the appointment only after scaling down the power of the office.[18] Catherine also conferred with Panin on matters of literary style and valued his opinion enough to give him the final say on whether certain items should be published.[19] The clearest evidence of the empress' confidence was that she entrusted exclusively to Panin's direction a most crucial matter of her own health and well-being. This was her much-heralded decision to undergo a smallpox inoculation.

In Russia, as elsewhere, smallpox was a major health menace, and the number of cases in the empire had increased substantially during the 1760s. Nikita Panin took a special interest in the problem.[20] Few persons felt the need for action more keenly, as the disease had claimed his fiancée, the beautiful and wealthy Countess Sheremeteva, on the very eve of their wedding. Through his advice and mediation Catherine decided to call the British physician Dr. Thomas Dimsdale to Russia to inoculate her and Paul, and she vested entire responsibility for the venture in Panin. He made all the arrangements, participated at every stage of the procedure, and shared in the success of the endeavor. Even the favorite Orlov was not informed of what was going on. Considering the state of medical technology and the occa-

---

obozreniia zhizni sanovnikov upravliavshikh inostrannymi delami v Rossii, vol. 2 (St. Petersburg, 1837), pp. 124–25; Poroshin, *Zapiski*, 24 September 1765.

[16]*Chteniia*, vol. 2, pt. 2, p. 67; Poroshin, *Zapiski*, 6 October 1764.

[17]Geisman and Dubovskoi, *Graf Petr Ivanovich Panin*, pp. 26–28.

[18]According to Macartney, Panin had no objection to the appointment so long as the empress prevented it "from being a status in statu, for it is an employment of great power and very extensive authority." Catherine abridged the power of the office by placing it under the supervision of the senate. Macartney to Sandwich, 18 March 1765, *SIRIO*, 12: 202–03.

[19]*GBL, f.* Pan. IV, *op.* 1, 242–43.

[20]Poroshin, *Zapiski*, 19 October 1765; Scheel to Copenhagen, 31 October 1768, *DRa*, TKUA, Russland A III 86, no. 14.

sional mishaps associated with inoculation, Catherine's decision was a tribute to her faith in Panin.[21] Following the inoculation she honored him with another important charge. He was to become founder and director of the new St. Petersburg Variolic Hospital *(Ospennyi Dom)*, established in recognition of Catherine's exemplary act.[22]

Besides these examples of Panin's position of confidence during the 1760s, Catherine bestowed many explicit expressions of regard. When Count Rzewuski wanted to obtain a private audience with her to relay some vital information, Catherine begged off and instead asked Panin to conduct the interview. She then added: "Try and get him to tell you about it, for if it concerns the interests of the empire, the utility of the service, or the security of my person, you ought to be informed just as well as I."[23] Another testimony of the empress' concern for her minister came in answer to a dispatch from Prince Repnin, ambassador to Warsaw, who expressed anxiety about some danger threatening Panin. While Panin merely remarked that the report deserved no credence, the empress added a footnote declaring, "And I, Catherine, say that Panin need be afraid of nothing."[24]

In short, during the mid 1760s Panin served as Catherine's most trusted minister, a man in charge of a vast range of affairs that he conducted with the full support and collaboration of the empress.[25]

[21]See his letter to Governor-General von Browne on arrangements for Dimsdale's journey in *Rizhskii Vestnik* (1869), no. 4. According to the British envoy, who owing to Dimsdale's participation had very detailed information about the matter, only Panin, Saldern and Cherkassov were present at the inoculation. Cathcart goes on to say that "having been the author and conductor of the whole affair, [Panin] is peculiarly happy in the success of the event, upon which so much depended." Also, "Mr. Panin . . . has the whole sway here, is trusted with the Empress's affairs, and has indeed been trusted with her life in the affair of the inoculation and all the important arrangements which preceded that operation." Cathcart to Weymouth, 17 September, 21 October, and 1 November 1768, *SIRIO*, 390–93. Descriptions of Dimsdale's trip may be found in W. J. Bishop, "Thomas Dimsdale, M.D., F.R.S. (1712–1800) and the Inoculation of Catherine the Great of Russia," *Annals of Medical History*, N.S. 4, no. 4 (1932), pp. 321–38; and Philip H. Clendenning, "Dr. Thomas Dimsdale and Smallpox Inoculation in Russia," *Journal of the History of Medicine*, vol. 28, no. 2 (1973), pp. 109–25, which, however, adds nothing of substance to Bishop's earlier study.

[22]Catherine to I. P. Elagin, 1773, *SIRIO*, 42: 304; Catherine to N. I. Panin, 3 April 1781, *GBL, f.* Pan. IV, *op.* 1, 358.

[23]*Chteniia*, vol. 2, pt. 2, p. 97.

[24]Solov'ev, *Istoriia Rossii*, 13: 512.

[25]The correspondence in *Chteniia*, vol. 2, pt. 2, is by itself sufficiently persuasive on this account; see also Shchebal'skii's review of this collection. "Perepiska Ekateriny Vtoroi s gr. N. I. Paninym," *Russkii Vestnik*, 45, (1863), pp. 748–62.

Moreover, Catherine gave public recognition to this fact in 1767 by conferring on him the title of count of the Russian Empire. The ukase read: "To N. I. Panin, who has demonstrated his devotion and energy in caring for the education of Our Son, while at the same time fulfilling with zeal and success a multitude of affairs both foreign and domestic."[26] In a more grudging fashion the broad range of Panin's responsibilities was likewise recognized by the foreign representatives stationed in St. Petersburg. They complained of the slowness with which government business was transacted in Russia and frequently blamed this lack of dispatch on Panin's dilatoriness and fondness for the good life. The accusation contained at least a grain of truth.[27] But in cooler moments the foreign envoys were gracious enough to acknowledge the real reason: all important affairs went through the hands of this single minister and weighed him down with enormous and time-consuming responsibilities.[28]

3. The Instruction and Legislative Commission

No survey of the 1760s can fail to discuss Catherine's famous *Instruction* on laws. The document is of great interest as a statement of the empress's political philosophy. It is also inextricably bound up with the whole question of the Panin party's relationship to Catherine, if only because Marxist scholars have interpreted it as part of a general counterattack by the empress on the Panin-led aristocrats. In composing the *Instruction* Catherine borrowed heavily from Montesquieu's *Esprit des lois*. Yet while employing his formulations

---

[26]*PSZ*, 17: no. 12682.

[27]Panin's fondness for women evidently distracted him from his government duties on occasion. Diplomats complained during the mid-1760s of his time-consuming involvement with Anna Mikhailovna Stroganova (née Vorontsova). For the background of the affair and letters relating to it, see *AKV*, 34: 333–52; comments of foreign envoys, see, among others, Macartney to Grafton, 4 April 1766, and Shirley to Conway, 28 May 1767, *SIRIO*, 12: 256–57, 301–03.

[28]"Dans un Pays où toutes les affaires sont entre les Mains d'un seul Ministre, on n'en fait aucune du Moment qu'on est éloigné de Sa Personne," Asseburg reported to his chief in Copenhagen. 2 February 1767, *DRa*, TKUA, Russland A III 85. See also, Macartney to Conway, 5 December 1766, and Shirley to Weymouth, 20 July 1768, *SIRIO*, 12: 290–91, 335–37. Even the former chancellor could get nothing accomplished without working through Panin, as he admitted in a letter to his nephew: "I will gladly make efforts with regard to Mr. Ferzen, only I have very few means to do so; for I scarcely ever see N. I. Panin, and my friend the vice-chancellor can hardly do something on his own. And so I cannot give you or him hopes about the success of my efforts." M. L. Vorontsov to A. R. Vorontsov, 19 April 1765, *AKV*, 5: 137.

she was always careful to make small alterations of the original that brought it into conformity with her view of Russia as an absolutist bureaucratic monarchy. This circumstance has led Marxist historians to contend that Catherine consciously chose the *Esprit des lois* as Panin's favorite text on government, gutted its argument for a limited estates monarchy, and twisted it into a rationale for Russian autocracy.[29] It would be more accurate, however, to see the *Instruction* and the Legislative Commission for which it was designed as works motivated by the reformist impulse of Catherine's early reign, and in this sense they were closely associated with the desires of the Panin party and the promises Catherine had made at her accession to bring greater legal form and system to Russian governance.

It was indeed true that the empress altered details of Montesquieu's writings in order to make them conform to absolutist bureaucratic monarchy rather than to the estates monarchy advocated in the *Esprit des lois*. This tendency appeared in her specific structural proposals, which located the depository of laws in the bureaucratic offices instead of the estates.[30] It was likewise reflected in her defini-

[29]"It was undoubtedly *solely due to Panin's aristocratic tendencies*," Sacke wrote, "that she saw herself compelled to defend the absolutist bureaucratic monarchy with the greatest energy and with the help of numerous citations from the works of modern writers." (Emphasis is Sacke's.) "Katharina II. im Kampf um Thron und Selbstherrschaft," pp. 203, 205. For similar views see the works cited in footnote 1 above.

[30]An example of this tendency was the instance when Catherine changed Montesquieu's meaning of the channels through which power flows and the role that these channels play as the depository of the laws. Compare the two texts:

Ces lois fondamentales supposent nécessairement des canaux moyens par où coule la puissance. [*Esprit des lois,* bk. II, chapter 4, sec. 1.]

Les lois fondamentales d'un Etat supposent nécessairement des canaux moiens, c'est à dire des Tribunaux [sirech' pravitel'stva] par où se communique la puissance souveraine. [*Nakaz,* Chechulin, ed., p. 20.]

In Montesquieu's scheme the intermediary channels occupied a very important position as the depository of the state's laws. By this he meant separate institutions, specifically the French parlements, which could refuse to register laws if they were in conflict with existing legislation or were thought to be injurious. Catherine rejected any such institution. With her added clarification ("c'est à dire des Tribunaux") she located the depository of laws in the bureaucracy. She restated this at another point: "This depository can be in no other place but in the state institutions (*Sie khranilishche inde ne mozhet byt' ni gde, kak v gosudarstvennykh pravitel'stvakh*). These institutions, upon receipt of laws from the ruler, examine them diligently and have the right to make representations when they detect that a certain law is in conflict with the Code, injurious, unclear, or impossible to execute." (*Nakaz,* pp. 21, 23, 24). According to Taranovskii, Catherine intended the depository to

tion of the role of government. Whereas Montesquieu recognized different forms of government as having only relative goals hedged around by various types of social or individual activity, Catherine gave to autocratic government an absolute goal covering all areas of social activity: "The achievement of the greatest good for the greatest number." She derived this theoretical position from the German cameralist school of the eighteenth century, which concerned itself directly with questions of absolutist rule. Baron Bielefeld's *Institutions politiques* anticipated her in this blend of Montesquieu and absolutism and Catherine clearly borrowed a great deal from him as well as from Justi and other cameralist writers. These points were made some time ago by F. V. Taranovskii and N. D. Chechulin, and students owe them a debt for focusing attention on this aspect of Catherine's political theory.[31]

Yet it is not at all clear that Catherine was distorting Montesquieu or using the *Instruction* as a polemic against Panin or anyone else. In modifying the *Esprit des lois* she stayed well within Montesquieu's own theoretical principles. To be sure, she identified Russia as a monarchy, while Montesquieu referred to it as a despotism. He observed that the country lacked the principle of honor, security of person, inviolability of property, due process of law and other attributes of true monarchy.[32] But, as Catherine seemed to recognize, from the point of view of his broad naturalistic theory, Russia also lacked the proper climatic conditions for pure or Asiatic despotism. Only its vast territorial expanse qualified it for this designation. Yet this special circumstance could just as well place Russia in a separate category identified as European despotism, a variety Montesquieu described merely as a degeneration of true monarchy, probably neglecting to spell out its characteristics for reasons of censorship.[33] Since the *Esprit des lois* also argued that a nation could

be merely an appellate *a principe male informato ad principem melius informandum,* and this function was to be performed by the bureaucracy. F. V. Taranovskii, "Politicheskaia doktrina Nakaza," in *Sbornik statei po istorii prava posviashchennyi M. F. Vladimirskomu-Budanovu* (Kiev, 1904), pp. 50–51, 80–82.

[31]These scholars did not, incidentally, draw any conclusions about these points giving an anti-Panin direction to the writing. Chechulin, *Nakaz,* p. 294; Taranovskii, "Politicheskaia doktrina Nakaza," pp. 77–78.

[32]Montesquieu, *Esprit des lois,* especially book III, chapter 8, book V, chapter 14, and book XII, chapters 12, 16, 18.

[33]For references in the *Esprit* and analysis, see Taranovskii, "Montesk'e o Rossii," in *Trudy russkikh uchenykh za-granitsei,* vol. 1 (1922), pp. 194–98, 204, 208, 211.

overcome its natural endowment as its level of civilization rose, Catherine would have good reason to believe that Russia could achieve a more perfect government through the growth of enlightenment and application of appropriate legislative measures.[34]

Seen in this light, Catherine was not so much distorting or corrupting Montesquieu's ideas as refining them to serve as a theoretical groundwork for legislative reform in Russia. She no doubt reasoned that since natural conditions defined political organization only in a state of nature, they posed no insurmountable barrier to improvement: Russia had long ago emerged from such a state. Furthermore, the French government Montesquieu held up for emulation did not necessarily represent the sole and perfect model of monarchical order, for like all others it reflected peculiar circumstances of time and place. It is somewhat hasty, therefore, to assume that Catherine cynically distorted her French mentor. More accurately, she restated his basic principles in light of German cameralist thinking in order to express her belief that absolutist monarchy was the government best adapted to Russian conditions in their present stage of development and that it was in no sense inferior to the French model, as it could obtain the greatest benefits for the Russian people.[35]

Neither did Catherine give any indication that she meant the *Instruction* to serve as a polemic. She seemed to believe that it would help solve the century-long problem of producing a new legal code. It should be recalled that she started writing the *Instruction* in 1764, showed off her draft with evident pride, and even defended some controversial points from criticism.[36] The first inkling that she had doubts about the project appeared as late as the summer of 1767, on the very eve of the Legislative Commission's gathering, and these doubts were prompted by an entirely new and unexpected experience: her exposure to non-Russian areas of the empire about whose administration and general condition she had previously known very little. The occasion was her trip down the Volga River into "Asia." From Kazan' she wrote to Voltaire:

These laws about which so much has been said are in the final analysis not yet enacted, and who can answer for their use-

[34]Taranovskii, "Montesk'e o Rossii," p. 213. Also Billington, *Icon and Axe*, p. 223.
[35]Taranovskii, "Montesk'e o Rossii," p. 222.
[36]See, for example, her commentary on Sumarokov's critique. *SIRIO*, 10: 87.

fulness? It is posterity, and not us, who will have to decide that question. Consider, if you will, that they must be applied to Asia as well as Europe, and what difference of climate, peoples, customs, and even ideas! Here I am in Asia: I wished to see it all with my own eyes. There are in this city twenty different peoples, which in no way resemble one another. We have nevertheless to design a garment to fit them all. They can agree on general principles well enough, but what about the details? And what details! I have come to realize that we have to create a world, unify and conserve it, etc.[37]

This experience certainly opened Catherine's eyes, perhaps for the first time, to the difficulty of unifying the diverse customs and practices of the empire's peoples into a single legal framework, but she did not seem the less enthusiastic for trying. She wrote to Panin about the same time: "This is a separate empire, and it is only here that one can see what an immense legislative undertaking this really is and how little our present laws conform to the state of the empire generally. They have exhausted an innumerable people whose condition up to this time has been moving in the direction of disappearance rather than increase; the same holds true for its property."[38] Though aware of the difficulties, she clearly still hoped that her *Instruction* and commission would create a new legal code for the empire. There were no grounds for believing that her ostensible purpose merely concealed a desire to attack the Panin party.

What little is known of Nikita Panin's reaction to the *Instruction* indicates that he too did not perceive it as an attack. He simply regarded it as another document reflecting the reformist spirit of the new regime, and Panin thought of it as in some respect too reformist. He was one of the first persons to whom Catherine showed her original draft, and after reading it he declared: "Ce sont des axiomes à renverser des murailles."[39] Although this remark has been interpreted as a horrified response to Catherine's defense of absolutist monarchy,[40] its explanation should be sought in a different direction

[37]Catherine to Voltaire, 29 May 1767, *SIRIO*, 10: 204.
[38]Catherine to N. I. Panin, 31 May 1767, *Chteniia*, vol. 2, pt. 2, p. 26; see also her comments on the widespread poverty in Simbirsk, *loc. cit.*, p. 30.
[39]"Zapiska Ekateriny ob uchrezhdeniiakh" (1779), *SIRIO*, 27: 175.
[40]Sacke explained it in the following terms: "At the time of the completion of the

entirely. The draft of the *Instruction* read by Panin contained explicit statements about the need to reform serfdom, and given this context, Panin's remark would most logically be understood as a warning against the consequences of publicly favoring an improvement in the lot of the serfs. To be sure, his brother Peter had earlier proposed restrictions on serfdom, but he also admonished that they be kept *secret* and not announced through a public ukase.[41] Catherine's proposals were, by contrast, not only to be published and distributed to large numbers of delegates from every area of the empire, but they went much farther than Peter Panin's recommendations and even included references to the eventual abolition of serfdom. These were truly "axioms to break down walls." A cautious minister like Nikita Panin, the minister most responsible for the tranquility of the empire, certainly knew of the many peasant rebellions sparked by rumors and forged ukases.[42] He could scarcely help being shocked at the thought of public references inspired by the empress herself that alluded to the eventual abolition of serfdom.[43] Panin's comment, therefore, bespoke his concern not for Catherine's "conservative" governing principles but for her too-eager public profession of an enlightened policy. As events soon proved, the concern for agrarian unrest was fully justified. Rumors about the *Instruction*

Instruction, just as in 1762, Panin was the leader of an aristocratic group which stood in outright hostile opposition to Catherine's political plans. He must, therefore, have recognized that Catherine sought with her document above all to defend unlimited autocracy. A monarchy, however, in which a legislative and executive institution on the lines of the Imperial Council was not available to the ruler, a monarchy, in which the regulation of state business depended upon so unpredictable a factor as the personal characteristics of the ruler, could not according to Panin be secure from either the despotism of the official head of state or from the arbitrary rule of her favorites. This form of government could in no way satisfy the author of the [Imperial Council] "Project." [The *Instruction*'s] theoretical justification must, therefore, have appeared to him as "axiomes à renverser des murailles." "Katharina II. im Kampf um Thron und Selbstherrschaft," p. 211. This explanation ignores the obvious fact that Panin had for some time been serving, if not leading, a government in which "an institution on the lines of the Imperial Council was not available to the ruler." So long as he and his clients enjoyed favor he seemed perfectly content to dispense with such a council.

[41] Semevskii, *Krest'ianskii vopros v Rossii,* 1: 22–23; this view was shared by other leading senators. Beliavskii, *Krest'ianskii vopros v Rossii nakanune vosstaniia,* p. 154.

[42] For a discussion of this question, see M. T. Beliavskii, "Vopros o krepostnom prave i polozhenii krest'ian v Nakaze Ekateriny II," in *Vestnik Moskovskogo Universiteta,* no. 6 (1963), p. 59.

[43] His feelings were probably similar to those of Sumarokov, who warned that any move toward freeing the serfs would lead to a general upheaval. *SIRIO,* 10: 82–87.

and Catherine's acceptance of peasant petitions during her trip down the Volga in 1767 combined to trigger numerous peasant insurgencies.[44]

If evidence fails to support the contention that the *Instruction* was an attack on the Panins, a similar notion that the Legislative Commission was a challenge to them is even less convincing. In fact, one could argue with equal cogency that the Panins were the chief inspirers of the Legislative Commission. Since the first days of the regime, they had been pressing for a reform of the legal system. Catherine consulted with Nikita Panin at every stage in developing the *Instruction* and commission programs. In convening the commission, she referred specifically to the manifesto of July 6, 1762, written by Panin, and announced that the commission represented a fulfillment of her promise at that time to establish the administration on a firm legal foundation.[45] This looked more like a victory for the Panins' reform aspirations than an assault on their leadership position.

Consider also their participation in the commission and the events surrounding it. When it came time to choose deputies for the body, Peter Panin turned out to be the representative of the Moscow nobility. He was furthermore named to sit on the commission's "Directional Committee," the board responsible for compiling the proposed legal code.[46] At the same time Nikita Panin, though too busy to participate as a deputy in the commission, took on the important preliminary task of composing the instructions for the Moscow assembly of nobles,[47] an undertaking that in no way dimin-

---

[44]John T. Alexander, *Autocratic Politics*, pp. 35–36.

[45]"From the day of Our accession to the throne to this day, We have pursued a single aim and have considered it Our duty toward God himself to fulfill what We had most solemnly promised on Our imperial word in Our manifesto of the sixth of July 1762," read the first paragraph of the decree establishing the Legislative Commission. *PSZ*, 17: no. 12801. See also Catherine's personal note on origin of the idea, cited in Solov'ev, *Istoriia Rossii*, 13: 498.

[46]Beliavskii, *Krest'ianskii vopros v Rossii nakanune vosstaniia*, pp. 248, 358. He was also elected to serve in a special delegation to express the Commission's gratitude to the empress. *RBS*, 13: 220; Dreyer to Copenhagen, 11 March 1768, *DRa*, TKUA, Russland A III 96, no. 11.

[47]The Danish envoy Asseburg, whose long personal friendship with Panin made him a particularly reliable witness, wrote: "Mr. le general de Panin a été nommé Depute de la noblesse du District de Moscou pour la Diete de Legislation, et Mr. le Grand Maitre Son frere a eu charge de dresser les Instructions dont il sera muni." Asseburg to Copenhagen, 22 March 1767, *DRa*, TKUA, Russland A III 85, no. 117; N. I. Panin to Catherine:

ished his ordinary responsibilities. He continued to manage all important affairs including foreign policy and supervision over the grand duke. About the same time (summer 1767) when Catherine was making her trip down the Volga, she left responsibility for matters of state in Panin's hands, while they discussed and decided current business through a daily exchange of letters.[48] This correspondence showed their relations to be characterized by a high degree of trust and intimate cooperation.

Further evidence of the Panin party's favor at this time appeared in Catherine's choice for Marshal of the Legislative Commission, A. I. Bibikov. Bibikov was a close friend and associate of long standing of both Panin brothers, one of the chief supporters of Nikita Panin's policies, and a person who must be counted as solidly in the Panin camp.[49]

One must certainly ask why, if Catherine were truly acting against the Panin party, she nevertheless maintained the Panins and their friends in their former positions and ranks, and even gave them important offices within the Legislative Commission. If that was not a sufficient mark of her trust and esteem, soon after the opening of the commission she raised both Panin brothers to the dignity of count.[50] Moreover, Catherine's satisfaction with Nikita Panin's service did not lessen during the months the commission sat. Toward the end of its proceedings, she granted him an outright gift of 50,000 rubles and increased his yearly spending allowance by 7,000 rubles.[51] This would be a curious method indeed of undermining the power of one's enemies.

The fact of the matter was that far from viewing the commission

---

"... I spent the entire morning in the assembly of nobles of this city of Moscow for the composition of the Instruction to the deputy," 1 May 1767, *GBL*, *f.* Barsk. XVIa, *d.* 29, 212; in another letter from the same collection Panin referred to his efforts to bring together in his instruction various points presented by the nobles. 9 June 1767, *loc. cit.*, p. 242. Also see Rossignol to Choiseul, 10 August 1767, *SIRIO*, 141: 331–32.

[48]Asseburg to Copenhagen, 20 May 1767, *DRa*, TKUA, Russland A III 85, no. 124; Catherine to N. I. Panin, 2 May 1767, *Chteniia*, vol. 2, pt. 2, p. 16.

[49]Bibikov, *Zapiski o zhizni i sluzhbe*, pp. 5, 11; *AKV*, 33: appendix, p. 22; Alexander, *Autocratic Politics*, p. 69.

[50]Petrov, *Istoriia rodov russkogo dvorianstva*, 1: 302.

[51]Dreyer to Copenhagen, 1 April 1768, *DRa*, TKUA, Russland A III 86, nos. 15, 16; other reports confirm that Panin's credit had never been higher. Shirley to Conway, 15 November 1767; Shirley to Weymouth, 28 February 1768 and 29 July 1768; *SIRIO*, 12: 323, 328–29, 335–37.

as a threat or challenge, the Panins seemed to look on it as an opportunity, the chance to realize some of the reform ambitions that had accompanied the new regime's coming to power. This attitude would certainly explain the Panins' active participation in the Moscow assembly of nobles. The two brothers guided the assembly's proceedings from beginning to end. As deputy of the Moscow nobility Peter Panin was given broad discretion in his charge of representing the assembly's views to the commission.[52] The instruction defining those views, while it undoubtedly included suggestions by other nobles of the province, was composed almost entirely by Nikita Panin and bore the unmistakable imprint of his ideas about the needs and desires of the Russian nobility.

As an important clue to Panin thinking at this time, the Moscow assembly instruction deserves a close examination. It not only reiterates the Panins' ideas about the nobility's needs and makes clear how much these ideas were conditioned by their position of social and political leadership; it also reveals their attitudes as representatives of the educated, westernized, bureaucratic elite toward participation in government by their less distinguished noble brethren. This knowledge, seen in the context of the demands of the rank-and-file nobility at the commission, will provide the background for analyzing the differences between Catherine's and the Panins' perceptions of Russia's needs.

4. Moscow Assembly Instruction

The first thing that strikes one about this document is its similarity with Panin's earlier report for the Commission on Noble Freedom. Again he emphasized the need to define once and for all the privileges of the nobility as an estate. The opening article of the Moscow assembly instruction asked the legislators to determine precisely what those privileges were, who may dispose of them, and how persons not of the nobility might acquire that distinction. Thereafter, in the manner of the noble freedom report, the author concentrated chiefly on property questions.[53] Among other things, he recommended finding sensible means for dividing inherited property without splitting up villages, ending ambiguity in transfers by marriage or to collateral relations so as to avoid the usual inter-

[52]*SIRIO*, 4: 226.
[53]Seven of the ten general articles dealt with real property.

minable litigation surrounding such affairs, and similar tightening of laws concerning property settlements in a divorce. Echoing a defunct 1737 law he much admired, Panin further cited the need for a strict statute of limitations on all property settlements.[54] The same objective appeared in his one article about peasants, which called for the final abolition of the *pistsovye knigi* of the early seventeenth century and establishment of the 1719 census as the standard for determining the ownership of serfs.[55] Although Panin went into detail in asking for regulation of these matters, the ideas themselves were scarcely exceptional and appeared in many other nobiliary instructions.

Much more significant was his attention to the right of entail, the longest article of the entire instruction. Characteristically, Panin brought to bear the authority of Peter the Great, who had decried the custom of dividing estates equally among heirs. Peter regarded this practice as the primary cause of the impoverishment of noble families, increasing burdens on the peasantry, and squandering of state resources. Following the example of well-regulated European states, Panin noted, Peter had issued a decree on March 24, 1714, ordering entailment of all family estates. Owing to its severe demands, the law soon ran up against the stubborn resistance of traditional attitudes, which brought about its repeal in 1731.[56] Panin insisted that Peter's objectives nevertheless remained valid. He advised that the law be resurrected in a slightly modified form that would allow landowners to place at least a portion of their holdings in entail while leaving the rest to be disposed of in the customary manner. "In this way," he explained, "the intent and benefit to the state sought by the provisions of the 1714 decree could be more precisely achieved."[57]

This recommendation, which had also appeared in the Panin-led

---

[54]Panin commented favorably on the law in an evaluation of the life work of its author, I. I. Nepliuev. Poroshin, *Zapiski,* 22 November 1764; Panin's remarks allow identification of the law as the decree of 1 August 1737, on disposal of mortgaged properties, *PSZ,* 10: no. 7339, repealed on 14 August 1740; *PSZ,* 11: no. 8206.

[55]The 13 May 1754 law to this effect had evidently gone unheeded.

[56]*SIRIO,* 4: 228–29; for the 1714 law see *PSZ,* 5: no. 2789; the 1730 repeal decree stated some of the reasons for its failure, *PSZ,* 8: no. 5653; for other reasons, see N. P. Pavlov-Sil'vanskii, *Gosudarevy sluzhilye liudi* (St. Petersburg, 1898), pp. 264–66.

[57]Panin distinguished three categories of property: familial estates or land acquired by direct inheritance, land acquired from a relative who died childless, and land acquired by special grant or purchase. A landlord could choose to entail any one of these types, but only one. *SIRIO,* 4: 228–29.

commission on noble freedom four years earlier, clearly set the Moscow assembly instruction apart. Of the 161 nobiliary instructions submitted to the Legislative Commission only Panin's and two others, also influenced by men of the bureaucratic elite, included a request for reviving the 1714 law on entail.[58] This fact bespoke the isolation of the educated, western-oriented elite from the aspirations of the vast majority of Russian noblemen, who saw no reason to abandon the traditional practice of providing for all their sons. Only the affluent, western-educated, politically motivated court nobles appreciated the advantages in economic power and corporate cohesion that would accrue from such a measure. If the Russian nobility was going to develop into a self-conscious corporate group like their western counterparts, measures had to be introduced to bring stability into the estate. Panin had already advised raising the standards for entrance into the nobility.[59] Another condition for producing stability was the opportunity of holding family properties intact through several generations; hence, the insistence on entail and clear definitions of qualifications for nobility.

Panin's instruction revealed the attitudes of the bureaucratic elite in less explicit ways as well. For example, instructions from other noble assemblies frequently complained of merchant serf holding and economic competition from merchants.[60] The Moscow instruction had nothing to say about these matters. Panin asked only that nobles have the right to engage in trade and manufacture (article 10). He did not want a special position for them and, in fact, insisted that nobles should be subject to the same rules and restrictions applied to all others engaged in enterprise.[61] The Moscow instruction also differed from others on the matter of electing local officials from the nobility. This had been a contentious issue during the earlier commission on noble freedom, in which Bestuzhev favored local election of nobles for provincial administration, a proposal defeated by the Panin-led majority. Now in the Legislative Commission a large number of noble instructions argued for the introduction of locally

[58]Paul Dukes, *Catherine the Great and the Russian Nobility* (Cambridge, 1967), pp. 161, 183; one might add to these the instruction of Kopor'e district, St. Petersburg *guberniia*, which included great landowners like Sievers and Chernyshev. Augustine, "Notes Toward a Portrait of the Eighteenth-Century Russian Nobility," p. 401.

[59]In 1763 commission report. Kulomzin, "Pervyi pristup," p. 37.

[60]Dukes, *Catherine the Great*, pp. 133–34.

[61]*SIRIO*, 4: 229–30.

elected officials. Although there were many variants in the degree of authority proposed for the elected offices, some suggestions went so far as to undermine altogether the power of the centrally appointed provincial governor.[62] In contrast, the Panin instruction, while this time agreeing to local election, narrowly restricted the scope of such "commissars." They should be allowed only to settle small disputes between nobles, investigate and report on breaches of the law, and see to the quartering of visiting troops. In other words, they should be no more than errand boys for the governor.[63]

These proposals clearly reflected the outlook of the westernized bureaucratic elite. They were interested in the overall development of the economy and did not want it hamstrung by special concessions that would weaken the established commercial groups. The idea was again to allow everyone capable and enterprising an opportunity to develop the productive capacity of the country. Second, Panin showed no sympathy for turning responsibility at the local level over to the provincial nobility. Such a policy would merely rob the central authorities of the power to control provincial administration, and the court elite naturally associated its interests with the central administration. Moreover, increased authority on the local level would permit the provincial nobility to intensify its exploitation of the serfs, the very thing Panin wanted to avoid by stricter government regulation of serf-lord relations.

Very revealing as well was the Panins' concern for the position of the central administration and general coordination of government action at the top. This came out quite clearly in the preamble to the Moscow instruction, which was evidently meant to serve as a guideline and admonition to other noble assemblies. It read that the Moscow assembly intended to present its needs to the throne "without touching in any way on general state institutions and statutes which require joint agreement *(soiuznoe soglasie)* regarding the various branches of the state administration and the peoples subject to it, nor [touching on] the state economy . . . which ought always to be regulated and governed by the central power."[64] This passage and other similar admonitions in the Moscow assembly instruction have been variously interpreted as everything from apathy toward

---

[62]Got'e, *Istoriia oblastnogo upravleniia*, 2: 201–08.
[63]*SIRIO*, 4: 230.
[64]*SIRIO*, 4: 227, and similar references, p. 226.

participation at the center to an attempt at prior censorship, the implication being that the censorship was imposed by the empress.[65] If historians had known of Panin's authorship, they would have better understood the import of these admonitions. The passages undoubtedly represented a form of censorship, but scarcely one imposed by the empress alone. The appearance of the guidelines in the Moscow assembly instruction and no others indicated that Catherine was not trying to restrain the Panins from touching on questions of the central government so much as the Panins themselves were warning the rank-and-file nobility to stay clear of matters that were the sole province of the bureaucratic elite. This jealousy in guarding elite prerogatives may likewise explain Nikita Panin's efforts to block participation in the Legislative Commission by the celebrated French jurist Mercier de la Rivière, whom Catherine had invited to Russia.[66]

5. Divergent Perceptions of Catherine and the Panins

While it is not clear whether the Panins hoped to turn the Legislative Commission to advantage or merely to keep it under control, the commission's impact on Catherine proved to be at variance with either of these expectations. This exposure to the views of a large number of rank-and-file nobles had the effect of freeing her from exclusive reliance upon the opinions of the court elite and brought her to the realization that she had to consider the role of the nobility as a whole from a different angle than the Panins. They viewed this issue from the standpoint of the bureaucratic elite, men who were western in education and outlook and who had come to regard the central state as their special preserve. Championing a modified version of the Vorontsov program of the past regime, they sought to distinguish a leadership stratum within the nobility consisting of men who through birth, education, and rank had earned the right to occupy the highest

[65]Indication of censorship in Veretennikov, "K istorii sostavleniia nakazov v Ekaterininskuiu komissiiu," in *Zapiski Khar'kovskogo Universiteta* (1911), no. 4, p. 7; indication of apathy in Dukes, *Catherine the Great*, pp. 177–78, where the author, oddly enough, set the passage in contrast with Panin's council project, evidently not realizing that Panin also wrote the Moscow instruction. For discussion of censorship in commission debates, see Knorring, "Ekaterininskaia zakonodatel'naia komissiia," p. 341.

[66]Panin's treatment of Mercier and the entire espisode connected with his visit to Russia has occupied an important place in the gentry opposition thesis debate. For a review of that case, see my article "Catherine II's Instruction to the Commission on Laws," pp. 24–27.

government posts.[67] More will be said about this in later chapters. It should, nevertheless, be pointed out here that this view more or less arbitrarily excluded the vast majority of Russian noblemen from consideration for a place in the kind of noble estate in which the Panins were interested.

Education was the most important qualification, and in the eighteenth century no less than today it was not cheap. Meeting the minimal standards of training for the elite normally required the services of a tutor in the home and involved considerable expense. Confino has reckoned the minimum cost of supporting an average noble family plus a tutor in 1795 at 2,700 rubles a year.[68] As the following tables on noble serfholding and rent income demonstrate,[69]

TABLE I. Percentage distribution of landowners according to the number of serfs in their possession in 1762 and 1777

Number of serfs per noble household	Percentage of landowners in 1762	Percentage of landowners in 1777
Fewer than 20	51	59
21–100	31	25
101–500	15	13
501–1000	2	2
Over 1000	1	1

TABLE II. Income of landowners in 1777 and 1795 based on the 1777 percentage distribution of landowners by number of serfs held

Percentage of landowners	Rent income in 1777	Rent income in 1795
32.0	Less than 35 rubles	Less than 50 rubles
30.7	35 to 105	50 to 150
13.4	105 to 210	150 to 300
7.7	210 to 350	300 to 500
5.0	350 to 525	500 to 750
11.2	More than 525	More than 750

that sum constituted the revenue from 540 revision souls, an income that (if one counts only revenue from serfholding) was beyond the reach of 95% of the Russian nobility.[70] In fact, well over 80%, those

[67]Raeff gives a fairly accurate summary of this view in *Origins*, pp. 102–06, although he makes too sharp a distinction between the aristocratic party and the bureaucratic elite.

[68]Confino, "A propos de la noblesse russe," pp. 1194–98.

[69]Tables are the work of Arcadius Kahan, "The Costs of 'Westernization,' " *Structure of Russian History*, ed., Michael Cherniavsky (New York, 1970), pp. 227–29, presented here as adapted in Confino, "A propos de la noblesse russe," pp. 1194, 1198.

[70]The study of noble wealth is only in its very beginnings, and these figures must be

with 100 serfs or less, were living on the very edge of impoverishment, quite unable to provide their sons with a good education, travel abroad, or a style of life appropriate to a nobleman. In the Russia of Catherine the Great only about 1000 families disposed of sufficient wealth to avail themselves of such opportunities, and it was to these families that the Panins' vision of the nobility applied.

Of course, these figures do not tell the whole story. Men of lesser means sometimes managed to obtain a superior education and climbed the ladders of imperial favor and party hierarchy to the highest ranks. The Panin party itself lifted a number of them, including several commoners, just as the Panin brothers had been helped early in their careers by their marital connections with the Kurakins and Nepliuevs. There was likewise a heavy attrition among the top 1000 families conditioned by division of inheritance, profligacy, and the imposition of disgrace, arrest, and confiscation, such that while the overall number remained fairly constant throughout the pre-emancipation period (about 870 families in the top 1% in 1834), only about 150 (ca. 17%) maintained themselves in the highest social ranks during the entire period. Considering the degree of turnover, it is easy to understand why the Panins wanted to stabilize the elite by upgrading the standards for acquiring nobility, introducing entail, and other similar measures. Of course, even if they had obtained these changes, they would only have stabilized the criteria for the elite and not the personnel. The turnover rate may not been have diminished. The Panins, for example, saw no contradiction in advancing their own clients from lower positions; such men presumably had exceptional merit by virtue of their attachment

---

viewed accordingly. Rent income from serfs was unquestionably the largest aggregate source of income for the nobility. But salaries, timber or mineral rights, government "loans" (often not repaid), and other such things were in some cases a supplement, in others the principal income of an individual nobleman. Likewise estimates of the cost of education for noblemen vary greatly. Confino's figure of 300 rubles for a tutor seems high; Kahan evidently uses a much lower figure. He also notes that in schools during the last decades of the century tuition plus room and board ran to about 150 rubles per noble student, and part of this expenditure was borne by government subsidies. Confino bases his figure of 2,700 rubles on a family of eight members.

No strict correlation between number of serfs and educational level can be established. For a significant contribution toward establishing a method to determine disparities in wealth and opportunity among the nobility, see Rex Rexheuser, "Besitzverhältnisse des russischen Adels im 18. Jahrhundert" (Inaugural Diss., Friedrich Alexander University, Erlangen-Nürnberg, 1971).

to the Panins. Other powerful patrons acted in the same manner. Finally, imperial favor accounted for a large part of the upward mobility,[71] and it could scarcely be subjected to the same criteria as bureaucratic promotion, at least not without undermining the autocratic authority on which the Panins' own power depended.

To return to the broader question of the role of the nobility as a whole, the empress could not lightly discount 95% of the estate. It constituted the social pillar on which autocracy and serf Russia ultimately rested. The nobiliary instructions and the debates in the Legislative Commission made her see more clearly than before the considerable gulf separating the aspirations of the bureaucratic elite and their rank-and-file brethren. She could observe, for example, the marked lack of interest on the part of the lesser nobility in such things as guarantees of residence abroad, service in foreign armies, and entailment of estates. Consider especially the matter of entail. Even if members of the lesser and middle nobility had been able to observe the West European gentry and weigh the possible benefits of an entail law, they would scarcely have wished to give up the minimal sustenance and status maintenance afforded by their small share of a small estate. They lacked the wealth, training, and opportunity to pursue successful careers in commerce or industry, and the Orthodox Church offered neither the wealth nor the prestige to provide an outlet for dispossessed younger sons. Under such circumstances, an entailing law could only appear as a threat. Still more ominous was the desire of the enlightened western-oriented nobles for government regulation of serfdom. The least mention of this possibility in the Legislative Commission raised a cry of indignation from all but a handful of the noble deputies. In fact, during the time the commission was sitting the authorities uncovered a number of conspiracies aimed at overthrowing the empress, the reasons given being the anti-nobility acts of the commission, including most prominently the proposals to regulate serfholding. The participants in one of these plots hoped to replace Catherine with Prince M. M. Shcherbatov, the leading spokesman for noble privilege.[72] Catherine was understand-

---

[71]For further discussion of these points, see my article "Bureaucracy and Patronage: The View from an Eighteenth-Century Russian Letter-Writer."

[72]G. V. Vernadskii, "Imperatritsa Ekaterina II i zakonodatel'naia komissiia," in *Sbornik Obshchestva Istorii i Sotsial'nykh Nauk pri Permskom Universitete,* vol. 1 (1918), pp. 1–23; *idem, Ocherk istorii prava russkogo gosudarstva* (Prague, 1924), pp. 23–24.

ably alarmed by the deep social antagonisms expressed at the commission,[73] and she soon realized that she could only accede to the
wishes of the westernized court nobles like the Panins at the risk of
incurring the enmity of the broad ranks of middle and lesser noblemen. So from this point forward Catherine relied less and less on the
Panin party's advice on domestic reform and gave greater consideration to the desires of their less exalted noble brethren.

While it is safe to say that the commission experiment made
Catherine aware of the impossibility of creating a new, not to mention
enlightened, legal code amid the bitter conflicts of the estates, there
is some dispute over her motivations in closing the Great Assembly of
deputies in December 1768 soon after the outbreak of war with
Turkey. Most historians believe that Catherine found the war to be a
convenient pretext to end the dangerous commission debates. She
seized the opprtunity with a great sense of relief and never intended to
reconvene the deputies.[74] All further work on legislative reform was
turned over to the commission's small and socially homogeneous
bureaucratic committees, where it could proceed more safely and
productively. On the other hand, as Kerry Morrison has pointed out,
there was really no possibility of continuing the commission debates
after December 1768. Nearly four of every five deputies held military
commissions and had to leave immediately for the front. Furthermore, Catherine expressed her desire in several subsequent decrees to
reconvene the full commission.[75] It is possible, of course, that these
professions were simply meant to quiet criticism from liberal journalists about the hasty abandonment of the legislative experiment. In
any event, Catherine failed to reassemble the commission and worked
out her later reforms during the 1770s and 1780s unassisted by
representatives of the estates.

6. Decline of the Panin Influence

The experience of the Legislative Commission and the outbreak of
the Turkish war together marked a turning point in the fortunes

[73]See her letter to the Marshal of the Commission A. I. Bibikov in A. A. Bibikov,
Zapiski o zhizni i sluzhbe, pp. 56–57.

[74]Firsov's comment was typical: "Catherine brought the great social conflicts of the
time into one large assembly, and Russia began to speak. The effect on the empress was
shocking, and having brought this capsule of social struggle into being, all she could do was
close it as soon as possible." *Petr III i Ekaterina II,* p. 102.

[75]Morrison, "Catherine II's Legislative Commission," pp. 480–81.

of the Panin party. The implications of the differences revealed in the commission were long range in nature and will be treated more fully in subsequent chapters. The war had immediate consequences for Nikita Panin's leadership, because in this area he bore the greatest responsibility. His policies had not left Russia in a good position to fight a major conflict in the south.

The Northern Accord foreign policy worked out by Panin had failed to mature. Pursuing basically conservative and defensive aims, Panin had sought to weld an alliance among Russia, Prussia, England, Poland, Saxony, and the Scandinavian powers. This north European bloc was to act as a counterweight to the Hapsburg-Bourbon alliance that emerged during the Seven Years' War. Panin sketched out the plan very well on paper. Russia, Prussia, Denmark, and England were to be the "active" powers, while under their leadership Sweden, Poland, and Saxony would serve as more or less passive partners. In time, however, Poland, too, would be given a more important role to play: it would replace Austria as Russia's chief ally against Turkey. But first some changes had to be made. The French influence at Warsaw would be curtailed and certain reforms made in Poland's governing order, such as abolishing the *liberum veto* and in other ways increasing monarchical authority. In Panin's view, a stable Poland would be a good ally, a buffer toward the west, and no threat to the now-powerful Russian Empire.[76]

Although this scheme looked good on the drawing boards, its practical realization proved to be extremely difficult. Panin managed to obtain defensive alliances with Denmark and Prussia, as these two powers had a great deal to gain in joining with Russia. Panin even succeeded in the less certain task of placing the Russian candidate Stanislaw Poniatowski on the Polish throne. After that, matters became more problematical. England agreed only to sign a commercial treaty and held aloof from political commitments. Sweden cost the Russian government dearly in bribe money just to maintain an uneasy neutrality, and the whole effort finally collapsed when a

[76]The two standard works on the Northern Accord are N. D. Chechulin, *Vneshniaia politika Rossii v nachale tsarstvovaniia Ekateriny II, 1762–74* (St. Petersburg, 1895), and P. A. Aleksandrov, *Severnaia sistema* (Moscow, 1914), the second being a rebuttal of Chechulin's central theme. More recent reviews include E. I. Druzhinina, *Kiuchuk-Kainardzhiiskii mir 1774 goda* (Moscow, 1955), especially pp. 84–89, and the very thorough treatment by David Griffiths, "Russian Court Politics and the Question of an Expansionist Foreign Policy under Catherine II, 1762–1783" (Ph.D. diss., Cornell University, 1967).

royalist coup brought a return of a pro-French absolutism in 1772.[77] Unquestionably the most difficult aspect of the whole scheme was Poland. Beyond the initial success with Poniatowski's election, everything the Russians attempted in Poland turned sour. Efforts to improve Poland's internal order met with stubborn resistance not only from native Poles but even from Russia's most important ally, Prussia. Frederick II preferred a weak, strife-ridden Poland and refused to go along with abolishing the *liberum veto*. The greater the chaos in Poland, the greater Frederick's chances for uniting his eastern territories by annexing intervening Polish lands. Native Catholic patriots resisted change, because reform threatened to bring an equalization of political and religious rights for Orthodox and Lutheran dissidents. When Russia finally tried to force the issue of civil rights for the dissidents in 1768, the Catholics formed into confederacies and plunged the country into the civil war that, more than any other factor, was responsible for drawing Russia into the conflict with Turkey.

The Turks had long viewed Russian actions in Poland with apprehension. They refused to recognize the election of Poniatowski, fearing it was part of a plot to unify the Polish and Russian crowns. They lodged numerous protests against Russian interference in Polish domestic affairs. Then, as the chaos in Poland deepened and military actions among the confederacies and Russian troops spread, a contingent of Russian Cossack irregulars breached the Ottoman Empire's border at Balta in September 1768 and put the town's inhabitants to the sword.[78] This direct injury, coming on top of a long string of Russian actions already viewed with abhorrence by the Porte, gave the war party in Constantinople the upper hand. The following month Turkey announced the opening of hostilities against Russia.

Until this time Catherine had given her full support to Panin's conduct of foreign affairs. Although personal enemies like Bestuzhev, Golitsyn, and the Chernyshevs had continued to snipe at him throughout the mid 1760s, the empress quickly squelched any intrigues against Panin's leadership. Now, however, with Panin's system in evident disarray, she was ready to listen to other opinions. One of

[77]E. Amburger, *Russland und Schweden 1762–1772* (Berlin, 1934), presents a thorough review of this question.

[78]Alan Fisher, *The Russian Annexation of the Crimea* (Cambridge, 1970), pp. 29–32.

the first signs of change was the recall of Panin's protégé N.V. Repnin as minister in Warsaw and his replacement by an Orlov client M. N. Volkonskii. About the same time (November 1768) the empress asked Panin to advise her on the formation of a state council to deal with questions of the war and foreign policy. As may be imagined, Panin did not respond favorably to the idea, which meant sharing leadership with his enemies. From being a champion of the state council idea in 1762, he now tried his best to dissuade Catherine from such a course.[79] His objections notwithstanding, the council came into being in January 1769 and included, in addition to Nikita Panin and his brother Peter, Kirill Razumovskii, Zakhar Chernyshev, Alexander Golitsyn, Grigorii Orlov, and Alexander Viazemskii, men unsympathetic to the Northern Accord policy. It must have been a hard blow for Nikita Panin. Even though he played a leading role in the council, his policies and actions were for the first time subject to immediate scrutiny and criticism by his opponents. At the opening council meeting his new colleagues rose to inquire, no doubt with a certain malicious satisfaction, whether Russia had any workable policy with regard to Turkey or any reliable allies.[80] It was not an easy question to answer. Panin's hoped-for ally, Poland, was not only torn by civil strife but was currently tying down substantial Russian forces in a futile pacification effort. England and Denmark held aloof. And Prussia was neither able nor committed to offer any more than subsidies. Under Panin's system Russia was very much on its own against Turkey.

In the final analysis, it was not the Northern Accord but the un-aided actions of the Russian army that saved Russia from Turkey. Although Panin had probably not counted on such an outcome, events demonstrated that Russia no longer required a strong ally in

[79]On Panin's opposition see above, chapter 5, section 5. Judging from the exchange between Catherine and Panin quoted there, the empress intended to establish a regular permanent council. It may, therefore, have been a partial victory for Panin that she set up only a temporary institution to deal with the war (although, to be sure, the council turned out to be more permanent than anyone at the time expected, lasting until the beginning of Alexander I's reign in 1801). Instructions and procedures in *PSZ*, 18: nos. 13232, 13233.

[80]*AGS*, 1, see also S. R. Vorontsov's evaluation of the change at this point in *AKV*, 10: 398–400; the British and French representatives likewise noted the sharp decline in Panin's credit and the emergence for the first time of serious challenges from his enemies. Cathcart to Rochford, 9 and 12 December 1768, *SIRIO*, 12: 411–12; Rossignol to Choiseul, 6 December 1768, *SIRIO*, 141: 495.

the south. So long as the western powers remained neutral, Russia could easily manage both Turkey and Poland, albeit at considerable cost of time and resources.

Russia's stunning victories in the Balkans yielded two contradictory effects. In the short run, they salvaged Panin's foreign policy system and made possible its continuation through the next decade. In the long run, however, they undermined that same system. The success of Russian arms awakened dreams of vast territorial conquest and imperial aggrandizement at the expense of the Turks. Visions of reestablishing the Byzantine Empire and the Kingdom of Dacia under Russian aegis were born in the victories of the first Turkish war, and these extravagant plans implied the liquidation of the status-quo oriented Northern Accord. Specifically, they required the cooperation of Austria. Hence, although Panin's policies and leadership continued through the 1770s, they did so with ever-diminishing authority and influence, while the ground was prepared for the shift to a pro-Austrian orientation culminating with the signing of a formal treaty of alliance in 1781. By that time Nikita Panin would be in self-imposed retirement. He left for his estate at Dugino in Smolensk Guberniia early that year in protest of the new policy, and no one bothered to recall him to the capital.[81]

His brother Peter broke with Catherine much earlier while the first Turkish war was still in progress. In 1769 he left the capital to take command of the Second Army and lay siege to the Turkish fortress Bendery. The next summer's campaign brought the fall of the previously impregnable bastion, but, unfortunately for Panin, this unprecedented conquest was overshadowed by the even more brilliant victories of General Rumiantsev's First Army that was covering the siege to the southwest. In recognition, Catherine awarded Rumiantsev a field marshal's baton, while Panin had to settle for the first rank of St. George. The personal rancor between Catherine and Peter Panin as well as his bickering over allocations for the two armies undoubtedly played a part in this slight to his dignity.[82] In

[81]The phasing out of the Northern System is traced in great detail by Griffiths, "Russian Court Politics and Expansionist Foreign Policy," chapters 4 through 9.

[82]Iu. R. Klokman, *Fel'dmarshal Rumiantsev*, (Moscow, 1951) pp. 74–87; Rumiantsev was the first to rush to Peter Panin's defense, and he stressed the enormous difficulties Panin had overcome in the siege. See his letter to N. I. Panin, 24 September 1770, *GPB f.* 563, no. 2. On Catherine's dissatisfaction with Peter Panin, see Geisman and Dubovskoi, *Graf Petr Ivanovich Panin*, pp. 45–46, 57; also note 85 below.

response, he immediately resigned his commission and retired in a huff to his Mikhalskoe estate near Moscow. The ostensible reason for his departure was the flare-up of intense headaches, side effects of wounds received in the Seven Years' War. As his letters during the Bendery siege indicate, he did indeed suffer constant debilitating pains for several months prior to his decision to leave the service. So he did not, as some historians suggest, simply dream up this excuse when he learned of Rumiantsev's promotion.[83] Nevertheless, he was definitely piqued at Catherine's refusal to grant him similar recognition.[84] On returning to Moscow, he became the center of the so-called "Moscow opposition," a collection of disgruntled nobles and former officeholders who devoted their leisure to carping criticism of the St. Petersburg court. His verbal barbs against the corruption and favoritism of Catherine's court were evidently very effective. He more than once provoked the empress to rail about "that big loudmouth" and "personal insulter." On at least one occasion she threatened to silence him by forceful means if necessary.[85]

The deterioration of the Panin party's position at the end of the 1760s dictated new tactics in the struggle for influence and control. There was no reason to consider a coup d'etat or as yet even to advance proposals for government reorganization as in 1762. Nikita Panin was after all still the leading government minister, even if he now had to share his authority with others. Moreover, several of his clients continued to occupy important posts, and any precipitous action would only serve to place them in jeopardy. These considerations as well as Panin's cautious nature convinced him to stay in office and operate within the established political framework to recapture the empress' confidence and goodwill. But now he had to

---

[83]Lebedev, *Grafy Paniny,* pp. 87–88; Pigarev, *Tvorchestvo Fonvizina,* p. 114. Peter Panin's letters to Nikita Panin, 9 October, 5 November, 2, 11, and 22 December 1769, *GBL, f.* Pan XV 5, 1, 17, 26–27, 30–31, 32–35; and letters of 23 February, 29 March, 3, 10, and 18 April, 3 July, *GBL, f.* Pan XV 6, 32, 44, 46, 57, and *f.* Pan XV 7, 9, 21–22. All bear his complaints of severe head pains as well as immobility from gout.

[84]The clearest commentary comes in a letter from his relative Princess Agrafena Kurakina to A. B. Kurakin, 7 February 1771, saying that in the last letter "I told you of uncle Peter Ivanovich's retirement . . . through it he merely carried out a whim of the side of him that tolerates no one and that is dissatisfied with everything on earth, and which makes him forever unhappy and leads us all to grief." *Arkhiv Kurakina,* 6: 273.

[85]See the correspondence between Catherine and the Moscow Governor-General M. N. Volkonskii, *Osmnadtsatyi vek,* 1: 96, 105; Catherine to G. A. Potemkin, July 1774, *SIRIO,* 13: 420.

employ means that were not previously part of his political repertory. As events soon revealed, he was not above using his own candidate for the imperial bedchamber to separate Catherine from the Orlov group and advance his own position with the empress.

Most important, Nikita Panin was still governor of Grand Duke Paul, a position that afforded considerable advantages not only in reinforcing his current position but also as a guarantee of a future opportunity to fulfill the party's reform aspirations. The independent political base Panin commanded from the "young court," not to mention his apparently strong paternal affection for the grand duke, nourished hopes that the party might reestablish its political dominance when Paul came into his majority in 1772. Since Panin's role as *oberhofmeister* constituted an important element in the party's cohesion and influence, it would be well to examine this aspect of Catherinian politics in some detail.

8

Oberhofmeister Panin

Despite Nikita Panin's many duties in the central government, he always regarded as crucial the office of *oberhofmeister* or governor to the grand duke. From his return to St. Petersburg in 1760 until Paul's marriage in 1773 Panin's leadership of the "young court" provided the secure foundation of his political career and the greatest hope of his party for continued influence. He refused to accept any official post that might appear in conflict with the *oberhofmeister* office. As early as 1761 the Shuvalovs tried unsuccessfully to dislodge him with an offer of the vice-chancellorship. On assuming leadership of foreign affairs two years later, he remained at the second rank with the designation "senior member" of the Foreign Affairs Collegium and left the title of chancellor to the exiled Vorontsov. After the latter's death in 1767, the Orlovs tried to tempt Panin into accepting the chancellorship, but he again refused. Although his admirers explained that he was "above the dignity and does not choose to accept it," it seems rather that he knew of the Orlovs' plans to use the promotion as a pretext for removing him as *oberhofmeister*.[1] Only after the grand duke's majority when his job of governor necessarily ended, did Panin finally move up to the post of "minister of Foreign Affairs" with a rank equal to that of chancellor.[2]

[1]Guyot to Choiseul, 15 July and 28 August 1767, *SIRIO*, 141: 325, 341; Macartney to Sandwich, 18 March 1765, *SIRIO*, 12: 203. It seems the Orlovs wanted to make I. I. Shuvalov governor. They may have chosen their candidate poorly, as Catherine had not been pleased with Shuvalov's behavior during his honorable exile in Europe. Bartenev, "I. I. Shuvalov," *Russkaia Beseda* (1857), no. 1, pp. 58–59.

[2]This case provides a good example of the general confusion about Panin's personal history. Two recent dissertations, otherwise excellent works, confound the meaning of this promotion. Brenda Meehan, "The Russian Generalitet of 1730" (Ph. D. diss., University of Rochester, 1970), p. 72, relates that he was given the "title" of actual privy counselor (a *rank* he had held since the early 1760s) but with the first rank. David Griffiths, "Russian Court Politics," p. 18, says that after October 1773 Panin was listed as Minister of Foreign Affairs, whereas before he had no formal state title. In fact Panin had since 1760 borne the office of *oberhofmeister* and the rank of actual privy counselor. In 1767 he was

The attractions of the governorship were several. In an aristocratic value system reputation counted for as much as wealth and official rank, and employment as governor to the heir carried considerable repute. After the imperial family, the governor was the most esteemed figure at court. It was understood that he commanded great learning and experience as well as the autocrat's confidence. Society looked upon him as the guardian of its wellbeing in years to come; his wisdom would mold the character of the future sovereign. Moreover, the position usually gave its bearer a large measure of independence. He administered the "young court" with an authority analogous to the ruler's in the imperial court. He chose and directed a considerable clientele of tutors, librarians, doctors, technicians, and servants, all appointed and retained at his discretion. In Panin's case this authority was reinforced by Empress Elizabeth's official charge to him in 1761. "In order that you would meet with no hindrance in arranging this important matter of state entrusted to you and in which you are alone responsible before God, Us and the Fatherland, Our desire is that no one be allowed to interfere in it and that you should be solely dependent upon Our personal orders, such that in all cases where anything should be required in addition to this instruction, you should report on it to Us personally."[3]

Catherine continued this policy. Her well-known attempt to enlist the French mathematician and philosopher D'Alembert to participate in Paul's education should not be viewed as an effort to replace Panin as governor. Catherine's invitation to D'Alembert said only that he should come to Russia "pour contribuer à l'éducation de mon fils,"[4] meaning, as the French ambassador interpreted it, that he would teach the grand duke mathematics.[5] If there were more to the offer, Catherine certainly would have spelled it out in a second appeal to D'Alembert after he refused her invitation. Catherine understood the alarm Panin's removal would have provoked. Many years later she explained to her secretary Khrapovitskii that even had she

granted the title of count. Upon ending his duties as governor in 1773, he had to relinquish his post as *oberhofmeister* and take an office corresponding to his duties as head of foreign affairs. Why this was minister rather than chancellor remains unclear, although he did receive the first rank and a salary equivalent to that of a chancellor.

[3]"Nastavlenie imperatritsy Elizavety Petrovny grafu N. I. Paninu o vospitanii velikogo kniazia Pavla Petrovicha (1761)," *Russkii Arkhiv* (1881), no. 1, p. 21.

[4]Catherine to D'Alembert, 13 November 1762, *SIRIO*, 7: 178–80.

[5]Bérenger to Choiseul, 2 August 1762, *SIRIO*, 140: 46–47.

wanted to take Paul from Panin, political considerations forbade it: "Everyone thought that if he were not with Panin, he would have perished."[6] This remark, which has been interpreted as a sign of Catherine's disfavor with Panin, seemed in the context merely an excuse for having neglected Paul's upbringing. But however much she regretted it later, she certainly showed no disfavor with Panin's work during the 1760s. She took little interest in supervising the grand duke's education or in placing restraints on Panin's discretion. Her correspondence with Panin during this period was remarkable for the absence of any substantive comments about Paul's education. She frequently inquired after health, never about his studies or the conduct of the "young court."[7] She left these matters entirely in Panin's hands. In 1766 when he decided to dismiss a member of the teaching staff, not even the personal intervention of the favorite Orlov could prevent the unfortunate scholar's reassignment to a distant military detachment.[8]

Very importantly, the "young court" provided a setting where the many people of the Panin clientele could gather. As has been suggested throughout this study, such clienteles formed the basic social unit of eighteenth-century Russian government. They were held together by a whole network of daily contacts, frequent calls, conversations, and exchanges; in short, by a myriad of face-to-face meetings that defined the group and built morale and cohesion. Maintaining

[6]Khrapovitskii, *Dnevnik* (1901 ed.), p. 254.

[7]See her letters to Panin in *Chteniia*, vol. 2, pt. 2, *passim*. Also see two letters from Catherine to I. P. Elagin indicating Panin's independence in caring for Paul, published in Lebedev, *Grafy Paniny*, pp. 309–11. The empress did, however, routinely sit in on Paul's examinations.

[8]This was the celebrated case of Poroshin's dismissal, the reasons for which have not been altogether satisfactorily explained. Solov'ev's summary is still the most convincing, *Istoriia Rossii*, 13: 508–15. See also Poroshin's appeal to Orlov and other notes in *Russkii Arkhiv* (1869), pp. 61–66. Asseburg reported to Copenhagen that there were "public reasons and secret ones" as well, which may have been a reference to the slight Poroshin allegedly made to Panin's fiancée, Sheremeteva. *DRa*, TKUA, Russland A III 84, no. 44 (21 April 1766); also Fonvizin's letter to his family in which he noted "M-r Porochine est congedié de la cour pour les impertinances qu'il a fait par raport de mademoiselle Cheremeteff." *FSS*, 2: 342. A French dispatch, while confusing the cause of the dispute, likewise confirmed Panin's precedence in all that concerned Paul. "M. le comte Orlov a été obligé de ployer et de faire des excuses à M. Panine, qui soutient son rang et sa dignité, surtout vis-à-vis de lui, en homme qui, sûr de l'appui de tous les grands qui sont de son parti, sent très bien qu'il n'a rien à redouter pour lui-même, et combien le rôle qu'il joue doit en imposer au favori et à sa Souveraine." Rossignol to the king, 19 April 1766, *SIRIO*, 141:139.

the setting for such a group entailed enormous expense, and few men possessed the resources to sponsor a clientele of national importance. Even the favorites had to be granted large palaces and huge subsidies by the empress to underwrite a household and table necessary to maintain the wide range of contacts appropriate to their position and vital to its retention. For the Panins, with their limited personal resources, the grand ducal court provided an ideal milieu. It was well supplied with staff, kitchen, and a prestigious location. Its chambers and dinner table daily received friends, relatives, clients, debtors, popular writers, passing foreign visitors, and members of the foreign affairs and commercial bureaus.[9] Panin was famous for keeping one of the best tables in town, and the contacts developed there added immeasurably to the influence of his circle. Significantly, the Panin party's importance steadily declined after the grand duke's majority and the closing of the *oberhofmeister*'s court.

Of course, the most obvious attraction of the governorship was the opportunity of affecting the future direction of state policy. Through Paul the Panins could still hope, despite their reverses in the late 1760s, to recoup their influence and to implement their reform ideas. The following review of Panin's educational plan and his influence on Paul up to the latter's majority in 1773 should help to clarify these ideas. Toward the end of the chapter something will be said about Paul's earliest political writings, as they not only provide a measure of Panin's influence but also form a background for "the crisis of Paul's majority," to be taken up in chapter 9.

1. An Enlightened Educational Plan

Among the specific problems in evaluating Panin's influence on Paul must be counted the fact that he became governor when the grand duke had already attained six years of age. The critical formative period of Paul's personality took place while Panin was still Russian minister in Stockholm and could not influence the boy's upbringing. Another important, if intractable, problem involved the potentially severe psychological conflicts Paul had to cope with. The question of his legitimacy, his early separation from his parents and their indifference to him, the existence of an illegitimate challenger to his rights in Bobrinskii, and the murder of his father in 1762 were sources of conflict for Paul. Some may not have been as critical as

---

[9]Poroshin, *Zapiski*, constitutes an invaluable catalog of visitors for the years 1764–65.

modern observers have rated them; for example, the separation from his parents was not far off the norm for his time and place and may have prevented other problems associated with a deep oedipal attachment complicated by the death of his father. Yet when one adds to these potential conflict situations the general frailty of Paul's health throughout his childhood, there had already formed a number of deep and abiding influences which his governor could scarcely control.

Within these limitations it is important to try and evaluate Panin's effect on the boy. To begin with, what was the proper education for a young prince? Panin had to approach this question altogether afresh. Recent Russian history offered no useful examples. The last tsar to be brought up in Russia was Peter II, and his training was hardly exemplary. Panin, who had naturally familiarized himself with that case, once related at table that the corruption of the court in those times very early caused the governor, Count Osterman, to abandon hope of doing the job properly, and he gradually withdrew altogether from participation in the young emperor's eduation.[10] Examples of the training of seventeenth-century tsars were equally unserviceable, since their instruction scarcely went beyond the rudiments of reading and writing.[11]

Obviously, the model for the grand duke's education would have to come from the west. Here Panin's mission abroad had prepared him admirably, for he had been able to acquire a great deal of information about princely education. During much of his stay in Sweden the issue of Prince Gustav Adolf's upbringing was being bitterly fought out between the royal family and the estates. Panin was well acquainted with Gustav's first governor, Count Carl Gustav Tessin, and he certainly knew Tessin's plan for the prince's education, as it was the subject of considerable public debate during the early 1750s.[12] When Tessin stepped down toward the middle of the decade, the Riksdag appointed Count Ulrik Scheffer as governor and supplied him with a new instruction, which Panin also studied care-

[10]For Panin's comments see Poroshin, *Zapiski*, 6 December 1764; note on Osterman's educational plan in protocols of Supreme Privy Council, *SIRIO*, 63:784.

[11][G. K. Kotoshikhin], "Grigorii Karpovich Kotoshikhin, *On Russia in the Reign of Alexis Mikhailovich:* An Annotated Translation," trans. and ed. Benjamin Uroff (Ph. D. diss., Columbia University, 1970), pp. 56–57.

[12]Tessin plan published in Johan Göransson, *Svea Rikes Konungars Historia ok Ättartal ifrån 2200 år före Skriftum intil 1749* (Stockholm, 1749), pp. 271–277.

fully.[13] As is clear from these observations as well as from Panin's later comments to friends, he followed the development of Gustav's education closely and knew many details of the subjects taught, exams taken, and books read.[14] Panin must have discussed these questions as well with his good friend Asseburg, the Danish minister in Stockholm, who in 1758 was twice offered the post of governor to Prince Fredrik of Denmark.[15] Another source of information was Leibnitz's tract *De educatione Principis commentario*.[16] Though first published in 1787, the plan was well known in manuscript copies at several German courts, and in Russia Jakob von Stälin employed its precepts in a belated and vain effort to improve the education of Peter Fedorovich (later Peter III).[17]

The Leibnitz, Tessin, and Riksdag plans mentioned above were all progressive documents incorporating the new ideas in educational thinking developed in the late seventeenth and early eighteenth centuries. These new views began with Rabelais and Montaigne and received fuller refinement and definition in the writings of Locke, Commenius, and Fénelon. They represented a strong current running against the former scholastic methods of rote learning and dry-as-dust drill in classical languages. The idea was to replace this dull business with living knowledge. Two means were proposed. The first called for basing instruction on visual experience: observation of nature, copper engravings, mechanical devices, globes, and the like. Commenius especially stressed this point. A concomitant approach

[13]This document, while similar to Tessin's in its general approach, is remarkable for its strong development of the natural law theory of popular sovereignty and the king's responsibility to the estates, a clear reflection of the bitter dispute between the Riksdag and the royal family over control of Gustav's education. Panin's translation, "Instruktsiia po kotoroi gospodin gofmeister postupat' imeet pri vospitanii ego korolevskogo vysochestva," in *LOII, f.* 36, *op.* 1, *d.* 1132, 93–99.

[14]Poroshin, *Zapiski*, 25 July 1765.

[15]"Nevesty velikogo kniazia tsesarevicha Pavla Petrovicha," *Russkaia Starina*, 19 (1877), p. 167.

[16]Published in French in Böhmers *Magazin für das Kirchenrecht, die Kirchen-und Gelehrten-Geschichte*, 1 (1787), pp. 177–96.

[17]Beth Henning, *Gustav III som kronprins* (Uppsala, 1935), p. 399n, date of first publication is mistakenly recorded here as 1887. On Peter III and Stälin, see Petschauer, "The Education and Development of an Enlightened Absolutist," pp. 278–79. Other works on childrearing were beginning to appear in Russia at this time. An article entitled "Pravila vospitaniia detei," translated from the *Patriot*, came out in *Ezhemesiachnye sochineniia* (pp. 414–21) in 1755, and the first translation of Locke's thoughts on education appeared in 1759. Berkov, *Istoriia russkoi zhurnalistiki*, p. 104; Kizevetter, "Odin iz reformatorov russkoi shkoli," in *Istoricheskie ocherki* (Moscow, 1912) p. 142.

was to encourage the child to develop his own thoughts and apply himself to independent study. For example, language learning would rely heavily on the pupil's immediate participation in conversation, the composition of brief epistles, reproduction. Also Latin would give way to greater emphasis on the native tongue and living foreign languages. History instruction might employ the child's own reflections as a point of departure for discussions and essays. Another innovation was for the governor and teachers to shed the role of stern fathers and become "friends" of their charge, an attitude better suited to an education whose purpose was to persuade and cultivate judgment rather than stuff one's head with learned pedantry.[18] Tessin's instruction (written in the King's name) provided a good example of this approach:

> An untimely flaccidity or thoughtless harshness on the governor's part would be equally burdensome, and I have confidence that he will scrupulously examine my son's temperament and inclinations, the knowledge of which ought to serve the governor as a guide in all his undertakings. It is especially important that the reflection [*eftertänken*] be strengthened and memorization not too heavily emphasized, so that the former would not be sacrificed to the latter.[19]

These modern attitudes, which prepared the ground for Rousseau's revolutionary restatement of educational philosophy, exerted an unmistakable influence on Nikita Panin's thinking. Many of the new concepts found their way into the "Most Humble Prospectus on the Education of His Imperial Highness Paul Petrovich," which Panin submitted to Empress Elizabeth in 1760 upon assuming his duties as governor to the heir.[20]

Panin began his prospectus with extended and effusive praise of the maternal care Elizabeth had showered on the young grand duke. Among Paul's forebears he naturally singled out "the founder and reconstructor" of Russia, Peter the Great, and Elizabeth herself as examples of the perfection one should strive for in training the heir. Most important, of course, a monarch had to exhibit a tender

[18]Henning, *Gustav III som kronprins*, p. 23.

[19]Göransson, *Svea Rikes Konungars Historia*, pp. 275–76.

[20]Title is here abbreviated from: "Vsepoddanneishee pred"iavlenie slabogo poniattiia i mneniia o vospitanii ego imperatorskogo vysochestva, gosudaria velikogo kniazia Pavla Petrovicha," ed. T. A. Sosnovskii, *Russkaia Starina*, 36 (November 1882), pp. 315–30.

care for his subjects, be "God-loving, just and kind." For "a good ruler neither possesses nor can possess any true interest or true glory apart from the prosperity and welfare of the subject peoples allotted to him by God's grace and who build altars to him in their hearts." Moral and religious training came first. The governor must strive assiduously to protect his charge from "words or deeds of any kind that could in the slightest corrupt the spiritual faculties for virtue with which man enters the world." Rather he should provide a milieu that would imperceptibly develop the boy's desire to imitate goodness and honor and detest all base and dishonorable acts.

The quality of religious instruction was considered of greatest consequence. Panin mentioned the three primary human virtues to be cultivated: "an appreciative knowledge of one's Creator, His holy purpose in creating us, and our consequent devoted duty to Him."

> The first occurs when the heart has already been filled with love and obedience to Him and to the powers He has established; the second arises from the sincere desire to fulfill the vocation for which we are brought into the world; the third from zeal and care in preparing oneself for carrying out the duties of that calling. Simple human existence implants in the understanding the first traces of these three rules of life; but our Orthodox Christianity illuminates them and opens the heart to the path of good. That is why instruction in the Scriptures is undoubtedly the most important point of a good education.[21]

These observations constituted "givens" in such an educational plan. More interesting was Panin's insistence on a religious instructor free of all prejudice or superstition, a characteristic, as he said, "only of false doctrines and ruinous to our piety in which faith is inseparably attended by good works." Although Elizabeth's own religious practice tended toward the ritualistic and superstitious, she no doubt viewed it in different terms and approved Panin's sentiments. Not until the accession of Catherine, however, did Panin find a religious instructor of the quality he desired. This was the monk and later metropolitan Platon Levshin, a most unusual cleric, probably one of the few Russian churchmen of his time who was thoroughly familiar with the literature of the Western Enlighten-

[21]N. I. Panin, "Vsepoddanneishee pred"iavlenie," p. 317.

ment.[22] Under his direction Paul developed an unusually tolerant and yet deeply pious religious outlook.

The remaining subject matter had a very modern ring. Mathematics was to occupy a central place in the curriculum, for its concepts were especially beneficial in "purifying reason and train[ed] more in the bases of truth than all other fundaments of reason." Next history instruction had to be given a high priority. The means proposed here were "brief clear essays," with particular attention to the history of Russia. This comment reflected the growing feeling of national pride that was developing in eighteenth-century Russia and which was particularly evident among the Panin group. The same sentiment revealed itself in the remarks about teaching of the native tongue. Concerning this, Panin wrote, "even if Russia did not already possess Lomonosovs and Sumarokovs, the reading of some ancient writings in the psalter during Scripture study would by itself partly fulfill the requirement. Besides, in the beginning short and easy written exercises on the thoughts and reflections of His Imperial Highness will facilitate this." All this was, of course, to be moderated "according to the child's years and the unfolding of his innate capabilities, so that in the beginning the studies need not be strictly scholastic but instead may be carried on by informal instruction."[23]

The same modern approach characterized Panin's advice in the area of foreign languages. French and German had to be given the highest priority. "But the one and the other, being living languages, can be learned in childhood by listening to conversation so as not to waste precious teaching time unnecessarily. And when the age is attained where maturity will without taxing the understanding make possible the teaching of grammatical rules, then His Highness will be in a position himself to correct those errors which almost invariably turn up in conversation." Beyond these subjects, he said, such things as cavalry exercises, dancing, and artistic drawing should

[22]On Panin's fondness for Platon and his views see Poroshin, *Zapiski*, 12 November and 10 December 1764; he sometimes joined Platon in quizzing Paul about theology, *idem*, 8 September 1765. On Platon's life there is a rather unsatisfactory biography by I. M. Snegirev, *Zhizn' moskovskogo mitropolita Platona*, 2 vols. in one (Moscow, 1856); also "K biografii mitropolita moskovskogo Platona," *Chteniia* (1875), no. 1, 161–62. For an excellent characterization of his personality see E. D. Clarke, *Travels*, (4th ed. London, 1816), vol. 1, *Russia, Tahtary and Turkey*, pp. 191–205.

[23]N. I. Panin, "Vsepoddanneishee pred"iavlenie," pp. 317–18.

be pursued to relieve the pressure of academic studies. Also an annual sum of money should be set aside for the "collection of books, mathematical and physical instruments, guns, copper engravings, collections of paintings, and other works of art, which if collected little by little before [His Highness'] eyes can imperceptibly give him a general inclination, love, and curiosity for all sciences and arts."[24]

In the later stages of the grand duke's education, that is after he had learned "all the appropriate sciences in the usual order, it will be very beneficial to organize a special consultation concerning the best approach to the study of statecraft." This subject, Panin continued, included a "knowledge of commerce, fiscal affairs, domestic and foreign policy, naval and land warfare, institutions of manufacture and factories, and other sectors constituting the government of his state, and the power and glory of the monarch." The inclusion here of the need to learn military science was, of course, common to much earlier instructions on monarchical education, and Panin in line with his personal antipathy to the military life-style and his stoic ideal of the virtuous peace-loving monarch in practice minimized this aspect of Paul's training.[25] The remaining comments on statecraft were somewhat novel and testified to the new appreciation of the monarch's important role in fostering the economic and industrial development of the country. It was no longer sufficient to have merely a military leader and tax collector at the head of government; the monarch had to be versed in all facets of modern administration. A second point to observe was Panin's cautious skirting of the issue of how to teach these matters. This implied the possibility of Paul's participation at some later date in the governing councils and actual administration of the country. Empress Elizabeth was certainly agreeable to this approach, as she included Peter Fedorovich in her state council. But Panin could not know how Paul's parents might react to this suggestion. In fact, the issue proved to be a very ticklish one when Paul reached his late teens and encountered his mother's jealous monopoly of authority.

Finally, with regard to the grand duke's daily regimen and living conditions, Panin's educational plan held to the view typical of the Leibnitz and Tessin models. It was a fairly Spartan ideal. The best results could be achieved "if every overindulgence, splendor and

---

[24]N. I. Panin, "Vsepoddanneishee pred" iavlenie," pp. 318–19.

[25]Kobeko, *Tsesarevich Pavel Petrovich*, p. 56.

luxury which tempt youth were kept from him and considered by him in no other wise than as the hope of future reward for zealous compliance in the eminent wish and desire of Her Imperial Majesty in those years when his education is completed." His court should correspond to his rank, but with decency and good behavior its principal decoration. Never missing an opportunity Panin added meaningfully, "there will be time enough for flatterers in the future."[26] The governor likewise recommended that no special ranks be conferred upon those chosen as companions (Cavaliers) and servants of the grand duke; their salaries and place of honor would be sufficient inducement to devoted service.

In brief outline, this was Panin's plan for rearing Paul. He did not present a systematic philosophy of education or even go into much detail on the specific points proposed. He merely set forth the precepts he intended to follow without elaborate design or exhaustive justification. Still, his plan expressed a clearly defined approach to childrearing, a set of learning priorities, and a considered method, all of which demonstrated his sympathy with the advanced educational ideas of the time. It should be noted further that Panin was one of the first Russians to put these ideas in written form. Contrary to the contention of Paul's biographer Kobeko,[27] Panin's views were not a mere reworking of the pedagogical theories of the famous Catherinian educationist I. I. Betskoi. To be sure, Betskoi made enormous contributions to Russian education, going well beyond Panin's ideas and even putting Rousseauean schemes into practice. All the same, Panin composed his plan three years prior to Betskoi's first writings on pedagogy and two years before Betskoi had returned to Russia from an extended stay abroad.[28] Had Panin written more extensively on the subject, he would undoubtedly be recognized as one of the pioneers of modern educational thought in Russia, a precursor rather than a follower of Betskoi.

2. *The Intellectual Milieu of the "Young Court"*

The substance of Paul's training indicates that Panin and his staff honestly strove to implement the ideas expressed in the edu-

---

[26]N. I. Panin, "Vsepoddanneishee pred"iavlenie," p. 319.

[27]Kobeko, *Tsesarevich Pavel Petrovich,* p. 28.

[28]On Betskoi's work see P. M. Maikov, *Ivan Ivanovich Betskoi, opyt ego biografii* (St. Petersburg, 1904), and Kizevetter, "Odin iz reformatorov russkoi shkoly," pp. 119–49.

cational plan and to make Paul an exemplary enlightened monarch. They gave him a firm grounding in the essential skills of language, mathematics, and military science, as well as a broad understanding of modern statecraft in both its theoretical and practical aspects. In addition, Paul became well versed in the principal literary and philosophical writings of the age. The intimate glimpse of his education at age ten and eleven given in the Poroshin diary showed him following regular courses in physics, astronomy, mathematics, and history, while at the same time cutting his teeth on Buffon's *Histoire naturelle*, Voltaire's *Dictionnaire philosophique*, as well as other Voltairian writings, plus a heavy diet of neo-stoicist moral works, especially those of Racine and Fénelon.[29] Another memoir about the grand duke's education during his middle teens showed him engrossed in studies of European history, the important sources at this stage being the Scottish historian Robertson's works and biographies of famous monarchs and ministers. At about the same time Paul began his practical training in statecraft. Here the main work was done by Grigorii Teplov, who introduced him to the details of office procedure and form of government papers and official documents. General guidance in these matters came primarily from Panin, Caspar von Saldern, and Baron L. H. Nicholay;[30] for a short time in 1772–1773 Catherine herself took Paul in hand and instructed him in the day-to-day operation of imperial decision making.[31]

In addition to his formal studies, the discussions and conversations at the grand ducal dinner table unquestionably played an important role in Paul's education. Nikita Panin presided there and daily brought visitors from among the government officials and court dignitaries as well as writers, scientists, and foreign representatives. This exposure gave Paul an exceptionally broad acquaintance with world affairs, current politics, and new cultural and scientific developments. Political and administrative topics regularly touched on included law, commerce, factories and manufactures, village economy, land surveying, and bureaucratic organization and personnel. Panin often illuminated these issues with remarks about conditions in other countries or by drawing on his own experience

[29]References to these matters in Poroshin, *Zapiski* are too numerous to list, but see especially 24 September, 20 October 1764; 8 January, 24 March, and 24 June 1765.

[30]Kobeko, *Tsesarevich Pavel Petrovich*, pp. 53–56; Heier, *L. H. Nicolay*, pp. 32–33. Catherine to Saldern, 26 May 1772, *SIRIO*, 118: 142.

[31]On this brief era of cooperation between Paul and his mother see below, chapter 9.

and giving examples from Russian and European history. As for cultural life, Paul had at his disposal the offerings of the court ballet and drama theater, and he often finished his day with attendance at the theater.[32]

It has already been mentioned that Panin and the grand ducal teaching staff imbued Paul's education with the ideals of the good ruler and enlightened monarchical order. The sources of this model lay in the natural law theorists and especially the neo-stoicist writers of seventeenth-century Europe, who did so much to turn the basic outlook of educated European society in a "modern" direction. Starting in the late sixteenth century and growing in numbers and influence, this new band of political moralists projected the values of reason, order, and moderation. They strove to break down the "undisciplined" and "primitive way of life" supposedly characteristic of medieval society and replace it with a more ordered, psychologically repressed polity governed by functionally differentiated institutions. They wanted to improve both public and private morality. Philip Ariès has recently brought attention to this process as it affected the family, which was retreating to a more private sphere and relinquishing many of its functions to more specialized institutions.[33] In the public arena these changes were accompanied by the growth of absolutism that was, ideally at least, enlightened and articulated on the basis of Christian morality and positive law as interpreted by the growing corps of skilled jurists and administrators in service to the crown.

After nearly one hundred years a similar intellectual climate began to manifest itself in Russia. Nikita Panin and Catherine were the most prominent representatives of this outlook, which was reflected in their early reform work and the program of the grand duke's education. But they did not stand alone. The same ideas had penetrated to a wider circle and found expression in the writings of the student journalists in the Sumarokov and Kheraskov circles. They enthusiastically embraced the principles of rationalism and stoic morality and filled their journals with translations of Lipsius, Racine, Fénelon and like-minded writers. This literature inevitably stimulated an intense interest in the quality of tsarist leadership, as

[32]Poroshin, *Zapiski, passim.*
[33]Philippe Ariès, *Centuries of Childhood* (New York, 1962) pp. 405–06; also his *Histoire des populations françaises* (Paris, 1948), pp. 447, 509, 511.

one of its basic themes was the contrast between the virtuous ruler and the despot. Personal moral rectitude and a concern for the welfare of the people characterized the first. The good ruler devoted his energy to maintaining peace abroad and with wise legislation secured his own people in their lives and possessions. Above all, he was an exemplar of moral virtue for his subjects. A despot, on the other hand, abandoned himself to his passions and sacrificed the people's welfare to the whims of his favorites. Instead of securing justice and prosperity, he preferred the role of military conqueror and in the interests of an adventurous foreign policy brought ruin to his country.[34]

It will be recalled that when Catherine ascended the throne in 1762 many of the student journalists saw her as the embodiment of the ideal monarch of their writings. They hailed her as Minerva enthroned and immediately abandoned their studies to take up service in the new regime. Hoping to act as instruments for the moral regeneration of the entire elite, the writers did more than just work in the government. They continued through the 1760s to propagandize for their ideas, fully expecting them to be implemented by the new regime. This ambition led them into close ties with the grand ducal court; of the ministers in Catherine's government *oberhofmeister* Panin was the one most in tune with the writers' outlook. They were attracted to his policies of peace, internal development, and his hostility to court favoritism. His reputation as an enlightener showed up in a popular broadside of the mid 1760s designating him as "an author of the *Encyclopedia*."[35] In turn, Panin gladly patronized the writers and frequently invited them to visit the "young court" and read their latest works. Even from the brief glimpse supplied by the Poroshin diary, one sees regular visits by A. P. Sumarokov, I. P. Elagin, I. F. Bogdanovich, Prince Belosel'skii, and several others, not to mention the literary men who partic-

[34]Walter Gleason, "Cultural Value Changes" does a splendid job of detailing this and other aspects of the moral outlook of the young writers. On the virtuous monarch see especially chapter 1.

[35]M. Loginov, ed., "Satiricheskii katalog pri dvore Ekateriny II," *Russkii Arkhiv* (1871), pp. 2039–54. Included in this catalog were some unflattering remarks about other persons at court. Interestingly enough, only a short time before the appearance of this catalog Panin had corrected and sent to the Moscow senate departments an ukase ordering such "abusive compositions" and catalogs publicly burned and those who possessed them punished. *SIRIO*, 7: 393–94; also *PSZ*, vol. 17, no. 12, 313. For additional evidence of Panin's popularity, see the letters in *Russkii Arkhiv* (1869), no. 1, pp. 68–72.

ipated directly in Paul's education: S. A. Poroshin, D. I. Fonvizin, G. N. Teplov, Baron Nicolay.[36]

Given this chummy relationship between Panin and the writers, it was not surprising that their works in some cases provided direct support of Panin's policy initiatives. This advocacy could be seen especially in Fonvizin's writings. At the time Panin's council plan was under consideration, Fonvizin presented a petition for a job as translator in which he offered a passage from Cicero defending the Roman Senate's deliberative role against Julius Caesar's despotic ambitions.[37] Just prior to the Legislative Commission, when the definition of the nobility was a central issue, Fonvizin translated an article on the "Noblesse commerçante" that agreed fully with the Panins' ideas about encouraging noble enterprise.[38] In another composition from the same time he promoted their views on the nobility's corporate rights and the need for a vigorous and enterprising middle class.[39] Interestingly enough, the work that most attracted Nikita Panin's attention and led to Fonvizin's inclusion in the inner circles of the Panin party was the play *Brigadier*, a merciless satire of the semi-educated provincial nobility. Panin warmly praised the authentic Russian characterizations and, of course, heartily approved of the central theme ridiculing the smug assumption that virtue and rank coincided. He insisted it be read several times for the edification of Paul and other members of the court.[40]

[36]Patronage naturally meant jobs as well as entry to the "young court." Bogdanovich worked as secretary to Peter Panin in 1763 and then transferred to Nikita Panin's foreign affairs chancery where he served as translator for 12 years. Belosel'skii, who worked in the same department, later became Russian ambassador in Saxony. Fonvizin was a translator in the foreign affairs department and secretary to Elagin before becoming Nikita Panin's personal secretary in 1769. Poroshin was, of course, Paul's tutor in science and mathematics until getting into trouble in 1766 (see note 8 above). Nicolay, who joined the teaching staff later in the 1760s and was not a member of the earlier literary circles, fully shared the other writers' moral views and, as his biographer phrased it, tried to educate Paul as a virtuous ruler in the Wielandian manner. Heier, *L. H. Nicolay*, pp. 40–41.

[37]"M. Tulliia Tsitserona rech' za M. Martsella," *FSS*, 2: 618–21. Makogonenko, *Denis Fonvizin*, pp. 18–19.

[38]"Torguiushchee dvorianstvo," *FSS*, pp. 117–88. The work was a partial translation of the German jurist Justi's translation of two French articles, one by Gabriel-François Coyer favoring commerce by nobles, another by the marquis de Lassay opposing it. Fonvizin translated only Justi's introduction and Coyer's discourse, thus indicating his preference for a trading nobility.

[39]"Sokrashchenie o vol'nosti frantsuzskogo dvorianstva i o pol'ze tret'ego china," *FSS*, 2: 109–16.

[40]For Panin's response see Fonvizin's "Chistoserdechnoe priznanie v delakh moikh

Other members of the literary circles of the early 1760s developed similar themes in their writings, but it should be noted that until the very end of the decade they made no distinction between their support of the Panin party and the empress. They still looked to Catherine as their standard-bearer; or better, they did not distinguish between the policies of Catherine and Panin. To be sure, her weakness for the favorite clashed with their vision of the ideal monarch. Yet, with a few notable exceptions like Sumarokov's poems "War of the Eagles," "Fist Fight," and "Ambassador Ass," criticism of favoritism was confined to vague generalities and not aimed directly at Catherine and Orlov.[41] Only in the last year of the decade, when the favorite and his clients began to play a larger role in policy formulation, did the tone change. Disillusioned with the shift away from social and legislative reform to a concentration on war and imperial expansion, the writers began to withdraw their praise for Catherine and instead to project their aspirations for enlightened rule on her son. This shift in attitude had an appreciable influence on the subsequent relations between Catherine and Paul.

3. The Literary "Opposition"

The parting of the ways between Catherine and her erstwhile literary allies accompanied the major policy changes of 1769. The downgrading of the Panin party unquestionably played a part, as it threatened the writers' most important patronage link. This change appeared all the more ominous in that it was directly connected with a shift in government priorities from domestic reform to an active, expansionist foreign policy. Most of the young writers had looked to the Legislative Commission with eager anticipation.[42] They viewed it as the fulfillment of Catherine's promise to give Russia an enlightened legal order. Then, just as the Commission was getting into

---

pomyshleniiakh," *FSS*, 2: 97–100. Varneke has some interesting comments on the play's value as an historical source, in *History of the Russian Theatre*, p. 142.

[41]"War of the Eagles," (Voina Orlov) caricatured the Orlovs' struggle to maintain imperial favor. The other two poems seem to refer more particularly to Aleksei Orlov in his capacities as spontaneous pugilist and envoy in the Adriatic. See Berkov's comments in Sumarokov, *Izbrannye proizvedeniia* (Leningrad, 1957), pp. 38–39, and for the poems, pp. 217, 224, 231.

[42]Several of them, in fact, participated directly in the Legislative Commission. For a partial list see Berkov, *Istoriia russkoi zhurnalistiki*, p. 160. For an interesting survey and discussion of this genre of satire *"na litso,"* see David Welsh, *Russian Comedy 1765–1823* (The Hague, 1966), pp. 19–27.

high gear, the empress seemed to be abandoning it and turning her attention to military action against Turkey and Poland. The change inevitably aroused the young writers' suspicions, especially in view of the fact that Panin's leadership role was receding, while the Orlovs and their adherents came forward with plans for the dismemberment of Poland and a vigorous offensive war against Turkey. The writers feared a turn to policies of imperial aggrandizement. As they saw it, Catherine was abandoning the role of the virtuous ruler, the great legislator concerned with the people's welfare, and adopting instead the attributes of a despotic ruler.

Catherine sensed this disillusionment. In an attempt to allay the doubts and retain the support of the writers, she launched a venture in satirical journalism in 1769 and invited them to follow her example. But this effort to divert and coöpt the young writers only served to emphasize the gap between the two sides' idea of what constituted acceptable social comment. Catherine's journal, *Anything and Everything*, besides offering excuses for the failure of the Legislative Commission, confined itself to poking fun at vices generally without reference to specific social and political problems. The point was to satirize common human foibles and then suggest healthy attitudes by which they could be improved. This approach fell far short of the journalists' aspiration. They wanted to discuss the burning issues of the day, serfdom, political corruption, education, and the moral bankruptcy of the nobility. In the first round of satirical journals in 1769 they not only commented on these broad and politically sensitive topics, but to the empress' horror, they went so far as to point the finger at particular individuals and government officials responsible for corruption.[43]

Catherine tried to moderate and control these expressions by a combination of witty and studied advice in her own columns, but with little success. Her antagonists responded with thinly veiled ridicule of "Madam Anything and Everything" and shifted to a debate on the proper limits of social satire. In a famous exchange of editorial letters, N. I. Novikov argued for the free expression of social opinion, for the journalist's right to be a spokesman for the interests of the people, while Catherine could only counter with depictions of her critics as idealistic dreamers. She accused them

[43]Berkov, *Istoriia russkoi zhurnalistiki*, pp. 174–75; Ryu, "Freemasonry under Catherine the Great," p. 90.

of longing for perfection and calumniating those who could not
instantly produce it. Governing required more than idle hopes and
dreams, she warned. Life was recalcitrant, not susceptible to simple
remedies. If her critics insisted on tilting at windmills, those who
understood the practical business of life would know well enough to
ignore their empty harpings. Yet, disturbed by the bold thrusts of
the "opposition" journals, Catherine failed to heed her own advice.
She began closing them down within the first year of publication.
New titles, which appeared in rapid succession through the next few
years, became progressively more timid as the writers maneuvered
to avoid censorship. Finally, the flare-up of the Pugachev Rebellion
led to an indefinite suspension of critical journalism in 1774.[44]

As the journalists became disappointed with Catherine, they
adopted postures indicating that their primary allegiance belonged
to Russia rather than to the empress and that their hopes for Russia's
future centered on the heir.[45] The earliest and most pointed reference
in this connection came in Denis Fonvizin's *Discourse on the Recovery
of His Imperial Highness, Crown Prince and Grand Duke Paul Petrovich in
1771*.[46] The occasion was Paul's recovery from a near fatal five-week
bout with influenza. Needless to say, this was one more source of
anxiety for the leading figures at court. The prolonged illness was
accompanied by such a high fever that Panin several times des-
paired of a cure and divided his time between berating the court
physician and abandoning himself to fits of depression. Catherine
was no less distraught, although her anguish expressed itself in an
entirely different fashion. She took walks in public every day and
tried to appear carefree and happy, as if there were not the least

[44]Admittedly, both the degree of suppression and the causal link between the Pugachev
Rebellion and suspension of journalistic activity are points subject to debate. K. A.
Papmehl's recent study, *Freedom of Expression in Eighteenth-Century Russia* (The Hague,
1971), advances a number of cogent arguments for Catherine's "liberal" attitude toward
press freedom, although even he grants her suppression of Novikov's *Drone*, evaluating
this and other cases of suppression as a warning to the editors to avoid offensive references
to individuals.

[45]For a thorough development of this theme, see Gleason's "Cultural Value Changes."

[46]"Slovo na vyzdorovlenie ego imperatorskogo vysochestva gosudaria tsesarevicha i
velikogo kniazia Pavla Petrovicha v 1771 gode," in Fonvizin, *FSS*, 2: 187–93, was
published in 1771 and then reprinted by Novikov the following year in "Zhivopisets,"
part 2, pp. 226–39. For additional comments, see Pigarev, *Tvorchestvo Fonvizina*, pp. 117–
18; and P. N. Berkov, "Teatr Fonvizina i russkaia kul'tura," *Russkie klassiki i teatr* (Leningrad, 1947), p. 46.

cause for concern about Paul's health.[47] It is not clear if she behaved this way merely to encourage calm among the citizenry or because she was so utterly terrified at the possibility of Paul's death that she tried to deny her fears. Aside from the natural concern of a mother for her child, Catherine certainly understood that if the popular young heir died so close to his majority, the public would inevitably raise questions about her involvement. Furthermore, Paul's death would strip the last pretense of legality from her own rule and open the way to challenges from any adventurer with the stomach to attempt one. So relief was great all around when Paul's fever finally broke, and he started on the road to recovery.

Fonvizin's discourse, while exclaiming this sense of relief, also included a disturbing political message. It clearly signalled the displacement of the young writers' hopes for reform from Catherine to Paul. The tip-off lay in the rhetorical associations rather than in the amount of space devoted to either personage. Fonvizin naturally included many kind words about the empress. He described her care and concern for her ailing son, told how she rushed to the capital to be at his side and give him the strength to fight off the menacing illness. He spoke too of her many successes and military victories that had brought fame to Russia. But these expressions had an air of formality, and, significantly, they failed to impart to Catherine the attributes of a virtuous ruler or to associate her with the feelings of the Russian people. In this respect, the statements of praise for Catherine paled beside the effusion of sentiment for Paul. He was symbolically bathed in the nation's tears. At the news of his illness, old people wept and begged God to take their lives in exchange for Paul's; grown men were cast into despair; even little children, seeing the uncontrollable weeping of their mothers, joined in the general bewailment. This bathos was followed by assurances that no one could be more deserving of popular affection than Paul. In the midst of his life and death struggle, Fonvizin emphasized, what tormented the grand duke most was the worry his illness was causing the people.[48]

The closing section of the discourse built the association between Paul and the moral qualities of a virtuous ruler. Paul's deep concern

[47]Heier, *L. H. Nicolay*, p. 164 and 164 note a. Fonvizin also makes reference to Catherine's behavior in his discourse on Paul's recovery, *FSS*, 2: 190.

[48]"Slovo na vyzdorovlenie," pp. 188–91.

for the Russian people, Fonvizin asserted, was implanted by his governor, Nikita Panin, "a man of true reason and honor, surpassing the highest morals of the century!" He instilled in Paul the virtues and sense of duty required of an enlightened monarch and "made him aware of the sacred bonds that unite him to the fate of millions of people and unite millions of people to him." Paul's recovery was a sign to the universe that he was created for the happiness of future centuries. He was the "hope of the fatherland" and "the *sole* and precious source of our tranquility."[49] Then Fonvizin ended with a lesson straight out of the *Telemach*. "Be just, kind, and sensitive to the misfortunes of the people, and you will always dwell in their hearts. Do not seek other glories. The people's love is the true glory of rulers. Be master of your passions and recall that he who is not master of himself cannot rule others with glory. Harken only to the truth, and regard flattery as treason, for there is no loyalty to the sovereign where truth does not abide. Acknowledge merit and reward services. In a word, leave your heart open to all virtues—and you will be glorious on earth and pleasing to heaven."[50] The sermon was at once an admonition to Paul and implicit criticism of Catherine's favoritism and expansionist foreign policy. The discourse left no doubt that while Fonvizin was willing to grant the empress credit for her personal achievements and military conquests, he no longer thought of her as the hope for establishing a rational, enlightened order in the Russian state and society.

This theme was echoed by other writers of the literary "opposition." In the same year Sumarokov produced an "Ode to Crown Prince Paul on His Nameday," which drew a similar distinction between the qualities of the empress and her son. And besides praising Nikita Panin, the ode also hailed his brother as the eternally unforgettable conqueror of Bendery, a reference that showed Sumarokov's sympathy for the fallen younger Panin.[51] Another significant

[49]"Slovo na vyzdorovlenie," pp. 187–92. (Italics mine.)

[50]"Slovo na vyzdorovlenie," p. 193. With respect to the *Telemach*, it is revealing to note that in the court-sponsored journal *Anything and Everything* this work was not treated favorably, whereas the "opposition" writers defended it vigorously and liberally borrowed from its wisdom, the reason being, it seems, that the *Telemach* stood as a quiet and yet palpable censure on the luxurious and corrupted court. A. S. Orlov, "'Tilemakhida' V. K. Trediakovskogo," *XVIII Vek*, 1: 33–34.

[51]Sumarokov, "Oda gosudariu tsesarevichu Pavlu Petrovichu v den' ego tezoimenitstva iiunia 29 chisla 1771 goda." *Izbrannye proizvedeniia*, pp. 74–77.

gesture was Novikov's dedication to the grand duke of his *Historical Dictionary of Russian Writers* (1772). Coming in the year Paul was to attain his majority, it recalled Sumarokov's bold dedication of his first journal in 1759 to the then-disgraced Catherine. The following year, 1773, Bogdanovich added his voice to the chorus with a poem entitled "The Bliss of Peoples." Though essentially only a crude reworking of Rousseau's evolutionary scheme, the piece was remarkable for its concluding appeal to Paul to promulgate laws that would enable man to recapture the blissful peace of earlier centuries.[52]

This shift in literary opinion clearly troubled Catherine. Her efforts to control the young journalists by a combination of satirical innuendo, threats, and in some cases outright suppression bespoke the success of the Panin party in capturing the "public opinion makers" as well as the growing importance of the latter in Catherinian Russia. Panin certainly welcomed this badly needed support for his faltering party, as the writers' backing narrowed Catherine's options and caused her to tread warily in dealing with the Panins. She realized that she would now have to prepare the ground carefully if she wanted to disgrace them. Yet the writers' support also had a negative effect on the relations between Catherine and the Panin party. It awakened the empress' suspicions about the Panins' hopes for Paul's elevation. Given the close association of the writers with the "young court," the empress could not but wonder if their disillusionment did not reflect a spirit permeating the entire Panin group, and her suspicions would seriously cloud efforts by the Panins to maintain Catherine's trust through the crisis of Paul's majority that was soon to follow. Catherine seemed to fear that the emphasis on Paul's virtues was a sign that the "young court" expected to come to power in the near future. Her concern only increased when it turned out that criticism by the young journalists went hand in hand with signs of Paul's desire to begin speaking out on government issues. For in his early efforts at political expression Paul was naturally very much influenced by the views of his mentors and the coterie of writers associated with the Panin party.

---

[52]Novikov's work in Efremov, *Materialy dlia istorii russkoi literatury* (St. Petersburg, 1867), p. 3; Bogdanovich, *Stikhotvoreniia i poemy* (Leningrad, 1957), pp. 187–94, both as cited in Gleason, "Cultural Value Changes," pp. 219–20.

4. Paul's First Political Writings

Panin's political influence on Paul must not be confused with his handling of personal relations between mother and son. Many writers have argued that Panin purposely fostered in Paul a feeling of ill will toward Catherine.[53] Yet the available evidence on this question gives quite the opposite impression. It shows Panin playing a positive role, actively working to expand and improve contacts between the two tsarist personages.

The clearest record of Panin's efforts in this regard appeared in connection with Catherine's trip down the Volga River in the spring and summer of 1767, when Panin stayed behind in Moscow with Paul and maintained daily contact with the empress by courier. Panin took this opportunity to persuade Paul to initiate a correspondence with the empress. Then in his own letters Panin took pains to explain that Paul composed his affectionate and well-formed epistles entirely on his own. He frequently reminded Catherine of how much the boy treasured the exchange, and he described in detail the joy with which the grand duke received each of her replies. Once, for example, he reported to Catherine that the grand duke had been moved to tears by her description of a reception at Kostroma that witnessed a touching scene of mutual good feeling between monarch and subjects. Panin also read Paul excerpts from his own letters when he thought they would increase the boy's admiration for his mother.[54] It is, of course, difficult to say whether this

---

[53]The view that Panin corrupted Paul and turned him against his mother has long been established in the historical literature. Lebedev, *Grafy Paniny*, especially pp. 135–36, 240, was the first to develop it as a central theme. The same interpretaion was carried over into two of the best-known biographies of Paul: Kobeko, *Tsesarevich Pavel Petrovich*, pp. 30–45; Shumigorskii, *Imperator Pavel I*, pp. 14–25. This view could only be supported by a highly distorted and sometimes amusingly naive selection of passages from the Poroshin diary, and at least two scholars, without going into the question in detail, have tried to offer a corrective. See the editorial note in *Russkaia Starina*, 36 (1882), pp. 313–15, and M. V. Klochkov, *Ocherki pravitel'stvennoi deiatel'nosti vremeni Pavla I* (Petrograd, 1916), pp. 95–96, 116, 133, 230. Braudo also addressed this question in his brief sketch of Panin's life with, if not the entire story, at least a measure of good sense and insight. "There is no basis," he wrote, "to suppose that N. I. Panin used his influence exclusively to set the young court against Catherine—he used it to strengthen his position against the hated favorites and to defend his political system from attack." *RBS*, 13: 201. For a detailed discussion of the historiography, see my thesis, "Nikita Panin's Role in Russian Court Politics," chapter 1.

[54]N. I. Panin to Catherine, 3, 6, 7, 13, 18, 21 May and 6 June 1767, *GBL, f.* Barsk XVIa, *d.* 29, nos. 213, 216, 217, 222, 226, 230, and 237. Catherine's replies in *Chteniia* vol. 2, pt. 2, pp. 17, 26, 38.

exchange typified the manner in which Panin handled relations between Catherine and Paul. During Panin's governorship the three persons in question lived regularly under the same roof, and consequently, except for a brief period of separation like the Volga journey, their contacts left little documentary trace. In any case, as the only detailed record of their relations during this period, this evidence stands in sharp contrast to the usual view that Panin cultivated animosity between mother and son.

Still, on another level, Panin provided Paul with a critical perspective from which to judge his mother's regime. This perspective derived in part from the suffusion of Paul's education with the model of the virtuous monarch and properly regulated government. But it owed something as well to the critical tone that began to characterize the "young court" after the downgrading of the Panin party in 1769. This can be seen in Paul's early political writings, which date from this period.

The first piece, written in 1772, was an academic exercise on the "Principles of Government." Paul began by sketching out a Hobbesian explanation of the origin of government, that in a state of nature the weak select rulers to protect them and voluntarily submit to the rulers' directives. In time, however, it becomes necessary to develop the concept of law and establish limitations on the supreme power. As Paul explained it, "These rulers, growing powerful and seeing nothing that could set limits to their passions, allow themselves to give vent to them and commit excesses. The society then takes care to moderate this power and prescribe limits for it, and that is the beginning of law. . . . It is the foundation of accumulated laws . . . that serves as a guide to the ruling power and [is] what one calls the principle of government." Then Paul concluded on the following critical note. "I am not at all speaking here of the abuses of the laws and of power, for to speak of the abuses would be like counting the drops of water in the sea."[55]

The essay quite accurately reflected Panin's embryonic *Rechtsstaat* notions of enlightened government. It did not speak of constitutionalism on the Anglo-French model but only of the need to set some recognized bounds *(préscrire des bornes)* to keep the ruling power within the framework of established law. The final remark showed that Paul

[55]"Reflections, qui me sont venus au sujet d'une expression qu'on m'a fait si souvent sonner aux oreilles, qui est: Principes du Gouvernement," *Russkaia Starina*, 9 (1874), p. 670.

understood the difference between the enunciation of such principles and their actual implementation, a possible reference to the gap between Catherine's *Instruction* and the actual governing practices of the time.

More interesting was Paul's second memoir, entitled "A Consideration of the State in General."[56] He composed it in the summer of 1774 and evidently intended it as a serious proposal for governmental consideration. The timing was important. It was not only the first political project of Paul's majority but it came in a moment of acute crisis. The Turkish war was just winding up in the south, while Pugachev and his rebel legions threatened the center of the empire.[57] The memoir spoke directly to these issues, appealing for the reestablishment of a long period of peace:

> Although the war has been to our advantage, how much we have at the same time lost through poor harvests, the plague—which was, of course, a result of the war—internal disorder, and, even more, through military recruitment! Now all that remains is to wish for a long peace by which we could attain a respite to restore calm, bring affairs into order and finally enjoy full public tranquility.

Although the desire for peace was hardly controversial in 1774, Paul's initiative implied a criticism of the war policy as such and especially of the mismanagement accompanying it. In the next section, for example, he inveighed against the imbalance in priorities and misallocation of resources. "Everything is done with the last [available] means," he wrote, "and nothing is held in reserve; and so if a breakdown occurs in some area, we have next to nothing with which to recover there; it is necessary to withdraw our resources from another place, thereby weakening it: hence, we act without having anything in reserve."

[56]"Rassuzhdenie o gosudarstve voobshche, otnositel'no chisla voisk, potrebnogo dlia zashchity onogo, i kasatel'no oborony vsekh predelov," the complete text of which I have found only in manuscript in *GBL, f.* Barsk XVII, *d.* 10, unnumbered. Excerpts have, however, been published in Lebedev, *Grafy Paniny*, pp. 184–98. and in Makogonenko, *Denis Fonvizin*, pp. 168–70. Quotes in the following paragraphs are from the manuscript copy.

[57]Internal evidence places it somewhere in the period from early July to October 1 (the day news of Pugachev's capture arrived in the capital), for the author speaks of the continuing rebellion. See analysis in Ia. L. Barskov, "Proekty voennykh reform tsesarevicha Pavla I," in *Russkii istoricheskii zhurnal*, vol. 1 (Petrograd, 1917), p. 118.

This situation accounted for the "Orenburg events," he went on, a clear case of not maintaining the proper balance of state commitments. The primary treasure of the state is its people, and so the preservation of the people is the state's salvation. But the people were overburdened, they abandoned their settlements, left the land uncultivated, and finally went into revolt. Paul then suggested a formula to remedy the situation. "The state should be regarded as a body," he asserted. "The ruler is its head, the laws are its soul, morals its heart, wealth and abundance its health, military power its arms and all other parts serving its defense, and religion is the law under which everything is constituted." These sections must be in proper balance. If too many resources are committed to military power, the health of all the other members suffers and undermines the overall strength of the state. The government should therefore allocate only sufficient resources for the external defense and maintenance of internal order without unnecessarily burdening the population. Then Paul followed these remarks with a number of specific proposals for bringing about a balanced arrangement of military and police forces.

While clearly meant to be helpful and instructive, the memoir had unmistakable political overtones. It repeated many of Panin's arguments for a properly regulated state administration, the need for peace and internal development. If it fell far short of expressing the "prejudice against the existing order and all of Catherine's institutions" that some authors have ascribed to Panin's influence,[58] it showed that Paul endorsed the principles his governor had imparted and was willing to speak out when he saw them violated by the ambitious imperial policies of Panin's enemies.

In anticipation of the crisis of Paul's majority, to be taken up in the next chapter, it should be noted that this evidence of the success of Panin's instruction could not have come at a more inopportune time for Catherine. War, inflation, crop failure, epidemics, and from late 1773 the massive upheaval of the Pugachev Rebellion had forced the government into a state of perpetual crisis. Bitter infighting among the court factions and dwindling support of public opinion added to Catherine's worries. In the midst of these difficulties Paul was coming into his majority and, if the empress needed reminding, the appearance of several plots told her that some people would gladly see

[58]The words are from Lebedev, *Grafy Paniny*, pp. 135–36, but as indicated above (note 52), it reflects a common view of Panin's influence on Paul.

her son on the throne. Under the circumstances, she could scarcely have derived any comfort from the fact that Paul chose this particular time to venture his first independent statements on government policy.

9

The Crisis of Paul's Majority and the Fall
of the Panin Party

Under normal conditions Paul would have come into his majority on his eighteenth birthday in September 1772. But owing to the unsettled political situation, Catherine decided to postpone official recognition of the change until the grand duke's marriage to Princess Wilhemina of Hesse-Darmstadt a year later.[1] It was a difficult time for the empress. She was aware that Paul, as his father's sole legitimate heir and last surviving male of the Petrine line, possessed claims much stronger than her own. Moreover, the grand duke enjoyed considerable popular support. In public appearances he often received warmer greetings than his mother. This was especially true in Moscow, where in 1768 a large crowd mobbed Paul and his governor, hailing the grand duke as their only true sovereign.[2] Since Catherine had no intention of stepping down or sharing rule with her son, she had to find a way of removing Paul from court without provoking popular resentment. The marriage offered an ideal pretext. It would engage Paul in the tasks of setting up a new household and producing an heir of his own, not to mention separat-

---

[1] Since 1771, in anticipation of Paul's majority, Catherine had been pressing the business of finding a marriage partner for him. Asseburg, *Denkwürdigkeiten*, pp. 249, 254.

[2] "Le jour que ce Prince est parti de Moscou, à peine la voiture, dans laquelle il était avec M. Panine, pouvait-elle [avancer] à cause de l'affluence de monde de toute espèce qui se trouvait sur son passage et qui le comblait de bénédictions. Cet entousiasme pour ce Prince chéri et d'une figure aimable a éclaté dans la plupart des stations où le peuple s'est assemblé pour le voir; il a été si nombreux dans une station que M. Panine, fort embarrassé, a été obligé de sortir de la voiture et de representer avec douceur et modération a cette multitude qui l'environnait les bornes de l'obéissance et du respect qu'il devait à sa Souveraine actuelle et de l'engager à se tenir dans le devoir. Le peuple appelait le Grand-Duc son unique Souverain, nommant M. Panine son père, son protecteur, lui disant qu'il était toute sa confiance et son espoir et lui recommandant le Prince." Rossignol to Choiseul, March 19, 1768, *SIRIO*, 141: 409–10. On Paul's popularity see further Ia. L. Barskov, "Pis'ma imp. Ekateriny II k gr. P. V. Zavadovskomu," *Russkii istoricheskii zhurnal*, no. 5 (1918), p. 225.

ing him from the tutelage of the Panin party. These circumstances would minimize the risk of his playing a political role.

The soundness of this plan did not, however, diminish tensions during the year and a half from the spring of 1772 to the grand duke's marriage in September 1773. Throughout this period individuals and factions engaged in complicated intrigues to protect themselves from the changes certain to follow Paul's majority. Interwoven with the intrigues were a number of important events, including a switch of imperial favorites, disturbances in the metropolitan guards, and a series of critical foreign policy decisions ranging from the Polish and Turkish involvements to the treaty with Denmark on the exchange of Holstein. In short, politics were in a state of almost constant turmoil, a situation that has led historians to characterize the period as "the crisis of Paul's majority."

The crisis has most often been presented in terms of a clash between the empress and the Panin party. The original version was concocted by the former Decembrist M. A. Fonvizin,[3] who asserted that the Panins planned to overthrow Catherine and establish Paul on the throne with a constitution limiting autocratic power.[4] Although some writers have since modified this interpretation contending that the Panin scheme went no further than to raise Paul to co-ruler, no substantial challenge has appeared to the view of a Panin-led conspiracy.[5] A second aspect of the same interpretation

[3]Not to be confused with D. I. Fonvizin, Panin's secretary and M. A. Fonvizin's uncle.

[4]In his work published in 1853, *Primechaniia k "Histoire philosophique et politique de Russie" par Enneau et Chennechot*, he wrote: "My deceased father related to me that in 1773 or 1774, when the Grand Duke Paul Petrovich attained majority and married the princess of Darmstadt, named Natal'ia Alekseevna, Count N. I. Panin, his brother fieldmarshal [sic] Peter Ivanov., Princess E. R. Dashkova, Prince Repnin, one of the archbishops, possibly even Metropolitan Gavriil, and many of the nobles and guards officers entered into a conspiracy with the goal of removing Catherine II, who had no right to rule, and instead of her to elevate her son. Paul knew about this, agreed to accept the constitution proposed to him by Panin, and affirming it with his signature he gave an oath to the effect that upon ascending the throne he would not abrogate that basic state law limiting [tsarist] power." Quoted from a later republication, "Zapiski M. A. Fonvizina," *Russkaia Starina*, 42, (1884), p. 62. It is difficult to say where Fonvizin got this story. Like many other assertions in his work, it contradicts known facts and finds no corroboration in the sources. It may, however, represent a garbled version of the Saldern plot (discussed below in this chapter) combined with a sketchy knowledge of a later constitutional plan composed by the Panin brothers and Denis Fonvizin (see chapter 10, below). For a detailed critique of the M. A. Fonvizin story see my thesis, "Nikita Panin's Role," pp. 13–19.

[5]To note just a few works that touch on this question, V. E. Iakushikin, *Gosudarstven-*

concerned Catherine's actions. Since nothing came of the alleged Panin conspiracy, it was naturally assumed that the empress had divined the scheme and skillfully mapped out her own strategy. She supposedly played one faction against another, frustrated her enemies' initiatives, and emerged victorious at the end of 1773.[6] The persistence of this interpretation may be explained by its undeniable dramatic impact, and perhaps even more importantly, because it cut a neat swath through the often intractable evidence. The problem with it, however, lies in the depiction of the principal figures as masterful schemers, a view that does considerable violence to the historical record.

First, no convincing evidence of a Panin conspiracy has ever emerged. On the contrary, the Panin party seemed to consider itself the victim of conspiracy. The atmosphere at the "young court" resembled a state of siege. Far from laying plans for a power grab, its members expected at any moment to be routed and cast into disgrace. Even less do the documents reveal Catherine as a confident and skillful manipulator cleverly setting traps for her enemies. The empress saw treachery everywhere and fluctuated between fits of despondency and frenzied activity to avert it. Both Catherine and Panin were struggling against confusion, mistrust, and occasional panic. In some instances they were reacting to real challenges posed by hostile elements in society or at court; in others they seemed to

---

naia vlast', pp. 53–55, and G. P. Makogonenko, *Denis Fonvizin*, pp. 160–62, accept the M. A. Fonvizin story in its essential outlines. An even more eager acceptance may be seen in the recent work of N. Ia. Eidel'man, *Gertsen protiv samoderzhaviia* (Moscow, 1973), pp. 97–130. Kobeko, *Tsesarevich Pavel Petrovich*, p. 77, and Braudo, "Nikita Ivanovich Panin," *RBS*, 200, leave the question up in the air, if not altogether confused, yet both make a strong point of the hostility between Catherine and the Panins and give the impression that there was definitely foul play; in the same vein, though handled with much greater analytical skill, K. V. Pigarev, *Tvorchestvo Fonvizina*, p. 135, rejects the M. A. Fonvizin story but then immediately clouds the issue by arguing that "where there is smoke, there is fire," though the nature of the fire is not spelled out. M. N. Pokrovskii may come closest to the truth, albeit more through an impressionistic evaluation than careful research, in stating that Paul's claims were more important for the fear they engendered than for any real threat they contained. Yet, oddly enough, he too cannot escape a suspicion that Panin was attached to a plot against Catherine, "if not to this one, then to previous conspiracies." *Istoriia Rossii s drevneishikh vremen* in *Izbrannye proizvedeniia*, 2: 118–19.

[6]For examples of this view see Alexander, *Autocratic Politics*, p. 85, who credits Catherine with an "intricate balancing act, performed with consummate skill" in handling the court parties. Also Griffiths, "Russian Court Politics," p. 81, who assumes that Panin wanted to act but was outmaneuvered by the empress.

respond irrationally to illusory threats, mere projections of their own
insecurities or groundless rumors planted by intriguers. In any event,
not cool calculation but fear and consternation most accurately
characterized their actions and statements.

As noted in chapter 7, one source of tension lay in the general
government crisis of the early 1770s. The troubles in Poland and the
lingering war with Turkey were severely straining the financial and
human resources at the regime's disposal. Beginning in 1769 the
state debt mounted at a rate of two to three million rubles annually,
while during the same period head-tax payments were falling into
ever-greater arrears. As a result, the treasury was soon exhausted and
foreign credit began to evaporate. Although the government managed to cover current expenses by printing paper *assignats,* this device
had the dangerous side effect of driving up bread prices, a problem
that became especially acute after a poor harvest in 1770–1771.[7] The
manpower drain was equally troublesome. The Turkish struggle had
settled into a war of attrition with injury, disease, and desertion taking a heavy toll of the Russian forces. Despite extraordinary levies,
the government experienced continual difficulty keeping its units up
to strength. To make matters worse, a plague epidemic hit the Danubian army in 1770 and then travelled north to ravage Kiev and, the
following year, Moscow and its environs. The scourge claimed nearly
100,000 victims in the latter region alone and provoked a popular
uprising that added one more domestic ill to a government already
harassed by insurgencies in such widely scattered areas as Kizhi in
the Lake Ladoga region and the Yaik Cossack territory north of the
Caspian Sea.[8]

Of course, Catherine had faced similar difficulties at the time of
her accession ten years earlier and managed to ride them out. But
those previous crises were not of her own making, and she had been
able to muster broad support to settle them. The critical institutions
of the senate, synod, guards, and court parties united in establishing
the new regime on a firm footing. In addition, Catherine had enjoyed
the enthusiastic backing of the young journalists of the Sumarokov
and Kheraskov circles. By the early 1770s, however, much of this
support had eroded. The senate and upper administration were split
among warring factions. The metropolitan guards were unruly and

[7]On financial problems and difficulties in tax collection, see the reports in the state
council for 9 May, 11 August, 20 October, and 28 November 1771. *AGS,* 1: 412–14.
[8]Much of the foregoing summarized from Alexander, *Autocratic Politics,* pp. 15–20.

excitable. One plot had been discovered in 1769, and another more serious one was soon to appear.[9] Finally, as previously indicated, the empress' erstwhile literary allies had not only turned from congratulations to criticism; they sounded an even more ominous note by projecting onto Paul the reform aspirations earlier associated with Catherine. To cap these difficulties, early in 1772 the empress got into a personal squabble with Grigorii Orlov over his infidelity and had to remove him from the court. Thus, in a most crucial moment of her reign, Catherine suddenly found herself threatened with an absence of support at every level of the society, from the overburdened peasants right up to the inner circles of court. This isolation and the fears it naturally engendered created ideal conditions for intriguers and adventurers, who were prepared to make the most of the crisis of Paul's majority.

1. The Panin Party's Changing Fortunes

For the Panin party Orlov's troubles came as an unexpected boon —although the device for his removal was not altogether to Panin's liking. Catherine appointed him head of the peace delegation to meet with the Turks at Focşani. Panin, who had worked hard to establish the peace conference, wanted a subtle and flexible diplomat capable of bringing the negotiations to a successful completion. Sending the inexperienced and temperamental Orlov was, as Fonvizin expressed it, just the kind of "willful stupidity" that could jeopardize a promising peace initiative.[10] Nevertheless, Panin believed that the combined influence of directives from the capital and the counsel of Ambassador Obreskov at Focşani would be sufficient to prevent Orlov from wrecking the peace conference.[11] On balance, it seemed much preferable to have him in Focşani than in St. Petersburg, where he could meddle directly in policy formulation.

With the stage thus set in the spring of 1772 the tempo of crisis and

[9]On the 1769 plot see V. Z. Dzhincharadze, "Iz istorii tainoi ekspeditsii pri Senate (1762–1801 gg)," *Uchenye zapiski*, Novgorodskii gosudarstvennyi pedogogicheskii institut, vypusk 2, no. 2 (1957,)pp. 97–99, cited in Alexander, *Autocratic Politics*, p. 30.

[10]D. I. Fonvizin to P. I. Panin, *FSS*, 2: 393–95. Peter Panin must have been worried that Orlov would rob his brother of the credit for running affairs and negotiating the peace, for in the same letter Fonvizin reassures him that all Europe knows who really manages Russian foreign policy. True merit will endure and be recognized, he concludes, while the favorite's glory will vanish as soon as he loses favor.

[11]D. I. Fonvizin to A. M. Obreskov, September 1772, *FSS*, 2: 403; also same to P. I. Panin, 6 April 1772, where he indicates that members of the Panin group will be at the peace conference as cavaliers, 2: 377.

intrigue increased steadily. Less than a month after Orlov's departure a plot was discovered among the metropolitan guards. Several non-commissioned officers of the Preobrazhenskii regiment decided to take advantage of the troubles at court to rid the country of the Orlovs' influence once and for all. They planned to sweep Catherine from the throne and proclaim Paul. The rebels would then occupy the places vacated by the Orlovs and their clients, naturally all for the good of the nation. The significant point was that the cause proved sufficiently popular for the rebels to enlist a large number of adherents before the government got word and moved against them.[12]

The plot left Catherine badly shaken. During investigation and sentencing of the rebels, she retreated to Finland with advisers and trusted guards officers to confer on measures to control the unruly regiments.[13] She would have liked to remove them from the capital, but this option was rejected as too risky. The social composition and established privileges of the guards made them a political force to be reckoned with. Moreover, Catherine, a non-Russian, did not want to appear to be reversing the traditions of Peter the Great who had first organized the regiments. People might attribute her action to a contempt for Russians and their institutions. Faced with these considerations, she took the safer course of keeping the entire corps well under full strength and heavily infiltrated with reliable agents.[14]

[12]Plot described in some detail by Solms to Frederick II, 26 June 1772, *SIRIO*, 72: 164–65, where he indicates the participation of 30 officers and men. The Swedish envoy Ribbing reported that 100 persons were involved; dispatch of 6 July 1772, *SRa*, Muscovitica 356, no 28. Also D. I. Fonvizin to P. I. Panin, 10 July 1772, *FSS*, 2: 390.

[13]As reported by the Swedish envoy, she was accompanied by "K. [G.] Razumovskii, Z. [G.] Chernyshev, I. [G.] Orlov, L. [N.] Naryshkin, [S.] Kuz'min, Hofmarshal Orlov, Prince Bariatinskii" (who had discovered the plot), and Kameriunker Potemkin. Reported by Ribbing to Chancellery President, 13 July 1772, *SRa*, Muscovitica 356, no. 29.

[14]In reporting Catherine's failure to disband the guards Solms gave an excellent précis of the position of this corps. "The officers composing the four regiments are mostly young men from the leading families of the country who are enrolled there to attain the quickest possible advancement, because on leaving these regiments they are placed in the army three ranks above those they had in the guards. A captain advances to a colonel rank and obtains command of a regiment . . . . . Being in the capital and always close to the court, the officers have more opportunity to be known and to make use of the protection and influence of their relatives in high positions to move them forward and get them appointments as the occasion arises. If you add to this the enjoyment of living in high society, participating in all the pleasures, and not being especially burdened by service, it is easy to understand that it would provoke discontent among all the nobility if one deprived them of the means for intrigues to advance their career . . . .. [They] would not view this

Shortly after her return from Finland, in a move clearly designed to mollify the guards, the empress took a new lover from among the young officers not associated with the Orlovs, and by September the new favorite, a lieutenant of the Horse Guards, A. S. Vasil'chikov, was officially installed at the palace in rooms adjoining the empress' chambers.[15] Though not initially a Panin candidate, Vasil'chikov understandably attached himself to the party opposing Orlov's return, and his advance brought with it several gains to the Panin group. Besides giving Nikita Panin much greater latitude in setting and executing policy, the empress granted Princess Dashkova 60,000 rubles to purchase an estate and honored another Panin client, General Bibikov, with the Alexander Nevskii order. About the same time she became exceptionally attentive to Paul. She dined with him regularly and even invited him to study government business with her.[16] These signs of renewed favor to the Panin group gave birth to rumors that Catherine was about to strip Grigorii Orlov of all his offices and give the most powerful of them, Master of Artillery, to Peter Panin, promoting him to field marshal in the bargain.[17] Although scarcely credible in view of the strained relations between the empress and the younger Panin, the rumor indicated that the recent

deprivation with indifference, and consequently, such a displacement could have dangerous consequences and occasion open rebellion in all four regiments." Solms to Frederick II, 27 July 1772, *SIRIO*, 72: 209–10.

[15]It has usually been assumed that Panin brought Vasil'chikov forward as his own candidate, but the first mention of the empress' favor included no references to Panin. Solms indicated that only after Orlov's return from Focşani did Vasil'chikov place himself under Panin's direction and patronage. Solms to Frederick II, 3 August and 11 September 1772, *SIRIO*, 72: 225–28, 257–60. On the selection of the new favorite as a means of satisfying the people who resented and feared Orlov influence, see Barskov, "Pis'ma Ekateriny k Zavadovskomu," p. 225.

[16]The good effect on the public of this change and the gains for the Panin group are described by Solms in his dispatch of 4 September 1772. As early as 27 March one sees a new buoyancy in Panin's conversation as he tells how he established his system against the objections of many who have since had to admit its superiority over the previous domination by Austria. It is clear that Panin feels himself firmly in the saddle again. Solms to Frederick II, 27 March and 4 September 1772, *SIRIO*, 72: 59–60, 254–56. Catherine herself described the warm relationship developing between her and Paul at this time to Mme. Bielke in letters of 25 June and 24 August, *SIRIO*, 13: 259–65. For additional comments see I. I. Kruk to A. B. Kurakin, 15 August 1772, *Arkhiv Kurakina*, 6: 397; and Barsukov, *Rasskazy iz russkoi istorii*, pp. 133–34. On the rewards to Dashkova and Bibikov, see Ribbing to Chancellery President, 7 September 1772, *SRa*, Muscovitica 356, no. 36. The awards came in conjunction with Vasil'chikov's promotion from *kamerger* to *kameriunker*.

[17]Ribbing to Chancellery President, 14 September 1772, *SRa*, Muscovitica 356, no. 37.

changes were viewed as a considerable victory for the Panin forces.

But the success was short-lived. Panin soon faced new difficulties on the diplomatic front. With partition staring them in the face, the Poles were proving more obdurate than ever. Among other things, the king refused to call a *seim* to ratify the seizure of his lands. Then while the Russians concentrated attention on events in Warsaw, Gustav III of Sweden staged a royalist coup in Stockholm that dealt a heavy blow to the Northern System, not to mention the danger of a military challenge from that side. These setbacks made success in the Turkish negotiations all the more urgent.[18] But here Orlov was in a position to frustrate Panin's initiatives and increase his difficulties. In an unmistakable reference to Orlov and his allies on the empress' council, Panin complained bitterly of the persons, not "true sons of the fatherland," who for their own reasons were sabotaging the peace negotiations.[19]

As if to confirm all Panin's fears, Orlov precipitously broke off the negotiations in August and hastily set out for St. Petersburg. The collapse of the peace conference had little to do with the negotiating issues. Panin had repeatedly urged moderation and had just obtained council approval to command Orlov to concede the difficult points and achieve a quick settlement.[20] The real reason for the rupture lay not at Focşani but, as Fonvizin told Obreskov, in the "new situation" at court, the installation of Vasil'chikov as favorite.[21] Orlov was not a man who backed down gracefully. Realizing that the change could mean disgrace and the end of influence for his party, he rushed to the capital for a desperate, last-ditch effort to restore his waning fortunes.

A four-week quarantine halted the former favorite outside St. Petersburg and averted an immediate personal confrontation.[22] Meanwhile, however, a correspondence ran daily between the court

[18]N. Panin's worried wait-and-see attitude toward Sweden described by Solms to Frederick II, 24 August 1772, *SIRIO*, 72: 247–52. Instructions to G. G. Orlov on 4 September 1772 indicate fear of the changes in Sweden as important cause for pushing negotiations with Turks, *SIRIO*, 118: 219–20; of course, Orlov was already en route to the capital when the instructions were sent.

[19]N. I. Panin to P. A. Rumiantsev, 4 September 1772, *SIRIO*, 118: 227–28; one may assume that Panin was much more to the point in his private comments, which, as he indicated in the same letter, he was sending with V. V. Dolgorukov, as they were inappropriate for commission to writing.

[20]Barsukov, *Rasskazy iz russkoi istorii*, p. 131; *AGS*, vol. 1, pt. 2, 23–24.

[21]D. I. Fonvizin to A. M. Obreskov, September 1772, *FSS*, 2: 403.

[22]I. I. Kruk to A. B. Kurakin, 16 September 1772, *Arkhiv Kurakina*, 6: 422–24.

and Orlov's estate south of the city, an exchange that took on the character of a bargaining session on the price of Orlov's removal. Not surprisingly, Panin spearheaded the drive to complete the favorite's disgrace, his advice being that Catherine should shower Orlov with such handsome rewards that he could not possibly refuse to withdraw. Catherine appeared to agree with this plan, and by the end of September the following package was offered. Orlov was to depart for at least a year and, except for the capital cities and environs, he could live where he pleased. In addition, he would receive a yearly pension of 150,000 rubles, an outright gift of 100,000 rubles to set up household, an estate of 10,000 peasants at a place of his choosing, the empress' newest Parisian silver service, plus an ordinary service.[23] But instead of accepting this generous offer, Orlov continued to make difficulties. In a gesture of defiance, he unilaterally proclaimed himself a prince of the Holy Roman Empire on the basis of a patent earlier negotiated for him by Catherine and then held up until he could first be made a Russian prince. Panin confidently predicted that this perverse behavior would hasten Orlov's downfall.[24] Yet to everyone's surprise it had the opposite effect. Catherine became more hesitant than before and refused to make a final break.[25]

Although the cause of Catherine's paralysis was not immediately clear, some clues were evident. Orlov still had many friends and clients at court feverishly working on his behalf. They carried a secret correspondence between Orlov and Catherine, carefully concealing the contents from Panin or any of his supporters. Presumably Orlov was again raising the spectre of Catherine falling into dependence on the Panin party, and he surely laid great stress on the dangers of such dependence at the time of Paul's approaching majority.[26] This tactic

[23]Solms to Frederick II, 18, 21, 25 and 28 September 1772, *SIRIO*, 72: 263–66.

[24]Solms to Frederick II, 9 October 1772, *SIRIO*, 72: 268.

[25]Solms to Frederick II, 23 October 1772, *SIRIO*, 72: 269–72.

[26]This was the understanding at the time, as Solms reported: "Des spéculatifs s'imaginent que l'Impératrice sera bien aise de l'avoir [Orlov] à portée, comme une personne de confiance, et pouvoir se serivir de lui, au cas que le comte Panin, sous le nom du grand-duc, voudrait un jour machiner quelque chose contre Elle, car on prétend savoir, que dans toutes les lettres, que le comte Orlow a écrites à S.M.I. avant son arrivée, il a toujours tâché d'exciter en Elle des soupçons contre les intentions de ce ministre, et quoiqu'ils ne paraissent pas avoir porté coup, il se pourrait pourtant, qu'ils ayant laisse quelque impression et que l'Impératrice croit nécessaire de se precautionner contre tout événement [sic]." Solms to Frederick II, 1 January 1773, *SIRIO*, 72: 310.

seemed to have the desired effect, as the conflicting pressures plunged the empress into a deep depression. During the closing months of 1772 contemporaries described her as utterly bewildered and sunk in indolence. Government business came to a complete standstill.[27] Catherine continued to keep Paul at her side and treated him with the same affection as in previous months. She maintained Vasil'chi- kov as the favorite and saw him regularly. At the same time, how- ever, she could not bring herself to a decision on Orlov's dismissal or even restrain his growing arrogance.[28]

One thing appeared certain. Political considerations and not a rekindling of personal affection accounted for the tolerance of Orlov's behavior. After the quarantine he met openly with friends and rel- atives, but more than two months passed before he was allowed to visit the court. Even then Catherine did not meet with him privately but in the presence of two ministers, I. P. Elagin and I. I. Betskoi, the first a friend of Panin, the other of Orlov.[29] At this meeting in late December it was agreed that Orlov would retire to the Baltic city of Revel the following week and wait until his future position could be clarified.[30] The decision was intended to reduce the unbearable tension at court. It in no way implied the disgrace of Orlov, whose influence was still formidable. The same week he obtained for his creature Prince Viazemskii a special decoration (the Grand Cordon Bleu) with a 15,000-ruble prize, an award long sought by such dis- tinguished ministers as Ivan Chernyshev, Vice-Chancellor Golitsyn, and Count Münnich.[31] Orlov had convinced Catherine of the need to hold him and his party in reserve as a counter to hostile moves from the Panin camp.

2. The Fight for Survival

Within a year the tables had turned full around. If Panin gloated over Orlov's apparent fall the previous spring, he now had to con-

[27]Solms to Frederick II, 14 December 1772, and on how the mood of uncertainty is affecting everyone and bringing all affairs to a halt, 25 December 1772, *SIRIO*, 72: 303– 05, 305–06.

[28]Solms to Frederick II, 29 January 1773, *SIRIO*, 72: 314–15.

[29]I. I. Kruk to A. B. Kurakin, December 1772, *Arkhiv Kurakina*, 7: 126; Solms to Fred- erick II, 25 December 1772, *SIRIO*, 72: 306–07.

[30]Solms to Frederick II, 25 December 1772, *SIRIO*, 72: 307.

[31]The Chernyshevs were especially incensed by this award, as they had stood by Orlov in his troubles only to see rewards go to people they disliked. Solms to Frederick II, 8 January 1773, *SIRIO*, 72: 310–13.

centrate all efforts on assuring his own survival. His relations with
Catherine deteriorated sharply in the first months of 1773 and continued on shaky ground right up to Paul's marriage in September.
The empress resented his vigorous advocacy of Orlov's removal and
may even have suspected some dangerous scheme behind it. Naturally, the Orlov brothers and their friends worked overtime to press
their advantage. They confounded the empress with rumors of plots
emanating from the "young court" and kept her suspicions constant-
ly aroused. The tactic forced Panin into a hopeless situation. Whatever he did to combat the Orlov party simply confirmed Catherine's
suspicions that he was trying to isolate and manipulate her. She
seemed to take for granted that anything happening in the "young
court" was designed to menace her.

One example involved Panin's harboring of some former Orlov
clients who had misread the signals and deserted their patron during
his absence at Focşani. When Orlov returned to court in late 1772,
the deserters were badly compromised and ran for cover to the opposing party. Panin found places for them as chamberlains at the
"young court" where they could ride out the storm. An awkward
confrontation ensued. Catherine believed that Panin was surrounding
Paul with men ill-disposed toward her, and, while unwilling to ad-
dress Panin directly, she let it be known through rumor and third-
hand—one intermediary was the Holstein diplomat Casper von
Saldern[32]—that she wanted these turncoats dismissed. But Panin
refused to truckle. He insisted that personnel for the "young court"
was his affair. In a pique poorly calculated to allay Catherine's
suspicions he retorted that she had no business telling him whom he
could have as friends.[33] A second source of recrimination appeared
in connection with Panin's attempt to control the arrangements for
Paul's marriage. Catherine's agents intercepted a letter to Paul's
future mother-in-law from Baron Asseburg, a close friend of Panin
and the Russian broker in negotiating the marriage with Princess
Wilhemina.[34] In the letter Asseburg admonished the princess' mother
to rely solely on Panin's advice and guidance when she arrived in
Russia and to confide in no one else, presumably including the em-

[32]See below, note 59.

[33]Solms to Frederick II, 30 July 1773, *SIRIO*, 72: 388–89.

[34]Catherine to Asseburg, 10 May 1771, *SIRIO*, 13: 82–88; Asseburg, *Denkwürdigkeiten*, pp. 55–75, 408–10.

press as well. Catherine flew into a rage over the letter. She complained that everyone in the world was trying to run her son's affairs for her, and she intended to put an immediate stop to such interference.[35] Matters came to such a pass that by early July she and Panin were no longer on speaking terms: a troublesome situation, as Panin observed, for a minister who had to meet with her frequently in council to decide affairs of state.[36]

Contributing to the growth of suspicion and ill-will between Catherine and her minister was Orlov's recall from Revel in March 1773 and restoration of his former ranks and offices.[37] What disturbed Panin most was that soon after his return Orlov began meddling directly in the marriage arrangements. He even went so far as to court Princess Wilhemina's sister, a relationship that could have led to the former favorite becoming Paul's brother-in-law by marriage.[38] Since Panin could only surmise that Catherine knew of and approved this audacious move, he was convinced that his days as first minister were numbered. In fact, by early August rumors circulated that he was about to be replaced at the head of foreign affairs by his long-time enemy Zakhar Chernyshev.[39] Faced with this threat, Panin clung more tightly than ever to his prerogatives as governor, and it was about this time that he rebuffed Catherine's request to purge the "young court" of men ill-disposed toward her. Though understandable enough under the circumstances, Panin's response simply reinforced the empress' fears about the intentions of the Panin party and the "young court." She let it be known that Panin was keeping

---

[35]Catherine to Baron Cherkassov, May 1773 [?], in Lebedev, *Grafy Paniny*, pp. 357–58.

[36]Solms to Frederick II, 19 July 1773, *SIRIO*, 72: 379–80.

[37]I. I. Kruk to A. B. Kurakin, 8 April 1773, *Arkhiv Kurakina*, 7: 179, tells of Orlov's return from Revel and regular appearance at court; also see Solms' dispatches of 12 March 1773, and his report on the ukase restoring Orlov's offices and ranks, 20 May 1773, *SIRIO*, 72: 348, 356–57.

[38]Panin seemed appalled by this development when he asked Solms to have Frederick II use his influence with the Darmstadt family to end the involvement of their daughter with Orlov. Of course, it is possible that Panin exaggerated the danger, either because of his own overly anxious perception of Orlov's designs or because he was then fighting Prussia's demand for Danzig and could use his alleged lack of influence as a pretext for not supporting the Prussian pretensions. Solms to Frederick II, 24 June 1773, *SIRIO*, 72: 367–68.

[39]Nolcken to Chancellery President, 2 August 1773, *SRa*, Muscovitica 386. About two weeks earlier Panin had warned Solms that he might soon have to retire. His disgrace, he was sure, had already been decided upon. Solms to Frederick II, 14 July 1773, *SIRIO*, 72: 372.

Paul in too great a state of dependence, and that she wanted the governor to relinquish supervision of the grand duke well in advance of the marriage. When Panin still refused to budge, Catherine had him removed from the palace on the pretext that the rooms had to be remodeled.[40] Another sign of the empress' anxiety, as well as the troubled position of the Panin party, was her surveillance of General Peter Panin, then living in retirement in Moscow and grumbling about the situation at the Petersburg court. Catherine ordered Moscow Governor-General Volkonskii to submit special reports on all of Peter Panin's activities, including the people visiting him and the substance of their communication.[41]

Catherine's fears were entirely misplaced. The Panin men, so far from plotting her overthrow, were girding themselves for what seemed a certain defeat and disgrace. Panin's grand-nephew A. B. Kurakin was warned about returning from Europe at this time because of the impending difficulties. His uncle Prince Repnin counseled patience and tried to prepare him for the danger that lay ahead. "[The Panin brothers] are the two most honest men in our country, and it is necessary to be entirely attached to them in good times or bad. It is better to share their misfortune than to be happy without them or with their enemies."[42] If Repnin, who was in London, sensed trouble, it was felt all the more keenly back home. Field Marshal Rumiantsev and General Bibikov, both Panin adherents, complained of the court's increasingly unfavorable treatment.[43] And Panin's secretary Fonvizin gave a vivid description of the group's fears. In reply to a request from his family to find his brother-in-law a post, he wrote that such favors were altogether out of the question; he did not know from one moment to the next whether he would have a job himself. He reported that Panin had just been driven from his rooms in the palace and "God knows where he will be living and on what footing." The Orlovs and Chernyshevs were maligning him

[40]D. I. Fonvizin to family, August 1773[?], *FSS*, 2: 355; Solms to Frederick II, 30 July 1773, *SIRIO*, 72: 389.

[41]M. N. Volkonskii to Catherine, 9 September 1773, *Osmnadtsatyi vek*, 1: 121–22, a report on the activities of P. I. Panin, made in answer to a request from Catherine 30 August 1773.

[42]N. V. Repnin to A. B. Kurakin, London, 22 March 1773, *Arkhiv Kurakina*, 7: 173–74; also Natal'ia Repnina to A. B. Kurakin, 17 August 1772, *Arkhiv Kurakina*, 6: 398.

[43]A. I. Bibikov to D. I. Fonvizin, 7 August 1772, and 28 February 1773, in Bibikov, *Zapiski*, pp. 72–75, and editorial remarks, pp. 105–08. Klokman, *Fel'dmarshal Rumiantsev*, pp. 142–49. See especially his letters to N. Panin, p. 143.

at every turn, and their chicanery simply beggared description. "Not in the meanest government bureau are there such pettifogging intrigues as occur every minute at our court," Fonvizin went on, "and it is overwhelming my poor count whose patience seems to have no end. He is afraid to bring his brother here lest they break his neck all the sooner, and there's not a single soul whom he could call a true friend." Then Fonvizin told that the final battle would come in September at Paul's wedding, when they would learn their ultimate fate. "I ask no more from God," he concluded, "than that I might emerge from this hell with honor."[44]

If Catherine's fears were misplaced, so too were the Panins'. Despite the efforts to compromise the Panin group, Catherine was not fully convinced of their treachery or bent on their destruction. Indeed, she may have feared that a public break with Nikita Panin would only increase the danger of a precipitous move in favor of Paul. So while guarding against this eventuality—she recalled all of the Orlov brothers to the capital during the crucial month of September—she also arranged for an amicable conclusion to Panin's governorship. A few days before Paul's marriage, she issued a decree thanking Nikita Panin for his great services to the country as preceptor of the grand duke,[45] and she sweetened the bitterness of his separation from his charge and commanding position at court with lavish rewards. He received estates totaling 9,000 peasants, a grant of 100,000 rubles to set up a new household, an annual pension of 30,000 rubles over and above an increased yearly salary of 14,000 rubles, a service worth 50,000 rubles, purchase at state expense of any house in the city, use of court livery, provisions and wine cellar for a year, and promotion to field marshal rank with the title of Minister of Foreign Affairs.[46] In one sense, these rewards reflected Catherine's feeling of relief at coming through the crisis of Paul's majority. They were a pay-off for Nikita Panin's cooperation and perhaps as well his pledge to dampen criticism by his supporters. Two days later Catherine wrote to Moscow Governor-General Volkonskii, who had been reporting on Peter Panin's murmurings against the court, that "since I recently showered his brother with undeserved riches, I

[44]D. I. Fonvizin to family, August 1773[?], *FSS*, 2: 353–56.

[45]Decree of 23 September 1773, published in *SIRIO*, 118: 466; French original in *LOII*, f, 36, d. 1157, 84 and verso; see also *AGS*, 1: 2, where Panin asks that the decree be read into the record.

[46]D. I. Fonvizin to Ia. I. Bulgakov, 27 September 1773, *FSS*, 2: 398.

hope that he will shut him up, and my house will be cleansed of chicanery."[47]

There was one bit of chicanery that Catherine evidently did not yet know about, one of the most bizarre and perplexing intrigues of this period. It involved the Holstein diplomat Caspar von Saldern. For reasons not yet satisfactorily explained, Saldern attempted earlier in the year to organize an anti-Catherine conspiracy at the "young court." Although Panin squelched the project at the very outset, it still evoked panicky feelings lest knowledge of it leak out and irretrievably compromise Paul and the entire Panin group. This was certainly one of the things Fonvizin had in mind when speaking of the hell they were going through. In a letter to Obreskov about that time he wrote that "Saldern's vile impudence began to be uncovered hourly after his departure. It is horrible to contemplate what is coming to light! There's not another such . . . on earth. He is already unmasked before Count Panin. I believe that we'll soon know even more about what kind of man Saldern is."[48] Since Saldern's murky designs have provided the basis for all later allegations of a Panin-led conspiracy to elevate Paul, the incident deserves a further examination.

Saldern was one of that long line of fugitives and expatriate adventurers who came to make their fortunes in eighteenth-century Russia. Born in 1710, the son of a Holstein official, he began government service at home in the office his father had previously held, *Amtsverwalter* in Neumünster. His taste for bribery and intrigue soon got him into trouble, and after a few years he had to flee to Russia in fear of arrest. There he ingratiated himself with Grand Duke Peter, who found a place for him among the Holstein faction at the St. Petersburg court.[49] He cooperated in Peter's plans to unite his homeland by absorbing Danish territories into Ducal Holstein. But after Peter was overthrown and murdered, Saldern aligned himself with the new leadership at the Russian court and supported efforts to annex Ducal Holstein into the Danish kingdom. Hence, insofar as he had any loyalties, they seemed to belong to a united Holstein,

[47]Catherine to M. N. Volkonskii, 25 September 1773, *Osmnadtsatyi vek*, 1: 96.

[48]D.I. Fonvizin to A. M. Obreskov, 28 September 1773, *FSS*, 2: 407–08.

[49]Saldern was in trouble within his first year of service but was protected by highly placed patrons. Later his patrons ran into troubles of their own and Saldern eloped to avoid sharing their fate. E. Holm, "Caspar v. Saldern og den dansk-norske Regering," *Historisk tidskrift*, vol. 4, no. 3 (Copenhagen, 1872–73), pp. 76–78.

and he cared little how this object was accomplished. He certainly had no fondness for either Denmark or Russia, both of which he used unscrupulously in his primary goal of advancing his own overweening ambition for wealth and power.[50]

Saldern managed to win Panin's trust and during the 1760s served as an unofficial adviser on German affairs and joined the "young court," participating in the education of the grand duke. In 1771 Panin appointed him Russian minister to Warsaw during the crucial final phase of negotiations on the partition of Poland. But in Poland Saldern's success finally ran out. Although Panin had apparently closed his eyes to the unsavory sides of Saldern's personality,[51] he quickly realized his mistake when the Holsteiner got to Warsaw and began giving free rein to his worst impulses. Apart from ordinary bribery demanded for even the smallest services, Saldern used his position in Poland to try to extort 20,000 écus from Prussia on the pretext of acting in Frederick II's interest. He forged Catherine's signature on an order to the Gottorp commission to pay himself 12,000 riksdollars, embezzled 12,000 rubles that the Danes were sending as a gift to Princess Dashkova, and to top everything he stole a diamond-studded gold snuffbox the empress had sent to a Polish dignitary.[52] If this were not enough, he arrested one of Panin's trusted embassy officials, an act that provoked Fonvizin, a personal friend of the unfortunate official, to write another colleague in

[50]In his conversations with Danes about Russia he spoke of the empire that had treated him so well with great distaste, saying on one occasion in his blunt fashion that one could "donnerait la Russie au diable." Holm, "Caspar v. Saldern," pp. 83–85. He sold his services to the Danes for 100,000 riksdollars, the amount he was to receive on conclusion of the treaty transferring Holstein to the Danish crown. On the background of this treaty see Holm, *Danmark-Norges historie fra den store nordiske krigs slutning til rigernes adskillelse (1720–1814)*, 5 (Copenhagen, 1906), pp. 165–94; S. C. Bech, *Danmarks Historie*, 9 (Copenhagen, 1965), pp. 404–07; Holm, "Caspar v. Saldern," p. 180.

[51]His arrogance and greed were, however, well known to subordinates in the Panin party. See, for example, Agrafena Kurakina to A. B. Kurakin, 21 December 1772, *Arkhiv Kurakina*, 7: 115–16; D. I. Fonvizin to P. I. Panin, 11 February 1771, and 26 June 1772, *FSS*, 2: 360–61, 389–90. The standard biography of Saldern by Otto Brandt, *Caspar von Saldern*, is rather unsatisfactory on Saldern's role in the crisis of 1773. The entire question is dismissed as an attempt to make Saldern the scapegoat for others' designs. The problem, says Brandt, is that all the sources are from people unfriendly to Saldern (pp. 261–64). It is, however, indicative of Saldern's personality that he left Russia without any friends who could state his side of the story.

[52]Holm, "Caspar v. Saldern," pp. 85, 171, 181–82; Solms to Frederick II, 27 August 1773, *SIRIO*, 72: 392–93.

Poland wishing him God's protection from disease and Ambassador Saldern.[53] What angered Panin most was Saldern's unrestrained bullying of the Poles. His arrogant intimidation and brandishing of military force endangered the partition negotiations and threatened to plunge the republic into greater disorder than ever. Thoroughly disabused, Panin recalled Saldern the moment the partition settlement was completed.[54]

The events following Saldern's return to St. Petersburg are as important as they are difficult to trace. According to the Prussian ambassador Solms, he came back bitterly resentful of Panin's turn against him and thirsting for revenge.[55] Saldern himself reported that he bore no grudge against Panin and even defended him to the empress.[56] In any case, soon after his return Saldern surprised foreign observers by abandoning ten years of unremitting hostility to the Orlov-Chernyshev faction and becoming what one diplomat called a regular "Orlowian."[57] About the same time (late 1772 or early 1773) he set in motion his plot to raise Paul to emperor and coregent. While much remains unclear about this episode, the following facts seem beyond doubt, as both Saldern and Panin affirmed them on separate occasions. Either just before or during Orlov's sojourn in Revel, Saldern approached the grand duke and persuaded him to sign a paper saying he would follow Saldern's advice. This document was to serve as the foundation for the conspiracy. Next Saldern went to Panin and, in the latter's words, advanced proposals that made one tremble just to listen to them. Panin flatly rejected any coopera-

[53]Panin ordered the official in question, A. I. Markov, to be released immediately and returned to Russia. The following year he sent Markov on a trusted mission to Western Europe. *SIRIO*, 118: 40. D. I. Fonvizin to Ia. I. Bulgakov, 30 December 1773, *FSS*, 2: 395–96.

[54]Solms to Frederick II, 20 July 1772, and 14 July 1773, *SIRIO*, 72: 197, 374; the feelings of the Panin group about this episode were aptly described in a letter from General Bibikov, who was then stationed with the Russian forces in Poland. "Affairs have gone their course here," he wrote, "but with all kinds of threats. Hunting sparrows with a blunderbuss, as the saying goes. Only will it last? That's the question. I'm overjoyed that this devilish ogre is unmasked and an honorable and esteemed man has been undeceived; I only regret that it happened so late. That malicious shyster has had time to do considerable harm with his machinations." A. I. Bibikov to D. I. Fonvizin, 26 April 1773, in Bibikov, *Zapiski*, p. 74; for further information on Bibikov's feelings about Saldern, see the same work, pp. 97–98.

[55]Solms to Frederick II, 14 July 1773, *SIRIO*, 72: 374.

[56]Solms to Frederick II, 23 August 1773, *SIRIO*, 72: 384.

[57]Nolcken to Chancellery President, 19 July 1773, *SRa*, Muscovitica 386.

tion and promptly relieved Saldern of the paper signed by Paul. Panin then went to the grand duke and convinced him to avoid further contact with Saldern. He did not, however, report Saldern's activities to the empress, as he feared unnecessarily compromising Paul. Exposing Saldern would have the further disadvantage of delaying ratification of the Holstein treaty, as Saldern was the only Danish representative empowered to carry the ratifications to Copenhagen. So Panin took this opportunity to finish the Holstein business and send Saldern out of the country for good.[58]

The motives behind Saldern's audacious scheme remain a mystery. It is hard to believe that he acted solely on his own initiative. He knew the Russian court well enough to understand the practical hindrances to establishing a coregency. Moreover, he could scarcely have believed that Panin would join him in such a design after what had happened in Poland. Nor does it seem likely, as one historian has suggested, that Catherine "might have been using Saldern as a stalking-horse to flush out the plans of the Panin faction."[59] Given

[58]Solms to Frederick II, 14 July and 27 August 1773, *SIRIO*, 72: 374–75, 394–95; another reason Panin gave—his humanitarian desire to save Saldern's head (see 27 August dispatch)—may well have validity, as Panin had intervened only a few months earlier on behalf of the Danish minister Struensee, whom he also regarded as a force for evil, in a vain attempt to convince the Danes to spare him from execution. See N.I. Panin to I. I. Mestmakher in Copenhagen, 26 January 1772, *SIRIO*, 118: 11–12. On Saldern's unexpectedly early departure, see Nolcken to Chancellery President, 26 July 1773, *SRa*, Muscovitica 386; N. I. Panin to I. M. Simolin in Copenhagen, 30 July 1773, *SIRIO*, 118: 441–442; he would have left even sooner had he not insisted with his usual imperiousness that the Danes send a frigate exclusively for his mission. Holm, "Caspar v. Saldern," p. 153.

[59]Alexander, *Autocratic Politics*, p. 269. The evidence for this surmise was Catherine's letter to Mme. Bielke in October 1773, containing the following message: "Tell Saldern, when you see him, that my house is completely or almost completely cleansed, and all the antics went as I had foreseen, but that God's will has anyway been done, as I had likewise predicted," *SIRIO*, 13: 361. To tie these words to Saldern's treasonous proposals it would be necessary to believe that Catherine casually encouraged a plot against herself at a time when it was just such a plot she feared most. One would also have to believe that Panin had no inkling of the source of Saldern's proposal. If he had the least suspicion the empress initiated it, he certainly would have told her. The letter seems rather to relate to a much more innocent assignment. Catherine had used Saldern to communicate to Panin her displeasure at the situation in the "young court." He told Panin that she wanted the grand duke's entourage purged of "ill-disposed" individuals and that Panin's own interests would be best served if he relinquished his duties as governor and moved out of the palace with his staff. Although Panin at first resisted these suggestions, he and his staff did leave the palace some time before Paul's marriage, and in September he gave up his post as governor. Catherine's letter to Mme. Bielke followed the last of these events by

the configuration of political forces in 1773, the most likely explanation would be that Saldern was cooperating in a scheme with the Orlovs and Chernyshevs. The Orlov faction had aroused Catherine's suspicions against Panin, but to defeat him they needed convincing evidence of his treachery. Since it would be provocative for the Orlovs themselves to approach Panin with a scheme to elevate Paul—not to mention the ammunition it would supply Panin against them—they had to find a suitable candidate for the task. Saldern was the perfect choice. He had long been close to the Panin party and could approach them without arousing suspicions. Moreover, the assignment must have appealed to Saldern. He had hopes of some day succeeding Panin as foreign minister,[60] but after bungling the mission to Poland he could no longer expect to receive Panin's support in this ambition. However, by helping the Orlovs undermine Panin, he might be able to replace his former patron all the sooner. Although only a surmise, this explanation is supported by circumstantial evidence. After returning from Poland nursing a grudge against Panin, Saldern cast about for a means to establish his career apart from the Panin group, and it was at this time that he ingratiated himself with the Orlovs and Chernyshevs and by early 1773 became a recognized "Orlowian." Yet after years of hostility toward the Orlovs he could not hope to win their backing without performing some useful service to prove his dissociation from the Panin group. What more useful service than to entrap the Panin party leaders in the very design the Orlovs were accusing them of? Finally, it should be noted that Catherine too seemed to understand the connection between Saldern's actions and the machinations of the Orlov group. For the disclosure of the Holsteiner's misdeeds in

---

little more than a week, and it would seem that her intention was merely to inform Saldern, who left St. Petersburg in July, of the satisfactory outcome of his earlier assignment. Four months later, when she learned of Saldern's plans to involve Paul in a conspiracy, her response was much different. She burst into anger and declared she "would have the wretch tied neck and heels and brought hither" for punishment. Her rage could scarcely have been feigned, as she issued orders to the border patrol to arrest the Holsteiner immediately if he appeared at the frontier. Only after some persuasion from Panin did she agree to let the matter drop with Saldern's retirement, provided he would return her jeweled snuffbox and pledge never again to set foot in Russia. Gunning to Suffolk, 11 and 14 February 1774, *SIRIO*, 19: 399–402; Solms to Frederick II, 7 February 1774, *SIRIO*, 72: 490–92.

[60]Or at least play a role equal to Panin's. Solms to Frederick II, 18 June and 30 July 1773, *SIRIO*, 72: 365–66, 386–87.

February 1774 led a short time later to the final phasing out and demise of the Orlov party.

In retrospect, the "crisis of Paul's majority" amounted to misunderstanding, a failure of communication between Catherine and the Panins. Nikita Panin had long hoped that the grand duke would be allowed to play a part in government when he came of age, and for a while in 1772, with Orlov out of the way and Catherine especially attentive to Paul, it appeared that this hope might be realized. But Panin also understood that the change had to be accomplished legally and peacefully. He lacked the temperament to risk a comfortable position on a daring move for supreme power. Moreover, it went directly contrary to his notions of ordered aristocratic government to permit the guards or urban crowd to influence decisions of state, especially the selection of a ruler. He abhorred political violence, and his reform proposals had consistently sought to eliminate unpredictability and interference from below in the political process. This explains why he could regard as fully justified the brutal repression of the rebels of the Preobrazhenskii regiment, notwithstanding their objectives of elevating Paul and banishing the Orlovs. Even when Panin came under vicious assault by Orlov and his adherents, his response was not to seek support among the guards or call his brother and other influential military figures to the capital. Least of all would he countenance Saldern's conspiratorial schemes. Rather he tried to allay Catherine's suspicions by keeping Paul in the background and then he clung desperately to the prerogatives of his offices and fortified himself in the moral rectitude of his course. He could perhaps have more effectively calmed Catherine's fears by silencing the criticism of his adherents and disbanding the "young court." But here his own apprehensions played a role. Even had he been able to exercise such control over his followers—which is doubtful—this virtual surrender to the opposing faction would have seriously weakened the morale and cohesion of his party, which not only constituted his sole protection against the intrigues of his enemies but also, paradoxically enough, was one of the things that made his leadership attractive and useful to the empress.

Of course, Catherine was in no position to understand Panin's fears. She faced grave difficulties with the war and internal unrest and had to be on guard against adventurers who might try to exploit these problems to stir up a revolt in Paul's name. Since she knew that such schemes could only succeed with the cooperation of Panin and the "young court," she was naturally concerned about Paul's entourage and became easily alarmed when intriguers tried to persuade her of the Panin party's disaffection. These circumstances prompted the increased surveillance and badgering of the Panin brothers and created a sense of resentment between them and Catherine that even the exceptional monetary rewards given to Nikita Panin in the fall of 1773 had trouble smoothing over.

This episode points up a number of lessons about the political organization of Imperial Russia. First, it shows the severe limitations on supreme authority. The supposedly all-powerful monarch could frequently be paralyzed by the action of subordinate patronage groups on which she relied for information and the articulation of imperial decisions. Throughout late 1772 and 1773 Catherine was virtually helpless in the face of conflicting rumors and threats generated by such groups. She could never be certain that the terrible conspiracy hinted at by the Orlovs was not actually congealing in the guards and "young court." Yet there was very little she could do to forestall such a move. The guards, always dangerous in troubled times, could not be removed or disbanded without inviting the very reaction their removal was intended to ward off. A direct attack on the Panin party could only be undertaken at the risk of arousing widespread fears about Paul's safety and possibly even driving the Panins into collaboration with other disaffected elements in society. Furthermore, an attack on the Panin party would seriously weaken, if not destroy, the empress' principal executive organization at a time when the combined pressures of foreign war and domestic discontent demanded effective, unified leadership. The dangers of acting decisively to block a potential threat from the Panins were at least as great as doing nothing and letting events take their course.

As in the similar crisis of the early 1760s Catherine opted to maintain a balance among the factions and wait out events. This seemed to be the safest choice, but it was also one of inefficiency—a situation that allowed one party to interfere with and hamstring the policies and activities of its opponents. To give but one crucial example, Orlov was permitted to sabotage the peace congress at Focşani, which Panin, if given his head, would unquestionably have brought to a successful conclusion as early as 1772 or the first months of 1773. The peace would then have released regular troops to quell internal unrest and may well have prevented the outbreak of the Pugachev Rebellion, or at the very least, have strictly limited its scope when it did occur. As it turned out, however, Catherine allowed the court parties to thwart and frustrate one another right up to the date of Paul's marriage, the very day the first rumors of the upheaval in Orenburg province reached the capital. It was another ten months before peace with Turkey was concluded and the government could finally begin to concentrate substantial military power against the rebel forces. But by that time the Pugachevshchina had wreaked havoc over vast sections of southeastern Russia.

3. Potemkin, the "Greek Project," and Panin's Fall

Although Nikita Panin survived the crisis of Paul's majority and even had the satisfaction of seeing the Orlovs fall from favor, his troubles were only beginning. Catherine soon found a new favorite, Grigorii Potemkin,[61] a man of such exceptional energy, ambition, and reckless daring as to prove far more dangerous to Panin's continued rule than the Orlovs had been.

Initially, however, Potemkin's arrival reinforced the recent Panin victory. Like his predecessor Vasil'chikov, Potemkin shared with the Panin party an interest in preventing the return of Orlov, and collaboration on this objective came quite naturally. The Pugachev Rebellion likewise contributed to their cooperation. Potemkin appeared at a crucial juncture. The commander sent against the rebels, General A. I. Bibikov, had died suddenly, and in the resulting confusion the insurgents managed to regroup and advance toward the heart of the empire. With the bulk of the army still at the Turkish front, the most able field commander available to replace Bibikov was Peter Panin, then living in retirement in Moscow. He was eager to take on the assignment, and his brother was pressuring Catherine to appoint him. But personal differences between

[61]Among the numerous studies of Potemkin are the well-known but rather unsatisfactory efforts by A. Brikner [Brückner], *Potemkin* (St. Petersburg, 1891), and G. Soloveytchik, *Potemkin* (New York, 1947). For a more serious treatment of his political and administrative achievements, see the lesser-known works of Theresia Adamczyk, *Fürst G. A. Potemkin, Untersuchungen zu seiner Lebensgeschichte* (Emsdetten, 1936), A. N. Fateev, *Potemkin-Tavricheskii*, in *Russkoe Nauchno-Issledovatel'skoe Ob"edinenie v Prage, Doklady i lektsii*, no. 3 (Prague, 1945), and A. Bogumil, *K istorii upravleniia Novorossii kn. Potemkinym* (St. Petersburg, 1905). Likewise E. I. Druzhinina, *Severnoe prichernomor'e, 1775–1800 gg.* (Moscow, 1959), contains valuable information on Potemkin's work in developing the southern borderlands.

the younger Panin and the empress made it difficult for them to agree on the nature and scope of his authority. While recognizing his abilities and anxious to conciliate his powerful friends, Catherine cringed at the thought of giving unlimited power over vast areas of the empire to a man known as her "personal insulter." Much to everyone's relief, Potemkin used his influence to smooth over these differences and facilitate Peter Panin's appointment.[62] Through the following year he continued to foster a working relationship between General Panin and the empress and performed other useful services for the Panin party.[63] The challenge of the Pugachev upheaval drew the elite together and gave the court a brief respite from the quarreling of political factions.

But the unity lasted only a short time. Potemkin differed so fundamentally from the Panins in outlook, interest, and temperament that conflict between them could not long be avoided. The hostility arose in part from the Panin's repugnance to favoritism. In their view, men who gained preferment by imperial favor were simply unworthy on the face of it. Moreover, Potemkin came from the lesser nobility of Smolensk province and could not boast the education, family connections, and service record the Panins regarded as essential for high office. His best-known client, the Ukrainian chancellery servitor A. A. Bezborodko, scarcely qualified as nobility at all.[64] More grating still was Potemkin's ill-concealed contempt for the Panins' standards of governmental and personal conduct. Where they perceived a potential conflict between one's

[62]For background to this appointment see Alexander, *Autocratic Politics*, chapter 8, especially 165–69. On the negotiations involving the two Panins, Potemkin and Catherine, see Bartenev's comments and accompanying letters in "Pugachevshchina (iz arkhiva P. I. Panina)," *Russkii Arkhiv*, no. 2 (1876), pp. 9–36. A. N. Samoilov, "Zhizn' i deianiia generala-fel'dmarshala kn. G. A. Potemkina Tavricheskogo," *Russkii Arkhiv* (1867), pp. 1021–22. See also Catherine's letter to G. A. Potemkin, July 1774, and her resolution on Panin's degree of authority in *SIRIO*, 13: 420–21.

[63]I. I. Kruk to A. B. Kurakin, 3 April 1775, and N. A. Repnina to A. B. Kurakin, 29 May 1776, *Arkhiv Kurakina*, 7: 391, 8: 211.

[64]Though he got his start with Field Marshal Rumiantsev, he attached himself to Potemkin soon after coming to St. Petersburg to serve as an imperial secretary following the first Turkish war. On his career, see the very favorable study by N. I. Grigorovich, *Kantsler Kniaz' Aleksandr Andreevich Bezborodko v sviazi s sobytiiami ego vremeni*, published as volumes 26 and 29 (1879, 1881) of *SIRIO*, which suffers the understandable bias of a work produced for a prize offered by one of Bezborodko's grandchildren. There is a lengthy critique, containing much additional information, by E. P. Karnovich, *Zamechatel'nye i zagadochnye lichnosti XVIII i XIX stoletii*, 2nd. ed. (St. Petersburg, 1893), pp. 171–273.

loyalty to a particular sovereign and one's duty to the nation or fatherland, Potemkin simply refused to recognize any contradiction. Whether he was serving Catherine in the bedchamber or in some official capacity he regarded himself as serving the fatherland and the interest of the people. The state and monarch were one.[65] As for the Panins' notions of aristocratic refinement, Potemkin not only viewed them with scorn but took positive pride in being thoroughly, boorishly Russian, even Eurasian. As he saw it, Russia was an asiatic empire, and its destiny lay not with Europe but to the south and "east," in the direction of the Ottoman Empire.[66] And much to the Panins' distress, he made no bones about his desire to translate this vision into action with schemes of imperial aggrandizement.

Not content to remain long in the empress' bedchamber, Potemkin was soon playing an active role in government. As early as 1774 Catherine gave him a seat in the council and made him vice-president of the War Collegium.[67] The following year he launched his first major policy initiative by organizing the breakup of the Zaporozhian Cossack host and incorporation of its territory into the regular sphere of Russian administration. Then came the opportunity he most desired: appointment as governor-general of the recently conquered southern provinces of New Russia, Azov, and Astrakhan, a territory larger than any European state. He immediately set in motion ambitious projects for developing the agricultural, commercial, scientific, and cultural life of the region.[68] At the same time, he did not forget his plans for further imperial expansion. Annexation of the Crimea was his initial objective, and in 1776, over Panin's strenuous objections, he won approval to exert military pressure on Ochakov, one of the remaining Turkish strongholds in the south, as the first

[65]See Potemkin's letter to Catherine, 27 February 1774, *Russkii Arkhiv* (1867), pp. 1016–17, and Adamczyk's comments on it, *Fürst G. A. Potemkin,* pp. 15–17.

[66]Potemkin's fondness for surrounding himself with Tatar and Greek regiments and affecting Asiatic and Greek dress are well known. Griffiths, "Russian Court Politics," pp. 157–58.

[67]There is some confusion in the literature on the dating of Potemkin's promotions, which Adamczyk, *Fürst G. A. Potemkin,* pp. 17–18, attempts to clear up.

[68]Adamczyk, *Fürst G. A. Potemkin,* pp. 28–50. On Panin's opposition to his harsh treatment of the Zaporozhians, see the letter to N. V. Repnin, 20 May 1775, *SIRIO,* 5: 185–87. On Potemkin's development of the southern territories generally, see especially Druzhinina, *Severnoe prichernomor'e,* and for the best brief exposition in English see Marc Raeff, "The Style of Russia's Imperial Policy and Prince G. A. Potemkin," in G.N. Grob, ed., *Statesmen and Statecraft in the Modern West* (Barre, Mass., 1967), pp. 1–51.

step toward this goal. The era of cooperation between the foreign minister and the favorite was now clearly at an end. Panin began complaining bitterly of Potemkin's highhanded actions. He "was ruling despotically and seizing control of everything," Panin wrote, and his rash moves were threatening renewed war with Turkey.[69]

If these initiatives disturbed Panin, he soon had much more to worry about. Potemkin's schemes were scarcely confined to annexing the Crimea and clearing the Turks from the northern Black Sea littoral. He wanted to drive them out of the Balkans and Anatolia as well and replace their power with a resurrected Byzantine Empire under the rule of a Russian prince. This was the so-called "Greek project," which also included plans for establishing an Orthodox Kingdom of Dacia in the Danubian Provinces for Potemkin himself to rule.[70] These grandiose designs encountered stiff opposition from the Panin party. They not only contradicted the principles of international politics Panin had striven so long to uphold; they were obviously calculated to overturn his leadership, since their fulfillment presupposed a complete reversal of Panin's Northern Accord system and a switch to a pro-Austrian foreign policy orientation.

Potemkin's influence was unlike that of previous favorites. His rapid promotions and ever-expanding responsibility belied a hold not only on the empress' affections but on her imagination as well. Try as they might, Panin and his supporters found it increasingly difficult to break this grip. Catherine seemed captivated by the enthusiasm and youthful vigor of her favorite. Moreover, his plans for a new active orientation in foreign affairs came at a particularly opportune moment. The Northern Accord had pretty much exhausted its usefulness, and Catherine was casting about for some alternative. Though lucid in conception, Panin's system never really materialized. By the late 1770s shifts in the European alliance system had rendered its main provisions meaningless. Two major northern powers, England and Sweden, remained outside the Northern Accord, and with the British now embroiled in North America,

[69]Barskov, "Proekty voennykh reform," p. 113; Panin was already concerned enough about Potemkin's authority that he was warning his young clients that he could no longer count on obtaining attractive positions for them. N. I. Panin to [S. S.] Apraksin, March 1776, *GBL, f.* Pan II, 1.

[70]Griffiths, "Russian Court Politics," pp. 144–75, gives an excellent resume of the "Greek project" and the politics surrounding its emergence in the late 1770s.

Panin himself no longer had any interest in bringing them into his system. Furthermore, the Hapsburg-Bourbon alliance it was designed to combat was now in the process of dissolution. Hence, little remained of the Northern Accord but the Prussian treaty, an arrangement that tended to isolate Russia and confine it to a purely passive role in European politics. Panin, too, realized the need for change, and while refusing to give up his anti-Hapsburg stance, he began making overtures to France, hoping in this way to extend Russian influence without upsetting the conservative European balance. Yet this was the very crux of the matter. Catherine had tired of a conservative role, and under Potemkin's prodding she was moving in the opposite direction, toward the exciting prospects offered by a pro-Austrian position.[71] With France and England occupied elsewhere, an Austrian alliance fulfilled all the conditions for a further imperial advance in the Balkans. Why not dream great dreams? What better way for Catherine to conclude her reign than by bringing Christianity and enlightenment to the Near East, to restore those unhappy people to the glorious path they trod before falling to the infidel Turks? By 1779 it was clear that Catherine had been won over to these views. That year saw the birth of Paul's second son, and Catherine left no doubt about the plans for his future. She christened the boy Konstantin after the last Byzantine emperor, ordered a medal struck showing him on the shores of the Bosphorus, and even supplied the child with Greek nurses and tutors.[72] The vision of a resurrected Byzantium began to acquire substance.

Still, it took time to bring the new system into being. Even though the Austrians made the first overtures and it was soon apparent that Joseph II was eager to move toward a rapprochement with Russia, his mother and coregent, Maria Theresa, did not share the enthusiasm. She opposed a radical alteration of the current European system, and accordingly, a formal treaty of alliance would have to await her death, which was expected in the near future. The delay suited Catherine's needs. She was then mediating the Bavarian Succession struggle between Austria and Prussia at Teschen and laying plans for the League of Armed Neutrality, which came into

[71]Catherine gladly gave Potemkin credit for establishing the new connection to Austria and noted that even Panin, before "he was blinded by Prussian flatteries," recognized the need for a different orientation to deal with the main enemy, which was the Turks. Catherine to Potemkin, 16 December 1787, in Lebedev, *Grafy Paniny,* p. 242.

[72]Griffiths, "Russian Court Politics," pp. 95–97, 158–60.

being in 1780. She did not want to upset these initiatives by an untimely shift to the Austrian alliance.[73] Besides, she had to contend with the opposition of the Foreign Affairs Collegium, still firmly under Panin's control. Since all the threads of policy, not to mention control of the foreign mails, ran through the collegium, Catherine needed time to build up a party of her own that could carry the new policy forward and eventually replace Panin's leadership in the collegium. Meanwhile, she took measures to neutralize the resistance of the Panin and grand ducal parties.

She began by inhibiting Panin's discretion in the choice of personnel. Instead of simply ratifying his appointments as in the past, the empress now insisted on selecting candidates of her own. In the summer of 1779 she replaced the Panin client A. S. Musin-Pushkin in London with the more pliant I. M. Simolin.[74] The following year she elevated Potemkin's protégé, A. A. Bezborodko, to a seat on the Foreign Affairs Collegium. Though outnumbered by Panin loyalists, Bezborodko could keep a close watch on the business of the collegium and report back to the empress and Potemkin any attempts to interfere with the Austrian negotiations. Early in 1781 another Panin stalwart, A. S. Stakhiev, was recalled from the crucial post of envoy to Constantinople and a younger man put in his place.[75] While these changes were occurring, the Austrian negotiations proceeded secretly outside the collegium. The groundwork was laid by Ambassador Cobenzl in talks with Potemkin. In the summer of 1780 Joseph II made an extended visit to Russia to firm up the basic agreement. All that remained was to await a favorable opportunity to complete formal treaty arrangements.

In November 1780 Maria Theresa's death removed the last obstacle from the Austrian side, and early the next year Cobenzl

---

[73]See Isabel de Madariaga, *Britain, Russia and the Armed Neutrality of 1780* (New York, 1962) for a superb clarification of this subject with many insights into the court politics of the time. Among other things, the author points out that the idea for the league of armed neutrality originated with Catherine and not Panin, as is usually contended. On the Teschen mediation see Paul Bernard, *Joseph II and Bavaria* (The Hague, 1965) and the literature cited therein.

[74]Madariaga, *Russia, Britain*, p. 104.

[75]Stakhiev had been with Panin since the 1750s when he assisted him in Sweden. The replacement was Ia. I. Bulgakov, a careerist who changed sides as Panin's influence waned. I.A. Markov likewise took this course (see below) and soon after replaced Panin's close friend I. S. Bariatinskii in Paris. Amburger, *Berhördenorganisation*, p. 450.

submitted his government's terms in writing. When the Foreign Affairs Collegium under Panin's direction predictably advised against the offer, Catherine simply ignored its recommendation and turned the negotiations over to the new party of Potemkin, Bezborodko, and S. R. Vorontsov. At the same time, she took the additional precaution of removing mail inspection from the collegium's jurisdiction to prevent Panin from intercepting Austrian dispatches and passing them on to his Prussian friends.[76] These rebuffs were the last straw for the aging statesman. In April Panin demanded a leave of absence and went sulking off to his Dugino estate near Smolensk to wait for the empress to come to her senses. But this tactic, which had worked so well in the past, now served the empress' plans. Her mind made up and Panin out of the way, she could bring the new alliance to a speedy conclusion. Likewise, Panin's absence made it easier to wrest the Foreign Affairs Collegium from his control. Seeing which way the wind was blowing, two key members of the collegium, P. V. Bakunin and A. I. Markov, now decided to desert to the other side in time to salvage their careers, a switch that brought a majority of the bureau in line with the new policy. Vice-Chancellor Osterman was then given the go-ahead to purge the remaining Panin clients.[77] The way was now clear to complete the foreign minister's formal dismissal.

Catherine delayed this last act until the fall, when Paul and the grand duchess were abroad on a grand tour of the continent. The empress had suggested and encouraged the trip, apparently still respectful enough of the combined influence of the Panin and grand ducal parties to prepare Panin's dismissal carefully. It was probably a needless precaution. The party was already in considerable disarray. Its prestigious military leaders were effectively dispersed:

[76]Younger members of the Vorontsov clan, despite the family's tactical support of Panin in the 1760s, evidently failed to give up their inclination for an Austrian and British alignment of Russian policy, and for this reason and, no doubt, to regain their lost position, they now sided with Potemkin. See S. R. Vorontsov to I. A. Osterman, 1 September 1787, and comments by Vorontsov's biographer D. D. Riabinin, "Biografiia grafa Semena Romanovicha Vorontsova," *Russkii Arkhiv*, no. 1 (1879), 102, 178. On the collegium's control of the mails see Griffiths, "Russian Court Politics," pp. 190–91.

[77]Grigorovich, *Kantsler Bezborodko* in *SIRIO*, 26: 332; Griffiths, "Russian Court Politics," p. 205. A thorough instruction from the empress on the reorganization of the collegium, dated 12 May 1781, may be found in *LOII, f.* 36, *op.* 1, *d.* 111, 14–21. Also A. A. Bezborodko to P. A. Rumiantsev, 5 September 1781, in P. M. Maikov, ed., *Pis'ma A. A. Bezborodko k grafu P. A. Rumiantsevu 1775–1793 gg.* (St. Petersburg, 1900), pp. 87–88.

Rumiantsev as governor-general of the Ukraine, Repnin as governor in Smolensk, and Peter Panin in his Moscow retirement. The Panin influence in the central administration had been broken by the steady advancement of Potemkin clients in recent years, and the "young court" was heavily infiltrated. Catherine took no chances. She waited for several days after Paul's departure and then ordered Panin to turn over his papers to Vice-Chancellor Osterman, who was henceforth to perform the duties of foreign minister.[78] The change occurred without fanfare or public notice. Panin retained the formal title of Minister of Foreign Affairs as well as his seat in council. He simply was given no more duties to perform. Quietly, yet decisively, the twenty-year reign of the Panin party came to a close.

4. The Panins and Russian Freemasonry

Catherine's hesitation may have been due in part to her fear of the Panin party's Masonic ties. In the last years of Panin's fight to keep his influence and system alive he flirted briefly with the idea of exploiting the domestic and international connections of Freemasonry. Although historians have yet to sort out all the political implications of Russian Masonry,[79] it seems clear that Panin allowed his name and the offices of the Foreign Affairs Collegium to be used in efforts to link Russian Masonry to the Swedish and north German Masonic unions. The movements in these countries were led by prominent statesmen and royalty, and Panin evidently hoped to bolster his faltering political system by welding strong ties among the political and social elites of the Northern Accord powers.

This effort began in earnest about the time of the consolidation of Potemkin's authority in 1776. There is no evidence of a previous Panin association with Masonry, although he no doubt enjoyed an informal relationship to the lodges organized in the early 1770s by his friend I. P. Elagin under a charter from London, and he may even have been initiated into Masonry as early as the 1750s during his stint as envoy to Sweden.[80] Whatever the case, Panin first appeared

[78]Griffiths, "Russian Court Politics," pp. 194–227.

[79]See especially A. N. Pypin, *Russkoe masonstvo XVIII i pervaia chetvert' XIX v.* (Petrograd, 1916); G. V. Vernadskii, *Russkoe masonstvo v tsarstvovanie Ekateriny II* (Petrograd, 1917); also a recent dissertation by In-Ho Lee Ryu, "Freemasonry under Catherine the Great: A Reinterpretation."

[80]Vernadskii suggests that Panin's surprising appointment as *oberhofmeister* in 1760 could be attributable to Masonic links with the chapter directed by R. L. Vorontsov. On

in a prominent position when the Elagin lodges amalgamated with Baron Reichel's Swedish-Berlin "Weak Observance" system in September 1776. Though apparently still not an active participant, the foreign minister lent the prestige of his name to the movement by becoming vice-grandmaster of the Elagin-led united Russian lodges.[81]

Even as this system formed, plans were afoot for an association of much greater political significance with Swedish Masonry. In late 1776 Panin sent his young relatives G. P. Gagarin and A. B. Kurakin to Stockholm, ostensibly to announce the grand duke's second marrige. But fortified with letters from Elagin, they had the additional assignment of obtaining a charter for Russian Masonry's adherence to the Swedish "Strict Observance" system.[82] This movement stood under the direction of Duke Karl of Södermanland, King Gustav III's brother, and was part of a broader north European province of Strict Observance, which was then undergoing a leadership struggle between Swedish Duke Karl and its present chief Duke Ferdinand of Brunswick.[83] Judging from the confusion in Stockholm during the Gagarin-Kurakin visit, there was a great deal of conscious manipulation on all sides. The Brunswick leaders, while planning to keep the province under their own control, appeared to be using the Swedes to draw in the Russian lodges. The Swedes seemed to hold out the possible incorporation of Russia as an enticement in bargaining for Duke Karl's pretensions.[84] Finally, although this is

---

this and the Elagin lodges of the early 1770s, see his *Russkoe masonstvo*, pp. 6–7, 13–37, 216. Also *Arkhiv Kurakina*, 8: vii.

[81]Vernadskii, *Russkoe masonstvo*, p. 36. For references to N. I. Panin in Masonic work and in songs of the lodges, see T. Bakounine, *Le répertoire biographique des francs maçons russes (XVIIIᵉ et XIXᵉ siècles)* (Brussels, 1940), and S. V. Eshevskii, *Sochineniia po russkoi istorii* (Moscow, 1900), pp. 462–63.

[82]Vernadskii, *Russkoe masonstvo*, pp. 38–40; *Arkhiv Kurakina*, 8: 255, 257, 294–95; T. O. Sokolovskaia, "Kapitul Feniksa. Vysshee tainoe masonskoe pravlenie v Rossii (1778–1882 gg.)" *Vestnik Imperatorskogo Obshchestva Revnitelei Istorii*, 2 (1915), pp. 232–33.

[83]Gu taf Iverus, *Hertig Karl av Södermanland, Gustav III's broder*, vol. 1, *Till ryska kriget* (Uppsala, 1925), pp. 147–48.

[84]At the time of the Russians' visit the dispute between Karl and Ferdinand had not been resolved and arrangements had to be made to send the papers for a Russian charter later in the year during King Gustav's journey to St. Petersburg. Vernadskii, *Russkoe masonstvo*, p. 39; Pypin, *Russkoe masonstvo*, pp. 154–56. Ferdinand and Karl finally arranged a preliminary settlement in August 1778, and the following year Karl was officially made master of the areas of Sweden, Finland, and All-Russia, as well as of a separate province in north Germany, *"vid Elbe och Oder."* But this drew so much protest from the Danes and

less certain, the Russians may have been looking forward to the time when they could propose the much more impressive candidacy of Grand Duke Paul for leadership of the province. Certainly, Paul was an important link in the whole business. His new wife, Maria Fedorovna, was niece to Duke Ferdinand of Brunswick, and her two brothers, Frederick and Ludwig, had connections through their tutor to the Berlin Rosicrucians led by the mystic Wöllner, later a minister of state under Frederick William II. During a sojourn in Russia by the two brothers in 1779–1780 there was talk of initiating Paul directly into the Berlin chapter, though apparently nothing came of the matter.[85] All this jockeying around was clearly attributable to the perceived political advantages of the Strict Observance system. It could be used as a powerful weapon. Apart from the prominent individuals involved, this order of Masonry was characterized by a secret and highly authoritarian chain of command that committed the subordinate levels to unquestioning fulfillment of directives handed down by their superiors.

In any event, the Gagarin-Kurakin mission to Sweden led to the establishment in 1778 of the first Russian Strict Observance lodge. Negotiations were immediately started to bring the existing Elagin lodges into the new system. But here some trouble arose. Even though Elagin had originally fostered this new link with Sweden, he balked after learning that the movement would owe allegiance to a foreign leader. Nikita Panin, too, seems to have remained aloof from this new chapter. Nevertheless, many former Elagin lodges broke away and on their own joined the Russian "Grand National Lodge" of Swedish Strict Observance, which, judging from its leadership, plainly represented a social extension of the Panin party. Its ranks included nearly the entire younger generation of Panin men. Along with its leader, or First Prefect, G. P. Gagarin, it counted as prominent members Gagarin's brother and cousins, the two Kurakin brothers, Alexander and Aleksei, the Apraksins, the Dologrukiis, A. S. Stroganov, A. I. Musin-Pushkin, and not least, N. V. Repnin, a man

[85]Barskov, "Proekty voennykh reform," pp. 139–40; Pypin, *Russkoe masonstvo*, pp. 222–28; Shumigorskii reports that Paul was introduced into masonry as early as 1772. See in Glassenapp, *Staat, Gesellschaft und Opposition*, p. 52, although there seems no solid evidence for this assertion.

second only to Nikita Panin among the party loyalists still in service. At its height in 1780 the system boasted fourteen lodges, seven in St. Petersburg, four in Moscow, and the remainder in provincial cities.[86]

The reason for the aloofness of the older Panin men like D. I. Fonvizin, G. N. Teplov, P. A. Rumiantsev, Ia. E. Sivers, and the two Panin brothers themselves, is not altogether clear.[87] Perhaps the enthusiasm of the younger men carried them beyond what their elders though prudent. Perhaps the political implications of allegiance to a foreign potentate, despite the proviso that the Russians could refuse to honor orders in conflict with duties to their legal sovereign and church,[88] were regarded as entirely too compromising. Such an association could easily be turned to their enemies' advantage, especially in view of the fact that the Gagarin lodges were in trouble with the empress from the very outset. Catherine was understandably concerned about the entire Masonic movement in Russia, as it included something between 1/12 and 1/3 of the top eight ranks of officialdom.[89] But she was particularly wary of the foreign connections of the Gagarin system. As early as 1779 she ordered the St. Petersburg police chief P. V. Lopukhin to visit the Gagarin lodges to investigate their correspondence with Duke Karl of Södermanland. Then two years later, in the general purge that accompanied Panin's dismissal, the empress transferred Gagarin to Moscow on a new government assignment. This move effectively intimidated his associates and led to a shutdown of the remaining St. Petersburg chapters of Strict Observance.[90]

Catherine's measures failed, however, to dampen interest in the Strict Observance systems that soon began to thrive in Moscow. The appeal of this "higher order" Masonry has been explained in a num-

[86]Vernadskii, *Russkoe masonstvo*, pp. 10–11, 40–41, 49; on Elagin's opposition to the spread of the Swedish system, see Sokolovskaia, "Kapitul Feniksa," pp. 232–33.

[87]Rumiantsev and Sivers were, of course, on assignments far from the capital cities and would not in any case have been able to participate actively.

[88]See Gagarin's speech denying submission to a foreign power and the oath proviso in Vernadskii. *Russkoe masonstvo*, pp. 42, 46–47.

[89]The highest figures (2,500 members) are given by Vernadskii, *Russkoe masonstvo*, pp. 86–90; on the basis of Prozorovskii's rather low estimates and lists in Bakounine's directory, Byu tries to arrive at a reasonable compromise figure. "Freemasonry under Catherine," pp. 125–26.

[90]M. N. Loginov, *Nikolai Novikov i moskovskie martinisty* (Moscow, 1867), p. 110; Pypin, *Russkoe masonstvo*, p. 165; Vernadskii, *Russkoe masonstvo*, pp. 47–48, 227 (although with the mistaken date of 1780 for Gagarin's move to Moscow).

ber of ways. The chapters boasted many more ranks than the former Elagin lodges and held out the enticement of greater knowledge at the highest levels, as new secrets unfolded with each step up the ladder. Moreover, a sense of increasing authority and in-group morale developed in the higher grades. Another seductive aspect was the system's pretended association with the chivalrous orders of the Middle Ages. The complex rites, trappings of medieval knighthood, and the strict hierarchical precedence all provided a feeling of aristocratic corporatism sorely lacking in the Russian nobility. Masonry apparently also served as a religious substitute for men who, though educated in Voltairian skepticism, were originally nourished on the traditional Orthodox beliefs of their peasant nannies and longed to return to a dogmatic view of human experience. And certainly, too, the moral tone and the emphasis on group loyalty and personal duty attracted many of those, like the former members of the student literary circles, who were seeking elevated standards of conduct by which to distinguish the elite. Finally, some of the brethren were able to combine their intellectual interests with a taste for private enterprise. Nikolai Novikov and his collaborators in Moscow managed for a time to earn a good livelihood through the publication and distribution of Masonic reading materials.[91] Hence, despite dwindling support for the Swedish system (due to its politically suspect and personally humiliating dependence on a foreign chief), the Moscow Masons made new efforts to link up directly with the Brunswick leaders in order to create a separate 8th Province of Strict Observance limited solely to Russia and under native Russian direction. When this, too, proved overtame, the Moscow brothers went over to the still more austere and mystical order of Rosicrucianism in 1784.[92]

Despite these other sources of interest in Freemasonry, political considerations, particularly the orientation toward Grand Duke Paul, were never far from the surface. As Nikita Panin lost his grip on power and could no longer find jobs and maintain an institutional setting for the party clientele, his younger supporters substituted the new bond of the Masonic movement. Looking to Paul as their hero

[91]Ryu, "Freemasonry under Catherine," especially pp. 260–93.

[92]On the Moscow Masons, in addition to the previously cited studies, see the more recent Soviet work by Makogonenko, *Nikolai Novikov i russkoe prosveshchenie XVIII veka* (Moscow, 1951).

and hope for a better future, they naturally wanted to draw him into this sphere of activity, and it seems that there were plans to initiate Paul into Masonry during his trip to Western Europe in 1781. Two prominent Masons and close personal friends, A. B. Kurakin and S. I. Pleshcheev, accompanied Paul on the journey, possibly to facilitate this enterprise. It is far from certain, however, that Paul joined the Masons at this time or had contacts of any kind with the Masonic movement abroad.[93] Catherine was fully aware of the possibility of such contacts and their political implications, and she had Paul's movements watched closely throughout his stay in Europe. Moreover, he was expressly forbidden to visit Berlin, where he might be subject to influence through Masonry or otherwise that could prove detrimental to the empress' planned switch to a pro-Austrian foreign policy.[94] Catherine's preventive measures included the interception of couriers to Paul, and at least one of these turned up with a very compromising letter to Kurakin from P. A. Bibikov (the son of the deceased Panin adherent General A. I. Bibikov). Though containing no references to Masonry, the letter was sufficiently damaging in its criticisms of Catherine and Potemkin and expressions of the hopes for the future with the grand duke to lead to Bibikov's arrest and exile as well as Paul's separation from Kurakin and other young friends upon his return to St. Petersburg.[95] Thus, having been cut off from political power and access to the grand duke, the young members of the Panin party settled into their

[93]Several sources contend that Paul joined the Masons during this trip abroad, including Loginov, *Novikov i moskovskie martinisty*, p. 159; L. Engel, *Geschichte des Illuminaten-Ordens* (Berlin, 1906), p. 193; and Barskov, "Proekty voennykh reform," p. 140, but little more than conjecture is offered in evidence.

[94]On denial of Mariia Fedorovna's petition, see Shumigorskii, "Puteshestvie Pavla Petrovicha i Marii Fedorovny za granitsa 1781–1782," *Russkii Arkhiv*, no. 2 (1890), pp. 26–28. The couple was even forbidden to leave the country via Moscow, no doubt as a precaution against their conspiring with the Masons and other opposition groups there. Paul to Metropolitan Platon, 5 August 1781, *Russkii Arkhiv*, no. 2 (1887), p. 24. One of Catherine's most trusted agents, N. I. Saltykov, was put in charge of the suite. Kobeko, *Tsesarevich Pavel Petrovich*, pp. 188–98.

[95]This episode is fully rehearsed in Shumigorskii, "Puteshestvie," *Russkii Arkhiv*, no. 2 (1890), pp. 17–78, and Griffiths, "Russian Court Politics," pp. 211–18. For an authoritative contemporary view by a relative of N. V. Repnin, see F. N. Golitsyn, "Zapiski," *Russkii Arkhiv*, no. 1 (1879), pp. 1284–85. Catherine continued to be concerned about a possible link between the Moscow Masons and Paul, as is clear from her questionnaires prepared for Novikov's interrogation in 1792. *SIRIO*, 42: 224.

Masonic lodges to wait out the long siege until Paul would come to the throne and restore their eclipsed ambitions.

While their younger sympathizers were taking refuge in various Masonic groups, the two Panin brothers and Denis Fonvizin decided on a more direct approach. They could not expect to wait out Paul's accession and had to make their case now or never. So instead of burying themselves for a long siege, they employed their enforced leisure to draw up a blueprint for Paul's future reign. Never having put their reform ideas into systematic order, they now set to work on a thorough exposition of their policies and aspirations. Until this time they had only spoken in a general way of the need to institute fundamental laws and move Russia in the direction of a modern constitutional order. Now, for the first time, they would sketch out an actual constitutional project, which they hoped would serve as a model for Paul's activity once he came to the throne. At the same time, with the help of Fonvizin's nimble pen, they confronted Catherine directly through the theatrical and journalistic media. In this latter approach, they relied not so much on the Masonic ideals that were now absorbing the attention of their younger followers, but instead returned to a theme that had served as a guidepost throughout their careers, the Petrine ethic. They wanted to identify themselves and their newly developed vision of a constitutional order as the proper heirs of the Petrine tradition and to point up the erosion of Petrine norms that had occurred under Catherine's rule. This was no easy task. Over the past twenty years, not without some help from the Panins, the empress had been very much in the business of appropriating the Petrine myth for her own purposes. So the Panins had first to challenge Catherine's already established claims to the mantle of Petrine tradition. Two events in the second half of 1782 marked the battle lines clearly.

10

The Last Battles:
Starodumstvo, the Constitutional Project, and
the Idealization of Petrine Values

On the afternoon of August 7, 1782, just one year after Nikita Panin's enforced retirement, the empress called all of official Russia to Senate Square in St. Petersburg. Thousands of spectators appeared. The two guard regiments of Peter I's time, the Preobrazhenskii and Semenovskii, paraded out in full dress to the center of the square, followed by other regiments, which deployed along the adjoining streets. State dignitaries of the first two ranks watched with their families from the windows of the senate building, while other ranking officials found places in galleries lining the Neva embankment. Behind them rose a dense thicket of masts from ships blanketing the waters. The empress arrived by boat and marched with her court to the senate balcony.[1] The occasion was the unveiling of Peter the Great's statue, the French sculptor Falconet's immense "bronze horseman," which Catherine had commissioned and brought to completion over the past fifteen years. She had come to lay claim to the Petrine heritage and bask in the reflected rays of the great tsar's glorious memory. The inscription Catherine ordered for the statue was simple and to the point: "Petro primo, Catarina secunda." The scene produced just the effect she anticipated. As the statue appeared from behind concealing walls and ships boomed salutes from the river, the empress looked around to see tears in the eyes of the spectators. Returning her gaze to the statue she sensed that Peter happily surveyed his creation. His image, she wrote to Baron Grimm, "had a look of contentment which also passed to me and encouraged me to do better in the future."[2]

[1]Description as given in *S.-Peterburgskie vedomosti,* cited in A. N. Radischev, *Polnoe sobranie sochinenii,* 1 (Moscow, 1938), pp. 461–62.
[2]Catherine to Baron Grimm, 10 December 1782, *SIRIO,* 23: 265.

The great statue culminated many years of effort by Catherine to clothe her reign in the mantle of Petrine tradition. Ever since the glorification of Peter I by the poets of Elizabeth's time,[3] it had been imperative to justify political action in terms of faithfulness to the Petrine heritage. Catherine, whose need for legitimation was especially great, had from the first days of her reign consciously sought to associate herself with the Petrine legend. She preceded all her reform efforts with a ransacking of the archives to learn what Peter had said or done about the matter,[4] and her most important legislative acts unfailingly cited his contributions. She stressed that her own reforms aimed merely at completing the work he had left unfinished, or, at most, were adjustments required by altered time and circumstance.[5] In less obvious ways, too, she played upon the Petrine legend. Prince de Ligne reported that she carried a snuffbox decorated with Peter's portrait and liked to explain that it reminded her "to ask each moment of the day: What would he have ordained, what would he have forbidden, what would he have done, if he were in my place?"[6] Catherine mastered the art of manipulating history for propagandistic purposes.[7] The "bronze horseman" and its accompanying inscription was one of her masterpieces.

[3] E. F. Shmurlo, "Petr Velikii v russkoi literature (opyt istoriko-bibliograficheskogo obzora)," *Zhurnal Ministerstva Narodnogo Prosveshcheniia*, 264 (1889), pp. 67–74.

[4] G. R. Derzhavin, *Sobranie sochinenii*, 7: 416, as cited in E. F. Shmurlo, "Petr Velikii v otsenke sovremennikov i potomstva," *Zhurnal Ministerstva Narodnogo Prosveshcheniia*, 37 (1912), p. 32n.

[5] An excellent example of this style may be found in her 1775 law on provinces. *PSZ*, vol. 20, no. 14392. Except for her laws on towns, which had no precedents in Peter's work, such references were frequent in her legislation. It is interesting to note, however, that while she assured Russians of her faithfulness to Peter's designs, she turned around and boasted to foreigners of her many innovations, an indication of her manipulative attitude toward the Petrine legend. On sources of the reforms, see A. A. Kizevetter, "Imperatritsa Ekaterina II, kak zakonodatel'nitsa," *Istoricheskie ocherki* (Moscow, 1912), pp. 277–79.

[6] Prince de Ligne, "Portrait de Catherine le Grand," *Oeuvres* (1860), 3: 17, cited in Shmurlo, "Petr Velikii v otsenke sovremennikov," p. 32n.

[7] Catherine's use of history, oddly enough, conflicted with her glorification of Peter. She was one of the first into the field to defend the pre-Petrine past. Outraged by the abbé Chappe d'Auteroche's unflattering picture of Russia past and present in his *Voyage en Sibérie fait par ordre du roi* (Paris, 1768), she launched an impassioned attack on the Frenchman's book. This *Antidote*, the title of her ambitious polemic, corrected many of the abbé's obvious errors and, without of course directly criticizing Peter the Great, developed a romanticized vision of pre-Petrine Russia replete with errors of its own. An outstanding feature of this too-often neglected work was its assertion of a common historical development between Russia and Europe up to the end of the sixteenth century. It was only the Time of Troubles that threw Russia off course and stalled its development for a few

Neither Catherine nor her most observant contemporaries were blind to the distance that separated their aspirations and life style from those of the Petrine age. The difference was most obvious to the few surviving relics of Peter's time like the aged statesman Ivan Nepliuev. When Catherine set as a condition of his retirement that he find a replacement equal to his merits, Nepliuev replied:

> No, My Lady, we pupils of Peter the Great, whom he led through fire and water, were educated differently, thought and behaved differently, while nowadays people are educated, behave, and think quite otherwise; hence, I cannot think of anyone to designate, not even my own son.[8]

Kirill Razumovskii revealed this awareness even more vividly at the *Te Deum* following the Russian naval victory over the Turks at Chesme. The service was another occasion for official Russia to hail its Petrine heritage. The empress and court assembled in SS. Peter and Paul Cathedral to hear the sermon of Metropolitan Platon, who waxed eloquent about Peter's many contributions and the merits of his successors. As the passion of Platon's words mounted, he strode over to the statue on the emperor's grave and exhorted it: "Arise now, Great Monarch, father of our country! Arise and view your lovely creation." The story runs that amid the mounting enthusiasm, Razumovskii turned to those around him and said, "Why on

---

decades. The *Antidote* even credited Peter's predecessors with initiating several of the reforms that he later carried to completion. Catherine repeated this idea many years later in her warning to Senac de Meilhan, a French emigré who asked permission to write a history of eighteenth-century Russia. She set as one condition that he could "not assert that pre-Petrine Russia possessed neither laws nor ordered governance, because the very opposite was the case." As further evidence of Catherine's manipulative attitude toward history, she demanded strict personal control over Senac's text, stressing that the history should be formed in such a way as to be in keeping with the highest glory of the state and should serve as a source of emulation and education for later generations. S. L. Peshtich, *Russkaia istoriografiia XVIII veka*, 3 vols. (Leningrad, 1961–1971), 2: 253–60, 263. On the authorship of the *Antidote*, which has been in dispute, see A. N. Pypin, "Kto byl avtorom Antidota?" in *Sochineniia imperatritsy Ekateriny II* 7 (St. Petersburg, 1901), pp. i–vi.

[8]From I. I. Golikov's *Dopolneniia k Deianiiam Petra Velikogo*, 17: 499; Nepliuev's reverence for Peter found expression in the following passage from his memoirs: "This monarch brought our country up to the level of others; he taught us to know ourselves as people,— in a word, everything that you see in Russia had its beginning with him, and everything that might be done in the future will derive from that source." Both cited in Shmurlo, "Petr Velikii v literature," p. 64.

earth is he calling him forth? If he rose up, we would all surely catch hell!"[9]

This tale, whether authentic or not, reflects a genuine shift in thinking among the most educated and perceptive men of Catherine's era. Enough distance now separated the thinkers of Catherinian Russia from Peter I that they could pierce the mists of legend and bloated rhetoric and see Peter the man and tsar more clearly. They could begin to evaluate him and his work by standards of their own. No less they could judge the court and themselves against the standards set by Peter. To be sure, most nobles simply accepted the official view and showed little concern about divergence from Petrine norms. They had acquired freedom from obligatory state service, expanded judicial and police authority over their serfs, and the tsarist government's solicitude in maintaining these privileges. They were altogether content to believe with Catherine that they were the rightful heirs to the Petrine tradition and that their privileges made up an essential part of that tradition. But there were also critical voices, people willing to appraise the Petrine heritage from new standpoints. While these reassessments came from a number of perspectives,[10] the critique developed by the Panin brothers and

[9]A. A. Vasil'chikov, "Semeistvo Razumovskikh. I. Grafy Aleksei i Kirila Grigor'evichi," *Osmnadtsatyi Vek*, 2: 490.

[10]Princess Dashkova, for example, branded Peter as a tyrant, saying his methods demonstrated contempt for Russians, especially the nobility. Wedded to notions of aristocratic prerogative, she could not accept what she considered Peter's useless humiliation of her noble confreres by commanding them to master trades of the lowborn. She failed, however, to appreciate how much her own exaggerated perception of "nobility" in Peter's Russia owed to Peter's efforts to create a Westernized elite. *AKV*, 21: 219–22. On the other hand, the historian Ivan Boltin defended many controversial acts of Peter, such as the succession law and the killing of Aleksei and applauded his efforts to increase Russia's power. But he criticized Peter's interference with the customs and mores of the country and believed that many aspects of the tsar's program alienated Russians from their country. For a brief review see O. E. Günther, "Peter der Grosse im Russischen Urteil des 18. Jh.," *Jahrbücher für Kultur und Geschichte der Slaven*, New Series 10, (1934), pp. 544–47. A somewhat similar, if more ambivalent, evaluation was offered by Prince M. M. Shcherbatov in three separate works. Compare his "On the Corruption of Morals in Russia," available in an English translation by A. Lentin (Cambridge, 1969), or his "Rassmotrenie o porokakh i samovlastii Petra Velikogo," in *Sochineniia kn. M. M. Shcherbatova*, 2 (St. Petersburg, 1896), pp. 23–50, with the "Approximate Evaluation of the Length of Time Russia Would Have Required, in the Most Favorable Circumstances, to Attain by Her Own Efforts, without the Autocratic Rule of Peter the Great, Her Present State of Enlightenment and Glory," trans. in Marc Raeff, ed., *Russian Intellectual*

Denis Fonvizin after their loss of power in 1780 was by far the most
challenging, because it strongly emphasized the values of service and
merit, so familiar from the legislation of Peter the Great.

1. The Foundation of the Panin Critique

The Panins considered themselves uniquely qualified to judge the
regime's faithfulness to Petrine norms. They had deep roots in the
Petrine system through their family connections to prominent statesmen of the reform era. Moreover, Nikita and Peter had both entered the guards in the 1730s when Peter's rules concerning education and beginning service in the lowest ranks were still in force.
They had to climb up the regular service hierarchy through years of
difficult duty. This career route was typical of other adherents to the
Panin party. General A. I. Bibikov, for example, began his service
at age fifteen in the engineering corps and received his first officer
assignment only five years later, when he went to work under Count
Luberas on the Kronstadt Canal.[11] Another Panin supporter, Prince
Ia. P. Shakhovskoi, proudly explained that in the Semenovskii
regiment he had served for a period at each rank, "private, corporal,
quarter-master sergeant, . . . not as afterward when many young
nobles got promoted through the noncommissioned ranks while
sitting at home, only to enter service when they reached a commissioned officer rank."[12] These men resented the deterioration of the
Petrine service system, especially the practice established during
Elizabeth's reign of nobles inscribing their sons in the guards at birth
and having them advance by seniority to ranks their elders had
achieved only after years of actual service. Even more they resented
the influence of court favoritism on promotions. With some bitterness
they had watched young flatterers and minions leap-frog from the
guards to the highest positions of state power, often bypassing men
who had worked faithfully and proved their abilities over many

---

History (New York, 1966), pp. 56–60. The radical A. Radishchev recognized Peter as a
great man but withheld similar praise of his actions as a ruler. In Radishchev's view, a
ruler could only be great if he gave his nation liberty. See his "Pis'mo k drugu, zhitel'-
stvuiushchemu v Tobol'ske, po dolgu zvaniia svoego," in *Polnoe sobranie sochinenii*, 1: 147–
51.

[11]Bibikov, *Zapiski o zhizni i sluzhbe*, pp. 10–14.

[12]Ia. P. Shakhovskoi, *Zapiski*, 1: 3; see N. I. Panin's comments to the same effect in
Poroshin, *Zapiski*, 26 September 1764 and 20 August 1765; also Romanovich-Slavatinskii, *Dvorianstvo*, pp. 428–29.

years. The swift rise of young men mocked the elder generation's long years of service and depreciated their conformity with Petrine standards.

The chief cause of this abuse, as the Panins saw it, was the lack of a stable governmental order and proper succession law. This situation had opened the way for frequent palace revolutions, with the result that any adventurer willing to stomach the risks could take hold of the government and modify or exploit it for his own purposes. Only toward the end of Elizabeth's reign under the brief ascendancy of the Vorontsovs had conditions been stabilized and an attempt made to secure the position of the established elite. Hardly had the process begun, however, when Peter III mounted the throne and again threatened to undermine the native elite. Under the impact of these events the Panin party first congealed and decided to act on behalf of Catherine's coup d'etat in hopes that they could work through her to end the influence of favorites, stabilize the elite, and reorganize the central government institutions. They viewed this program as a return to Petrine standards, and all their early reform efforts—the Imperial Council project, the report of the Commission on Noble Freedom, and the Moscow Assembly Instruction—appealed to Peter I's authority and claimed to represent the intentions of the Great Reformer. Although Catherine went only part way in implementing these reforms, she satisfied the Panins' primary goal by elevating their party to the leading place in government. In the decade that followed the Panins were able to steer Russia into their Northern Accord foreign policy and to introduce a number of reforms in military, commercial, and administrative affairs. Though still interested in general legal reform, they withdrew their proposals for a state council to coordinate legislative policy, because under the circumstances it would merely have provided an entering wedge for their competitors and inhibited their own exercise of power. Only later when Catherine turned them out and replaced their leadership with the upstart Potemkin group did the Panins return to their critique of arbitrary power. They interpreted their dismissal as a betrayal of Petrine values, which in their way of thinking they alone truly represented, and they were prepared on this basis to challenge Catherine's claim to the Petrine heritage. It was scarcely a coincidence that the principal public expression of the Panin party's ideas, Fonvizin's play *The Minor*, appeared on stage in St. Petersburg the same autumn (1782) that Catherine unveiled the monument to Peter the Great and proudly proclaimed her association with his work. Instead of echoing this smug assertion, *The Minor* shouted back a warning to the empress and society alike that not only had they failed to build according to Peter's designs but they were well on the way to destroying the edifice he had worked so hard to construct. The Panins had decided to employ their enforced leisure to develop and refine their earlier critique into a coherent program of reform, including this time an outline of a constitutional order for Russia.

The critique is of interest for two reasons. First, the Panins confronted what they regarded as Catherine's self-serving exploitation of the Petrine legend with a different model of how the legacy of Peter's charismatic authority should be routinized. They suggested that Peter's effort to produce a Westernized and enlightened elite was a preparation for a modern constitutional order in Russia, in which the educated nobility would play a leading political role. Personal despotism, necessary in its time to shake Russia out of backwardness, should now be transformed into a legal monarchy with the rights of the various estates defined in law and protected from the arbitrary intervention of despotic authority. Above all, the fundamental values of life, property, and honor should be guaranteed against the capricious action of autocrat and favorite. Along with this went a conception of what the nobility should be: patriotic, enterprising, enlightened servants of the nation and exemplars of moral virtue.

The second reason for interest is the Panins' influence on Grand Duke Paul. They worked to instill in him the belief that he was a new Peter the Great, but one who would devote himself to realizing the constitutional program developed by the Panins. They did not conceal from Paul the despotic nature of Peter's rule. He had forced the challenge of Westernization on the elite, driven the nobles to get educated in the European spirit, and exhorted them to continue to learn from the West and to introduce into Russia the best of Western institutions. Yet the Panins impressed on Paul that although Peter had ruled despotically, his plan was to create conditions that would make despotism unnecessary. Hence, Paul could best make himself worthy of his great-grandfather's ambitions by implementing constitutional guarantees that would achieve these aims.

2. Starodumstvo

The Panins' first move was to enlist the satirical pen of Denis Fonvizin and thereby find a forum for their ideas in the theatrical and journalistic media. An ardent participant in his boss' political views, Fonvizin eagerly joined the battle. Through the late 1770s and 1780s he produced a number of works bringing together all the party's reform ideas into a general conceptual schema that might be characterized as *starodumstvo* after Mr. Starodum, the protagonist of Fonvizin's play *The Minor*, and, as the author liked to call him, "the friend of honorable people."

Starodumstvo meant literally "old-thought," although a more accurate rendering would be "old-fashioned moral virtue." Again the Petrine orientation was evident: the "old fashion" stretched only as far back as Peter the Great's time. Unlike the conservative publicist Prince Shcherbatov or (after 1767) Catherine herself, the Panins were not given to idealizations of the pre-Petrine past. Their few scattered references to early Russia revealed a belief that Russian history first began with Peter's reforms. Nikita Panin liked to entertain and appall his listeners with stories of the uncouthness of early Russians, the backwardness of the military organization, and boyars going around lopping heads off one another.[13] In his Imperial Council project he even included a reference to their "barbarous" forebears, which Catherine asked him to delete as it did a disservice to the memory of her predecessors.[14] In Panin's view, it was Peter who "first established the government of the empire" in the face of enormous obstacles bequeathed by old Russia. Human materials for the enterprise had to be entirely remolded with less than delicate means. "It is sufficient to recall in this connection," Panin wrote, "that the vice-chancellor mounted the scaffold only to teach the new senators how to attend and discuss properly in the senate."[15]

This uncharitable view of the pre-Petrine past contrasted sharply with the Panin party's idealized picture of the men who collaborated with Peter during the reform era. Mr. Starodum proudly noted:

My father brought me up in the old-fashioned way [po-tog-

[13]Poroshin, *Zapiski*, 1 July, 14 September, and 14 October 1765.
[14]Solov'ev, *Istoriia Rossii*, 13: 148.
[15]From his memoir on the Imperial Council project, *SIRIO*, 7: 204.

dashnemu], and I haven't found any need to reeducate myself.
He served Peter the Great. In those days a man was addressed
as "thou" and not "you." In those days they still didn't know
how to corrupt people so much that each would think of himself
as plural. But the many now aren't worth one then.[16]

As was clear from Fonvizin's later didactic biography "The Life of
Count Nikita Ivanovich Panin," he modeled Mr. Starodum at least
in part on Panin's life and work.[17] The biography emphasized Panin's
Petrine background and attributed to its subject all the sterling
virtues possessed by Mr. Starodum.

As for the concept of *starodumstvo* as expressed in *The Minor* and
other works by Fonvizin, it may be reduced to two basic concerns:
the monarch as initiator of reform and moral leader of his people,
and the education of the nobility to the Petrine ideals of duty, service,
and enterprise, plus the more recent demands of refinement and
culture.

Starodumstvo began with the assumption that all human beings
possessed the germs of evil in childhood; it had no truck with Rousseauean theories of the inherent goodness in human nature.[18] Accordingly, education was vital as a means of rooting out the evil
instincts and setting man on the path of virtue.[19] If education was
necessary to the ordinary man, it was many times more important
for a monarch, who had to be an exemplar of moral goodness and
justice for his people. Yet the mere provision of a moral upbringing
and education, however excellent, afforded no guarantee of goodness
in a ruler. So long as he was clothed in absolute power and surrounded by flatterers, his human nature would easily succumb to
corruption. Flatterers and favorites, being by definition unworthy

---

[16]*FSS*, 1: 129.

[17]I am indebted to Walter Gleason for pointing out that the character of Starodum may
have included elements as well of Fonvizin's father, whom the writer portrayed in his
memoirs as an exemplar of the old virtues of Petrine Russia.

[18]*FSS*, 2: 84; also N. Panin to Zavadovskii (1776) *Russkii Arkhiv*, no. 1 (1892), p. 487.
The attitude toward education was, however, similar to the model portrayed in Rousseau's *Emile*, a work which, of course, presented a fundamental philosophic conflict with
the author's principal political studies.

[19]*Starodumstvo* is a construct of the historian, not a concept developed systematically by
Fonvizin or the Panins. As this and the following notes indicate, I have drawn elements
from the entire body of Fonvizin's work to form this composite picture. *FSS*, 1: 317; 2: 85,
280, and 377.

since they did not attain rank through service and merit, always blinded the ruler to the truth and made him forget his duty to serve the whole people.[20]

Since the monarch and his court set the tone for society, corruption spread outward from the center. After Peter's death, *starodumstvo* implied, a general decline in moral values set in. Bribery flourished at all levels of the state administration, especially in the law courts where dishonesty was habitual. Judges were appointed not because of moral or intellectual fitness but by means of patronage and venality. The unworthy seized the most important offices, while truly qualified persons were left to languish and often went into retirement rather than kowtow.[21] As a result, the state was turning into an unfeeling monster, trampling on honor, justice, and personal integrity in the interests of preserving the privileges of its crooked and unqualified agents. Unable to retain the loyalty of righteous men, the government would someday meet the impassioned resistance of its subjects and crumble into anarchy.[22]

The best way to prevent this mishap was to remove the vices leading to it. Since these derived from the corrosive effects of absolute power, the monarch should understand that it was not only his duty but his interest to institute fundamental laws setting limits to the exercise of autocratic power. Averse to revolutionary means, *starodumstvo* stayed strictly within the Enlightenment approach of persuasion, education, and gradualism. It placed the onus for reform on the monarch himself, appealing to him with a blend of arguments culled from Christian morality, natural law theory, and simple common sense, philosophically based in a kind of vulgar deism.[23] The most consistent appeal was to the sovereign's moral

[20]*FSS*, 1: 132, 152, 168, 208, 270; 2: 29, 31, 41, 213–14, and 279.

[21]*FSS*, 1: 11, 55, 61, 81, 131, 183, 211, 225, 228; 2: 13, 27, 43, 52–55, 69, 82, and 272.

[22]This passage sums up a central theme of the party's best-known critical work, "Rassuzhdenie o nepremennykh gosudarstvennykh zakonakh," in *FSS*, 2: 254–67, especially 258.

[23]The following may serve as an example: "The reason why God is almighty is that He cannot do anything except good; and that this inablility might be an eternal token of His perfection, He instituted principles of everlasting truth, unalterable by Himself, whereby He governs the universe, and which He Himself cannot transgress without ceasing to be God. In the same way, a sovereign, like unto God and the recipient on earth of His almighty power, cannot signify his might and worth except by instituting in his state unalterable rules, based on the common weal, which he himself could not infringe without ceasing to be a worthy sovereign." From the "Rassuzhdenie" cited above, *FSS*, 2: 254–

duty to protect the rights of each estate as constitutionally defined. Only in this way could he safeguard the general security and advance the welfare of his people.

In order to give more concrete expression to the *starodumstvo* ideas of government, the two Panin brothers and Denis Fonvizin drafted a series of papers on constitutional reform shortly before Nikita Panin's death in 1783. The papers, which the Panins hoped would serve as a model for Grand Duke Paul's later rule, included the well-known "Discourse on Permanent State Laws," a constitutional outline, a manifesto of 18 articles setting out the goals of Paul's reign, a model succession law, and two letters by Peter Panin with additional comments on certain aspects of the accompanying documents.[24]

Of the items listed above the constitutional outline illustrated most succinctly the form of government preferred by the Panins. At the very outset it proclaimed that Russia should have "a monarchical government with unalterable fundamental laws."[25] This statement underlined the Panins' differences with Catherine. It rang out their response to her Instruction for the Legislative Commission of 1767 in which she had rejected Montesquieu's definition of Russia as a despotism and, by identifying Russian autocracy as a special form of European monarchy, strained to adapt his analysis of monarchical government to Russia.[26] The Panins objected to this resolution of the issue and in the "Discourse" preceding the constitutional outline argued that Russia fit none of the Montesquieuan ideal types. It was

> a state not despotic, for the nation has never surrendered itself to the arbitrary rule of the sovereign and has always had civil and criminal tribunals responsible for defending innocence and punishing crimes; a state not monarchic, since it lacks fundamental laws; [a state] not aristocratic, for its higher administration is a soulless machine controlled by the whim of the ruler; [a state not democratic, for how] can a land have any resemblance to a

---

55; translation by Ronald Hingley in Marc Raeff, ed., *Russian Intellectual History*, p. 96.

[24]All of which are published together in Shumigorskii, *Imperator Pavel I*, appendix, pp. 1–35.

[25]Article 1, Shumigorskii, *Imperator Pavel I*, appendix, p. 13.

[26]For an analysis, see F. V. Taranovskii, "Politicheskaia doktrina Nakaza," *Sbornik statei po istorii prava posviashchennyi M. F. Vladimirskomu-Budanovu* (Kiev, 1904), pp. 44–86.

democracy when the common people, groveling in the darkness of deepest ignorance, silently bear the yoke of cruel slavery?[27]

Despite the disclaimer, the authors of this passage left little doubt that Russia most nearly approximated a despotic rule. The disclaimer merely indicated their belief that Russia was not condemned by nature to despotism but could become a true monarchy if the autocratic power were brought within constitutional limits.

The constitutional outline then went on to enumerate guarantees of religious tolerance, a succession law, definitions of rights of property and inheritance, and the rights of each estate defined separately. It divided the society into five corporations: nobility, clergy, merchantry, lesser towndwellers *(meshchanstvo)*, and peasantry.[28] Other articles concerned the judiciary and called for all criminal proceedings to be carried on in properly constituted courts open to the public. They also demanded clear, substantive definitions of all crimes of lèse-majesté. Furthermore, all civil suits were to be handled exclusively by officers of the judiciary. The investigative functions previously belonging to administrative agencies should be given to the judicial branch to insure that "administrative power cannot be put to evil purposes" in deciding property cases.[29] Finally, the constitution defined the most important government institutions. There was to be a supreme supervisory organ to serve as guarantor of the fundamental laws, an institution that combined the functions of a chief procurator and a supreme court whose task was defending the constitution against infringement.[30] As for legislative matters, they were to be handled through a state council, the provisions of which repeated in all essential details those of the Imperial Council project of 1762.[31]

[27]*FSS*, 2: 266; trans. from Raeff, *Russian Intellectual History*, p. 104.

[28]Unfortunately, these articles were left without any explanation of content, noting merely "O prave Dvorianstvu," "O prave Dukhovenstvu," etc.

[29]Article 39, Shumigorskii, *Imperator Pavel I*, appendix, p. 18.

[30]Compare this with Catherine's *Nakaz*, chapter 4, and with Paul's idea for the same body (see below in text).

[31]Shumigorskii, *Imperator Pavel I*, appendix, p. 18. Article 38 defined the council as the sole channel through which business reached the monarch; all decrees and acts would be read there and each minister's opinion submitted in writing for entry in the protocols, and the monarch would have a deciding vote in all cases. The same two objectives pursued in the earlier Imperial Council project were evident here. First, Panin wished to eliminate

In sum, the *starodumstvo* concept of the state called for a well regulated government in accordance with principles of German cameralist statecraft. Judicial and administrative authority would be separated and the continuity of legislative policy guaranteed by the permanent establishment of a state council and senate as the sole channels for the articulation of sovereign power. Moreover, the Panins introduced elements of Western constitutionalism that went beyond the cameralist writers. They stressed the rights of each estate based in fundamental laws unassailable even by the monarch and protected from infringement by a quasi-representative senate. While contradictory in some respects, this proposal opened the way toward a political structure with the potential to check supreme power. In this form of government the Panins professed to see the realization of Peter the Great's plan for Russia.

The second issue to which *starodumstvo* addressed itself was the role of the nobility. This matter did not come up so much in the constitutional project as in the other documents prepared for Paul and especially in the writings of Denis Fonvizin. The contrast between an idealized "true nobility" and the selfish, ignorant provincial gentry formed the central theme of Fonvizin's plays and essays.

The true nobleman had to be an enlightened, patriotic servant of the nation, an embodiment of enterprise, culture, and moral virtue. Only through such high standards of conduct could he justify his position of privilege. Above all, he must conform to the Petrine standards of education and service. Military service was the first duty of every nobleman. Thereafter he might choose to work in the civil administration, engage in the development of commerce, or contribute to the enlightenment of his fellow man.[32] However interpreted, service to the state and society constituted the very essence of nobility. Those nobles who understood the 1762 decree granting freedom from obligatory state service as an excuse to return home and

---

the influence of favorites by forcing the monarch to act within a firmly defined decision-making hierarchy and subject all decisions to a formal process of deliberation, and second, he hoped to attach responsibility to ministers by exposing their opinions to "public" scrutiny.

[32]See especially P. I. Panin's "Pis'mo k Nasledniku Prestola dlia podneseniia pri zakonnom vstuplenii Ego na Prestol," and "Formy Manifestu, kakoi rassuzhdaiutsia, ne mozhet li byt' ugoden k izdaniiu pri zakonnom po predopredeleniiu Bozheskomu vosshestvii na Prestol Naslednika," in Shumigorskii, *Imperator Pavel I,* appendix, pp. 20–32. *FSS,* 1: 22, 24, 28, 131, 153, 169; 2: 17–18, 228, 272–73, and especially his "Torguiushchee dvorianstvo," 2: 117–86.

vegetate on their estates had, according to *starodumstvo*, abandoned their responsibilities. There was no excuse for living off the labor of one's peasants and contributing nothing in return. Such nobles deserved to be treated as parasites, not as patricians.

Worse yet, of course, were landlords like the Prostakovs (the Simpletons) and Skotinins (the Pigs) in *The Minor*, who mercilessly oppressed and tormented their peasants. Then with galling ignorance they appealed to the law to justify their lawlessness. Fonvizin summed up this lesson in a single climactic scene. Here a virtuous official (Pravdin) restrains Mrs. Prostakov, who is on the way to thrash her peasants, and warns her that "no one is free to tyrannize others." Mrs. Prostakov responds: "Not free! A noble, when he feels like it, isn't free to beat his servants? Then what's this law about the freedom of the nobility given us for?"[33] When she persists in her brutality, the playwright brings in the power of the enlightened government to confiscate her peasants and place her under arrest.

As Kliuchevskii observed in his analysis of *The Minor*, "Mrs. Prostakov was speaking nonsense, and in this nonsense was the whole sense" of the play. Fonvizin was warning his fellow nobles that there could be no such thing as a law absolving one estate from obedience to the laws any more than there could be rights without corresponding obligations. The first was a juridical impossibility, the second social suicide, a despotism no less destructive than the autocracy itself. If the nobility wished to survive, it had to serve and make itself useful to society. Otherwise the state, in the interests of its own survival, would have to treat the nobility as a whole in the same manner it treated Mrs. Prostakov.[34]

The defenders of *starodumstvo* blended a profoundly conservative view of estate privilege with their ideas of enlightened constitutional reform. They wanted to retain all the privileges the nobility had achieved in recent decades and even to extend nobles' participation in the political sphere. Yet they realized that in the long run privilege could only be justified by corresponding responsibilities. Since enforced service contradicted the very essence of estate right and merely enhanced the autocratic power, they could not advocate a return to the obligatory service requirement of Peter I's time. The

[33]*FSS*, 1: 172.
[34]V. O. Kliuchevskii, "Nedorosl' Fonvizina (Opyt istoricheskogo ob"iasneniia uchebnoi p'esy)," in *Kurs russkoi istorii*, 5 (Moscow, 1937), pp. 489–514.

answer was rather to convince people of their *moral obligation* to serve. In this sense *starodumstvo* stood for the original spirit of the 1762 law on freedom of the nobility. The law did not imply freedom from service altogether, to say nothing of Mrs. Prostakov's absurd interpretation. It merely ended the obligatory 25-year term of service. The language left no doubt that the government expected the nobility to continue to get educated and serve, just as Peter the Great had intended. In contrast to their earlier glowing portrayal of the nobility's service ambitions, the Panins now argued that many nobles were abandoning these responsiblities. Some did so in a cynical trade-off for relinquishing any demands for political participation; others, the most qualified men at the top, were being pushed into early retirement by favoritism and corruption in high government. The Panins attributed both these phenomena, so deleterious to the longrun interest of their estate, to the continuation of despotic rule. Once the autocracy recognized its obligation to society and brought its power within the rule of law, they argued, all nobles worthy of the name would willingly heed the call of duty.[35]

The *starodumstvo* concept of nobility went beyond the Petrine demands for service and a narrowly utilitarian education. As with the updating of Peter I's views to justify a constitutional order, the Panins' idea of nobility was likewise fed by more recent Western influences. They required a nobleman to be patriotic in the broader sense of having a love for native culture and language. This precept, directed against Francomania and the wholesale rejection of Russian culture by some nobles, did not mean to exclude beneficial foreign borrowing. The point was that such borrowing should be selective and not deracinate the noble or breed a contempt for everything Russian.[36] Religion also had a place. A noble should be tolerant, enlightened, he might even criticize superstitious churchmen—but a religious element unquestionably dwelled in the heart of a true nobleman.[37]

The important thing was *blagonravie*. This concept, which Fonvizin

[35]Kulomzin, "Pervyi pristup," pp. 38–40; they may have been thinking here of Montesquieu's axiom that "those commands are more strongly insisted upon, when they happen not to be commanded by law." *Esprit des lois,* chapter 1, no. 35. The clearest expression of this attitude toward the freedom of nobility decree is in the "Formy manifestu," sections 9–10, Shumigorskii, *Imperator Pavel I,* appendix, pp. 26–27.

[36]*FSS,* 1: 152, 231–32; 2, 64–65, 275, and 308–09.

[37]*FSS,* 1: 175, 207, 211, 230; 2: 15, 414, and 459.

identified as the source of success in government as well as in family life and society generally, resembled Montesquieu's "honor," the essential spring of monarchical government. But *blagonravie* had stronger moral overtones and was more inner-directed than "honor," whose reality was principally defined in recognition by others. *Blagonravie* embraced ideas of right conduct generally: being an example to others, aiding one's fellow man, and having good morals in private and family life. It sprang from within, more a quality of soul and a good heart than a motive for recognition. Opposed to this idea was *zlonravie*, broadly interpreted as acting contrary to laws prescribed for the general good. Fonvizin illustrated this concept in the behavior of the ignorant and brutal Prostakov family. Their arrest and ruin, as Mr. Starodum remarked, were the fruits of *zlonravie*.[38]

Education again held the key. Fonvizin laid great stress on education precisely because of its role in making people *blagonravnye*.[39] His plays mercilessly satirized the two types of education commonly pursued by the provincial nobility. The first was that of Mitrofan in *The Minor*, an education provided by ignoramuses and foreign coachmen posing as tutors, which amounted to no education at all.[40] The second type, represented by Ivanushka in *The Brigadier*, the product of a foreign sojourn, turned out to be Francomania compounded by imbecility.[41] Contrasted to these was the truly moral education of Fonvizin's heroes, men whose fathers had served Peter the Great and had instilled in their offspring a love of country and zeal for service. Their early training aimed at giving them a good heart and consisted of reading the *Telemachus* and other moralist writings. The rest they learned in the service, where they entered at the lowest ranks and advanced according to merit. If they found their path to further promotion blocked by favorites, they turned to commercial enterprise or other useful pursuits.[42]

3. The Paradox of the Would-Be Reformer in Eighteenth-Century Russia

Bloodless models of virtue like Mr. Starodum, Pravdin (Mr.

[38]*FSS*, 1: 177.
[39]*FSS*, 1: 168–69, 183; 2: 196.
[40]*FSS*, 1: 53, 149; 2: 71.
[41]*FSS*, 1: 98, 174; 2: 202.
[42]*FSS*, 1: 129, 130, 134, 149, 191; 2: 279–80.

Righteous), Nel'stetsov (Mr. Non-Flatterer), had almost no life as stage characters. They paled beside the animated portrayals of their fatuous, *zlonravnye* antagonists. But Fonvizin intended them as no more than spokesmen for the ideals of civic virtue. *Starodumstvo* was an expression of moral sentiment, an indignant protest against the unworthy upstarts who had replaced the Panin party in power. The defenders of *starodumstvo* never pretended that ordinary mortals could live up to such high standards. Indeed, the Panins themselves engaged in the behavior condemned by their literary spokesmen. While working to move Russia in the direction of a *Rechtsstaat*, they continued to operate out of the traditional political formation of a familial patronage clique. They advanced the careers of their relatives and protégés over men from competing hierarchies, and Nikita Panin was not above using a favorite like Vasil'chikov when it served his interest. The contradictions between the ideals the Panins held up for emulation and their own efforts to cope with the political and social reality of eighteenth-century Russia speak volumes about the problem of reform in that context.

As much as would-be reformers like the Panins appreciated the benefits of legal relations and constitutional order, they still had to operate in a world governed by personal relations. In eighteenth-century Russia the chief guarantee of life, honor, property, personal expression, or any other social value was the power and cohesion of one's clientele group. Such groups were not only valued by the members themselves as the surest avenue to career advancement, economic well-being, and political influence; in their capacity as unified executive organizations they were likewise indispensable to rulers, who needed disciplined hierarchies to implement policy. Rulers may have been ambivalent toward clientele groups and suspicious of their power, but monarchs had no more effective means of exerting their will. Given the central role of these groups, the first interest of any statesman was to protect his patronage organization. This implied, in turn, the preservation, at least in form, of the autocratic power that sanctioned the action of these essentially illegal bodies. Even Panin, in spite of his distaste for despotism, understood the necessity of this relationship. In proposing his early reforms, he explained that the empress would have to implement them in such a way as "not to seem to alter her despotic authority."[43] Hence,

[43]Breteuil to Praslin, 23 February 1763, *SIRIO*, 140: 162.

from the very outset, a reformer's scope was severely circumscribed. He needed to maintain the cohesion and morale of his clientele as an effective shield for his own interests and an attractive executive organization for the sovereign, and he needed to uphold the legitimizing force of autocratic authority. He could not go very far in establishing objective standards for government service or constitutional restrictions on autocratic power without at the same time undermining the patronage clique and autocratic sanction on which his own power ultimately rested. This conflict ran through all the Panins' political activity and has caused some confusion about the extent of their reform ambitions.

Much of the confusion has stemmed from the Panins' frequent appeals to legal standards based on merit and service. These concepts have a very modern ring and seem to belong to the bureaucratic reform era of the nineteenth century, when they came to be associated with notions of objective standards of performance. To aristocrats of the age of absolutism the terms merit and service, while certainly implying a minimum level of competence, were most prominently associated with such ideas as the status and quality of one's family over several generations, the proved merits of one's forebears through long service to the crown, and a level of culture and refinement that reflected not merely technical expertise but, more important, an aristocratic moral tone and courtly manner. *Starodumstvo* expressed this idea quite clearly with its emphasis on *blagonravie* as the chief object of a noble education. Accordingly, the Panins perceived no conflict when, in addressing the issue of governmental recruitment at the Commission on Noble Freedom in 1763, they recommended not reform along bureaucratic lines but the introduction into Russia of the longstanding, aristocratically oriented patronage system of the Baltic Provinces. It was altogether in keeping with their understanding of service and merit that they believed these concepts should be embodied in an aristocratic and strictly hierarchical system of rewards and recruitment. This view was a conventional wisdom of the day and certainly not peculiar to the Panins. It reappeared in much the same form in Catherine's own Charter of Nobility of 1785.[44]

In assessing the Panins' political activity, one must always keep in mind both their view of themselves as an aristocratic elite and the overriding need they felt to maintain the power of their clientele.

44*PSZ*, vol. 22, no. 16187.

The party's first major undertaking, the action that in fact launched the Panin group as something different from a wing of the Vorontsov family alliance, was the coup d'etat of June 1762. It revealed these assumptions quite clearly. Although Nikita Panin abhorred the unstable succession practices and court coups that had disrupted Russian government since 1725, he did not shrink from fostering this revolt against the legally designated monarch and in so doing helped to bring to power a woman who, of all eighteenth-century rulers, had the least claim to legitimacy. Catherine was the very kind of "accidental personage" Panin considered the bane of Russian government. To be sure, he spoke of elevating Paul and restricting Catherine to the role of regent. He could also justify the move against Peter III on grounds of his "despotic" attacks on established state institutions and his arbitrary plan to alter the succession by setting aside Catherine and Paul. Yet behind these rationalizations was another compelling motivation for participation in the conspiracy: the defense of the Panin clientele and its leading position in the grand ducal court. Peter's actions threatened to destroy the Panin party, and in the face of this crisis the survival of the clientele outweighed considerations of the ruler's legitimacy. Of course, it would be misleading to say that Panin acted merely from expediency. More accurately, he perceived no distinction between issues of principle and party survival. In Panin's view, he and his allies were the true representatives of the established order, whose protection was the monarch's chief duty. When Peter menaced that order, he automatically forfeited his legitimacy. It certainly did not occur to Panin that the order he was defending was in its own way as illegal as Peter's despotism and, in fact, derived its sanction from that same despotic power.

A similar observation may be made in regard to the Imperial Council project. Its explicit objectives were to remove the glaring inefficiencies of a collegial administration combining legislative, judicial, and executive functions in the same institutions and to assert the principles of merit and service over personal favoritism. Yet, as the battle surrounding the reform revealed, its roots lay in the traditional competition among patronage groups in high government. The primary purpose of the reform was to secure the Panin party's position in the new regime. When Catherine guaranteed this position in other ways, the Panins not only dropped their council proposal but even resisted a similar plan in 1768 that would have allowed their competitors a share in government decisions. Moreover, even if the Imperial Council reform had been implemented, it was unlikely that the procedural restraints it imposed on autocratic power would have endured, because the reformers could no more dispense with the arbitrary authority of the sovereign than they could divest themselves of their patronage organizations. The one and the other constituted the sole means of accomplishing positive action, and as ministers responsible for governing the country they had to be interested first of all in practical results.

From their position of leadership during the 1760s the Panins did not try to reform the basic power relationships in Russian government but worked for policies that would give a firm economic and political foundation to the system as it existed. They fostered a conservative foreign policy to provide an era of peace during which Russia could restore its economic strength and expand the faltering domestic administration. They pushed for liberal trade policies and government subsidization of commerce. They addressed the anomalous situation of a nobility enjoying privileges without obligations by appealing to the nobles' moral obligation to serve the state or otherwise make themselves useful to society. Finally, the Panins spoke in favor of greater state regulation of serf-landlord relations with an eye toward removing the abuses of serfdom. Though narrowly reformist, this was essentially a conservative program, the object being to make the present system function more efficiently and humanely. The Panins' proposals for constitutional change came when they were out of power. Only at these times did they clearly perceive the need for a legally established order that would guarantee the position of men truly worthy to serve in the highest government posts.

Thus it was that after 1780 they returned to their early critique of arbitrary rule and sought to lay the groundwork for constitutional government. They had not altogether lost sight of this reform ambition during their tenure in power. At the time it had simply seemed unnecessary to insure the kind of leadership they valued and, in the competition of informal power groupings, incompatible with effective action. Of course, the time had passed when the senior members of the Panin group could expect to realize the changes they now proposed. They could only hope that their pupil Paul might in the future bless Russia with the benefits of legal monarchy. They had spent many years communicating to him their political principles and moral sentiments, and the projects they now drew up were intended chiefly as a kind of final testament and guide to Paul's future actions as monarch. Accordingly, a few words about Paul's understanding and adaptation of this program will serve as a concluding appraisal of the Panins' political hopes and stance.

4. Paul's Adaptation of the Panin Program

It should be mentioned at the outset that the Petrine ethic also had an important place in the Panins' education of Grand Duke Paul. As noted in chapter 8, Paul's training was characterized by the most recent methods and subjects undergirded with a strong moral and religious foundation. Yet the well established approach of studying the lives of great rulers was not neglected. Two European monarchs, Henry IV and Frederick II, served as important models. Paul read Henry IV's biography and took extensive notes on the memoirs of his adviser Duke Sully. The Grand Duke's library likewise abounded with volumes on Frederick II's statecraft.[45] But it was unquestionably the life of his great-grandfather Peter the Great that contributed most to Paul's image of himself as ruler. As one of but two Russian-born and Russian-educated male heirs since Peter's time, he could scarcely avoid comparison with his illustrious forebear. Because of the Panins' interest in reasserting Petrine values, this identification went further in Paul than might normally be expected. Peter the Great was a frequent topic of discussion at the "young court,"[46] and Paul was often reminded of this heritage and the expectations it imposed. An exceptionally sensitive and impressionable child, Paul even reported having a vision in which Peter appeared and offered advice about his future actions as tsar.[47] It is

[45]For a brief catalogue of his private library, see M. V. Klochkov, *Ocherki*, pp. 587–88; also "Vyderzhki velikogo kniazia Pavla Petrovicha iz zapisok gertsoga Siullii," *Russkaia Starina* (1874), pp. 735–42; "Pavel Petrovich: uchebnye tetradi i raznye ego rassuzhdeniia 1772–1776," *Russkaia Starina* (1873), pp. 649–90, 853–84; (1874), pp. 37–56, 277–300, 473–512.

[46]Poroshin, *Zapiski, passim*.

[47]Oberkirch, *Mémoires*, 2: 96–100. Psychological studies have differed on the issue of Paul's hallucinations. P. I. Kovalevskii, "Imperator Petr III, Imperator Pavel I," *Psikhiatricheskie eskizy iz istorii*, 1 (St. Petersburg, 1909), pp. 61–172, accepts them as authentic material for analysis; V. T. Chizh, "Imperator Pavel I," *Voprosy filosofii i psikhologii* (1907), nos. 88, 89, 90, however, questions the validity of this particular vision (see especially no. 90, pp. 672–74).

scarcely surprising, therefore, that Paul many times referred to Peter I in his writings and conversation and regarded it as his "greatest ambition to resemble [Peter] one day and to continue the work that he had commenced."[48] Not to be outdone by his mother in publicly proclaiming his association with Peter's work, after coming to the throne he ordered Rastrelli's equestrian statue of Peter moved to the entrance of his Mikhailovskii castle and engraved with the words: "To Great-Grandfather from Great-Grandson."[49]

Although Paul was separated from the Panins in 1773 and sent into enforced exile at Gatchina, they did not lose their influence with him. Besides the imprint their ideas left on his education, members of the Panin party continued to correspond with the grand duke and, as already mentioned, in the early 1780s the two Panin brothers and Fonvizin composed their constitutional outline and other political projects for Paul's guidance when he assumed the throne. Paul drew much of his political program from these sources and, with some important exceptions to be noted in due course, remained faithful to the original *starodumstvo* conceptions. Even before becoming monarch he implemented enlightened governing practices at his Gatchina estate, whose administration was characterized by religious tolerance, a progressive school system (including schools for peasants), comprehensive welfare facilities, and several manufacturing enterprises.[50] But the best indication of Paul's adoption of the Panin party program may be seen in his *Nakaz* of 1788, a document written on the eve of his departure for the Swedish warfront and intended to serve his heirs as a guide to policy should he die at the front. So many points in this *Nakaz* resembled those in the Panin-Fonvizin "Discourse" and accompanying papers that one recent investigator has argued that Paul had access to the papers when he composed the *Nakaz*.[51]

[48]Oberkirch, *Mémoires*, 2: 272, and other stories of his attachment to Peter in 1: 300, and 2: 122. Snegirev, *Zhizn'*, pp. 24–25. See also Paul's discussion of Peter in one of his early political writings, published in part in P. S. Lebedev, *Grafy Paniny*, pp. 232–35.

[49]B. N. Kalinin and P. P. Iurevich, *Pamiatniki Leningrada i ego okrestnostei* (Leningrad, 1965), pp. 159–61.

[50]S. V. Rozhdestvenskii, "Gatchinskaia votchina Pavla I," *Uchenye zapiski RANIION, institut istorii*, (1928), 6: 127–45.

[51]Claus Scharf, "Staatsauffassung und Regierungsprogramm eines aufgeklärten Selbstherrschers, Die Instruktion des Grossfürsten Paul von 1788," in *Gedenkschrift Martin Göhring*, Studien zur europäischen Geschichte, ed. Ernst Schülin (Wiesbaden, 1968), p. 98, note 22. The following interpretation owes much to Scharf's analysis. The *Nakaz* is published along with Paul's will and letters to his wife and children in M. I. Semevskii,

Again in Paul's *Nakaz* each estate was treated separately with stress on different roles and duties for each, reflecting the grand duke's belief in a strictly corporate organization of society. The document set as the overall goal of society the "general well-being of each and all" and posited as the object of government to define each estate's proper contribution to this goal. With regard to the nobility he emphasized its role as the principal support of state and ruler and, accordingly, its obligation to serve. Here he repeated the Panins' admonitions to exclude unworthy persons from this estate. The *Nakaz* went on to define the contributions of other estates— clergy, middle class, and peasants—saying each of them deserved respect for providing a necessary spiritual or material sustenance to the body politic. But it was not enough merely to give legal definition to the various estates. Education was likewise required, so that men could understand how they personally fit into the broader social scheme. "Hence, schools and institutes [are needed] . . . to instill a knowledge of the prescribed goals and a desire on the part of each person, according to his estate, to fulfill his duties for the common goal of society."[52]

On specific items of policy the *Nakaz* gave, among other things, a foreshadowing of Paul's later efforts to ease peasant burdens. Although his recommendations paled beside the vigorous critique of peasant conditions in the Panin-Fonvizin "Discourse," they did follow closely Peter Panin's earlier proposals for defining peasant obligations in law and protecting peasants from the unbridled caprice of their overseers. Even closer to the Panin party's ideas were the articles on financial policy. Paul insisted on a strict division between revenue belonging to the state and revenue for the royal family. "State income is for the state, and not for the ruler." So far as expenditures for the court, royal grants, and family maintenance were concerned, they should be provided exclusively by crown lands. The Panins' moral precepts likewise found an echo here with Paul calling for a reduction of the liquor monopoly, which corrupted good morals, and its replacement by more intensive development of other resource areas such as mining and manufacture. Finally, Paul spoke of striking

---

ed., "Materialy k russkoi istorii XVIII veka (1788 g.)," *Vestnik Evropy*, no. 2 (March 1867), pp. 297–330.

    [52]The above points are included in articles 1 and 8 through 13. Semevskii, "Materialy," pp. 316–18.

a proper balance between internal and external security arrangements. He saw the foundation of domestic peace in the "good faith" of all subjects united in a common striving toward this end and assisted by efficient rural and urban police forces. In the area of foreign affairs he repeated Nikita Panin's *dicta* on morality in international relations and Russia's chief reliance on its own great strength within the framework of an alliance among the northern powers.[53]

All these points revealed the strong influence of the Panin party's reinterpretation of Petrine policies. Yet Paul left out something of fundamental importance. While adopting the cameralist approach to practical policy approved by the Panins, the *Nakaz* simply continued the same emphasis when it came to questions of constitutional rights and guarantees against arbitrary state power. In contrast to the Panin-Fonvizin outline of fundamental laws with its concern for the rights of various estates, Paul nowhere referred to rights as such. He spoke rather of the contributions each group must make to the general good of society. While the definition of each estate's function may have implied rights, the stress fell heavily on the obligations of each to serve for the good of all. Even the idea of instituting fundamental laws disappeared in Paul's *Nakaz*. Except for a permanent, unchanging succession law, Paul advised against making new laws and merely suggested bringing the present laws into systematic order.

The extent to which he had abandoned the Panin party's constitutional program can best be seen in his approach to three basic institutions: the monarchy, the council, and the senate. He dropped altogether the Panin formulation that Russia should be "a monarchical government with fundamental, immutable laws," and announced, in full conformity with his mother's views, that "there is no better form [of government] than autocracy, for it combines the strength of law with the executive dispatch of a single authority."[54] His idea of a council likewise departed from Panin's. Instead of a body to share in decision-making and serve as the locus of legislative development, a body whose membership would furthermore be subject to review by a quasi-representative senate, Paul opted for a

[53]Semevskii, "Materialy," pp. 318–22. Compare in the Panin constitutional outline articles pp. 40–42, Shumigorskii, *Imperator Pavel I,* appendix, pp. 18–19. Comparisons summarized by Scharf, "Staatsauffassung," pp. 102–03.
[54]Semevskii, "Materialy," Article 2, p. 316.

purely bureaucratic institution, a kind of council of ministers that would include the chancellors and vice-chancellors of justice and foreign affairs, a naval minister, finance minister, commerce minister, and state treasurer. In other words, he gave up the constitutional checks implied in the Panin scheme and viewed the council as another device for increasing the effective articulation of an un-encumbered autocratic power.[55]

Similarly, with the issue of "pouvoirs intermediaires" Paul followed his mother's cameralist leanings rather than the Montes-quieuan formulae preferred by the Panins. He located the depository of laws in the bureaucratic institutions of the senate and its subor-dinate judicial bodies rather than in a special supervisory organ responsible for upholding the law. Compare the two drafts:

Paul's Nakaz	*Panin-Fonvizin Outline*
Laws are to be observed. Nonobser-vance should be watched. The Ruler, being human, cannot look after every-thing, even if he desired; therefore, for the one and the other administrative institutions are necessary. Such are the senate, other judicial offices and etc. (Article 5)	Establishment and confirmation of a single chief state organ directly under the Monarch for supervision through-out the state of all other offices and of the entire state administration and judiciary, for the precise and impartial observance of noninfringement of the fundamental laws. (Article 36)

Obviously, Paul was not prepared to confine his powers within the *Rechtsstaat* limitations proposed by his mentors, let alone to follow up their cautious suggestions for a constitutional check on sovereign authority. His formulae did not advance beyond the "legal des-potism" practiced by his mother. The Panins wanted a supervisory organ *(nadzor)* to be the eye of the law. Paul kept it as it had been, the "eye of the sovereign" whose personal will alone determined the validity of statutes.[56]

But if these constitutional checks were lost as early as 1788, the situation became still worse after Paul took the throne. By that time

[55]It is difficult to accept Scharf's view ("Staatsauffassung," p. 100) that this change arose from Paul's unconscious transferral of N. I. Panin's moral precept for binding the monarch to the laws. The council Paul proposed fit too neatly into his thoroughgoing cameralist approach to statecraft to have been an unconscious adaptation. It is worth noting that the implementation of this council idea during Paul's reign helped to pave the way toward the full-scale ministerial system developed under Alexander I. Klockhov, *Ocherki,* pp. 113–15, 160–80.

[56]For a discussion of this point, see Ditiatin, "Verkhovnaia vlast'," pp. 626–27.

he had also dispensed with the Panins' gradualist approach. They succeeded in giving him a thorough grasp of the *starodumstvo* social and moral objectives. They also successfully nurtured an identification with Peter the Great. Like his great-grandfather, Paul saw himself as first servant of the state, a ruler above class, and a reformer with the task of creating a stable, modern government order for Russia. Yet he seemed to misunderstand altogether the measured approach of his mentors. They had advised education, persuasion, and the gradual establishment of a legal and institutional framework that would provide inducement to loyal service and virtuous conduct. Of course, as autocrat Paul may have seen no reason to confine himself to methods advocated by a beleaguered opposition party. Perhaps, too, the French Revolution impressed Paul with the urgent need for positive action and he felt compelled to shelve the gradualist approach. Or, finally, Paul may have suffered a mental breakdown once the full burden of supreme authority fell on his shoulders. In any case, where the Panins had proposed moderation and education, Paul applied naked force. Where his mentors advised persuasion and example, Paul decided to cram his program down the throats of his unwilling subjects.

Was there a need to reorder government institutions? Paul abolished 34 departments, rearranged several others, and created many new offices of his own. Did *starodumstvo* stress the importance of finding worthy government servants and removing those who neglected their duty? Paul discharged more civil and military servitors in a shorter time than any tsar before or since. In the military alone he dismissed nearly 3,000 officers in three years, including 7 field marshals, 333 generals, and 2,261 commissioned officers.[57] The Panins wanted to encourage the nobility to serve in the Petrine spirit. Paul went a step further and through piecemeal legislation abrogated the decree on freedom of nobility. *Starodumstvo* advocated education as the means of implanting *blagonravie*. Paul ruthlessly suppressed all cultural expression not conforming to his statist ideals and, again much like Peter the Great, defined education in narrowly utilitarian terms—it should provide the knowledge necessary to fulfill the duties of one's station in life. Finally, where the Panins

[57]Klochkov, *Ocherki*, pp. 119, 130, 158–59; dismissals from service listed in P. S. Lebedev, "Preobrazovateli russkoi armii v tsarstvovanie Pavla Petrovicha," *Russkaia Starina* (1877) no. 2, p. 247.

sought to create a respect for law by the institution of permanent fundamental laws, Paul turned the idea inside out. He flooded his chancelleries with a stream of contradictory decrees, abolishing today what he had yesterday erected; he demanded strict conformity to a seemingly endless series of idiotic norms in dress, speech, and behavior, and eventually he created the very nightmare of despotic rule and personal insecurity the Panins had worked so hard to prevent. It was as if Kirill Razumovskii's worst fears had been realized. Peter the Great had indeed reappeared, and everyone was certainly catching hell.

Among other things, this story points up a problem of Russian reformers generally. Peter the Great had thrust the challenge of Westernization upon the elite. He had left the example of his own reforming zeal, his desire to regulate and modernize the government order. He insisted on the elite having a Western education and continuing his reform work. But he also left a legacy of autocratic rule from which all power in the state necessarily derived its legitimacy. In order to reform, therefore, statesmen had to rely upon a despotic authority that rendered reform of a constitutional nature virtually meaningless. In the end, moderate reformers like the Panins were reduced to the uncertain method of exerting moral suasion on the ruler to convince him to abandon irrationality and govern in accordance with reason. They could not escape the paradox of having to ask the monarch to establish the rule of reason through an act of personal will.

Finally, on a somewhat different level, the Panin party's experience provides a lesson in the dangers of manipulating powerful myths. It was natural for the Panins and their supporters, especially given their age and social background, to advertise their views as Petrine ideals. In a certain sense, they possessed a stronger title to this identification than did Catherine. But to inspire Paul's education with the same myth courted the very disaster the Panins feared most. Holding Peter up as a model of service and selfless devotion to duty may have afforded an effective critical contrast with Catherine's court. But the Panins too quickly forgot that Peter was also a ruthless despot. One day Paul would succeed to that same despotic authority, much distressed with what he perceived as an intolerable deterioration of the Petrine system. What motivation would he then have to restrict the powers necessary to return the state to its proper course? If he were to act in Peter's spirit, he would need Peter's authority. Indeed, Paul proved to be so averse to any division of his authority that he confined the discretion of his ministers within even narrower limits than had Peter the Great. Had the Panin brothers lived into Paul's reign, their chagrin would have been complete. To compound the irony, one of the chief conspirators in Paul's overthrow and assassination turned out to be N. P. Panin, Peter Panin's son and Nikita's nephew, who, furthermore, justified his actions on the basis of his uncle's principles of statecraft.[58]

[58]His explanations are included in a letter to Mariia Fedorovna (autumn 1801?) in *Tsentral'nyi Gosudarstvennyi Istoricheskii Arkhiv, Leningrad, f.* 651, *d.* 1134.

Bibliography

Archives

No attempt has been made to list all the collections consulted. The purpose of the entries is limited to acquainting the reader in a general way with the scope and nature of the papers used in this study. The Russian citations are given in the following form: *fond* (collection), *opis'* (inventory) *razriad* (category), *delo*, pl. *dela* (affair).

LENINGRAD

Leningradskoe otdelenie instituta istorii akademii nauk SSSR (*LOII*).
Fond 36, *opis'* 1, *dela*: 111, Bezborodko's letters and reports; 115, notes from the Konferentsiia; 117, M. L. Vorontsov's notes on conferences with foreign envoys, 1756–63; 127, N. Panin's dispatches from Stockholm, 1748–51; 132, letters and dispatches to the chancellor, 1762; 133, letters to the chancellor and empress, 1763; 134, dispatches of A. R. Vorontsov from the Hague, 1765–68; 142, diplomatic papers (including Count Bestuzhev's memoir on Konferentsiia); 145, papers of the Bestuzhev family, 1740–60; 317, varied information on Sweden in eighteenth century; 362, registers of imperial ukases, 1762–79; 398, documents relating to the empress's personal cabinet and the senate; 400, various letters and state projects, 1762–68; 631, letters of N. Panin to A. M. Stroganova, 1760s; 645, reports submitted to Peter III, 1762; 703, memoranda on political, military, and internal affairs, 1762–82; 1067, reports and proposals of R. L. Vorontsov; 1072, papers of M. L. Vorontsov; 1073, papers and projects of M. L. Vorontsov; 1087, correspondence of M. L. Vorontsov with Teplov, Repnin, Rebinder, Poniatowski, P. Panin, and others; 1132, letters and papers sent to M. L. Vorontsov; 1133, correspondence of M. L. Vorontsov with N. Panin, 1748–66; 1134, letters of K. G. Razumovskii to M. L. Vorontsov, 1754–62; 1154, opinions on peasant question submitted, ca. 1764; 1157, decree on ending N. Panin's duties as *oberhofmeister*, and other affairs; 1190, correspondence of A. R. Vorontsov with various persons, 1763–1805.

Gosudarstvennaia publichnaia biblioteka, rukopisnyi otdel (*GPB*).
Fond 563. Letters of P. A. Rumiantsev to N. Panin.

MOSCOW

Tsentral'nyi gosudarstvennyi arkhiv drevnikh aktov (*TsGADA*).
  Fond 5, *opis'* 1, *delo* 94, correspondence of the empress with N. Panin, 1762–75.
  Fond 11, *razriad* XI, *dela* 660–64, 666, 669–71, 677, 682, 684, and 686, correspondence of N. Panin with various persons, including Teplov, Burturlin, the Vorontsovs, the Shuvalovs, de la Riviere, Browne, Dolgorukov, and others during the 1760s.
  Fond 1261, *opis'* 1, *dela*: 190, dispatches from N. Panin in Stockholm and A. M. Golitsyn in London, 1758–59; 468, correspondence of A. R. Vorontsov with N. Panin and others, 1774–95; 1616, letters of N. Panin to Catherine II.
  Fond 1261, *opis'* 2A, *delo* 226, reports and notes by M. L. Vorontsov, 1760–62.
  Fond 1263, *opis'* 1, *dela*: 2652–56, correspondence between N. Panin and A. M. Golitsyn, 1756–60; 2662, letters and notes from N. Panin, 1760–62.
  Fond 1274, *opis'* 1, *delo* 136, registers of imperial ukases written in Catherine II's hand and given to N. Panin.

Gosudarstvennaia biblioteka im. Lenina, rukopisnyi otdel (*GBL*).
  Fond, razriad, and *delo* follow respectively.
  Barsk, XVIa, 24, letters from N. Panin to various persons in 1760s; 27, letters from N. Panin to various persons; 28, letters from N. Panin to Elizabeth I; 29, letters from N. Panin to Catherine II, 1762–75; 30, letters from N. Panin to various persons in 1760s.
  Barsk, XVII, 10, papers and projects of Grand Duke Paul and Paul's correspondence with N. V. Repnin and the Panins.
  222, II, 25, 27, 28, letters from N. Panin to Stanislaw Poniatowski.
  222, V, 1, letters from Grand Duke Paul and Mariia Fedorovna to the Panins in the 1770s.
  Pan, I, 3, letters from N. Panin to Osterman, Stakhiev, Browne, Sievers, Sumarokov, and others, 1770; 5, letters from N. Panin to various persons, 1771.
  Pan, II, 1, 10, 11, 14, letters from N. Panin to A. G. Orlov and others; 30–32, letters from N. Panin to the Kurakins and others, 1770.
  Pan, IV, 1, letters and notes from Catherine II to N. Panin.
  Pan, XIV, 13, correspondence of Grand Duke Paul with P. Panin.
  Pan, XV, 1–12, letters from various persons to N. Panin, 1763–83.
  Pan, XVII, 2, dispatches and letters from A. G. Orlov to N. Panin, 1772–74.

COPENHAGEN

Danske Rigsarkivet *(DRa)*
  Collection TKUA RUSSLAND
    A I, 12, letters from Russian emperors and empresses to Danish kings
    A II, 26, acts and documents concerning political relations with Russia, 1746–1770
    A III, 80, dispatches of G. C. Haxthausen, June–December 1762; 84, dispatches of A. F. Asseburg, 1766; 85, dispatches of A. F. Asseburg and C. Scheel, 1767–1768; 178, Asseburg's ambassadorial archive, 1765–1767

STOCKHOLM

Svenska Riksarkivet *(SRa)*
  Collection Muscovitica
    298, Posse's letters to the king, 1757–1763; 307, Posse's dispatches to Chancellery President, January–June, 1762; 308, Posse's dispatches, July–December, 1762; 309, Posse's and Jahnke's dispatches, 1763; 310, Posse's dispatches to Chancellery College, 1752–1763; 339, Jahnke's dispatches to Chancellery President and Chancellery College, 1763–1764; 343, Düben's dispatches to Chancellery President, 1763–1764; 351, Ribbing's dispatches to Chancellery President, 1767; 356, Ribbing's dispatches to Chancellery President, 1772; 357, Ribbing's and Kiöring's dispatches to Chancellery President, 1773; 386, Nolcken's dispatches to Chancellery President, 1773; 628, N. Panin's letters to Chancellery College

Primary Sources

Documents cited from such well-known serials as *Chteniia v imperatorskom obshchestve istorii i drevnostei rossiiskikh, Russkii Arkhiv, Russkaia Starina, Russkii Vestnik,* and *Sbornik imperatorskogo russkogo istoricheskogo obshchestva* are not listed separately.

Arkhiv gosudarstvennogo soveta, 1, Sovet v tsarstvovanie Imperatritsy Ekateriny II (1768–1796). Ed. I. A. Chistovich. St. Petersburg, 1869.
Arkhiv Kniazia Vorontsova. 40 vols. Ed. P. Bartenev. Moscow, 1870–1895.
Arkhiv kniazia F. A. Kurakina. 10 vols. Ed. M. I. Semevskii. St. Petersburg, 1890–1902.
Asseburg, A. F. *Denkwürdigkeiten.* Berlin, 1842.
Baranov, P. I. *Opis' vysochaishim ukazam i poveleniiam khraniashchimsia v Sankt Peterburgskom Senatskom Arkhive, 1740–1762.* Vol. 3. St. Petersburg, 1878.

Barskov, Ia. L. *Perepiska moskovskikh masonov XVIII-go veka 1780–1792 gg.* Petrograd, 1915.

Beer, Adolph, and Fiedler, J. R., eds. *Joseph II und Graf Ludwig von Cobenzl: Ihr Briefwechsel.* In *Fontes Rerum Austriacarum*, vol. 53. Vienna, 1901.

Bibikov, A. A. *Zapiski o zhizni i shluzhbe A. I. Bibikova.* St. Petersburg, 1865.

Broglie, Duc de. *Le Secret du Roi, correspondance secrète de Louis XV avec ses agents diplomatiques, 1752–1774.* Vol. 2. Paris, 1878.

Brückner, A. [Brikner]. *Materialy dlia zhizneopisaniia grafa Nikity Petrovicha Panina.* 7 vols. St. Petersburg, 1888–1892.

Buganov, V. I., ed. *Razriadnaia kniga 1475–1598 gg.* Moscow, 1966.

Catherine II. *Sochineniia imperatritsy Ekateriny II.* 12 vols. Ed. A. N. Pypin. St. Petersburg, 1901–1907.

―――. *Nakaz imperatritsy Ekateriny II.* Ed. N. D. Chechulin, St. Petersburg, 1907.

Clarke, E. D. *Travels in Various Countries of Europe, Asia and Africa, Russia, Tahtary and Turkey.* 4th ed. 2 vols. London, 1816.

Corberon, Chevalier de. *Un diplomate français à la cour de Catherine II 1775–1780.* 2 vols. Paris, 1901.

Correspondence of Catherine the Great with Sir Charles Hanbury-Williams. Eds. Illchester and Langford-Brooke. London, 1928.

Dashkova, E. R. *Mémoires de la Princesse Dashkaw d'aprés le manuscrit revu et corrigé par l'auteur.* Published as vol. 21 of *AKV*. Moscow, 1881.

―――. *Memoirs of the Princess Daschkaw, Lady of Honour to Catherine II.* Ed. W. Bradford. 2 vols. London, 1840.

Derzhavin, G. R. *Sobranie sochinenii.* 7 vols. St. Petersburg, 1864–72.

The Despatches and Correspondence of John, Second Earl of Buckinghamshire, Ambassador to the Court of Catherine II of Russia 1762–1765. 2 vols. Ed. A. Collyer. London, 1900.

Engel'gardt, L. N. *Zapiski L'va Nikolaevicha Engel'gardta 1766–1836.* Moscow, 1868.

Fénelon, François de Salignac de La Mothe. *Adventures of Telemachus.* Trans. Hawkesworth. New York, n.d.

Fonvizin, D. I. *Sobranie sochinenii.* 2 vols. Ed. G. P. Makogonenko. Moscow, 1959.

Fonvizin, M. A. *Primechaniia k "Histoire philosophique et politique de Russie" par Enneau et Chennechot.* Tobolsk, 1853. Republished as "Zapiski M. A. Fonvizina." In *Russkaia Starina*, vol. 42 (1884).

Fortunatov, P. K. *P. A. Rumiantsev, materialy po istorii russkoi armii.* 2 vols. Moscow, 1953.

Frederick II. *Politische Correspondenz Friedrichs des Grossen.* 46 vols. Berlin, 1879–1939.

Göransson, Johan. *Svea Rikes Konungars Historia ok Ättartal ifrån 2200 år före Skriftum intil 1749*. Stockholm, 1749.

Harris, James. *Diaries and Correspondence of James Harris*. Vol. I. London, 1844.

Heier, Edmund. *L. H. Nicolay (1737–1820) and His Contemporaries*. The Hague, 1965.

Helbig, G. Ad. W. *Russische Günstlinge*. Tubingen, 1809.

Khrapovitskii, A. V. *Dnevnik za 1782–1793*. Ed. N. Barsukov. St. Petersburg, 1874.

Kleinschmidt, A. "Vom Tode Peters III bis zum Tode Iwans VI. Gesantschaftsberichte aus dem Haager Reichsarchive." In *Russische Revue* 23: 534–59.

[Kotoshikhin, G. K.] "Grigorii Karpovich Kotoshikhin *On Russia in the Reign of Alexis Mikhailovich*: An Annotated Translation." Trans. and ed. Benjamin Uroff. Ph.D. dissertation, Columbia University, 1970.

Kulomzin, A. N., ed. "Pervyi pristup v tsarstvovanie Ekateriny II k sostavleniiu Vysochaishei Gramoty dvorianstvu rossiiskomu." In N. Kalachov, *Materialy dlia istorii russkogo dvorianstva*, vol. 2. St. Petersburg, 1885.

Leibnitz, G. W. "Projet de l'éducation d'un prince." In *Magazin für das Kirchenrecht, die Kirchen- und Gelehrtengeschichte*. Göttingen, 1787. 1: 177–96.

Maikov, P. M., ed. *Pis'ma A. A. Bezborodka k grafu P. A. Rumiantsevu 1775–1793 gg*. St. Petersburg, 1900.

Malyshev, I. V., ed. *N. I. Novikov i ego sotrudniki, izbrannye sochineniia*. Moscow, 1961.

Masson, Charles. *Secret Memoirs of the Court of Petersburg*. Philadelphia, 1802.

Münnich, B. C. *Ébauche pour donner une idée de la forme du Gouvernement de l'empire de Russie*. Copenhagen, 1774.

———. *Zapiski fel'dmarshala Minnikha*. St. Petersburg, 1874.

Nepliuev, I. I. *Zapiski Ivana Ivanovicha Nepliueva 1693–1773*. St. Petersburg, 1893. Also in *Russkii Arkhiv*. No. 1. (1871).

Oberkirch, H. L. *Mémoires de la Baronne d'Oberkirch*. 2 vols. Paris, 1853.

Perevorot 1762 g., sochineniia i perepiska uchastnikov i sovremennikov. Moscow, 1908.

Polnoe sobranie zakonov rossiisskoi imperii s 1649 goda. 45 vols. St. Petersburg, 1830.

Poroshin, S. A. *Zapiski*. St. Petersburg, 1881.

Raeff, Marc, ed. *Plans for Political Reform in Imperial Russia, 1730–1905*. Englewood Cliffs, New Jersey, 1966.

———. *Russian Intellectual History, An Anthology*. New York, 1966.

Recueil des instructions données aux ambassadeurs de France. Vol. 9, *Russie, 1749–1789.* Paris, 1890.

Reddaway, W. F., ed. *Documents of Catherine the Great, the Correspondence with Voltaire and the Instruction of 1767 in the English Text of 1768.* Cambridge, 1931.

Russkii Arkhiv. 1863–1917.

Russkaia Starina. 1870–1918.

Sakhanev, V. V. "Iz istorii Rossii kontsa XVIII stoletiia (tri neopublikovannykh dokumenta iz istorii roda grafov Paninykh)." *Zapiski russkogo nauchnoissledovatel'skogo ob"edineniia v Prage.* Vol. 10 [old series 15]. No. 71. Prague, 1940.

Saldern [C. von]. *Histoire de la vie de Pierre III.* Frankfurt on Main, n.d.

Sbornik imperatorskogo russkogo istoricheskogo obshchestva. 148 vols. St. Petersburg, 1867–1916.

Semevskii, M. I. ed. "Materialy k russkoi istorii XVIII v." *Vestnik Evropy.* No. 2 (1867), 297–330.

Shakhovskoi, Ia. P. *Zapiski Ia. P. Shakhovskogo pisannye im samin.* 2 vols. Moscow, 1810.

Shcherbatov, M. M. *Sochineniia kniazia M. M. Shcherbatova.* 2 vols. St. Petersburg, 1896–1898.

Speranskii, M. M. *Plan gosudarstvennogo preobrazovaniia grafa M. M. Speranskogo.* Moscow, 1905.

———. *Proekty i zapiski.* Moscow, 1961.

Strube de Piermont, F. H. *Lettres russiennes.* St. Petersburg, 1760.

Sumarokov, A. P. *Izbrannye proizvedeniia.* Ed. P. N. Berkov. Leningrad, 1957.

Turgenev, A. *La cour de la Russie il y a cent ans 1725–1783.* Berlin, 1858.

Voskresenskii, N. A. *Zakonodatel'nye akty Petra I.* vol. 1. Moscow, 1945.

Zavadovskii, P. V. *Pis'ma Grafa P. V. Zavadovskogo k fel'dmarshalu P. A. Rumiantsevu 1775–1791.* Ed. P. M. Maikov. St. Petersburg, 1901.

Secondary Sources

Adamczyk, Theresia. *Fürst G. A. Potemkin.* Emsdetten, 1936.

Alef, Gustave. "The Crisis of the Muscovite Aristocracy: A Factor in the Growth of Monarchical Power." *Forschungen zur osteuropäischen Geschichte.* Berlin, 1970. 2: 15–58.

Alefirenko, P.K. *Krest'ianskoe dvizhenie i krest'ianskii vopros v Rossii v 30-50-kh XVIII veka.* Moscow, 1958.

———. "Obshchestvennoe dvizhenie v Moskve vo vtoroi polovine XVIII stoletiia." *Izvestiia AK. Nauk. SSSR,* seriia istorii i filosofii. Vol. 4, no. 6 (1947): 521–35.

Aleksandrov [Ol'minskii], M. S. *Gosudarstvo, biurokratiia i absolutizm v istorii Rossii.* 2nd ed. Moscow, 1919.

Aleksandrov, P. A. *Severnaia sistema.* Moscow, 1914.

Alekseev, A. S. "Sil'nye persony v verkhovnom Tainom Sovete, Petra II i rol' kniazia Goltsyna pri votsarenii Anny Ioannovny." In *Russkoe obozrenie.* 45: 740–59; 46: 175–98, 616–58; 47: 67–93, 432–60; 48: 160–75.

Alexander, John T. *Autocratic Politics in a National Crisis.* Bloomington, Ind., 1969.

Alexeiev, N. N. "Beiträge zur Geshichte des russischen Absolutismus im 18. Jahrundert." In *Forschungen zur osteuropäischen Geschichte.* 6 (1958): 7–81.

Allen, Robert V. "The Great Legislative Commission of Catherine II of 1767" (Ph.D. dissertation, Yale University, 1950).

Amburger, E. *Geschichte der Behördenorganisation Russlands von Peter dem Grossen bis 1917.* Leiden, 1966.

———. *Russland und Schweden 1762–1772.* Berlin, 1934.

Andreev, V. *Predstaviteli vlasti v Rossii posle Petra I.* St. Petersburg, 1871.

Andreevskii, I. *O namestnikakh, voevodakh i gubernatorakh.* St. Petersburg, 1864.

Arheim, Fritz. "Beiträge zur Geschichte der nordischen Frage in der zweiten Hälfte des 18 Jahrhunderts." In *Deutsche Zeitschrift für Geschichtswissenschaft.* Vols. 2, 3, 4, 5, and 8 (1889–1892).

Ariès, Philippe. *Centuries of Childhood, Social History of Family Life.* New York, 1862.

———. *Histoire des populations françaises et de leurs attitudes devant la vie depuis le XVIIIᵉ siècle.* Paris, 1948.

Augustine, Wilson R. "Notes Toward a Portrait of the Eighteenth-Century Russian Nobility." In *Canadian Slavic Studies.* Vol. 4, no. 3 (Fall, 1970): 373–425.

Bakounine, T. *Le répertoire biographique des francs maçons russes (XVIIIᵉ et XIXᵉ siècles).* Brussels, 1940.

Barskov, Ia. L. "Pis'ma imp. Ekateriny II k gr. P. V. Zavadovskomu (1775–1777)." In *Russkii istoricheskii zhurnal.* No. 5 (1918): 223–57.

———. "Proekty voennykh reform tsesarevicha Pavla I." In *Russkii istoricheskii zhurnal.* Vol. 1, nos. 3–4 (Petrograd, 1917): 104–45.

Barsukov, Aleksandr. "Batiushkov i Opochinin, popytka dvorianskoi oppozitsii v tsarstvovanie Ekateriny II." *Drevniaia i novaia Rossiia.* Vol. 3 (1878): 287–309.

———. *Rasskazy iz russkoi istorii XVIII veka.* St. Petersburg, 1885.

Bartenev, P. "I. I. Shuvalov." In *Russkaia Beseda* no. 1, (1857): 1–80.

Batz, C. W. *Catharina die Grosse, Historisches Drama in Fünf Acten.* Leipzig, 1869.

Bech, Svend Cedergreen. *Danmarks Historie,* vol. 9 *Oplysning og Tolerance 1721–1784.* Eds. John Danstrup and Hal Koch. Copenhagen, 1865.

Behre, Göran. "Postspionaget under 1700-talet." In *Scandia,* 29 (1963): 292–319.

Beliavskii, M. T. *Krest'ianskii vopros v Rossii nakanune vosstaniia E. I. Pugacheva.* Moscow, 1965.

———. "Vopros o krepostnom prave i polozhenii krest'ian v Nakaze Ekateriny II." In *Vestnik Moskovskogo Universiteta.* No. 6 (1963): 44–63.

Bellanger, Justin. "Un Czarowitz à Paris." In *Revue des Etudes historiques.* No. 4 (1898): 206–17.

Berkov, P. N. *Istoriia russkoi zhurnalistiki XVIII veka.* Moscow, 1952.

———. "Teatr Fonvizina i russkaia kul'tura." In *Russkie klassiki i teatr.* Leningrad, 1947: 7–108.

———. *Vladimir Ignat'evich Lukin.* Moscow–Leningrad, 1950.

Bernadskii, V. N. *Ocherki iz istorii klassovoi bor'by i obshchestvenno-politicheskoi mysli Rossii v tret'ei chetverti XVIII veka.* Published in *Uchenye zapiski LGPI im. A. I. Gertsena.* Vol. 229. Leningrad, 1962.

Bernard, Paul. *Joseph II and Bavaria.* The Hague, 1965.

Betiaev, Ia. D. *Obhschestvenno-politicheskaia i filosoficheskaia mysl' v Rossii v pervoi polovine XVIII v.* Saransk, 1959.

Bil'basov, V. A. "Pamiati imperatritsy Ekateriny II." In *Russkaia Starina.* Vol. 88 (1896): 240–80.

———. *Istoricheskie monografii.* 5 vols. St. Petersburg, 1901.

———. *Istoriia Ekateriny II.* Vols. 1, 2, and 12. Berlin, 1900.

Billington, James. *Icon and Axe.* New York, 1966.

Bishop, W. T. "Thomas Dimsdale, M.D., F.R.S., and the Innoculation of Catherine the Great." In *Annals of Medical History.* N.S. Vol. 4, (1932): 321–38.

Bittner, Konrad. "Beiträge zur Geschichte des Lebens und Wirkens Heinrich Johann Friedrich (Andrej Ivanovic) Ostermanns." In *Jahrbücher für Geschichte Osteuropas.* Vol. 2, no. 5 (1957): 106–26.

Blanc, Simone. "La Franc-Maçonnerie sous Catherine II." Seminar notes from the Russian Research Center, Harvard University. 8 December 1966.

Blum, K. L. *Ein Russischer Staatsmann: Denkwürdigkeiten des Grafen J. J. Sievers.* 4 vols. Leipzig, 1857.

Bogoslovskii, M. M. *Byt i nravy russkogo dvorianstva v pervoi polovine XVIII veka.* 2nd ed. Petrograd, 1918.

———. *Istoriia Rossii XVIII veka 1725–1796.* Moscow, 1915.

———. *Konstitutsionnoe dvizhenie 1730 g.* 2nd ed. Petrograd, 1918.

————. *Oblastnaia reforma Petra Velikogo: Provintsiia 1719–1727.* Moscow, 1902.

Bogumil, A. *K istorii upravleniia Novorossii kn. Potemkinym.* St. Petersburg, 1905.

Bolkhovitinov, N. N. *Stanovlenie russko-amerikanskikh otnoshenii, 1775–1815.* Moscow, 1966.

Bondarenko, V. N. *Ocherki finansovoi politiki Kabineta Ministrov Anny Ioannovny.* Moscow, 1913.

Brandt, Otto. *Caspar von Saldern und die nordeuropäische Politik im Zeitalter Katharinas II.* Kiel, 1932.

Braudo, A. I. "Nikita Ivanovich Panin." In *Russkii biograficheskii slovar'.* Vol. 3. St. Petersburg, 1902: 189–205.

Brückner, A. *Die Europäisierung Russlands.* Gotha, 1888.

————. *Istoriia Ekateriny Vtoroi.* 3 vols. St. Petersburg, 1885.

————. "Vskrytie chuzhikh pisem i depesh pri Ekaterine II." In *Russkaia Starina.* Vol. 7 (1873): 75–84.

————. *Potemkin.* St. Petersburg, 1891.

————. "Zur Charakteristik der Kaiserin Katharina II." In *Russische Revue.* Vol. 7 (Aug.–Sept. 1875): 139–64, 193–214.

Cederberg, Arno Rafael. *Heinrich Fick: ein Beitrag zur russischen Geschichte des XVIII Jahrhunderts.* In the series *Acta et Commentationes Universitatis Tartuensis.* B. Humaniora. Vol. 17. Tartu, 1930.

Chechulin, N. D. *Ekaterina II v bor'be za prestol. Po novym materialam.* Leningrad, 1924.

————. *Ocherki po istorii russkikh finansov v tsarstvovanie Ekateriny II.* St. Petersburg, 1906.

————. "Proekt Imperatorskogo Soveta." In *Zhurnal Ministerstva Narodnogo Prosveshcheniia.* No. 3 (1894): 68–87.

————. *Russkoe provintsial'noe obshchestvo vo vtoroi polovine XVIIIogo veka.* St. Petersburg, 1889.

————. *Vneshniaia politika Rossii v nachale tsarstvovaniia Ekateriny II 1762–74.* St. Petersburg, 1895.

Chicherin, B. N. *Oblastnye uchrezhdeniia v Rossii v XVII-m veke.* Moscow, 1856.

Chistovich, N. *Istoricheskaia zapiska o sovete v tsarstvovanie Ekateriny II.* St. Petersburg, 1870.

Chizh, V. F. "Imperator Pavel I." In *Voprosy filosofii i psikhologii.* (May–June 1907): 221–90; (Sept.–Oct.): 391–468; (Nov.–Dec.): 585–678.

Commons, J. R. *Legal Foundations of Modern Capitalism.* Madison, Wisconsin, 1959.

Confino, Michael. "A propos de la noblesse russe au XVIIIe siècle." In *Annales E. S. C.* Vol. 22, no. 6 (November–December 1967): 1163–1205.

————. *Domaines et seigneurs en Russie vers la fin du XVIIIe siècle.* Paris, 1963.

————. "La politique de tutelle des seigneurs russes envers leurs paysans vers la fin du XVIIIe siècle." In *Revue des Études slaves.* Vol. 37 (1960): 39–69.

————. "Le paysan russe jugé par la noblesse au XVIIIe siècle." *Revue des Études slaves.* Vol. 38 (1961): 51–71.

Cross, A. G. "British Freemasons in Russia during the Reign of Catherine the Great." *Oxford Slavonic Papers.* N.S., 4 (1971): 43–72.

Crusenstolpe, M. J. *Der russische Hof von Peter I. bis auf Nicolaus I.* Vol. 2. Hamburg, 1855.

Dahlgren, Stellan. "Kansler och kungamakt vid tronskiftet 1654." In *Scandia.* Vol. 26 (1960): 99–144.

Danevskii, P. N. *Istoriia obrazovaniia gosudarstvennogo soveta v Rossii.* St. Petersburg, 1859.

Danielsson, J. R. *Die nordische Frage in den Jahren 1746–51. Mit einer Darstellung der russisch-schwedisch-finnischen Beziehungen 1740–1743.* Helsingfors, 1888.

Demidov, N. F. "Biurokratizatsiia gosudarstvennogo aparata absoliutizma v XVII-XVIII vv." In N.M. Druzhinin, ed. *Absoliutizm v Rossii.* Moscow, 1964: 206–42.

Ditiatin, I. I. *Ekaterininskaia komissiia 1767 g. "O sochinenii proekta novogo ulozheniia."* Rostov on Don, 1905.

————. *Stat'i po istorii russkogo prava.* St. Petersburg, 1896.

Dmitriev, F. *Istoriia sudebnykh instantsii i grazhdanskogo appelliatsionnogo sudoproizvodstva ot Sudebnika do Uchrezhdeniia o guberniiakh.* Moscow, 1859.

Druzhinin, N. M. "Prosveshchennyi absoliutizm v Rossii." In *Absoliutizm v Rossii.* Moscow, 1964: 428–59.

Druzhinina, E. I. *Kiuchuk-kainardzhiiskii mir 1774 goda.* Moscow, 1955.

————. *Severnoe prichernomor'e v 1775–1800 gg.* Moscow, 1959.

Dukes, Paul. *Catherine the Great and the Russian Nobility.* Cambridge, 1967.

Easum, Chester V. *Prince Henry of Prussia, Brother of Frederick the Great.* Madison, Wisconsin, 1942.

Eidel'man, N. Ia. *Gertsen protiv samoderzhaviia,* Moscow, 1973.

Eisenstadt, S. N. "Internal Contradictions in Bureaucratic Polities." In *Comparative Studies in Society and History.* Vol. 1 (1958–59): 58–75.

————. *The Political Systems of Empires.* Glencoe, Illinois, 1963.

Engel, L. *Geschichte des Illuminaten-Ordens.* Berlin, 1906.

Eroshkin, N. P. *Ocherki istorii gosudarstvennykh uchrezhdenii dorevoliutsionnoi Rossii.* Moscow, 1960.

Esipov, G. "Fridrikh II i graf Panin. Prusskaia politika v pervom razdele Pol'shi." In *Beseda.* No. 1 (1871): 269–303.

Fateev, A. N. *Potemkin-Tavricheskii.* In *Russkoe Nauchno-Issledovatel'skoe Ob"ednenie v Prage, Doklady i lektsii.* No. 3. Prague, 1945.

Fedosov, I. A. *Iz istorii russkoi obshchestvennoi mysli XVIII stoletiia: M. M. Shcherbatov.* Moscow, 1967.

Firsov, N. N. *Petr III i Ekaterina II v pervye gody ee tsarstvovaniia.* Moscow, 1915.

———. *Pravitel'stvo i obshchestvo v ikh otnosheniiakh k vneshnei torgovle Rossii v tsarstvovanie imperatritsy Ekateriny II.* Kazan', 1902.

Fisher, Alan W. *The Russian Annexation of the Crimea 1772–1783.* Cambridge, 1970.

Fleischhacker, Hedwig. "Porträt Peters III." In *Jahrbücher für Geschichte Osteuropas.* Vol. 2, no. 5 (1957): 127–89.

Gay, Peter. *The Party of Enlightenment: Essays in the French Enlightenment.* New York, 1964.

Geisman, P. A., and Dubovskoi, A. N. *Graf Petr Ivanovich Panin, 1721–1789.* St. Petersburg, 1897.

Geyer, Dietrich. " 'Gesellschaft' als staatliche Veranstaltung, Bemerkugen zur Sozialgeschichte der russischen Staatsverwaltung im 18. Jahrhundert." In *Jahrbücher für Geschichte Osteuropas,* Vol. 14, no. 1 (March 1966): 21–50.

Gierke, Otto. *Natural Law and the Theory of Society 1500–1800.* 2 vols. Cambridge, 1934.

Glasenapp, Igor. *Staat, Gesellschaft und Opposition im Zeitalter Katharinas der Grossen.* Munich, 1964.

Gleason, Walter. "Cultural Value Changes among Certain Russian Writers 1759–1772." Draft of doctoral thesis, University of Chicago, 1973.

Glinskii, B. B. *Bor'ba za konstitutsiiu 1612–1861 gg., istoricheskie ocherki.* St. Petersburg, 1908.

Golikova, N. V. "Organy politicheskogo syska i ikh razvitie v XVII-XVIII vv." In *Absoliutizm v Rossii.* Moscow, 1964: 243–80.

———. *Politicheskie protsessy pri Petre I. Po materialam Preobrazhenskogo prikaza.* Moscow, 1957.

Golitsyn, P. *Pervyi vek Senata.* St. Petersburg, 1910.

Got'e, Iu V. *Istoriia oblastnogo upravleniia v Rossii ot Petra I do Ekateriny II.* 2 vols. Moscow, 1913, 1941.

———. *Ocherk istorii zemlevladeniia v Rossii.* Sergiev Posad, 1915.

———. " 'Proekt o popravlenii gosudarstvennykh del' Artemiia Petrovicha Volynskogo." In *Dela i Dni, istoricheskii zhurnal.* Vol. 3 (1922): 1–31.

Gradovskii, A. D. *Nachala russkogo gosudarstvennogo prava.* Vol. 2. St. Petersburg, 1899.

Gradovskii, S. A. *Vysshaia administratsiia XVIII veka: General-prokurory*. St. Petersburg, 1866.

Grau, C. *Der Wirtschaftsorganisator, Staatsmann und Wissenschaftler Vasilij N. Tatiščhev (1686–1750)*. Quellen und Studien zur Geschichte Osteuropas. Vol. 13. Berlin, 1963.

Gribovskii, V. M. *Vysshii nadzor i sud v Rossii XVIII v*. St. Petersburg, 1901.

Griffiths, David M. "The Rise and Fall of the Northern System: Court Politics and Foreign Policy in the First Half of Catherine II's Reign." In *Canadian Slavic Studies*, Vol. 4, no. 3 (Fall 1970): 547–69.

————. "Russian Court Politics and the Question of an Expansionist Foreign Policy under Catherine II, 1762–1783." Ph.D. dissertation, Cornell University, 1967.

Grigor'ev, V. *Reforma mestnogo upravleniia pri Ekaterine II*. St. Petersburg, 1910.

Grigorovich, N. I. *Kantsler Kniaz' Aleksandr Andreevich Bezborodko v sviazi s sobytiiami ego vremeni*. Published as volumes 26 and 29 (1879, 1881) of *SIRIO*.

Grunwald, Constantin de. *Trois siècles de diplomatie russe*. Paris, 1945.

Gukovskii, G. A. *Ocherki po istorii russkoi literatury XVIII veka, dvorianskaia fronda v literature 1750-kh—1760-kh godov*. Moscow, 1936.

Günther, O. E. "Peter der Grosse im Russischen Urteil des 18. Jh." *Jahrbücher für Kultur und Geschichte der Slaven*. N. S., vol. 10 (1934): 529–57.

Hans, N. A. *History of Russian Educational Policy 1701–1917*. London, 1931.

Hassell, James Edward. "The Vicissitudes of Russian Administrative Reform, 1762–1801." Ph.D. dissertation, Cornell University, 1967.

Haumant, E. *La Culture française en Russie 1700–1900*. Paris, 1910.

Haxthausen-Abbenburg, August F. *The Russian Empire, Its People, Institutions and Resources*. London. 1856.

Henning, Beth. *Gustav III som kronprins*. Uppsala, 1935.

Hjärne, Erland. *Från Vasatiden till Frihetstiden, några drag ur den svenska konstitutionalismens historia*. Stockholm, 1929.

Hjärne, Harald. "Ryska konstitutionsprojekt år 1730 efter svenska förebilder." In *Historisk tidskrift*. Vol. 4. Stockholm, 1884: 189–272.

————. "Storpolitiska villobilder från frihetstiden." In *Samlade skrifter*. Vol. 2. Stockholm, 1932.

————. Svenska reformer i tsar Peters välde." In *Ur det förgångna*. Stockholm, 1912.

Holm, Edvard. "Caspar v. Saldern og den dansk-norske Regering." In *Historisk Tidskrift*. Vol. 4, no. 3. Copenhagen, 1873: 73–190.

————. *Danmark-Norges historie fra den store nordiske krigs slutning til rigernes adskillelse (1720–1814)*. Vol. 5. Copenhagen, 1906.

Humphreys, Lester Jay. "The Vorontsov Family: Russian Nobility in a

Century of Change, 1725–1825". Ph.D. dissertation, University of Pennsylvania, 1969.

Iablochkov, M. *Istoriia dvorianskogo sosloviia v Rossii.* St. Petersburg, 1876.

Iakushkin, V. E. *Gosudarstvennaia vlast' i proekty gosudarstvennoi reformy v Rossii.* St. Petersburg. 1906.

Ikonnikov, V. S. "Arsenii Matseevich, istoriko-biograficheskii ocherk." In *Russkaia Starina.* (1879) Vol. 24: 731–52; vol. 25: 1–34, 577–608; vol. 26: 1–34, 177–98.

"Imperator Ioann Antonovich 1740–1764." In *Russkaia Starina* (1879), Vol. 24: 497–508; vol. 25: 291–306, 493–574.

Istoriia diplomatii. 3 vols., 2nd ed. Moscow, 1963.

Istoriia Pravitel'stvuiushchego Senata za dvesti let, 1711–1911. Vol. 2. St. Petersburg, 1911.

Istoriia russkoi literatury. Vol. 4. Moscow, 1947.

Ivanov-Razumnik, P. V. *Istoriia russkoi obshchestvennoi mysli.* 2 vols., 4th ed. St. Petersburg, 1914.

Iverus, Gustaf. *Hertig Karl av Södermanland, Gustav III's broder.* Vol. 1, *till ryska kriget.* Uppsala, 1925.

Jägerskiöld, Olof. *Den svenska utrikespolitikens historia, II:2, 1721–1792.* Stockholm, 1957.

———. *Hovet och författningsfrågan 1760–1766.* Uppsala, 1943.

Jauffret, E. *Catherine II et son regne.* 2 vols. Paris, 1860.

Jones, Robert E. *The Emancipation of the Russian Nobility 1762–1785.* Princeton, 1973.

———. "The Russian Gentry and the Provincial Reform of 1775." Ph.D. dissertation, Cornell University, 1968.

Kabuzan, V. M. *Narodonaselenie Rossii v XVIII-pervoi polovine XIX v. (po materialam revizii).* Moscow, 1963.

Kafengaus, B. B. "Voprosy istoriografii epokhi Petra Velikogo." In *Istoricheskii zhurnal.* No. 9 (1944): 24–33.

Kahan, Arcadius. "The Costs of 'Westernization' in Russia: The Gentry and the Economy in the Eighteenth Century." In Michael Cherniavsky, ed. *The Structure of Russian History, Interpretative Essays.* New York, 1970.

Kalinin, B. N. and Iurevich, P. P. *Pamiatniki Leningrada i ego okrestnostei.* Leningrad, 1965.

Kaplan, Frederick I. "Tatiščev and Kantemir, Two Eighteenth Century Exponents of a Russian Bureaucratic Style of Thought." In *Jahrbücher für Geschichte Osteuropas,* n.s. (1965) vol. 13, no. 4: 497–510.

Kaplan, Herbert. *The First Partition of Poland.* New York, 1962.

———. *Russia and the Outbreak of the Seven Years' War.* Berkeley, 1968.

Karabanov, P. F. "Freiliny russkogo dvora v XVIII i XIX stoletiiakh." In *Russkaia Starina* (October 1871): 379–404.

Karnovich, E. P. *Zamechatel'nye bogatstva chastnykh lits v Rossii: Ekonomiches-koe istoricheskoe issledovanie.* St. Petersburg, 1874.

————. *Zamechatel'nye i zagadochnye lichnosti XVIII i XIX stoletii.* 2nd ed. St. Petersburg, 1893.

Kashtanov, S. M. "Kommentarii k dvadtsat' piatomu i dvadtsat' shesto-mu tomam 'Istorii Rossii s drevneishikh vremen.' " In S. M. Solov'ev. *Istoriia Rossii s drevneishikh vremen.* Vol. 13. Moscow, 1965: 597–619.

"K biografii mitropolita moskovskogo Platona." In *Chteniia.* (1875) No. 1: 161–62.

Kizevetter, A. A. *Gorodovoe polozhenie Ekateriny II 1785 g.* Moscow, 1909.

————. "Imperatritsa Ekaterina II, kak zakonodatel'nitsa (Rech' pered doktorskim disputom)." In *Istoricheskie Ocherki.* Moscow, 1912: 274–83.

————. *Istoricheskie siluety.* Prague, 1931.

————. *Mestnoe samoupravlenie v Rossii IX-XIX st., Istoricheskii ocherk.* Moscow, 1910.

————. "Odin iz reformatorov russkoi shkoli." In *Istoricheskie ocherki.* Moscow, 1912: 119–49.

————. "Pervoe piatiletie pravleniia Ekateriny II." In *Sbornik statei posviashchennyi P. N. Miliukovu.* Prague, 1929.

————. *Posadskaia obshchina v Rossii XVIII st.* Moscow, 1903.

Kjellén, R. "Samuel Åkerhielm den yngre och de ryska stämplingar i Sverige åren 1746–49." In *Historisk tidskrift.* Vol. 14. Stockholm, 1894: 1–36.

Kliuchevskii, V. O. *Boiarskaia duma drevnei rusi.* 5th ed. St. Petersburg, 1919.

————. *Istoriia soslovii v Rossii.* 3rd ed. Petrograd, 1918.

————. *Kurs russkoi istorii.* Vols. 4 and 5. Moscow, 1937.

Klochkov, M. V. *Ocherki pravitel'stvennoi deiatel'nosti vremeni Pavla I.* Petro-grad, 1916.

Klokman, Iu. R. *Fel'dmarshal Rumiantsev v period russko-turetskoi voiny 1768–1774 gg.* Moscow, 1951.

————. *Sotsial'no-ekonomicheskaia istoriia russkogo goroda, vtoraia polovina XVIII veka.* Moscow, 1967.

Knorring, N. N. "Ekaterininskaia zakonodatel'naia komissiia 1767 goda v osveshchenii inostrannykh rezidentov pri russkom dvore." In *Sbornik statei posviashchennyi P. N. Miliukovu.* Prague, 1929: 327–50.

Kobeko, D. I. *Tsesarevich Pavel Petrovich (1754–1796).* 2nd ed. St. Peters-burg, 1883.

Kochetkova, N. D. "Ideino-literaturnye pozitsii masonov 80-90-kh godov XVIII v. i N. M. Karamzin." In *XVIII vek.* Vol. 6 (1964): 176–96.

Kogan-Bernshtein, F. A. "Vliianie idei Montesk'e v Rossii v XVIII veke." *Voprosy istorii*. No. 5 (1955): 99–110.

Korf, S. A. *Dvorianstvo i ego soslovnoe upravlenie*. St. Petersburg, 1906.

Korkunov, N. M. "Dva proekta preobrazovaniia Senata vtoroi poloviny tsarstvovaniia Ekateriny II." In *Zhurnal Ministerstva Iustitsii* (May 1899). Also separately, St. Petersburg, 1899.

———. *General Theory of Law*. Translated by W. G. Hastings. Boston, 1909.

———. *Istoriia filosofii prava*. St. Petersburg, 1908.

———. "S. E. Desnitskii, pervyi russkii professor prava." Offprint of speech to St. Petersburg Juridical Society, Nov. 1894.

Korsakov, D. A. "Anna Ioannovna." In *Russkii biograficheskii slovar'*. Vol. 2. St. Petersburg, 1900: 158–98.

———. "Art. Petr. Volynskii." In *Drevniaia i novaia Rossiia*. No. 1 (1876): nos. 1 and 2 (1877).

———. *Iz zhizni russkikh deiatelei XVIII veka*. Kazan', 1891.

———. "Sud nad Kniazem D. M. Golitsynym." In *Drevniaia i novaia Rossiia*. No. 10 (1879): 20–62.

———. *Votsarenie Imperatritsy Anny Ioannovny*. Kazan', 1880.

Kovalevskii, E. P. *Graf Bludov i ego vremia*. St. Petersburg, 1866.

Kovalevskii, P. I. "Imperator Petr III, Imperator Pavel I." In *Psikhiatricheskie eskizy iz istorii*. Vol. 1. St. Petersburg, 1909: 61–172.

Krieger, Leonard, and Stern, Fritz, eds. *The Responsibility of Power: Historical Essays in Honor of Hajo Holborn*. New York, 1967.

Krummel, W. *Nikita Ivanovič Panins aussenpolitische Tätigkeit 1748–1760*. Breslau, 1941.

Kucherov. A. Ia. "Frantsuzskaia revolutsiia i russkaia literatura XVIII veka." In *XVIII vek: Sbornik statei i materialov*. Vol. 1. Ed. A. S. Orlov. Moscow–Leningrad, 1935: 259–307.

Lagerroth, F. *Frihetstidens författning. En studie i den svenska konstitutionalismens historia*. Stockholm, 1915.

Lang, D. M. *The First Russian Radical, Alexander Radishchev 1749–1802*. London, 1959.

Larivière, Charles de. *La France et la Russie au XVIIIe siècle*. Paris, 1909.

Latkin, V. N. *Uchebnik istorii russkogo prava perioda Imperii (XVIII-XIX st.)*. 2nd ed. St. Petersburg, 1909.

———. *Zakonodatel'nye kommissii v Rossii v XVIII stoletii*. St. Petersburg, 1887.

Lauber, Jack Moore. "The Merchant-Gentry Conflict in Eighteenth-Century Russia." Ph.D. dissertation, University of Iowa, 1967.

Lebedev, P. S. *Grafy Nikita i Petr Paniny, Opyt razrabotki noveishei russkoi istorii po neizdannym istochnikam*. St. Petersburg, 1863.

Leeds, Anthony. "Brazilian Careers and Social Structure: A Case History and Model." In Dwight Heath and Richard Adams, eds. *Contemporary Cultures and Societies in Latin America.* New York, 1965.

Leikhtenbergskii, G. N. *Istoriia leibgvardii konnogo polka.* Vol. 1. Paris, 1938.

―――., ed. "Iz zapisok o Rossii grafa fon Gertsa, prusskogo poslannika pri dvore Ekateriny II." In *Vestnik Obshchestva Revnitelei Istorii.* Vol. 1 (1914): 1–37.

Leontovitsch, V. *Geschichte des Liberalismus in Russland.* Frankfurt-am-Main, 1957.

Ley, Francis. *Le Maréchal de Münnich et la Russie au XVIIIᵉ Siècle.* Paris, 1959.

Liutsh, A. "Russkii absoliutizm XVIII veka." In Liutsh, A., et al. *Itogi XVIII veka v Rossii.* Moscow, 1910: 1–256.

Loginov, M. N. *Nikolai Novikov i moskovskie martinisty.* Moscow, 1867.

―――. "Satiricheskii katalog pri dvore Ekateriny II". In *Russkii Arkhiv.* (1871): 2039–54.

Lortholary, A. *Le mirage russe en France au XVIIIᵉ siècle.* Paris, 1951.

McArthur, Gilbert H. "The Novikov Circle in Moscow, 1779–1792." Ph.D. dissertation, University of Rochester, 1968.

Madariaga, Isabel de. *Britain, Russia and the Armed Neutrality of 1780.* New Haven, 1962.

Maikov, P. M. *Ivan Ivanovich Betskoi, opyt ego biografii.* St. Petersburg, 1904.

Makogonenko, G. P. *Denis Fonvizin, tvorcheskii put'.* Moscow, 1961.

―――. *Nikolai Novikov i russkoe prosveshchenie XVIII veka.* Moscow, 1951.

―――. *Radishchev i ego vremia.* Moscow, 1956.

Malmström, C. G. *Sveriges politiska historia från konung Karl XII's död till statshvalfningen 1772.* 6 vols. Stockholm, 1893–1901.

Manuel, Frank E. *The Eighteenth Century Confronts the Gods.* New York, 1967.

Marcham, Frederick George. *A Constitutional History of Modern England, 1485 to the Present.* New York, 1960.

Martynov, I. F. "English Literature and Eighteenth-Century Russian Reviewers." In *Oxford Slavonic Papers,* n.s. Vol. 4 (1971): 30–43.

Maurach, Reinhart. *Der russische Reichsrat.* Berlin, 1939.

Mavrodin, V. V. *Klassovaia bor'ba i obshchestvenno-politicheskaia mysl' v Rossii XVIII v.* Leningrad, 1964.

―――., et al. *Krest'ianskaia voina v Rossii v 1773–1775 godakh: Vosstanie Pugacheva.* 2 vols. Leningrad, 1961 and 1966.

Meehan, Brenda M. "The Russian Generalitet of 1730: Towards a Definition of Aristocracy." Ph.D. dissertation, University of Rochester, 1970.

Menshutkin, B. N. *Russia's Lomonosov: Chemist, Courtier, Physicist, Poet.* Princeton, 1952.

Merry, Henry J. *Montesquieu's System of Natural Government*. West Lafayette, Indiana, 1970.

Miliukov, P. N. *Glavnye techeniia russkoi istoricheskoi mysli*. 2nd ed. Moscow, 1898.

————. "The Influence of English Political Thought in Russia." In *Slavonic Review*. Vol. 5 (December, 1926): 258–70.

————. *Iz istorii russkoi intelligentsii*. 2nd ed. St. Petersburg, 1903.

————. *Ocherki po istorii russkoi kul'tury*. Vol. 3, *Natsionalizm i obshchestvennoe mnenie*. 2 parts. St. Petersburg, 1913.

————. *Russia and Its Crisis*. Chicago, 1906.

Mohrenschildt, Dimitri von. *Russia in the Intellectual Life of Eighteenth-Century France*. New York, 1936.

Morane, Pierre. *Paul I de Russie*. Paris, 1907.

Mork, Gordon. "German Constitution of 1866–71: Pseudo-Constitutional Absolutism." Paper presented to Duquesne History Forum. October, 1971.

Morrison, Kerry R. "Catherine II's Legislative Commission: An Administrative Interpretation." In *Canadian Slavic Studies*. Vol. 4, no. 3 (Fall, 1970): 464–84.

Mousnier, Roland. *La vénalité des offices sous Henri IV et Louis XIII*. Rouen, 1946.

Nilzén, Göran. *Studier i 1730-talets partiväsen*. Licentiat dissertation published in limited edition, Stockholm, 1971.

Ocherki istorii SSSR, period feodalizma, v pervoi chetverti XVIII v. Moscow, 1954.

Odhner, C. T. *Gustav III och Katarina II, åren 1783–1784*. Stockholm, 1879.

Okun', S. B. *Ocherki istorii SSR konets XVIII-pervaia chetvert' XIX veka*. Leningrad, 1956.

Olsson, G. "Fredrik II och Sveriges författning." In *Scandia*. Vol. 27, no. 2 (1961): 337–65.

Orlov, V. N. *Russkie prosveteteli 1790–1800-kh godov*. Moscow, 1950.

Ovsianiko-Kulikovskii, D. N. *Istoriia russkoi intelligenstsii*. Vols. 7–9 of *Sobranie sochinenii*. St. Petersburg, 1910.

Palme, Sven Ulric. "Vom Absolutismus zum Parliamentarismus in Schweden." In *Ständische Vertretungen in Europa im 17. und 18. Jahrhundert*. Ed. D. Gerhard. Göttingen, 1969: 368–97.

Papmehl, K. A. *Freedom of Expression in Eighteenth-Century Russia*. The Hague, 1971.

Pavlov-Sil'vanskii, N. P. *Gosudarevy sluzhilye liudi, proiskhozhdenie russkogo dvorianstva*. St. Petersburg, 1898.

————. *Proekty reform v zapiskakh sovremennikov Petra Velikogo*. St. Petersburg, 1896.

Pekarskii, P. P. *Dopolneniia k istorii masonstva v Rossii XVIII stoletiia*. St. Petersburg, 1869.

―――. *Istoriia imperatorskoi Akademii Nauk v Peterburge*. Vol. 1. St. Petersburg, 1870.

―――. *Nauka i literatura v Rossii pri Petre Velikom*. 2 vols. in 1. St. Petersburg, 1862.

Peshtich, S. L. *Russkaia istoriografiia XVIII veka*. 3 vols. Leningrad, 1961–1971.

Petrov, P. N. *Istoriia rodov russkogo dvorianstva*. St. Petersburg, 1886.

Petrova, V. A. "Politicheskaia bor'ba vokrug senatskoi reformy 1763 goda." In *Vestnik Leningradskogo Universiteta*. Vypusk 2, No. 8 (1967): 57–66.

Petrovskii, S. *O Senate v tsarstvovanie Petra Velikogo*. Moscow, 1875.

Petschauer, Peter. "The Education and Development of an Enlightened Absolutist: The Youth of Catherine the Great, 1729–1762." Ph.D. dissertation, New York University, 1969.

Pfeiderer, Edmund. *Gottfried Wilhelm Leibnitz: Patriot, Staatsmann und Bildungsträger*. Leipzig, 1870.

Piatkovskii, A. P. "Zamechatel'nye russkie deiateli. Ivan Ivanovich Betskii, istoriko-biograficheskii ocherk." In *Delo*. (1867), no. 4: 287–308; no. 5: 171–97; no. 7: 270–302; no. 8: 81–117; no. 9: 58–79.

Pigarev, K. V. *Tvorchestvo Fonvizina*. Moscow, 1954.

Platonov, S. F. *Stat'i po russkoi istorii*. St. Petersburg, 1912.

Pokrovskii, M. N. *Istoriia Rossii s drevneishikh vremen*. In *Izbrannye proizvedeniia*. Vol. 2. Moscow, 1965.

Pokrovskii, S. A., ed. *Iuridicheskie proizvedeniia progressivnykh myslitelei*. Vol. 1, *Vtoraia polovina XVIII veka*. Moscow, 1959.

Pokrovskii, S. P. *Ministerskaia vlast' v Rossii*. Iaroslavl' , 1906.

Polenov, D. V. "A. Ia. Polenov, russkii zakonoved XVIII veka." *Russkii Arkhiv* (1865): 445–70, 703–36.

Porai-Koshits, I. A. *Ocherk istorii russkogo dvorianstva ot poloviny IX do kontsa XVIII veka, 862–1796*. St. Petersburg, 1874.

Predtechenskii, A. V. *Ocherki obshchestvenno-politicheskoi istorii Rossii v pervoi chetverti XIX veka*. Moscow-Leningrad, 1957.

Protasov, G. A. " 'Konditsii' 1730 g. i ikh prodolzhenie." In *Uchenye zapiski*. Tambovskii gosudarstvennyi pedogogicheskii institut. Vyp. 15 (1957): 215–30.

―――. "Zapiska Tatishcheva o 'proisvol'nom rassuzhdenii' dvorianstva v sobytiiakh 1730 g." In *Problemy istochnikovedeniia*. AN SSSR Institut Istorii, Moscow, 1963: 237–65.

Puttkamer, E. "Einflüsse schwedischen Rechts auf die Reformen Peters des Grossen." In *Zeitschrift für ausländisches öffentliches Recht und Völkerrecht*. No. 19 (1958): 369–84.

Pypin, A. N. "Ekaterina II i Montesk'e." In *Vestnik Evropy*. Vol. 38, no. 5 (1903): 272–300.

———. "Russkoe masonstvo do Novikova." *Vestnik Evropy*. Vol. 3 (June, (1868): 546–89; (July, 1868): 187–222.

———. *Russkoe masonstvo XVIII i pervaia chetvert' XIX v*. Petrograd, 1916.

Raeff, Marc. "The Domestic Policies of Peter III and His Overthrow." In *American Historical Review*. Vol. 75, no. 5 (June, 1970): 1289–1310.

———. "Home, School, and Service in the Life of the 18th Century Russian Nobleman." In *Slavonic and East European Review*. Vol. 40, no. 99 (June, 1962): 295–307.

———. "Les Slaves, les Allemands et les 'Lumières'." In *Canadian Slavic Studies*. Vol. 1, no. 4 (Winter, 1967): 521–51.

———. *Michael Speransky, Statesman of Imperial Russia 1772–1839*. The Hague, 1957.

———. *Origins of the Russian Intelligentsia: The Eighteenth-Century Nobility*. New York, 1966.

———. "Pugachev's Rebellion." In *Preconditions of Revolution in Early Modern Europe*, eds. Robert Forster and Jack P. Greene. Baltimore, Maryland, 1970.

———. "The Russian Autocracy and its Officials." In H. McLean, et al., eds. *Russian Thought and Politics*. Vol. 4 (Harvard Slavic Studies), Cambridge, 1957: 77–91.

———. "The Style of Russia's Imperial Policy and Prince G. A. Potemkin." In G. N. Grob, ed., *Statesmen and Statecraft of the Modern West*, Barre, Mass., 1967: 1–51.

Ransel, David L. "Bureaucracy and Patronage: The View from an Eighteenth-Century Russian Letter-Writer." In *The Rich, the Well-Born, and the Powerful: Elites and Upper Classes in History*, ed. Frederic Cople Jaher. Urbana, 1973: 154–78.

———. "Catherine the Great's Instruction to the Commission on Laws: An Attack on Gentry Liberals?" *Slavonic and East European Review*. Vol. 50, no. 118 (January, 1972): 10–28.

———. "The Constitutional Crisis of 1730: Political Perceptions of the Russian Nobility." *Laurentian University Review*. Vol. 4, no. 3 (June, 1972): 20–38.

———. "The 'Memoirs' of Count Münnich." *Slavic Review*. Vol. 30, no. 4 (December, 1971): 843–52.

———. "Nikita Panin's Imperial Council Project and the Struggle of Hierarchy Groups at the Court of Catherine II." In *Canadian Slavic Studies*. Vol. 4, no. 3 (Fall, 1970): 443–46.

Recke, W. "Die Verfassungspläne der russischen Oligarchen im Jahre 1730." In *Zeitschrift für Osteuropäische Geschichte*. Vol. 2 (1911–1912): 1–64, 161–203.

Remgård, Arne. *Carl Gustaf Tessin och 1746–1747 års Riksdag.* Doctoral dissertation published as vol. 20 of *Bibliotheca Historica Lundensis.* Falkenberg, 1968.

Rexheuser, Rex. "Besitzverhältnisse des russischen Adels im 18. Jahrhundert. Historische Fragen, methodische Probleme." Inaugural Dissertation, Friedrich-Alexander University, Erlangen-Nürnberg, 1971.

Riabinin, D. D. "Biografiia grafa Semena Romanovicha Vorontsova." In *Russkii Arkhiv.* No. 1 (1879): 58–82, 168–96, 305–45, 444–502.

Roberts, Clayton. "The Growth of Ministerial Responsibility to Parliament in Later Stuart England." In *Journal of Modern History.* Vol. 28, no. 3 (September, 1956): 215–33.

Roberts, Michael. *Essays in Swedish History.* Minneapolis, 1966.

Roetter, J. H. "Russian Attitudes Toward Peter the Great and His Reforms Between 1725 and 1910." Ph.D. dissertation, University of Wisconsin, 1951.

Rogger, Hans. *National Consciousness in Eighteenth-Century Russia.* Cambridge, Massachusetts, 1960.

Romanovich-Slavatinskii, A. *Dvorianstvo v Rossii ot nachala XVIII v. do otmeny krespostnogo prava.* 2nd ed. Kiev, 1912.

Rozhdestvenskii, S. V. "Gatchinskaia votchina Pavla I." In *Uchenye zapiski RANIION.* Institut istorii (1928) 6: 127–45.

Rubinshtein, N. L. *Sel'skoe khoziaistvo v Rossii vo vtoroi polovine XVIII v.* Moscow, 1957.

———. "Ulozhennaia komissiia 1754–1766 gg. i ee proekt novogo ulozheniia 'O sostoianii poddannykh voobshche' (K istorii sotsial'noi politiki 50-kh-nachala 60-kh godov XVIII v.)." In *Istoricheskie zapiski.* Vol. 38 (1951): 208–51.

Rudbeck, Johannes. *Kanslirådet Karl Fredrik Eckleff, det svenska frimuraresystemets fader.* Stockholm, 1930.

Ruffmann, Karl-Heinz. "Russischer Adel als Sondertypus der europäischen Adelswelt." In *Jahrbücher für Geschichte Osteuropas.* Vol. 9, no. 2 (1961): 161–78.

Russkii biograficheskii slovar. 25 vols. St. Petersburg, 1896–1918.

Ryu, In-Ho Lee. "Freemasonry under Catherine the Great: A Reinterpretation." Ph.D. dissertation, Harvard University, 1967.

Sacke, Georg von. "Adel und Bürgertum in der gesetzgebenden Kommission Katharinas II. von Russland." In *Jahrbücher für Geschichte Osteuropas.* Vol. 3 (1938): 408–17.

———. "Katharina II. im Kampf um Thron und Selbstherrschaft." In *Archiv für Kulturgeschichte.* Vol. 23, no. 2 (1932): 191–216.

———. "Zur Charakteristik der gesetzgebenden Kommission Katharinas

II. von Russland." In *Archiv für Kulturgeschichte*. Vol. 21, no. 2 (1931): 161–91.

Samoilov, A. N. "Zhizn' i deianiia generala-fel'dmarshala kniazia Grigoriia Aleksandrovicha Potemkin-Tavricheskogo." In *Russkii Arkhiv* (1867): 575–606, 993–1027, 1203–62.

Scharf, Claus. "Staatsauffassung und Regierungsprogramm eines aufgeklärten Selbstherrschers, Die Instruktion des Grossfürsten Paul von 1788." In *Gedenkschrift Martin Göhring*. Studien zur europäischen Geschichte. Ed. Ernst Schulin. Wiesbaden, 1968: 91–106.

Schlözer, Kurd von. *Friedrich der Grosse und Katharina II*. Berlin, 1859.

Schmidt, K. Rahbek. "The Treaty of Commerce between Great Britain and Russia, 1766: A Study in the Development of Count Panin's Northern System." In *Scandoslavica* (1954): 115–34.

———. "Wie ist Panins Plan zu einem Nordischen System entstanden?" In *Zeitschrift für Slawistik*. Vol. 2, no. 3 (1957): 406–22.

Schmidt, S. O. "La politique intérieure du Tsarisme au milieu du XVIIIᵉ siècle." In *Annales*. Vol. 21, no. 1 (January–February, 1966): 95–110.

Segel, H. G., ed. *The Literature of Eighteenth-Century Russia*. 2 vols. New York, 1967.

Semennikov, V. P. *Radishchev*. Petrograd, 1923.

Semevskii, V. I. *Krest'iane v tsarstvovanie imperatritsy Ekateriny II*. Vol. 2. St. Petersburg, 1901.

———. *Krest'ianskii vopros v Rossii v XVIII i pervoi polovine XIX veka*. 2 vols. St. Petersburg, 1888.

———. "Literatura ekaterininskogo iubileia, 1873." In *Russkaia Starina*. Vol. 9 (1874): 796–817.

———. "Volneniia krepostnykh krest'ian pri Ekaterine II 1762–1789." In *Russkaia Starina*. Vol. 8 (1877), nos. 1–4: 193–226.

———. "Vopros o preobrazovanii gosudarstvennogo stroia v Rossii v XVIII i v pervoi chetverti XIX veka." In *Byloe*. No. 1 (1906): 150–200.

Seredonin, S. M. *Istoricheskii obzor deiatel'nosti Komiteta Ministrov*. Vol. 1. St. Petersburg, 1902.

Sergeevich, V. I. *Lektsii i issledovaniia po drevnei istorii russkogo prava*. St. Petersburg, 1910.

Shampai, D. D. "Ob izdateliakh pervogo chastnogo zhurnala (Po materialam kadetskogo korpusa)." In *XVIII vek*. Moscow, 1935: 377–85.

Shchebal'skii, P. K. "Perepiska Ekateriny Vtoroi s gr. N. I. Paninym." In *Russkii Vestnik*. Vol. 45 (1863): 748–62.

———. *Politicheskaia sistema Petra III*. Moscow, 1870.

Shcheglov, V. G. *Gosudarstvennyi sovet v Rossii*. St. Petersburg, 1892.

Shchepkin, E. N. *Padenie Kantslera A. P. Bestuzheva-Riumina*. Odessa, 1901.

––––––. *Russko-avstriiskii soiuz vo vremia semiletnei voiny 1746–1758 gg.* St. Petersburg, 1902.

Shmurlo, E. F. "Petr Velikii v otsenke sovremennikov i potomstva." In *Zhurnal Ministerstva Narodnogo Prosveshcheniia.* (October, 1911): 315–40; (November–December, 1911): 1–37, 201–73; (May–June, 1912): 1–40, 193–259.

Shtrange, M. M. *Demokraticheskaia intelligentsiia Rossii v XVIII veke.* Moscow, 1965.

Shumigorskii, E. S. *Imperator Pavel I, zhizn' i tsarstvovanie.* St. Petersburg, 1907.

––––––. "Puteshestvie Pavla Petrovicha i Marii Fedorovny za granitsa 1781–1782." In *Russkii Arkhiv,* no. 2 (1890): 17–78.

Simmons, E. S. *English Literature and Culture in Russia 1553–1840.* Cambridge, Massachusetts, 1935.

Sivkov, K. V. "Samozvanstvo v Rossii v poslednei tret'i XVIII v." In *Istoricheskie zapiski,* (1950): 88–135.

Slany, William. "Russian Central Government Institutions 1725–1741." Ph.D. dissertation, Cornell University, 1958.

Small, Albion W. *The Cameralists: The Pioneers of German Social Policy.* Chicago, 1909.

Snegirev, I. M. *Zhizn' moskovskogo mitropolita Platona.* 2 vols. in 1. Moscow, 1856.

Sokolovskaia, T. O. "Kapitul Feniksa. Vysshee tainoe masonskoe pravlenie v Rossii (1778–1822 gg.)." In *Vestnik imperatorskogo Obshchestva Revnitelei Istorii.* Vol. 2 (1915): 217–316.

––––––. "O masonstve v prezhnem russkom flote." In *More* (1907), no. 8: 216–52.

Solov'ev, S. M. *Istoriia Rossii s drevneishikh vremen.* n. s. 15 vols. Moscow, 1960–1966.

––––––. "Rasskazy iz russkoi istorii." In *Russkii Vestnik* (1861): 303–40.

Solov'ev, S. "Zametki o samozvantsakh v Rossii." In *Russkii Arkhiv* (1868): 266–81.

Soloveytchik, George. *Potemkin.* New York, 1947.

Sprinchorn, C. "Ett bidrag till den väpnade neutralitetens historia i Norden." In *Historisk tidskrift* (1881): 247–73.

Stavenow, Ludvig. "Det adertonde århundradets parlamentarism i Sverige." In *Uppsala Universitets Årsskrift* (1923). Program 1: 1–31.

––––––. *Frihetstiden.* Vol. 9, *Sveriges historia till våra dagar.* Stockholm, 1922.

Strömberg-Back, Kerstin. *Lagen, rätten, läran. Politisk och kyrklig debatt i Sverige under Johan III's tid.* Lund, 1963.

Svatikov, S. G. *Obshchestvennoe dvizhenie v Rossii 1700–1895.* Rostov on Don, 1905.

Syromiatnikov, B. I. *"Reguliarnoe" gosudarstvo Petra Pervogo i ego ideologiia.* Moscow–Leningrad, 1943.

Taranovskii, F. V. "Montesk'e o Rossii (K istorii Nakaza imperatritsy Ekateriny II)." In *Trudy russkikh uchenykh za-granitsei.* Vol. 1 (1922): 178–223.

———. "Politicheskaia doktrina Nakaza." In *Sbornik statei po istorii prava posvaishchennyi M. F. Vladimirskomu-Budanovu.* Kiev, 1904: 44–86.

Taylor, N. W. "Adam Smith's First Russian Disciple." In *Slavonic and East European Review.* Vol. 45 (1967): 425–38.

Tengberg, N. *Om Kejsarinnan Catharina II's åsyftade stora nordiska alliance.* Lund, 1863.

Tereshchenko, A. *Opyt obozreniia zhizni sanovnikov upravliavshikh inostrannymi delami v Rossii.* Vol. 2. St. Petersburg, 1837.

Thompson, G. S. *Catherine II and the Expansion of Russia.* New York, 1950.

Trefolev, L. "Aleksei Petrovich Mel'gunov, General-gubernator Ekaterininskikh vremen." In *Russkii Arkhiv* (1865): 931–78.

Troitskii, S. M. *Finansovaia politika russkogo absoliutizma v XVIII veke.* Moscow, 1966.

———. "Istoriografiia 'dvortsovykh perevorotov' v Rossii XVIII v." In *Voprosy istorii.* Vol. 41, no. 2 (1966): 38–53.

———. "Sotsial'nyi sostav i chislennost' biurokratii Rossii v seredine XVIII v." In *Istoricheskie zapiski.* Vol. 89 (1972): 295–352.

Utechin, S. A. *Russian Political Thought: A Concise History.* New York, 1964.

Varneke, B. V. *History of the Russian Theatre.* Trans. B. Brasol. New York, 1951.

Vasil'chikov, A. A. "Semeistvo Razumovskikh. I. Grafy Aleksei i Kirila Grigor'evichi." In *Osmnadtsatyi Vek.* Vol. 2: 260–502.

Veidemeier, A. *Dvor i zamechatel'nye liudi v Rossii,* St. Petersburg, 1846.

Veretennikov, V. I. *Istoriia tainoi kantseliarii Petrovskogo vremeni.* Khar'kov, 1910.

———. "Iz istorii instituta prokuratury nachala Ekaterininskogo tsarstvovaniia." In *Russkii istoricheskii zhurnal* (1918), no. 5: 86–100.

———. *Iz istorii tainoi kantseliarii 1731–1762.* Khar'kov, 1911.

———. "K istorii sostavleniia nakazov v Ekaterininskuiu Komissiiu." In *Zapiski Khar'khovskogo Universiteta* (1911), no. 4: 1–32.

———. *Ocherki istorii general-prokuratory v Rossii doekaterininskogo vremeni.* Khar'kov, 1915.

Vernadskii, G. V. "Imperatritsa Ekaterina II i zakonodatel'naia kommissiia." In *Sbornik Obshchestva Istorii i Sotsial'nykh Nauk pri Permskom Universitete.* Vol. 1 (1918): 1–23.

———. "Manifest Petra III o vol'nosti dvorianskoi i zakonodatel'naia kommissiia 1754–1766." In *Istoricheskoe Obozrenie.* Vol. 20 (1915): 51–59.

————. *Ocherk istorii prava russkogo gosudarstva.* Prague, 1924.

————. *Russkoe masonstvo v tsarstvovanie Ekateriny II.* Petrograd, 1917.

Veselovskii, S. B. *Issledovaniia po istorii klassa sluzhilykh zemlevadel'tsev.* Moscow, 1969.

Viazemskii, B. L. *Verkhovnyi Tainyi Sovet.* St. Petersburg, 1909.

Viazemskii, P. A. *Fon-vizin.* St. Petersburg, 1848.

Vierhaus, Rudolf. "Montesquieu in Deutschland. Zur Geschichte seiner Wirkung als politischer Schriftsteller im 18. Jahrhundert." In *Collegium Philosophicum. Studien Joachim Ritter zum 60. Geburtstag.* Basel, Stuttgart, 1965.

Vladimirskii-Budanov, M. F. *Obzor istorii russkogo prava.* 7th rev. ed. Petrograd-Kiev, 1915.

Vodovozov, V. *Ocherki iz russkoi istorii XVIII-ogo veka.* St. Petersburg, 1882.

Volkov, M. Ia. "Otmena vnutrennikh tamozhen." In *Istoriia SSSR* (1957), no. 2: 78–95.

Vucinich, A. *Science in Russian Culture: A History to 1860.* Stanford, 1963.

Weber, Max. *From Max Weber: Essays in Sociology.* New York, 1946.

————. *Max Weber on Law in Economy and Society.* Cambridge, Massachusetts, 1954.

Welsh, David J. *Russian Comedy 1765–1823.* The Hague, 1966.

Winter, E., et al. *Die deutsch-russische Begegnung und Leonhard Euler: Beiträge zu den Beziehungen zwischen der deutschen und der russischen Wissenschaft und Kultur im 18. Jahrhundert.* Quellen und Studien zur Geschichte Osteuropas. Vol. 1. Berlin, 1958.

Wolff, H. M. *Die Weltanschauung der deutschen Aufklärung in geschichtlicher Entwicklung.* 2nd ed. Bern–München, 1963.

Wootton, A. C. *Chronicles of Pharmacy.* 2 vols. London, 1910.

Yaney, George. *The Systematization of Russian Government.* Urbana, 1973.

Zagoskin, N. P. *Verkhovniki i shliakhetstvo 1730-go goda, Po povodu sochineniia D. A. Korsakova: "Votsarenie imperatritsy Anny Ioannovny."* Kazan', 1881.

Zanta, L. *La Renaissance du stoïcisme au XVI siècle.* Paris, 1914.

Zapadov, A. V., ed. *Istoriia russkoi zhurnalistiki XVIII veka.* Moscow, 1963.

Zav'ialov, A. *Vopros o tserkovnykh imeniiakh pri Ekaterine II.* St. Petersburg, 1900.

Zutis, Ia. Ia. *Ostzeiskii vopros v XVIII v.* Riga, 1964.

Index